The Best AMERICAN ESSAYS College Edition

The *Best* AMERICAN ESSAYS College Edition

Fifth Edition

Edited and with an Introduction
by ROBERT ATWAN

*Director, The Blue Hills Writing Institute
at Curry College*

Houghton Mifflin Company   Boston   New York

Publisher: Patricia Coryell
Assistant Editor: John McHugh
Project Editor: Aimee Chevrette/Katherine Leahey
Senior Art and Design Coordinator: Jill Haber Atkins
Photo Editor: Jennifer Meyer Dare
Composition Buyer: Chuck Dutton
Associate Manufacturing Buyer: Susan Brooks
Senior Marketing Manager: Annamarie Rice
Marketing Assistant: Bettina Chiu

Cover image: © Ralph Mercer

Printed in the U.S.A.

Library of Congress Number:

Instructor's exam copy
ISBN-13: 978-0-618-83299-6
ISBN-10: 0-618-83299-8

For orders, use student text ISBNs:
ISBN-13: 978-0-618-83259-0
ISBN-10: 0-618-83259-9

123456789-EB-10 09 08 07 06

Contents

1. THE PERSONAL VOICE: IDENTITY, DIVERSITY, SELF-DISCOVERY • 37

ANWAR F. ACCAWI, *The Telephone* • 38

"When I was growing up in Magdaluna, a small Lebanese village in the terraced, rocky mountains east of Sidon, time didn't mean much to anybody, except maybe to those who were dying, or those waiting to appear in court because they had tampered with the boundary markers on their land."

MARCIA ALDRICH, *Hair* • 47

"In maturity, I'm incapable of assuming a coherent or consistent philosophy. I have wayward hair: it's always becoming something else."

LYNDA BARRY, *Two Questions* • 55

"It turns out there are also drawings which can make people dislike you. Drawings that make people think you are dirty or stupid or lame. One by one most kids I knew quit drawing and never drew again. It left behind too much evidence."

"The men drank Palo Viejo rum, and some of the younger ones got weepy. The first time I saw a grown man cry was at a New Year's Eve party: he had been reminded of his mother by the smells in the kitchen."

"Though there was graffiti on most of the walls of Westbury Court, and hills of trash piled up outside, and though the elevator wasn't always there when we opened the door to step inside and the heat and hot water weren't always on, I never dreamed of leaving Westbury Court until the year of the fire."

"Did education mean moving from one class to the next? My grandmothers told me again and again that one could scale a mountain with a good education. But could I still talk to them, to my parents, my siblings? I would try to live in two worlds — at the very least. That was now my task."

"I have known Lodovico for twenty-three years, as long as I have lived in New York. After all these years, I keep asking myself the same question: Why do I continue to visit this mute, overdressed, imperious young man?"

"What terrified me that late summer day was the sudden greenness of the trees, the way their beauty insinuated itself into my vision — peripherally at first, vaguely, and without my consent. I blinked to stop what felt like tears, which I hadn't tasted for so long I'd forgotten that they were made of salt, that they were something my body was producing on its own, long after I thought I had shut down. O.K., I said to the steering wheel, the padded dashboard, the pines. If I can think of five reasons not to die, I won't."

"It has been alleged that when I was in college she heard that I had stayed up all night playing poker and wrote me a letter that used the word 'shame' forty-two times. I do not recall this."

"I understood right away without being told or knowing why, beyond their same beak-like nose and large black eyes, that she was connected to my father, the way you usually know when someone is about to betray you or hurt you, even though there aren't any obvious signs and warnings, you feel it along your skin."

"The tools in my workbench are a double inheritance, for each hammer and level and saw is wrapped in a cloud of knowing."

"And so a part of me began to learn about living outside the disease, cultivating appreciation for a few free moments. It was nothing I would have wished for myself, nothing to noisily celebrate. But it was something, and I could choose it, even while mourning the paralyzed parts of me, the pill that had failed me."

"Language is the tool of my trade. And I use them all — all the Englishes I grew up with."

2. THE ATTENTIVE MIND: OBSERVATION, REFLECTION, INSIGHT • 168

"A week before his twenty-sixth birthday, the nimble Petit clandestinely strung a cable between the not-yet-completed Twin Towers, already dominating Manhattan's skyline, and for the better part of an hour walked back and forth over the void, demonstrating his astonishing obsession to one hundred thousand or so wide-eyed gawkers gathered so far below."

"Nothing on earth is more gladdening than knowing we must roll up our sleeves and move back the boundaries of the humanly possible once more."

"Every creature on earth has approximately two billion heartbeats to spend in a lifetime. You can spend them slowly, like a tortoise, and live to be two hundred years old, or you can spend them fast, like a humming-bird, and live to be two years old."

"What does it mean that some of my fondest memories are of technology? Have we begun our slide toward the ineluctable merging of man and machine? Are Walkman headphones in the ears the first step toward a computer chip implanted in the brain?"

"You took a sentence, threw it against the wall, picked up the pieces, and put them together again, slotting each word into its pigeonhole. When you got it right, you made order and sense out of what we used all the time and took for granted: sentences."

"'What are you *doing?*' The question pursues me still. When I go fishing and catch no fish, the idea that it's fun simply to be out on the river consoles me for not one second. I must catch fish; and if I do, I must then catch more and bigger fish."

"I waited until I held his eye. I assured him I would not tell anyone else how to get there. He looked at me with stoical despair, like a man who had been robbed twice, whose belief in human beings was offered without conviction."

"Thread holds together, and restricts, while yarn stretches and gives. Thread is the overall theme that gives meaning to our words and thoughts — to lose the thread is to be incoherent or inattentive. A yarn is a long, pointless, but usually amusing story whose facts have been exaggerated. It is infinitely more relaxing to listen to a yarn than to a lecture whose thread we must follow."

"As a woman and a writer, I have long wondered at the wellsprings of female masochism. Or what, in despair of a more subtle, less reductive phrase, we can call the congeries of predilections toward self-hurt, self-erasure, self-repudiation in women."

"It was the business of dealing with dead things, coupled with the questionable enterprise of making dead things look like live things. In spite of its scientific value, it was usually regarded as almost a black art, a wholly owned subsidiary of witchcraft and voodoo."

"The road to Fidel Castro's Palace of the Revolution leads through a memory lane of old American automobiles chugging along at about twenty-five miles an hour — springless, pre-embargo Ford coupes and Plymouth sedans, DeSotos and LaSalles, Nashes and Studebakers, and various vehicular collages created out of Cadillac grilles and Oldsmobile axles and Buick fenders patched with pieces of oil-drum metal and powered by engines interlinked with kitchen utensils and pre-Batista lawn mowers and other gadgets that have elevated the craft of tinkering in Cuba to the status of high art."

"Inhabiting a male body is much like having a bank account; as long as it's healthy, you don't think much about it. Compared to the female body, it is a low-maintenance proposition. . . ."

3. THE PUBLIC SPHERE: ADVOCACY, ARGUMENT, CONTROVERSY • 293

"Education doesn't end until life ends, because you never know when you're going to understand something you hadn't understood before."

"Justice Oliver Wendell Holmes's classic example of unprotected speech — falsely shouting 'Fire!' in a crowded theater — has been

Should anything be inferred from the fact that the first form of defense failed and the second succeeded?"

"In the world as it is now, I can see no escape from the conclusion that each one of us with wealth surplus to his or her essential needs should be giving most of it to help people suffering from poverty so dire as to be life-threatening. That's right: I'm saying that you shouldn't buy that new car, take that cruise, redecorate the house, or get that pricy new suit. After all, a thousand-dollar suit could save five children's lives."

"And why, then, is it an injury — compensated in countable cash — for an airline passenger to be forced to watch (and, yes, feel) the last seconds of his life hurdle into the past? Whereas a medieval man might have been grateful for the chance to pray, and a Victorian might have choked out a last word for his family, we sue."

"As I picked out six limes, not a bruise or blemish on them, it occurred to me that I was not really worried about robots becoming sentient, human, indistinguishable from us. That long-standing fear — robots who fool us into taking them for humans — suddenly seemed a comic-book peril, born of another age, as obsolete as a twenty-five-year-old computer."

"To kill is to put to death, extinguish, nullify, cancel, destroy. But from the hunter's point of view, it's just a tiny part of the experience."

Preface

What Is *The Best American Essays* Series?

Back in the 1970s Edward Hoagland wondered why no one had compiled an annual collection of the year's best essays, especially since comparable short story volumes had been around for decades. I agreed with Hoagland, and after a few false starts (I thought at first of calling the series "The E. B. White Awards" and later "The Emerson Awards"), I founded *The Best American Essays* as a companion volume to Houghton Mifflin's *The Best American Short Stories*. The first volume was published in 1986. Since then, the series has grown in popularity; each year more and more readers seem drawn to the vitality and versatility of the contemporary American essay.

For readers unfamiliar with the series, a brief introduction may be useful. As the series editor, I screen hundreds of essays from an enormous variety of general, specialized, and literary magazines. I then turn over roughly one hundred of these to a guest editor, a prominent American writer, who makes the final selection of approximately twenty essays. To qualify for selection, the essays must be works of high literary quality intended as fully developed, independent essays on subjects of general interest, originally written in English for first appearance in an American periodical during a calendar year. In general, selections for the book are included on the basis of literary achievement: they must be admirably written and demonstrate an awareness of craft as well as a forcefulness of thought. Since each guest editor, of course, possesses a different idea about what comprises a fine essay, each book also represents a unique literary sensibility. This variety of literary taste and opinion (which can be sampled in the prologue, "Essayists on the Essay") keeps the series healthy and diverse.

The College Edition

This version of *The Best American Essays* is designed for college students and classroom use. Essays have long been a staple of writing courses, so why not a collection of the "best" contemporary essays for today's students? I believe that many writing instructors wish to expose their students to high-quality, socially relevant, and intellectually challenging prose. With this end in mind, I selected particular essays from *The Best American Essays* series that I thought would work best for writing instructors and their students. Among the considerations for selection were length, topicality, diverse perspectives, and rhetorical and thematic variety.

Since the majority of essays we encounter today tend to fall into three general, though fairly distinct, categories — personal, informative, and argumentative — I arranged the selections accordingly. The book reflects the types of writing most often taught in introductory and even advanced composition courses. Instructors will find a generous number of selections to use if they want to teach excellent writing within the context of personal narratives, expository patterns, and persuasive strategies. In addition, I included within these three categories selections that also reflect many of the topics and issues that currently enliven discussion and debate: multiculturalism, race and gender, sexual and identity politics, popular culture, and media studies.

I've also drawn from the various "Forewords" I contribute to the annual volumes to develop an introduction to the literary and compositional features of the contemporary American essay. And, though space would not permit the inclusion of all the guest-editor introductions, I orchestrated incisive excerpts into a prologue that should stimulate critical discussion of the genre and lead to writing assignments.

In addition, to help orient student readers, the volume contains an informative "lead-in" to each essay and a brief biographical note. "Reflections and Responses," a set of questions designed to assist class discussion or to instigate ideas for papers, follows each selection. The questions range from a consideration of compositional details to broader reflections on theme and issue. Instructors who wish to delve deeper into the literary and rhetorical features of the essays should appreciate the thorough instructor's manual that I've prepared by Elizabeth Huyck. The manual can be found online.

For instructors who prefer to teach essays along different lines, the manual now includes three alternative arrangements: (a) a rhetorical table of contents that rearranges the essays into ten traditional modes or patterns; (b) a table of contents that focuses on salient literary and journalistic features; and (c) a thematic and topical organization that places the essays in a context of current issues.

Given its arrangement, flexibility, and emphasis on recently published essays, the college edition of *The Best American Essays* is suitable for various writing courses. It can be used in mainstream freshman composition programs with a focus on personal, expository, and argumentative essays. Instructors who want to concentrate on the contemporary essay, creative nonfiction techniques, or the essay as a literary genre will also find the collection and its instructional apparatus extremely suitable.

New to the Fifth Edition

For this fifth college edition, I expanded the Introduction to cover the issue of truth in the memoir and personal essay, a topic that has received a great deal of recent attention. I have added four new authors to the *Prologue: Essayists on the Essay*, a unique feature that has proved to be popular with instructors who enjoy the wide range of bite-sized comments on the art and craft of the genre from many of the nation's premier essayists. I have also revised a third of the book; of the thirty-seven selections, thirteen are new. With one exception, all of these selections are drawn from the most recent volumes of *The Best American Essays*. My choices were partially guided by several useful reviews from writing instructors who shared with me some of their classroom experiences with particular selections.

Marcia Aldrich, *Michigan State University*
Ted Anton, *DePaul University*
Andrea De Fusco, *Boston College*
Brennan Enos, *Palm Beach Community College*
Andrea Herrmann, *University of Arkansas at Little Rock*

Elizabeth Hutton, *University of Michigan*
Tom Irish, *Western Illinois University*
Bonnie J. Marshall, *Grand Valley State University*
Christine Murray, *University of Texas at Arlington*
Lad Tobin, *Boston College*

Instructors familiar with previous editions of the book will notice a bold new look this time. The collection now contains a generous array of visual material. Because certain selections are so textually dependent on specific images (such as David Masello's "My Friend Lodovico" or Ashraf Rushdy's "Exquisite Corpse"), it now seems pedagogically necessary to include the pictures along with the essays. Each year as I select candidates from numerous periodicals, I also come across the essays and creative nonfiction of graphic and comic artists. I am finding that more and more prestigious literary periodicals now include cartoons and comics. I do not select this material for *The Best American Essays*, but, with my editor John McHugh's encouragement, I saw no reason this time not to include in the college edition "graphic essays" that have impressed me. For this edition, I've selected Lynda Barry's "Two Questions," which I originally found in *McSweeney's* (and which was appropriately also selected by Anne Elizabeth Moore and Harvey Pekar for the inaugural edition of *The Best American Comics 2006*). I hope instructors will find this selection a refreshing — and relevant — addition to the book.

No collection, of course, can entirely please everyone. I have listened carefully to reviewers and have relied on my own classroom and writing workshop experiences in choosing contemporary essays that — in their variety of subject, style, and structure — would best serve as an introduction to the genre. I ought to add that I based my choices on the essays themselves, considering mainly their relevance to writing courses, not the reputations of their authors. You will certainly find many well-known essayists in the collection; but you will also discover several unfamiliar writers, some of whom have rarely been anthologized. A large part of my purpose in editing *The Best American Essays* series is to introduce to the reading public young and emerging writers.

I am always interested in comments and suggestions, especially regarding the book's classroom utility, and invite responses from teachers and students. Please address responses to Robert Atwan/

Series Editor/The Best American Essays/P.O. Box 220/Readville, MA 02137.

Although anthologies such as this one may appear simple to construct, they actually involve the professional efforts of many people. I appreciate the enthusiasm for the project and the help I've received from the Houghton Mifflin college staff: I especially appreciate the advice and support I received from my editors, Suzanne Phelps Weir and John McHugh. I would also like to thank Project Editors, Katherine Leahey and Aimee Chevrette, who handled production; permissions editors Craig D. Mertens and Katie Huha; and the copyeditor, Vici Casana. I'm especially indebted to my wife Helene and my son Gregory for their indispensable support and advice.

R. A.

The Best
AMERICAN
ESSAYS
College Edition

Encountering the Essay

What Are Essays?

Like poems, plays, novels, and short stories, essays resist simple definition or classification. There are so many types of essays that any attempt to come up with a single, authoritative description of *the* essay is likely to be overly general or critically useless. A well-known handbook of literary terms, for example, doesn't even attempt to define the form: "A moderately brief prose discussion of a restricted topic," the entry begins. But it then goes on to say: "Because of the wide application of the term, no satisfactory definition can be arrived at; nor can a wholly acceptable 'classification' of essay types be made." So much writing today goes under the name of essay — celebrity profiles, interviews, political commentary, reviews, reportage, scientific papers, scholarly articles, snippets of humor, and newspaper columns — that it's virtually impossible for readers to obtain any clear and consistent impression of the form.

Though many illustrious examples of "brief prose discussion" can be found in classical Greek and Latin literature, the modern essay had its origins in the European Renaissance. At a time when writers and artists throughout Europe were exploring ways to express their personalities more freely in painting and literature, a French magistrate, Michel de Montaigne, retired to his Bordeaux estate in 1570 and began experimenting with a new kind of prose. Impatient with formal philosophy and academic disquisition, he soon found a way to create a more flexible and personal discourse. Realizing that his efforts fit no conventional category — they could not be termed letters, or memoirs, or treatises—he simply referred to them by the French word *essais,* meaning *attempts, trials,* or *experiments.* By adopting a casual, everyday word to describe his endeavors, Montaigne called attention to the informal character of this new literary genre. His essays were personal, tentative, highly digressive, and wholly unsystematic in their approach to a topic.

Montaigne's brand of essay became for many later writers *the* genuine essay. For William Hazlitt, Virginia Woolf, and E. B. White, this was the only type of essay that could be considered a literary form. It went under different names; sometimes it was called the periodical, informal, or familiar essay. This was to differentiate it from types of prose discourse composed in a more systematic and formal fashion, writing that conformed to objective rather than subjective standards. Some examples of the formal essay are philosophical and ethical arguments, historical and scientific papers, dissertations, and critical articles. Today the informal essay is best represented by the personal essay, whereas the most popular type of formal essay is the magazine article. Although writers and editors may use the terms interchangeably, many periodicals routinely distinguish between essay and article in their tables of contents, a distinction that usually boils down to personal memoir or reflection as opposed to reportage, interviews, or feature stories.

Essays and Articles

If it's impossible to produce an airtight definition of an essay, it's equally impossible to define an article. Like "essay," this all-purpose literary label has a long, complex history. The word goes back to the Latin term for a joint (*artus*) connecting two parts of a body, and its literal use was eventually extended to include the components of writing and discourse. By the eighteenth century, "article" was used regularly for literary compositions that treated a specific topic. The first to use the term in its modern journalistic sense was one of English literature's foremost essayists, Joseph Addison.

Articles require not just a topic, but a timely topic. Unlike essays, articles are usually (a) about something specific and (b) about something of *current* interest. Essays, on the other hand, can take large liberties with subject, theme, organization, and point of view. Essay-ists tend to be personal, reflective, leisurely; article writers (they used to be called "articlers") usually stay close to the facts, rarely stray from "the point," and seldom interrupt the flow of information with personal opinion or reflection. The essayist will feel comfort-able writing about various general topics — friendship, envy, man-ners, nature. The article writer is often looking for an angle, or "hook," that will directly relate the article to some current event or fashionable trend.

For example: assign the topic of "revenge" to two authors — one who prefers to write personal or familiar essays and one who specializes in journalistic articles or feature stories. Chances are the essayist will take a first-person, reflective look at the nature of revenge, blending together personal experience and literary refer-ences. The journalist will most likely conduct several interviews with psychologists and then skillfully choreograph these into an informative piece on how to deal constructively with vengeful emo-tions. These are, of course, extremes, but they suggest the diver-gent routes of the essay and article in today's literature. In general, the personal, reflective essay is often found in the literary quarterlies and periodicals; articles, like the example above, are the mainstay of popular magazines.

With a few exceptions, our major magazines print relatively few personal essays. Editors believe that their readers want news and information, not personal reminiscence or leisurely reflection. As a result, the weekly and monthly magazines depend on hard news stories, interviews, profiles, and "service articles" that offer readers practical advice on everything from child rearing to the latest diet. Few of these pieces could be called "literary"; most of them fall rapidly out of date and are not likely to be read even a few months after their appearance. If the personal essayist faces the challenge of making his or her experiences and reflections interesting and relevant, the article writer faces a different chal-lenge: how to handle current issues and topics in such a way that people will still read the work with pleasure long after those issues and topics have vanished from public discussion.

Yet, as the selections in this volume show, most good prose is not easy to pigeonhole. At either end of the spectrum, it's fairly easy to distinguish a literary essay from a journalistic article. But as we move toward the center of the spectrum, the distinctions become less clear. We begin to find a compositional mix: personal essays that depend on research and reporting, topical articles that feature a personal voice and individual viewpoint. Such literary mixtures have become increasingly prevalent in today's magazines and literary periodicals. Note, for example, the selection by Gay Talese, the writer who was one of the founders of a literary movement known as "The New Journalism." This movement attracted many prominent authors (Joan Didion, Truman Capote, Norman Mailer, among others) who wanted to incorporate a variety of literary techniques — many borrowed from novels and essays — into the conventionally "objective" magazine article. In Talese's talented hands, the ordinary celebrity profile becomes infused with mood, atmosphere, and conflict as personalities develop within a narrative that bristles with dramatic tension. Many readers coming across "Ali in Havana" (see page 265) in *Esquire* magazine would naturally consider Talese's profile of the world's most famous athlete an article; yet a close reading will demonstrate not only Talese's meticulous skills as a journalist but also his mastery of dramatic irony and literary form. Readers will want to note, too, how Annie Dillard (see page 180) elevates a "profile" of a famous stunt pilot into an essay of astonishing lyric power. In a number of the essays collected here, the writers move between the topical requirements of an article and the literary demands of an essay, adroitly balancing fact and observation with the nuances of voice and style, irony and wit.

Essays and Fiction

What ultimately makes a piece of prose an essay is usually found in the personal quality of its writing. Many of the essays in this book are not only written in the first-person singular, but they are also *about* the first-person singular. As Montaigne proved long ago, the essay is the perfect literary vehicle for both self-disclosure and self-discovery: "The wisdom of my lesson," he wrote, "is wholly in truth, in freedom, in reality." Writers today use the essay to explore their personal relationships, their individual identities, and their ethnic or racial heritages. Personal essays like Judith Ortiz Cofer's "Silent Dancing" (see page 70) and Scott Russell Sanders's "The Inheritance of Tools" (see page 131) are intimate, candid, revealing, close to the pulse of everyday human experience. Yet *personal* can be a tricky term. Its roots reach back to the Latin *persona*, the literal term for "mask." The word was traditionally used for a theatrical character, a *dramatis persona*. Thus, oddly enough, the word we use to convey intimacy and sincerity — we often approvingly speak of someone's *personal* touch — has hidden overtones of disguise and performance. Readers may overlook this double sense of the term, but personal essayists rarely do. They know that the first-person singular is not a simple equivalent of the self, a mere matter of slapping down the word "I" in front of every sentence. They know that the single letter "I" is one of the English language's most complex words.

Who is the "I" of the essay — a real person or a *dramatis persona*? Did Scott Russell Sanders really bang his thumb with a hammer just before learning of his father's death? Did Rebecca McLanahan actually come across the intriguing marginal comments in used books that she writes about? Or have these essayists contrived incidents and fabricated moods in the interests of creating a story or endorsing a position? Unless we personally know the writers, how can we verify their accounts?

When the essay is philosophical or argumentative, we can decide whether we accept an essayist's opinions or not on the basis of logic, evidence, proof, or internal consistency. For example, we would base our agreement or disagreement with Ashraf Rushdy's "Exquisite Corpse" (page 356) entirely on information that has nothing to do with the author's personal life. But once essayists begin to tell stories — about sampling dog food or playing with their children — they move dangerously close to fiction, especially when they add characters, dialogue, episodes, and climaxes. When constructing personal narratives, the essayist confronts the toughest challenge of the craft: telling stories that are at once artful, true, and *believable*. One of the essayist's most frustrating moments is when he or she relates a true story with the utmost candor and discovers that nobody believes it.

The personal essayist, then, must balance craft and credibility, aesthetics and accuracy. The first-person singular is both person and *persona*, a real person and a literary construct. The "I" is both reporting a story and simultaneously *shaping* one. If essayists hope to be wholly believable, however, they need to worry about too much shaping. A true story doesn't usually come prepackaged in a compellingly dramatic shape — many elements just don't fit in. To be believable, the essayist may narrate a story that doesn't — like much of life itself — possess a satisfying narrative closure. Sometimes what one expects to happen doesn't happen. "The writer in me," writes Frank Conroy in "Think About It," "is tempted to create a scene here — to invent one for dramatic purposes — but of course I can't do that." His literary impulse as a novelist is to create a scene; his honesty as an essayist won't let him. An essay like "Think About It" places the reader directly inside the conflict between essay and story. In fact, the tension between personal essays and stories recurs throughout this collection and is especially apparent in such selections as Anwar F. Accawi's "The Telephone" and Robert Polito's "Shame."

Autobiography and Truth

The boundary lines between a memoir and a novel (or a personal essay and a short story) can often be confusing. Many memoirs are written in a first-person narrative, and so are many novels. Great novels like Mark Twain's *The Adventures of Huckleberry Finn,* F. Scott Fitzgerald's *The Great Gatsby,* or J. D. Salinger's *The Catcher in the Rye* sound very much like memoirs, especially in their opening sections, though they are entirely fictional. Today, many memoirs and personal essays borrow heavily from the novelist's toolbox and seem indistinguishable from fiction. Note how the poet Yusef Komunyakaa opens his autobiographical essay (see page 86):

> "I feel like I'm part of this damn thing," Frank said. He carried himself like a large man even though he was short. A dead cigarette dangled from his half-grin. "I've worked on this machine for twenty-odd years, and now it's almost me."

Short story writers commonly open their stories with dialogue, often introducing a character abruptly and without establishing any situational context. This is precisely the way Komunyakaa decides to start an essay that recounts his experiences one summer when he took a job as a factory worker.

Contrast Komunyakaa's opening to the way Harper Lee begins her famous novel *To Kill a Mockingbird:*

> When he was nearly thirteen, my brother Jem got his arm badly broken at the elbow. When it healed, and Jem's fears of never being able to play football were assuaged, he was seldom self-conscious about his injury. His left arm was somewhat shorter than his right; when he stood or walked, the back of his hand was at right angles to his body, his thumb parallel to his thigh. He couldn't have cared less, so long as he could pass and punt.
>
> When enough years had gone by to enable us to look back on them, we sometimes discussed the events leading to his accident. . . .

Which opening passage sounds like it belongs in a work of fiction, and which sounds closer to a memoir? With only the two passages in front of them, most people, assuming that they weren't familiar with the original works, would say the first sounded fictional and the second truthful. And yet the opposite is the case.

If its prose style is no indication of whether a piece of writing is factual or fictional, then how can we tell the difference between an essay and a short story or between a memoir and a novel? As any cautious reader can see, it's nearly impossible to establish internal characteristics — such as voice, tone, or diction — that help us to easily distinguish one genre from the other. Therefore, if we are curious about the degree of fabrication, we usually need to rely on verifiable external factors — facts, actual events, people, places and institutions, dates, and so forth. Once the writer begins to disclose concrete or factual information, then other issues come quickly into play. The reader, if so inclined, can now use those details to test the writer's veracity or can begin inferential processes that can damage authorial credibility. Records can be discovered that prove someone didn't spend nearly as much time in the Peace Corps as claimed, or was never admitted to a certain psychiatric hospital, or hadn't served as much prison time as reported. According to many accounts, the publishing sensation of 2005, James Frey's *A Million Little Pieces,* was originally widely submitted (and widely rejected) as a *novel.* It was only when resubmitted as a *memoir* that publishers jumped.

Therefore, anyone writing a memoir (or an autobiographical essay) needs to be careful when recounting verifiable details or risks being called a liar, a phony, or an opportunist. The unverifiable world is vast and accommodating. The classic memoir, in which a celebrated individual offers an account of his or her public life and adventures, along with profiles of the important people encountered along the way, usually depended upon verifiable details — at least it is possible to confirm whether Benjamin Franklin ever met the famous Methodist preacher George Whitefield or lived for a time in London. But the modern memoir is different since it so often focuses on the private life of a not well-known or perhaps even an obscure person. Who's to say if the author ever really took a life-transforming midnight swim all alone in Buzzard's Bay when she was fifteen? And unless a description is biologically or physically implausible, who would bother to question it? Perhaps a question to ask of a memoir is something the American philosopher William James might have asked: If a report of something is wholly unverifiable, should we even concern ourselves with the issue of truth?

We have thousands of critical studies dealing with the art of fiction, but very little exists on the art of the memoir aside from a growing number of "how-to" books. One reason for this situation is that despite its present popularity, the memoir has not yet become a fully accredited genre in our universities. Most educated readers are still uncertain about how best to evaluate a memoir or an autobiographical essay. What makes one memoir or essay outstanding and another forgettable? Does it largely depend on the quality of the prose? Will the particulars of an author's life bias our aesthetic responses either positively or negatively? Why is the first question that readers ask of a memoir "Is it true?" Is it a critical error to apply modern journalistic fact-checking standards to memoirs and essays intended as works of literature? If a personal essay turns out to have some fictional elements and details, does that automatically turn it into a short story — or does it become something else: a fictive essay? a fable? an outright lie? Does using the term *creative nonfiction* solve anything?

In the eighteenth and nineteenth centuries, writers like Addison and Steele and Washington Irving could invent characters and situations for their nonfiction works (many of these were published in the newspapers of their day), and readers found their essays and sketches delightful. As you encounter the autobiographical essays in this volume, you might ask yourself to what extent your enjoyment and appreciation of a selection depends on whether you are convinced that the writer is telling the truth. When do you think it matters, and when do you think it doesn't?

The Autobiographical "I"

In college writing courses years ago, instructors referred to a syllogism that may help explain the enormous popularity of the personal memoir. It went something like this: "You write best when you write about what you know; what you know best is yourself; therefore, you write best when you write about yourself." As a syllogism, this seemed valid: The conclusion followed logically from its premises, no? So why didn't teachers always receive better essays when they assigned personal topics?

As anyone can see, the conclusion rests on dubious assumptions. The premises sound reasonable, but they raise some fundamental questions. Do people really write best about the subjects they know best? We see evidence all the time of experts being unable to communicate the basic concepts of their professions, which explains why so many technical books are authored by both an expert and a writer. Brilliant academics so committed to their vast research that they can't bear to part with any detail thus clog up their sentences with an excess of information. If a little knowledge is a dangerous thing, too much can sometimes be an impediment to clear and robust expression. Shakespeareans do not always write the best books on Shakespeare.

Can we also safely conclude that we know ourselves best of all? If so, then why do so many of us spend so much time in psychotherapy or counseling sessions? Surely, the pursuit of the self — especially the "hidden" self — has been a major industry. Self-knowledge, of course, confronts us with another logical problem: How can the self be at the same time the knower and the known? That's why biographies can be so much more revealing than autobiographies. As Dostoyevsky said in his *Notes from Underground:* "A true autobiography is almost an impossibility . . . man is bound to lie about himself."

Yet the illusion that we do know ourselves best must serve as both comfort and inspiration to the growing wave of memoirists who seem to write with one finger glued to the shift key and another to the letter *I*, which on the keyboard looks nothing like it does on the page, thus appropriately symbolizing the relationship between that single letter and the "self" it presumes to represent. Today's writer's market is flooded with autobiography — now more likely to be labeled "memoir" in the singular, as though the more fashionable literary label promises something grander. Memoirs (the term was almost always used in the plural) were customarily written by public figures who recorded their participation in historical events and their encounters with other prominent individuals. General Ulysses S. Grant's two-volume *Personal Memoirs* (1885–86) were bestsellers. The old memoirs were penned by well-established individuals in the twilight of their careers; the new memoir is frequently the work of an emerging writer aspiring to be well established.

The memoir is easily abused by those who believe the genre automatically confers upon the author some sort of importance. It's only natural, isn't it, to be the heroes or heroines of our own lives? And as the main protagonists, how can we resist the impulse to occupy center stage and not consider ourselves gifted with greater sensitivity, finer values, higher moral authority, and especially keener powers of recollection than any member of our supporting cast of characters? The most interesting autobiography ever conceived must be Mark Twain's. Partly written, partly dictated, never published in its entirety, and never according to his intentions — in many ways a colossal failure of a book — Twain's autobiography grappled with every psychological and compositional difficulty characteristic of the genre. Twain knew how easy it was to exhibit ourselves in "creditable attitudes exclusively" and tried to display himself as honestly as he could. It was a noble experiment, but it proved impossible: "I have been dictating this autobiography of mine," he wrote, "for three months; I have thought of fifteen hundred or two thousand incidents in my life which I am ashamed of but I have not gotten one of them to consent to go on paper yet."

To say that memoir, autobiography, and the personal essay are easily abused is not to disparage these vigorous genres. Democratizing the memoir has resulted in many wonderful books, not a few crafted by young or relatively young writers who have learned to ask themselves how to prevent their personal writing from deteriorating into narcissism and self-absorption. This is a question anyone setting out to write personally must face sooner or later. The solution requires a healthy regimen of self-skepticism and a respect for uncertainty. Though the first-person singular may abound, it should be a richly complex and mutable "I," never one that designates a reliably known, wholly static entity. In some of the best memoirs and personal essays, the writers are mysteries to themselves, and the work evolves into an enactment of surprise and self-discovery. These elements keep "life writing" *live* writing, as a mysterious "I" converses with an equally mysterious "I."

Writing the "Standard" Essay

Many students who enter their first-year writing courses already know how to manufacture the "perfect paper." For some reason, they know it should begin with an introductory paragraph that contains a thesis statement and often cites an expert named Webster. It then pursues its expository path through three paragraphs that develop the main idea until it finally reaches a concluding paragraph that industriously summarizes all three previous paragraphs. The conclusion often begins, "Thus we see that. . . ." If the paper tells a personal story, it might conclude, "Suddenly I realized. . . ." Epiphanies abound.

What is especially maddening about the typical five-paragraph paper has less to do with its tedious, predictable structure than with its implicit message that writing should be the end product of thought and not the enactment of its process. Many students seem unaware that writing can be an act of discovery, an opportunity to say something they had never before thought of saying. The worst papers instructors receive are largely the products of premature conclusions, of unearned assurances, of minds irrevocably made up. As Robert Frost once put it, for many people thinking merely means voting. Why go through the trouble of writing papers on an issue when all that's required is an opinion poll? Do you agree? Disagree? It makes sense to call such productions "papers" (or "themes" or "assignments") since what is written has almost no connection with the true sense of "essaying" — trying out ideas and positions, writing while in a state of uncertainty, of not knowing.

The five-paragraph theme is also a charade. It not only parades in lock-step toward its conclusion; it begins with its conclusion. It is all about its conclusion. Its structure permits no change of direction, no reconsideration, no wrestling with ideas. It is — and has long been — the perfect vehicle for the sort of reader who solemnly likes to ask: "And your point is . . . ?"

The most talented essayists have aims other than merely getting a point across or a position announced or an identity established. It may help to imagine an essay as a sort of Cubist rendition of an idea: the essayist would rather you consider all sides and aspects of a thought or concept, much in the same multiperspectival fashion that Picasso or Braque portrayed an ordinary table on canvas. Some essayists — Montaigne again was the first — seem literally to be turning ideas over in their minds. The intellectual essay is nothing if not ruminative; the autobiographical essay may continually lose its sense of direction. Both kinds of essays, like Samuel Johnson's eighteenth-century fable, *Rasselas,* will often reach a "conclusion in which nothing is concluded."

Evaluating the "Standard" Essay

Can a computer evaluate an essay? This question has been on people's minds since Educational Testing Service recently unveiled e-rater®, its new computer program that will grade essay questions on the Graduate Management Admissions Test. As news of e-rater spread, newspaper reports appeared across the nation nervously wondering how essays can be machine scored. Objective tests, with their multiple choices, are one thing; but aren't sentences, paragraphs, and organization quite another?

The answer is that a computer can very easily score the results of essay questions, assuming that all anyone wanted to know was whether the writing conformed to standard English usage and reflected a few other elements of style, like syntactic variety, that can be measured conveniently and objectively. Computers have been able to do this for quite some time, and most word-processing applications currently provide a few (though still rudimentary) tools to check grammar and style. But can a computer detect humor and irony (which skilled readers themselves sometimes fail to catch)?

Can it evaluate the use of imagery and metaphor, or discern the nuances of a writer's tone of voice? E-rater's developer honestly admitted to the *New York Times* that it cannot: "It's not designed to score Montaigne," she said. "It's designed for a specific purpose: to score the kinds of essays we see on standardized tests." Admittedly, these would be "standard" essays.

Are these what we talk about when we talk about essays? Montaigne's term for his eccentric and digressive meditations is now employed so broadly and indiscriminately that its traditional literary meaning is all but forgotten. An essay, it seems, is anything we want it to be. Our dailies, weeklies, and monthlies are chock full of nonfiction prose, but little of it is either creative or literary. Most of it is informative, functional, or advisory, and that's as it should be. Produced with built-in obsolescence, such writing is made for the month (at best) and not for the years. E-rater may do fine evaluating standardized expression, but it is educationally unfortunate that its name and use will continue to confuse people about the true literary nature of essays.

Essays Can Be a Risky Business

"Where there's a will there's a way," an excited William Hazlitt says to himself as he hurries down Chancery Lane "about half-past six o'clock, on Monday the 10th of December, to enquire at Jack Randall's where the fight the next day was to be." The year is 1821, the city is London, and Hazlitt is pursuing his way to an out-of-town boxing match, his first fight ever. He's eager to see big Bill Neate, the raging Bristol "Bull," take on the "Gas-Man," Tom Hickman, the bravest and cruelest fighter in all of England. "I was determined to see this fight, come what would, and see it I did, in great style."

You can consult all the handbooks on literary fiction for all the elements of style, structure, and composition, but you'll rarely find mention of what Hazlitt just noted — *determination*. Yet its literary value is inestimable.

This collection is filled with determination. You can see the fight in great style. You can narrate it with equally great style. But as Hazlitt reminds us, you first have to get there. No sitting in your study with a boxing encyclopedia, no telephone interviews with experts, no electronic highway; and the travel involved takes you beyond your local library.

Such narratives can be a risky business. For one thing, the destinations are often uncertain. When Jamaica Kincaid decides to see England for the first time, or when Barry Lopez strays far from the beaten track in search of an ancient stone horse, or even when Ian Frazier journeys around his Ohio and Montana neighborhoods, they have no idea what surprising emotions or events they will encounter. But there's an additional risk. After writing "The Fight," Hazlitt was surprised to find that people considered his eyewitness report a "vulgar thing." This wasn't simply because his story took readers into an unfamiliar subculture, but because it took them into unfamiliar prose territory as well. In other words, Hazlitt risked the unliterary; he was determined to find a way to develop an essay out of "unsuitable" material. We can find a similar determination throughout this volume: Look at how such writers as Marcia Aldrich, Rebecca McClanahan, or Frank Conroy creatively confront ordinary, unpromising, uncomfortable, or even intractable subjects. Where there's a will, there's a way.

Risk and determination — at both a personal and creative level — will often transform a piece of nonfiction prose into a memorable literary work. Our finest essayists seek out challenges, go for the toughest questions on the board. The challenges may spring from the demands of the assignment or of the composition — or both. These essayists resist the plodding memoir, the facile discovery of identity, the predictable opinion, or the unearned assertion. What many of the essays collected here have in common is their determination to take on the tough assignment, to raise the difficulty level of the game.

The Contemporary American Essay: A Diversity of Forms and Voices

The personal essay has long existed in a literary twilight zone. Because it presumes to tell a true story yet often employs fictional or poetic techniques, it stands awkwardly with one foot in and one foot out of "imaginative" literature. It was partially for this reason that one of America's foremost essayists, E. B. White, complained in 1977 that the essayist "unlike the novelist, the poet, and the playwright, must be content in his self-imposed role of second-class citizen." Writers who have their eyes on a Nobel Prize or "other earthly triumphs," White continued, "had best write a novel, a poem, or a play." White was responding not only to the critical reception of his own work but also to a general decline in the literary quality of the American essay. Essays struck a lot of readers as "old-fashioned." When readers thought of essays, they thought of writing that was stiff, stuffy, textbookish — things teachers forced them to read and write in school.

A century ago, however, the essay occupied a prominent position in American literature. It fell into the class of writing that critics called "polite letters." The essayists, mostly men, addressed the literate world in an urbane, congenial, comfortable manner. These gentlemen, it seemed, always possessed three names — James Russell Lowell, Oliver Wendell Holmes, Thomas Wentworth Higginson — and more often than not lived in New England. In this era, when "coming out" referred only to a young woman's debut, the typical essay was proper, genteel, and Anglophilic. Although it atrophied during the 1930s, the polite essay retained for many years an insidious power over American students, who were often forced to imitate its polished civility in that shadow genre known as the "freshman theme." The goal of English teachers, Kurt Vonnegut recalls, was to get you "to write like cultivated Englishmen of a century or more ago."

Essays began to seem old-fashioned to the American reader mainly because they were too slow in coming to terms with twentieth-century modernism. While William Faulkner, T. S. Eliot, and Eugene O'Neill were radically transforming fiction, poetry, and drama, the essay retained much of its relaxed, genteel manner. Adventurous writers considered the essay a holdover from Victorian times. With few exceptions, the essay broke no new ground, violated no literary conventions. Instead of standing as modern works of literature in themselves, essays simply tried to explain those works. For the academic community as well as for many general readers, the essay gradually grew synonymous with literary criticism. Essays were written *about* literature, not *as* literature.

Since E. B. White issued his complaint, the literary status of the essay has been steadily improving. As Annie Dillard says, the essay "has joined the modern world." Essays are now written in the same imaginative spirit as fiction and poetry. Contemporary essays can rival the best fiction and poetry in artistic accomplishment. Far from being hesitant about literary aims and methods, today's essayists delight in the use of imagery, symbol, and metaphor, often interweaving them into such complex mosaic patterns as those we find in Kyoko Mori's "Yarn" and Joyce Carol Oates's "They All Just Went Away." Boundary lines — between life and art, prose and poetry, truth and fiction, the world and self — are often blurred as essayists take greater liberties with language and form. This is now true even of essays grounded in information and explanation.

Nor can the essay be characterized any longer by its homogeneity. In fact, its diversity may now be its most noticeable feature. In light of the essay's transformation, today's poetry and fiction appear stagnant: The essay may be our most exciting literary form. We see narrative essays that are indistinguishable from short stories, mosaic essays that read like prose poems. We find literary criticism with an autobiographical spin, journalism sensitively attuned to drama and metaphor, reflection with a heavy dose of information. Some essayists write polemic that sounds like poetry. Physicists, mathematicians, and philosophers are finding that complex ideas and a memorable prose style are not irreconcilable. Even law review articles have taken a literary turn. Today's essays are incredibly difficult to categorize and pin down.

This volume collects and celebrates the contemporary American essay. Never before — except perhaps in the days of Ralph Waldo Emerson and Henry David Thoreau — have so many fine young American writers begun to explore the essay's literary possibilities. They come to the form with a renewed enthusiasm for its astonishing flexibility and versatility — the essay can incorporate an enormously wide range of subjects and styles. The personal essay has grown increasingly candid, more intimate, less polite. Essayists seem willing to take greater emotional risks. Essayists today seem less relaxed and more eager to confront urgent social questions. Journalism has contributed to this sense of risk and urgency, encouraging essayists to fuse within a single style both personal experience and public issues, dual themes that Barry Lopez brilliantly combines in "The Stone Horse."

The Essay and Public Events

As Stephen Jay Gould was making selections for the 2002 volume
of *The Best American Essays*, he observed how everything seemed
"shaped by 9/11," regardless of whether it was written before or
after. Later, I realized how every few years some pivotal event dominates the national attention and dramatically narrows the literary
scope of this series. In 1995 it seemed that half the essays published in magazines dealt either directly or tangentially with the
O. J. Simpson trial. The nation couldn't stop talking about it, and
many distinguished writers weighed in with insightful and sometimes brilliant commentary. In a similar occurrence toward the
end of 2000, the American political process was put on hold
during the most bizarre presidential election in our history. Yet
coverage of these events — as influential and absorbing as they
still are — did not necessarily find their way into the volumes
featuring the best essays of those years.

But the terrorist attacks of 9/11 and their aftermath were altogether another story. The written response was overwhelming, and
not merely because of the immediate and massive news coverage.
One could expect the coverage, commentary, and reportage;
unexpected was their astonishingly high quality. Anticipating that
thoughtful essays would require months of reflection and deliberation, the "literature of 9/11" was surely several years away. But
essays of high literary quality began appearing within weeks of the
incident.

In fact, we should have expected the abundance of fine 9/11
essays. The essay always seems to be revitalized in times of war
and conflict — and usually with the return of peace and prosperity,
fiction and poetry regain their literary stature. The First World War
resulted in an eruption of essays and introduced the work of some
of our finest nonfiction writers, many of whom, like Randolph
Bourne, took up the pacifist cause. But then the postwar years
saw the flourishing of some of our most celebrated poets and
novelists, those members of the "lost generation." This was true,
too, in the Second World War (E. B. White published his greatest
essay collection in 1942) and especially true during Vietnam. It
seems to me no coincidence that the Vietnam years saw the emer-
gence of the New Journalism, an exciting and innovative brand of

nonfiction pioneered (as mentioned earlier) by Gay Talese, a writer included in this volume.

This theory about essays in time of war is not easily proven, but the idea also appears in Czeslaw Milosz's brilliant long poem, A *Treatise on Poetry*, which appeared shortly before the 9/11 carnage. Though he promotes the value of poetry in difficult times, Milosz, who won the Nobel Prize in 1980, prefaces *Treatise* with the recognition that in our time, "serious combat, where life is at stake, is fought in prose." Perhaps in times of conflict and crisis, people want to be in the presence of less mediated voices; we need more debate and directives; we desire more public discourse. We instinctively turn to writing that displays a greater sense of immediacy and urgency. "These are the times that try men's souls," Tom Paine memorably wrote in 1776, in what would be the first essay of *The American Crisis*. At that moment in history, radicalism and nationalism could go hand in hand.

Whatever other consequences arise from 9/11, the attacks have had enormous cultural repercussions. One of these is the reemergence of the essay as a broadly relevant, even indispensable, genre — a vital source of voices, ideas, and personal histories that the public will turn to with perhaps greater attention than ever before. A fine example of how the events of 9/11 resulted in politically astute responses from essayists is Elaine Scarry's "Citizenship in Emergency" (see page 367).

The Essay's Future

The year 1995 marked the 400th anniversary of the first complete edition of Montaigne's essays. As we progress into the twenty-first century, it will be natural to speculate on how the essay will change. Will essays be shaped in new, surprising ways by the digital revolution? Will cyberspace breed new essayists and new kinds of essays? Will original, literary prose works begin appearing in underground sites without benefit of agents, editors, publishers, and prestige periodicals? Will young, struggling writers find a quicker and less stressful way to break into print? As voice and video become increasingly common, will a new age of graphic/audio texts dramatically alter the reading habits of a future generation? In 2020, as one commentator wondered, will book publishers as a trade be as obsolete as blacksmiths?

Predictions of a bookless future have, of course, been commonplace for decades, and there's good reason to be skeptical about the announced "end" of anything, whether it be books, literature, or history itself. When Bill Gates wanted to evangelize on America's electronic future, he didn't go online but instead produced an old-fashioned thirty-dollar hardcover book with a first printing of 800,000 copies. The first thing most young people probably did when they got the book, however, was run the inserted "companion interactive CD-ROM" that contained the complete text, multimedia hyperlinks, video demonstrations, and an audio interview with Gates. Unbelievers continually say that nobody wants to read a book on a screen, and for that reason alone they consider books to be irreplaceable. But for the next generation, books may routinely be read on a screen, a cozy lightweight "papery" screen you can pop a CD into, carry anywhere, and comfortably curl up with and read in the dark. Why not? The practical advantages will be tremendous, and parents will finally be able to lift their kids' backpacks.

There's no reason to oppose technology; the digital revolution is here to stay, and one can amply enjoy its products and conveniences. A younger generation may be more comfortable reading electronic books, but if they are reading something worth reading, they will more than likely — to borrow the title of critic Ruben Brower's seminal essay — do their "reading in slow motion." Though retrieving and downloading *Walden* or *Portrait of a Lady* can be done in the blink of an eye, savoring the prose, word by word, sentence by sentence, will always take time. One danger, of course, is that as people become more accustomed to instantaneous acquisition of texts, they will simultaneously grow so impatient with the time-consuming process of reading them that reading itself may become as obsolete as Sunday family strolls down Main Street.

The issue really isn't the future of books but of reading, and since people were reading long before the paginated book was developed some five hundred years ago, chances are good that they'll be reading long after it has been radically transformed. It is hardly a coincidence that the essay was invented not long after the book, for we owe to the physical feature of books the personal essay's idio-syncratic and circuitous manner. Montaigne equipped his home office with one of the earliest book-lined studies, where he loved to spend his time *browsing*. His mind too mercurial to concentrate wholeheartedly on any one volume, he would "leaf through now one book now another, without order and without plan, by discon-nected fragments." An idea took hold; he began to write just the way he read. His medium became his message, and the personal essay was born.

For those who enjoy leisurely reading, the essay remains the ideal form, as the selections in this volume amply demonstrate. A rumi-native, unhurried style has long been part of the essay's tradition. Early in the twentieth century, literary critics were predicting that the slow-paced "old-fashioned essay" would soon disappear. It was, as William Dean Howells observed in 1902, being driven out by newsworthy articles with no interest in the "lounging gait," and the "wilding nature" that characterized what Howells called the "right" essay. His concerns about a readership so corrupted and depraved, so bereft of a lyrical sense that they preferred articles to essays, were echoed through every decade of the twentieth century. Yet somehow "right" or true essays still manage to be written, pub-lished, and admired. This volume — with its many sinuous selections that wind through time and memory, that blur the distinctions be-tween past and present, that take us intimately into the multilay-ered processes of thought — attests to that fact.

Robert Atwan

Essayists on the Essay

Each edition of The Best American Essays *features a guest editor who makes the final selections and writes an introduction to the volume. The guest editors themselves are distinguished American writers, many of whom have excelled in various literary forms. In their introductions, they almost always address the question of the essay: its history, definition, style, audience, composition. Their essays on the essay would in themselves make an interesting collection. What follows are some of their most incisive remarks.*

What Is an Essay?

What *is* an essay, and what, if anything, is it about? "Formal" and "informal," "personal," "familiar," "review-essay," "article-essay," "critical essay," essays literary, biographical, polemic, and historical — the standard litcrit lexicon and similar attempts at genre definition and subclassification in the end simply tell you how like an eel this essay creature is. It wriggles between narcissism and detachment, opinion and fact, the private party and the public meeting, omphalos and brain, analysis and polemics, confession and reportage, persuasion and provocation. All you can safely say is that it's not poetry and it's not fiction.
— Justin Kaplan

Resisting Definitions

AN ESSAY! The fixed form or the fixed category of any kind, any definition at all, fills me with such despair that I feel compelled to do or be its opposite. And if I cannot do its opposite, if I can in fact complete the task that is the fixed form, or fill the fixed category, I then deny it, I then decline to participate at all. Is this a complex view? But I believe I have stated it simply: anything that I might do, anything that I might be, I cannot bear to be enclosed by, I cannot bear to have its meaning applied to me.

The Essay: and this is not a form of literary expression unfamiliar to me. I can remember being introduced to it. It was the opinions and observations of people I did not know, and their opinions and observations bore no relationship to my life as I lived it then. But even now, especially now, I do not find anything peculiar or wrong about this; after all, the opinions and observations of people you do not know are the most interesting, and even the most important, for your own opinions and observations can only, ultimately, fix you, categorize you — the very thing that leads me to dissent or denial.

— Jamaica Kincaid

The Ideal Essay

In reading an essay, I want to feel that I'm communing with a real person, and a person who cares about what he or she's writing about. The words sound sentimental and trite, but the qualities are rare. For me, the ideal essay is not an assignment, to be dispatched efficiently and intelligently, but an exploration, a questioning, an introspection. I want to see a piece of the essayist. I want to see a mind at work, imagining, spinning, struggling to understand. If the essayist has all the answers, then he isn't struggling to grasp, and I won't either. When you care about something, you continually grapple with it, because it is alive in you. It thrashes and moves, like all living things.

When I'm reading a good essay, I feel that I'm going on a journey. The essayist is searching for something and taking me along. That something could be a particular idea, an unraveling of identity, a meaning in the wallow of observations and facts. The facts are important but never enough. An essay, for me, must go past the facts, an essay must travel and move. Even the facts of the essayist's own history, the personal memoir, are insufficient alone. The facts of personal history provide anchor, but the essayist then swings in a wide arc on his anchor line, testing and pulling hard.

— Alan Lightman

The Essay as Object

If kids still write essays in school the way people my age used to, they meet the essay first as pure object. In school, it is (or was) a written paper

of a certain length, on an assigned subject, with specified margins and
neatness, due on the teacher's desk at a certain date. From about fourth
grade on, I wrote many essays. "An essay a week" was a philosophy lots of
grammar school teachers subscribed to back then. Recently I came
across an essay of mine I'd saved from the fifth grade. It's called "If I Had
Three Wishes." My first wish, as I described it, was for lots of fishing
equipment, my second was for a canoe in which to go fishing, and my
third was for a cabin in the woods somewhere near good fishing. I have
more or less gotten those wishes, writing occasional essays about fishing
all the while. Even in its present state as childhood artifact, "If I Had
Three Wishes" retains its purposeful object-ness: the three-ring-binder
paper with regular lines and space at the top for student's name, teacher's
name, and date; the slow, newly learned script, in blue ballpoint, almost
without mistakes; and the circled good grade in the teacher's hand.

— Ian Frazier

The Essay as Action

Beneath the object, the physical piece of writing with its unpredictable
content, is the action that produced it. The action, it seems to me, is easier
to predict. The difference is like that between a golf ball in the air and the
swing of the golfer that propelled it; the flight of a struck ball varies, but
the swing tends always to be the same. An essay is a golf swing, an angler's
cast, a tennis serve. For example, say, an experience happens to you, one
that seems to have literary potential. You wait for it to grow in your mind
into a short story or even just an episode of "Friends," but somehow it
doesn't. Then a further experience, or an odd chance, or something a
friend says, or something in the newspaper chimes with the first experience, and suddenly you understand you can write about it, and you do.
You quit longing for form and write what's there, with whatever serviceable
prose comes to hand, for no better reason than the fun and release of saying. That sequence — that combination of patience with sudden impatience, that eventual yielding to the simple desire to tell — identifies the
essay.

— Ian Frazier

Essays and the Real World

The essay can do everything a poem can do, and everything a short story
can do — everything but fake it. The elements in any nonfiction should
be true not only artistically — the connections must hold at base and

must be veracious, for that is the convention and the covenant between the nonfiction writer and his reader. Veracity isn't much of a drawback to the writer; there's a lot of truth out there to work with. And veracity isn't much of a drawback to the reader. The real world arguably exerts a greater fascination on people than any fictional one; many people, at least, spend their whole lives there, apparently by choice. The essayist does what we do with our lives; the essayist thinks about actual things. He can make sense of them analytically or artistically. In either case he renders the real world coherent and meaningful, even if only bits of it, and even if that coherence and meaning reside only inside small texts.

— Annie Dillard

The Essay's Subjectivity

As near as I can figure, an essay can be . . . a query, a reminiscence, a persuasive tract, an exploration; it can look inward or outward; it can crack a lot of jokes. What it need not be is objective. An essay can certainly present facts and advocate a position, but that seems quite different from objectivity, whereby a writer just delivers information, adding nothing in the process. Instead, essays take their tone and momentum from the explicit presence of the writer in them and the distinctiveness of each writer's perspective. That makes essays definitely subjective — not in the skewed, unfair sense of subjectivity, but in the sense that essays are conversations, and they should have all the nuances and attitude that any conversation has. I'm sure that's why newspapers so rarely generate great essays: even in the essay-allowed zone of a newspaper, the heavy breath of Objective Newspaper Reporting is always blowing down the writer's neck. And certainly there is no prescribed tone that is "correct" for essays. Sometimes it seems that they have a sameness of manner, a kind of earnest, handwriting solemnity. Is this necessary? I don't think so. Many of the essays that intrigued me this year were funny, or unusually structured, or tonally adventurous — in other words, not typical in sound or shape. What mattered was that they conveyed the writer's journey, and did it intelligently, gracefully, honestly, and with whatever voice or shape fit best.

— Susan Orlean

No Standard Essay

As there is no standard human type who writes essays, so is there no standard essay: no set style, length, or subject. But what does unite almost all successful essays, no matter how divergent the subject, is that a strong personal presence is felt behind them. This is so even if the essayist never comes out to tell you his view of the matter being discussed, never attempts directly to assert his personality, never even slips into the first-person singular. Without that strong personal presence, the essay doesn't quite exist; it becomes an article, a piece, or some other indefinable verbal construction. Even when the subject seems a distant and impersonal one, the self of the writer is in good part what the essay is about.

— Joseph Epstein

The Essay's Diversity

It is not only that the essay *could* be about anything. It usually was. The good health of essay writing depends on writers continuing to address eccentric subjects. In contrast to poetry and fiction, the nature of the essay is diversity — diversity of level, subject, tone, diction. Essays on being old and falling in love and the nature of poetry are still being written. And there are also essays on Rita Hayworth's zipper and Mickey Mouse's ears.

— Susan Sontag

The Memorable Essay

I am predisposed to the essay with knowledge to impart — but, unlike journalism, which exists primarily to present facts, the essays transcend their data, or transmute it into personal meaning. The memorable essay, unlike the article, is not place- or time-bound; it survives the occasion of its original composition. Indeed, in the most brilliant essays, language is not merely the medium of communication; it *is* communication.

— Joyce Carol Oates

The Author's Gumption

Given the confusion of genre minglings and overlaps, what finally distinguishes an essay from an article may just be the author's gumption, the extent to which personal voice, vision, and style are the prime movers and shapers, even though the authorial "I" may be only a remote energy, nowhere visible but everywhere present. ("We commonly do not remember," Thoreau wrote in the opening paragraphs of *Walden*, "that it is, after all, always the first person that is speaking.")

— Justin Kaplan

Essays and the Imagination

An essay is a thing of the imagination. If there is information in an essay, it is by-the-by, and if there is an opinion in it, you need not trust it for the long run. A genuine essay has no educational, polemical, or sociopolitical use; it is the movement of a free mind at play. Though it is written in prose, it is closer in kind to poetry than to any other form. Like a poem, a genuine essay is made out of language and character and mood and temperament and pluck and chance.

— Cynthia Ozick

Essays Versus Articles

And if I speak of a genuine essay, it is because fakes abound. Here the old-fashioned term poetaster may apply, if only obliquely. As the poetaster is to the poet — a lesser aspirant — so the article is to the essay: a look-alike knockoff guaranteed not to wear well. An article is gossip. An essay is reflection and insight. An article has the temporary advantage of social heat — what's hot out there right now. An essay's heat is interior. An article is timely, topical, engaged in the issues and personalities of the moment; it is likely to be stale within the month. In five years it will have acquired the quaint aura of a rotary phone. An article is Siamese-twinned to its date of birth. An essay defies its date of birth, and ours too.

— Cynthia Ozick

Essays Versus Stories

In some ways the essay can deal in both events and ideas better than the short story can, because the essayist — unlike the poet — may introduce the plain, unadorned thought without the contrived entrances of long-winded characters who mouth discourses. This sort of awful device killed "the novel of idea." (But eschewing it served to limit fiction's materials a little further, and likely contributed to our being left with the short story of scant idea.) The essayist may reason; he may treat of historical, cultural, or natural events, as well as personal events, for their interest and meaning alone, without resort to fabricated dramatic occasions. So the essay's materials are larger than the story's.

— Annie Dillard

Essays Versus Poems

The essay may deal in metaphor better than the poem can, in some ways, because prose may expand what the lyric poem must compress. Instead of confining a metaphor to half a line, the essayist can devote to it a narrative, descriptive, or reflective couple of pages, and bring forth vividly its meanings. Prose welcomes all sorts of figurative language, of course, as well as alliteration, and even rhyme. The range of rhythms in prose is larger and grander than that of poetry. And it can handle discursive idea, and plain fact, as well as character and story.

— Annie Dillard

Why Essays Can Confuse People

I picked up my pen again and began to write, began to write directly, honestly, began to converse, showing, telling, pausing, contradicting, setting the frayed contents of my mind down on plain paper to be plainly seen by anyone who cared to look. That doesn't mean there isn't art and artifice involved in the writing of an essay. But it does mean that the art is in revealing the voice of the writer, as opposed to trying to transform it to suit the requirements of a fictional character or narrator. Essay writing is not about facts, although the essay may contain facts. Essay writing is about transcribing the often convoluted process of thought, leaving your own brand of breadcrumbs in the forest so that those who want to can find their way to your door.

Essays, therefore, confuse people. They occupy a quirky place in the general genre of nonfiction, a place many people seem not to understand. It has been my experience that people not acquainted with the literary essay expect it to behave like an article or a piece of journalism. Journalism is a broad category unto itself, but it is probably finally defined by its mission to report to readers clear facts that have been thoroughly investigated and digested by the journalist. One does not expect to read a piece of journalism filled with tentative reflections or outright contradictions. However, essays thrive on these, because contradiction, paradox, and questioning best reflect the moving, morphing human mind, which is what the essayist wants to capture.

— Lauren Slater

Essays Are Not Scientific Documents

An essay is not a scientific document. It can be serendipitous or domestic, satire or testimony, tongue-in-cheek or a wail of grief. Mulched perhaps in its own contradictions, it promises no sure objectivity, just the condiment of opinion on a base of observation, and sometimes such leaps of illogic or superlogic that they may work a bit like magic realism in a novel: namely, to simulate the mind's own processes in a murky and incongruous world. More than being instructive, as a magazine article is, an essay has a slant, a seasoned personality behind it that ought to weather well. Even if we think the author is telling us the earth is flat, we might want to listen to him elaborate upon the fringes of his premise because the bristle of his narrative and what he's seen intrigues us. He has a cutting edge, yet balance too. A given body of information is going to be eclipsed, but what lives in art is spirit, not factuality, and we respond to Montaigne's human touch despite four centuries of technological and social change.

— Edward Hoagland

The Essayist's Defensiveness

No poet has a problem saying, I am a poet. No fiction writer hesitates to say, I am writing a story. "Poem" and "story" are still relatively stable, easily identified literary forms or genres. The essay is not, in that sense, a genre. Rather, "essay" is just one name, the most sonorous name, bestowed on a wide range of writings. Writers and editors usually call them "pieces." This is not just modesty or American casualness. A certain defensiveness now surrounds the notion of the essay. And many of the best essayists today are quick to declare that their best work lies elsewhere: in writing that is more "creative" (fiction, poetry) or more exacting (scholarship, theory, philosophy).

— Susan Sontag

On Being an Essayist

As someone who takes some pride in being known as "Joseph Epstein, an essayist"— or, even better, "the essayist Joseph Epstein"— who takes the term "essayist" as an honorific, I have both an interest and a stake in the form. I hate to see it put down, defamed, spat upon, even mildly slighted. The best luck that any writer can have is to find his or her form, and I feel fortunate in having found mine some twenty years ago in the familiar essay. It happened quite by luck: I was not then a frequent reader of Montaigne and Hazlitt; in those days I was even put off by Charles Lamb, who sometimes seemed to me a bit precious. For me the novel was the form of forms, and easily the one I most admired and should most have liked to master. Although I have published a dozen or so short stories, I have not yet written a novel — nor have I one in mind to write — and so I have to conclude that despite my enormous regard for that form, it just isn't mine. Perhaps it is quite useless for a writer to search for his perfect form; that form, it may well be, has to find him.

— Joseph Epstein

Essayists Must Tell the Truth

I work by Hemingway's precept that a writer's root charge is to distinguish what you really felt in the moment from the false sentiment of what you now believe you should have felt. The personal essay, autobiography, has been a red flag to professional classifiers and epistemologists; a critical industry has flourished for the refinement of generic protocols (many in French, with as much fine print as an installment purchase agreement), subcontracted principally to skeptics. In the judgment of Northrop Frye, for instance, a piece of work is shelved with autobiography or with fiction according to whether the librarian chooses to believe it.

Well. I've written one, and I've written the other, and I'm here to testify that the issue is at once weightier and simpler: a personal essayist means to tell the truth. The contract between a personal essayist and a reader is absolute, an agreement about intention. Because memory is fallible, and point of view by its nature biased, the personal essayist will tell a slant tale, willy-nilly. But not by design.

— Geoffrey Wolff

The Essayist's Voice

The influential essayist is someone with an acute sense of what has not been (properly) talked about, what should be talked about (but differently). But what makes essays last is less their argument than the display of a complex mind and a distinctive prose voice.

— Susan Sontag

Voice and Personality

Writing that has a voice is writing that has something like a personality. But whose personality is it? As with most things in art, there is no straight road from the product back to the person who made it. There are writers read and loved for their humor who are not especially funny people, and writers read and loved for their eloquence who, in conversation, swallow their words or can't seem to finish a sentence. Wisdom on the page correlates with wisdom in the writer about as frequently as a high batting average correlates with a high IQ: they just seem to have very little to do with one another. Charming people can produce prose of sneering sententiousness, and cranky neurotics can, to their readers, seem to be inexhaustibly delightful. Personal drabness, through some obscure neural kink, can deliver verbal blooms. Readers who meet writers whose voice they have fallen in love with usually need to make a small adjustment in order to hang on to their infatuation.

— Louis Menand

The Demands of the First Person Singular

The thoroughgoing first person is a demanding mode. It asks for the literary equivalent of perfect pitch. Even good writers occasionally lose control of their tone and let a self-congratulatory quality slip in. Eager to explain that their heart is in the right place, they baldly state that they care deeply about matters with which they appear to be only marginally acquainted. Pretending to confess to their bad behavior, they revel in their colorfulness. Insistently describing their own biases, they make it all too obvious that they wish to appear uncommonly reliable. Obviously, the first person doesn't guarantee honesty. Just because they are committing words to paper does not mean that writers stop telling themselves the lies that they've invented for getting through the night. Not everyone has Montaigne's gift for candor. Certainly some people are less likely to write honestly about themselves than about anyone else on earth.

— Tracy Kidder

The "Who Cares?" Factor

Not every voice a great soliloquy makes, a truth at odds with the education of many an American writer, with the education of *this* American writer. I remember (see how difficult, even now, to break the habit of that pronoun, that solipsistic verb), at boarding school in England, writing about Cordelia in the moment when she recognizes how mistaken is her father's measurement of affection. I spent the greater part of my allotted space telling about a tangled misunderstanding between my dad and myself: "So I understand just how Cordelia felt." Of course my teacher wrote "who cares?" Of course he was right to write that: to filter all data through the mesh of personal relevance is the voice's tyrannical sway over listener and speaker alike. Sometimes it should be okay to take facts in, quietly manipulate them behind an opaque scrim, and display them as though the arranger never arranged. It should be all right to mediate, let another voice speak through your spirit medium, pretend as a writer not to be front and center on stage.

— Geoffrey Wolff

What "Confessional Writing" Must Do

I knew that "confessional writing" now enjoys quite a vogue, but I had no idea how pervasive the practice of personal storytelling has become among our finest writers. I can't help asking myself (although all lives are, by definition, interesting, for what else do we have?): why in heaven's name should I care about the travails of X or Y unless some clear generality about human life and nature emerges thereby? I'm glad that trout fishing defined someone's boyhood, and I'm sad that parental dementia now dominates someone's midlife, but what can we do in life but play the hand we have been dealt?

— Stephen Jay Gould

How the Essayist Acquires Authority

Essays are how we speak to one another in print — caroming thoughts not merely in order to convey a certain packet of information, but with a special edge or bounce of personal character in a kind of public letter. As a writer you multiply yourself, gaining height as though jumping on a trampoline, if you can catch the gist of what other people have also been feeling and clarify it for them. Classic essay subjects, like the flux of friendship, "On Greed," "On Religion," "On Vanity," or solitude, lying, self-sacrifice, can be major-league yet not require Bertrand Russell to handle them. A layman who has diligently looked into something, walking in the mosses of regret after the death of a parent, for instance, may acquire an intangible authority, even without being memorably angry or funny or possessing a beguiling equanimity. *He* cares; therefore, if he has tinkered enough with his words, we do too.

— Edward Hoagland

The Conversational Style

While there is no firmly set, single style for the essayist, styles varying with each particular essayist, the best general description of essayistic style was written in 1827 by William Hazlitt in his essay "Familiar Style." "To write a genuine familiar or truly English style," Hazlitt wrote, "is to write as any one would speak in common conversation who had a thorough command and choice of words, who could discourse with ease, force, and perspicuity, setting aside all pedantic and oratorical flourishes." The style of the essayist is that of an extremely intelligent, highly commonsensical person talking, without stammer and with impressive coherence, to him- or herself and to anyone else who cares to eavesdrop. This self-reflexivity, this notion of talking to oneself, has always seemed to me to mark the essay off from the lecture. The lecturer is always teaching; so, too, frequently is the critic. If the essayist does so, it is usually only indirectly.

— Joseph Epstein

The Essay as Dialogue

Human storytelling was once all breath, the sacred act of telling family stories and tribal histories around a fire. Now a writer must attempt to breathe life into the words on a page, in the hope that the reader will discover something that resonates with his or her own experience. A genuine essay feels less like a monologue than a dialogue between writer and reader. *This is a story I need*, we conclude after reading the opening paragraph. *It will tell me something about the world that I didn't know before, something I sensed but could not articulate.*

An essay that is doing its job feels right. And resonance is the key. To be resonant, the dictionary informs us, is to be "strong and deep in tone, resounding." And to resound means to be filled to the depth with a sound that is sent back to its source. An essay that works is similar; it gives back to the reader a thought, a memory, an emotion made richer by the experience of another. Such an essay may confirm the reader's sense of

things, or it may contradict it. But always, and in glorious, mysterious ways that the author cannot control, it begins to belong to the reader.
— Kathleen Norris

The Attractions of Autobiography

Contemporary critical theory lends authority to the autobiographical impulse. As every graduate student knows, only a fool would try to think or bear witness to events objectively anymore, and only an intellectual crook would claim to have done so. There's a line of reasoning that goes like this: writers ought to acknowledge that they are subjective filtering agents and let themselves appear on the page; or, in greater honesty, describe themselves in detail; or, most honest of all, make themselves their main subject matter, since one's own self is the only subject one can really know. Maybe widespread psychotherapy has made literary self-revelation popular. Certainly there are economic reasons. Editors and agents seem to think that the public's hunger for intimate true-life stories has grown large enough to include the private lives of literary figures as well as those of movie stars, mass murderers, and athletes. And the invitation to write about oneself has intrinsic attractions. The subject interests most writers. The research doesn't usually require travel or phone calls or hours in a library. The enterprise *looks* easy.
— Tracy Kidder

The Essayist's Audience

Essays are addressed to a public in which some degree of equity exists between the writer and the reader. Shared knowledge is a necessity, although the information need not be concrete. Perhaps it is more to be thought of as a sharing of the experience of reading certain kinds of texts, texts with omissions and elisions, leaps. The essayist does not stop to identify the common ground; he will not write, "Picasso, the great Spanish painter who lived long in France." On the other hand, essays are about something, something we may not have had reason to study and master, often matters about which we are quite ignorant. Elegance of presentation, reflection made interesting and significant, easily lead us to engage our reading minds with Zulus, herbaceous borders in the English garden, marriage records in eighteenth-century France, Japanese scrolls.
— Elizabeth Hardwick

Essays Start Out in Magazines

Essays end up in books, but they start their lives in magazines. (It's hard to imagine a book of recent but previously unpublished essays.) The perennial comes now mainly in the guise of the topical and, in the short run, no literary form has as great and immediate an impact on contemporary readers. Many essays are discussed, debated, reacted to in a way that poets and writers of fiction can only envy.

— Susan Sontag

The Importance of Being Edited

A few years ago, the author of an autobiographical essay I was planning to publish in *The American Scholar* — a very fine writer — died suddenly. The writer had no immediate relatives, so I asked his longtime editor at *The New Yorker* if he would read the edited piece, hoping he might be able to guess which of my minor changes the writer would have been likely to accept and which he would have disliked. Certainly, said the editor. Two days later, he sent the piece back to me with comments on my edits and some additional editing of his own. "My suggestions are all small sentence tweaks," he wrote. "I could hear ———'s voice in my head as I did them and I'm pretty sure they would have met with his approval — most of them, anyway." Some examples: "A man who looked unmusical" became "a man so seemingly unmusical." "They made a swift escape to their different homes" became "They scattered swiftly to their various homes." "I felt that that solidity had been fostered by his profession" became "That solidity, I felt, had been fostered by his profession." These were, indeed, only small tweaks, but their precision filled me with awe. Of *course* you couldn't look unmusical. Of *course* it was awkward to use "escape" (singular) with "homes" (plural). Of *course* I should have caught "that that." I faxed the piece to my entire staff because editors rarely get a chance to see the work of other editors; we see only its results. This was like having a front-row seat at the Editing Olympics.

Five days later, the editor sent the piece back to us, covered with a second round of marginalia. "No doubt this is more than you bargained for," he wrote. "It's just that when the more noticeable imperfections have been taken care of, smaller ones come into view . . . I've even edited some of my own edits — e.g., on page 25, where I've changed 'dour,' which I inserted in the last go-round, to 'glowering.' This is because 'dour' is too much like 'pinched,' which I'm also suggesting."

If you're not a writer, this sort of compulsiveness may seem well nigh pathological. You may even be thinking, "What's the difference?" But if you *are* a writer, you'll realize what a gift the editor gave his old friend. Had not a word been changed, the essay would still have been excellent. Each of these "tweaks"— there were perhaps a hundred, none more earthshaking than the ones I've quoted — made it a little better, and their aggregate effect was to transform an excellent essay into a superb one.

  — Anne Fadiman

On Certain Magazine Interviews

I myself have been interviewed by writers carrying recorders, and as I sit answering their questions, I see them half-listening, nodding pleasantly, and relaxing in the knowledge that the little wheels are rolling. But what they are getting from me (and I assume from other people they talk to) is not the insight that comes from deep probing and perceptive analysis and old-fashioned legwork; it is rather the first-draft drift of my mind, a once-over-lightly dialogue that — while perhaps symptomatic of a society permeated by fast-food computerized bottom-line impersonalized workmanship — too frequently reduces the once-artful craft of magazine writing to the level of talk radio on paper.

  — Gay Talese

Listening to People Think

Quoting people verbatim, to be sure, has rarely blended well with my narrative style of writing or with my wish to observe and describe people actively engaged in ordinary but revealing situations rather than to confine them to a room and present them in the passive posture of a monologist. Since my earliest days in journalism, I was far less interested in the exact words that came out of people's mouths than in the essence of their meaning. More important than what people say is what they think, even though the latter may initially be difficult for them to articulate and may require much pondering and reworking within the interviewee's mind — which is what I gently try to prod and stimulate as I query, interrelate, and identify with my subjects as I personally accompany them whenever possible, be it on their errands, their appointments, their aimless peregrinations before dinner or after work.

Wherever it is, I try physically to be there in my role as a curious confidant, a trustworthy fellow traveler searching into their interior, seeking to discover, clarify, and finally to describe in words (my words) what they personify and how they think.

— Gay Talese

On the Subjects of Essays

Those with the least gift are most anxious to receive a commission. It seems to them that there lies waiting a topic, a new book, a performance, and that this is known as material. The true prose writer knows there is nothing given, no idea, no text or play seen last evening until an assault has taken place, the forced domination that we call "putting it in your own words." Talking about, thinking about a project bears little relation to the composition; enthusiasm boils down with distressing speed to a paragraph, often one of mischievous banality. To proceed from musing to writing is to feel a robbery has taken place. And certainly there has been a loss; the loss of the smiles and ramblings and discussions so much friendlier to ambition than the cold hardship of writing.

— Elizabeth Hardwick

The Essay's Unlimited Possibilities

The essay is, and has been, all over the map. There's nothing you cannot do with it; no subject matter is forbidden, no structure is proscribed. You get to make up your own structure every time, a structure that arises from the materials and best contains them. The material is the world itself, which, so far, keeps on keeping on. The thinking mind will analyze, and the creative imagination will link instances, and time itself will churn out scenes — scenes unnoticed and lost, or scenes remembered, written, and saved.

In his essay "Home," William Kittredge remembers Jack Ray, his boyhood hero, whom he later hired as a hand on his Oregon ranch. After a bout in jail, Jack Ray would show up in the bunkhouse grinning. "Well, hell, Jack," Kittredge would say. "It's a new day."

"Kid," he would say, "she's a new world every morning."

— Annie Dillard

1

The Personal Voice: Identity, Diversity, Self-Discovery

ANWAR F. ACCAWI

The Telephone

Newspapers and popular magazines indirectly encourage readers to think essays are synonymous with opinion pieces—columns and articles in which writers speak their minds and air their views on topics in the news. But essays can be effective means of storytelling, as Anwar Accawi proves in the following account of his childhood in a tiny village in southern Lebanon. In "The Telephone," Accawi offers an unpretentious description of how the modern world began its intrusion into a timeless and insulated culture, where "there was no real need for a calendar or a watch to keep track of the hours, days, months, and years." As Accawi says of village life: "We lived and loved and toiled and died without ever needing to know what year it was, or even the time of day."

Accawi, who was born in Lebanon in 1943 and came to the United States in 1965, began writing essays as a way to preserve a disappearing culture for his young children, who knew nothing of the old country. A teacher at the English Language Institute at the University of Tennessee, Knoxville, he is the author of a memoir, The Boy from the Tower of the Moon *(1999). "The Telephone," which originally appeared in* The Sun *(1997), was one of Accawi's first publications and was selected by Cynthia Ozick for* The Best American Essays *1998.*

When I was growing up in Magdaluna, a small Lebanese village in the terraced, rocky mountains east of Sidon, time didn't mean much to anybody, except maybe to those who were dying, or those waiting to appear in court because they had tampered with the boundary markers on their land. In those days, there was no real need for a calendar or a watch to keep track of the hours, days, months, and years. We knew what to do and when to do it, just as the

Iraqi geese knew when to fly north, driven by the hot wind that blew in from the desert, and the ewes knew when to give birth to wet lambs that stood on long, shaky legs in the chilly March wind and baaed hesitantly, because they were small and cold and did not know where they were or what to do now that they were here. The only timepiece we had need of then was the sun. It rose and set, and the seasons rolled by, and we sowed seed and harvested and ate and played and married our cousins and had babies who got whooping cough and chickenpox — and those children who survived grew up and married *their* cousins and had babies who got whooping cough and chickenpox. We lived and loved and toiled and died without ever needing to know what year it was, or even the time of day.

It wasn't that we had no system for keeping track of time and of the important events in our lives. But ours was a natural — or, rather, a divine — calendar, because it was framed by acts of God. Allah himself set down the milestones with earthquakes and droughts and floods and locusts and pestilences. Simple as our calendar was, it worked just fine for us.

Take, for example, the birth date of Teta Im Khalil, the oldest woman in Magdaluna and all the surrounding villages. When I first met her, we had just returned home from Syria at the end of the Big War and were living with Grandma Mariam. Im Khalil came by to welcome my father home and to take a long, myopic look at his foreign-born wife, my mother. Im Khalil was so old that the skin of her cheeks looked like my father's grimy tobacco pouch, and when I kissed her (because Grandma insisted that I show her old friend affection), it was like kissing a soft suede glove that had been soaked with sweat and then left in a dark closet for a season. Im Khalil's face got me to wondering how old one had to be to look and taste the way she did. So, as soon as she had hobbled off on her cane, I asked Grandma, "How old is Teta Im Khalil?"

Grandma had to think for a moment; then she said, "I've been told that Teta was born shortly after the big snow that caused the roof on the mayor's house to cave in."

"And when was that?" I asked.

"Oh, about the time we had the big earthquake that cracked the wall in the east room."

Well, that was enough for me. You couldn't be more accurate than that, now, could you? Satisfied with her answer, I went back to playing with a ball made from an old sock stuffed with other, much older socks.

And that's the way it was in our little village for as far back as any-body could remember: people were born so many years before or after an earthquake or a flood; they got married or died so many years before or after a long drought or a big snow or some other dis-aster. One of the most unusual of these dates was when Antoinette the seamstress and Saeed the barber (and tooth puller) got mar-ried. That was the year of the whirlwind during which fish and oranges fell from the sky. Incredible as it may sound, the story of the fish and oranges was true, because men — respectable men, like Abu George the blacksmith and Abu Asaad the mule skinner, men who would not lie even to save their own souls — told and retold that story until it was incorporated into Magdaluna's calendar, just like the year of the black moon and the year of the locusts before it. My father, too, confirmed the story for me. He told me that he had been a small boy himself when it had rained fish and oranges from heaven. He'd gotten up one morning after a stormy night and walked out into the yard to find fish as long as his forearm still flop-ping here and there among the wet navel oranges.

The year of the fish-bearing twister, however, was not the last remarkable year. Many others followed in which strange and won-derful things happened: milestones added by the hand of Allah to Magdaluna's calendar. There was, for instance, the year of the drought, when the heavens were shut for months and the spring from which the entire village got its drinking water slowed to a trickle. The spring was about a mile from the village, in a ravine that opened at one end into a small, flat clearing covered with fine gray dust and hard, marble-sized goat droppings, because every afternoon the goatherds brought their flocks there to water them. In the year of the drought, that little clearing was always packed full of noisy kids with big brown eyes and sticky hands, and their mothers — sinewy, overworked young women with protruding collarbones and cracked, callused brown heels. The children ran around playing tag or hide-and-seek while the women talked, shooed flies, and awaited their turns to fill up their jars with drinking water to bring home to their napping men and wet babies. There were days when we had to wait from sunup until late afternoon just to fill a small clay jar with precious, cool water.

Sometimes, amid the long wait and the heat and the flies and the smell of goat dung, tempers flared, and the younger women, anxious about their babies, argued over whose turn it was to fill up her jar. And sometimes the arguments escalated into full-blown, knockdown-dragout fights; the women would grab each other by the hair and curse and scream and spit and call each other names that made my ears tingle. We little brown boys who went with our mothers to fetch water loved these fights, because we got to see the women's legs and their colored panties as they grappled and rolled around in the dust. Once in a while, we got lucky and saw much more, because some of the women wore nothing at all under their long dresses. God, how I used to look forward to those fights. I remember the rush, the excitement, the sun dancing on the dust clouds as a dress ripped and a young white breast was revealed, then quickly hidden. In my calendar, that year of drought will always be one of the best years of my childhood, because it was then, in a dusty clearing by a trickling mountain spring, I got my first glimpses of the wonders, the mysteries, and the promises hidden beneath the folds of a woman's dress. Fish and oranges from heaven . . . you can get over that.

But, in another way, the year of the drought was also one of the worst of my life, because that was the year that Abu Raja, the retired cook who used to entertain us kids by cracking walnuts on his forehead, decided it was time Magdaluna got its own telephone. Every civilized village needed a telephone, he said, and Magdaluna was not going to get anywhere until it had one. A telephone would link us with the outside world. At the time, I was too young to understand the debate, but a few men — like Shukri, the retired Turkish-army drill sergeant, and Abu Hanna the vineyard keeper — did all they could to talk Abu Raja out of having a telephone brought to the village. But they were outshouted and ignored and finally shunned by the other villagers for resisting progress and trying to keep a good thing from coming to Magdaluna.

One warm day in early fall, many of the villagers were out in their fields repairing walls or gathering wood for the winter when the shout went out that the telephone-company truck had arrived at Abu Raja's *dikkan*, or country store. There were no roads in those days, only footpaths and dry streambeds, so it took the telephone-company truck almost a day to work its way up the rocky terrain from Sidon — about the same time it took to walk. When the truck came into view, Abu George, who had a huge voice and, before the telephone, was Magdaluna's only long-distance communication system, bellowed the news from his front porch. Everybody dropped what they were doing and ran to Abu Raja's house to see what was happening. Some of the more dignified villagers, however, like Abu Habeeb and Abu Nazim, who had been to big cities like Beirut and Damascus and had seen things like telephones and telegraphs, did not run the way the rest did; they walked with their canes hanging from the crooks of their arms, as if on a Sunday afternoon stroll.

It did not take long for the whole village to assemble at Abu Raja's *dikkan.* Some of the rich villagers, like the widow Farha and the gendarme Abu Nadeem, walked right into the store and stood at the elbows of the two important-looking men from the telephone company, who proceeded with utmost gravity, like priests at Communion, to wire up the telephone. The poorer villagers stood outside and listened carefully to the details relayed to them by the not-so-poor people who stood in the doorway and could see inside.

"The bald man is cutting the blue wire," someone said.

"He is sticking the wire into the hole in the bottom of the black box," someone else added.

"The telephone man with the mustache is connecting two pieces of wire. Now he is twisting the ends together," a third voice chimed in.

Because I was small and unaware that I should have stood outside with the other poor folk to give the rich people inside more room (they seemed to need more of it than poor people did), I wriggled my way through the dense forest of legs to get a firsthand look at the action. I felt like the barefoot Moses, sandals in hand, staring at the burning bush on Mount Sinai. Breathless, I watched as the men in blue, their shirt pockets adorned with fancy lettering in a foreign language, put together a black machine that supposedly would make it possible to talk with uncles, aunts, and cousins who lived more than two days' ride away.

It was shortly after sunset when the man with the mustache announced that the telephone was ready to use. He explained that all Abu Raja had to do was lift the receiver, turn the crank on the black box a few times, and wait for an operator to take his call. Abu Raja, who had once lived and worked in Sidon, was impatient with the telephone man for assuming that he was ignorant. He grabbed the receiver and turned the crank forcefully, as if trying to start a Model T Ford. Everybody was impressed that he knew what to do. He even called the operator by her first name: "Centralist." Within moments, Abu Raja was talking with his brother, a concierge in Beirut. He didn't even have to raise his voice or shout to be heard.

If I hadn't seen it with my own two eyes and heard it with my own two ears, I would not have believed it — and my friend Kameel didn't. He was away that day watching his father's goats, and when he came back to the village that evening, his cousin Habeeb and I told him about the telephone and how Abu Raja had used it to speak with his brother in Beirut. After he heard our report, Kameel made the sign of the cross, kissed his thumbnail, and warned us that lying was a bad sin and would surely land us in purgatory. Kameel believed in Jesus and Mary, and wanted to be a priest when he grew up. He always crossed himself when Habeeb, who was irreverent, and I, who was Presbyterian, were around, even when we were not bearing bad news.

And the telephone, as it turned out, was bad news. With its coming, the face of the village began to change. One of the first effects was the shifting of the village's center. Before the telephone's arrival, the men of the village used to gather regularly at the house of Im Kaleem, a short, middle-aged widow with jet-black hair and a raspy voice that could be heard all over the village, even when she was only whispering. She was a devout Catholic and also the village *shlikki* — whore. The men met at her house to argue about politics and drink coffee and play cards or backgammon. Im Kaleem was not a true prostitute, however, because she did not charge for her services — not even for the coffee and tea (and, occasionally, the strong liquor called arrack) that she served the men. She did not need the money; her son, who was overseas in Africa, sent her money regularly. (I knew this because my father used to read her son's letters to her and take down her replies, as Im Kaleem could not read and write.) Im Kaleem was no slut either — unlike some women in the village — because she loved all the men she entertained, and they loved her, every one of them.

In a way, she was married to all the men in the village. Everybody knew it— the wives knew it; the itinerant Catholic priest knew it; the Presbyterian minister knew it— but nobody objected. Actually, I suspect the women (my mother included) did not mind their husbands' visits to Im Kaleem. Oh, they wrung their hands and complained to one another about their men's unfaithfulness, but secretly they were relieved, because Im Kaleem took some of the pressure off them and kept the men out of their hair while they attended to their endless chores. Im Kaleem was also a kind of confessor and troubleshooter, talking sense to those men who were having family problems, especially the younger ones.

Before the telephone came to Magdaluna, Im Kaleem's house was bustling at just about any time of day, especially at night, when its windows were brightly lit with three large oil lamps, and the loud voices of the men talking, laughing, and arguing could be heard in the street below— a reassuring, homey sound. Her house was an island of comfort, an oasis for the weary village men, exhausted from having so little to do.

But it wasn't long before many of those men — the younger ones especially— started spending more of their days and evenings at Abu Raja's *dikkan*. There, they would eat and drink and talk and play checkers and backgammon, and then lean their chairs back against the wall — the signal that they were ready to toss back and forth, like a ball, the latest rumors going around the village. And they were always looking up from their games and drinks and talk to glance at the phone in the corner, as if expecting it to ring any minute and bring news that would change their lives and deliver them from their aimless existence. In the meantime, they smoked cheap, hand-rolled cigarettes, dug dirt out from under their fingernails with big pocketknives, and drank lukewarm sodas they called Kacula, Seffen-Ub, and Bebsi. Sometimes, especially when it was hot, the days dragged on so slowly that the men turned on Abu Saeed, a confirmed bachelor who practically lived in Abu Raja's *dikkan*, and teased him for going around barefoot and unshaven since the Virgin had appeared to him behind the olive press.

The telephone was also bad news for me personally. It took away my lucrative business— a source of much-needed income. Before the telephone came to Magdaluna, I used to hang around

Im Kaleem's courtyard and play marbles with the other kids, waiting for some man to call down from a window and ask me to run to the store for cigarettes or arrack, or to deliver a message to his wife, such as what he wanted for supper. There was always something in it for me: a ten- or even a twenty-five-piaster piece. On a good day, I ran nine or ten of those errands, which assured a steady supply of marbles that I usually lost to Sami or his cousin Hani, the basket weaver's boy. But as the days went by, fewer and fewer men came to Im Kaleem's, and more and more congregated at Abu Raja's to wait by the telephone. In the evenings, no light fell from her window onto the street below, and the laughter and noise of the men trailed off and finally stopped. Only Shukri, the retired Turkish-army drill sergeant, remained faithful to Im Kaleem after all the other men had deserted her; he was still seen going into or leaving her house from time to time. Early that winter, Im Kaleem's hair suddenly turned gray, and she got sick and old. Her legs started giving her trouble, making it hard for her to walk. By spring she hardly left her house anymore.

At Abu Raja's *dikkan*, the calls did eventually come, as expected, and men and women started leaving the village the way a hailstorm begins: first one, then two, then bunches. The army took them. Jobs in the cities lured them. And ships and airplanes carried them to such faraway places as Australia and Brazil and New Zealand. My friend Kameel, his cousin Habeeb, and their cousins and my cousins all went away to become ditch diggers and mechanics and butcher-shop boys and deli owners who wore dirty aprons sixteen hours a day, all looking for a better life than the one they had left behind. Within a year, only the sick, the old, and the maimed were left in the village. Magdaluna became a skeleton of its former self, desolate and forsaken, like the tombs, a place to get away from.

Finally, the telephone took my family away, too. My father got a call from an old army buddy who told him that an oil company in southern Lebanon was hiring interpreters and instructors. My father applied for a job and got it, and we moved to Sidon, where I went to a Presbyterian missionary school and graduated in 1962. Three years later, having won a scholarship, I left Lebanon for the United States. Like the others who left Magdaluna before me, I am still looking for that better life.

Reflections and Responses

---

1. Why do you think Accawi begins his recollections of childhood by focusing on the way the passage of time was measured by the villagers? Does Accawi see the village's attitude toward time in positive or negative ways? How do his word choices and images reflect his position?

2. Consider the way Accawi introduces the telephone into the village. How does he prepare for its appearance? From whose perspective do we view the installation? How are the class lines of the village drawn when the telephone is installed? Finally, why did the telephone turn out to be "bad news" for the village as a whole?

3. How would you assess Accawi's attitude in the final paragraph? How did the telephone personally change his life? Do you think the change was for the worse? Do you think Accawi himself believes it was for the worse? How do you interpret his final sentence?

MARCIA ALDRICH

Hair

Montaigne, the first essayist, would have enjoyed Marcia Aldrich's wonderful meditation on hairstyles and the way they reflect our personal identity. When Montaigne began writing personal essays in the 1570s, he initiated a new style of self-portrayal. He brought his whole body into his writing, inviting his readers to see his essays not simply as thoughts on a page but as an extension of his physical being. Not having (as he put it) an "imposing presence" in actual life, he tried to create one in and through his remarkable essays. A very "physical" writer, he would discuss his looks, height, voice and complexion, the way he walked, and his habit of scratching the inside of his ears. A persistent self-reviser, Montaigne would also appreciate Aldrich's resistance to a settled style ("a new hairstyle," she says, "will write over the last") and to a coherent philosophy.

Marcia Aldrich is a professor of English who specializes in twentieth-century poetry at Michigan State University. She is the author of a memoir about growing up in the '50s, Girl Rearing *(1998). She is also working on a study of the poet Louise Bogan. "Hair" originally appeared in* The Northwest Review *(1992) and was selected by Joseph Epstein for* The Best American Essays *1993.*

I've been around and seen the Taj Mahal and the Grand Canyon and Marilyn Monroe's footprints outside Grauman's Chinese Theater, but I've never seen my mother wash her own hair. After my mother married, she never washed her own hair again. As a girl and an unmarried woman — yes — but, in my lifetime, she never washed her hair with her own two hands. Upon matrimony, she began weekly treks to the beauty salon where Julie washed and styled her hair. Her appointment on Fridays at two o'clock was never cancelled or rescheduled; it was the bedrock of her week, around which she pivoted and planned. These two hours were indispensable to my mother's routine, to her sense of herself and what, as a woman, she should concern herself with — not to mention their being her primary source of information about all sorts of things she wouldn't otherwise come to know. With Julie my mother discussed momentous decisions concerning hair color and the advancement of age and what could be done about it, hair length and its effect upon maturity, when to perm and when not to perm, the need to proceed with caution when a woman desperately wanted a major change in her life like dumping her husband or sending back her newborn baby and the only change she could effect was a change in her hair. That was what Julie called a "dangerous time" in a woman's life. When my mother spoke to Julie, she spoke in conspiratorial, almost confessional, tones I had never heard before. Her voice was usually tense, on guard, the laughter forced, but with Julie it dropped much lower, the timbre darker than the upper-register shrills sounded at home. And most remarkably, she listened to everything Julie said.

As a child I was puzzled by the way my mother's sense of self-worth and mood seemed dependent upon how she thought her hair looked, how the search for the perfect hairstyle never ended. Just as Mother seemed to like her latest color and cut, she began to agitate for a new look. The cut seemed to have become a melancholy testimony, in my mother's eyes, to time's inexorable passage. Her hair never stood in and of itself; it was always moored to a complex set of needs and desires her hair couldn't in itself satisfy. She wanted her hair to illuminate the relationship between herself and the idea of motion while appearing still, for example. My mother wanted her hair to be fashioned into an event with a complicated narrative past. However, the more my mother attempted to impose a hairstyle pulled from an idealized image of herself, the more the hairstyle seemed to be at odds with my mother. The more the hairstyle became substantial, the more the woman underneath was obscured. She'd riffle through women's magazines and stare for long dreamy hours at a particular woman's coiffure. Then she'd ask my father in an artificially casual voice: "How do you think I'd look with really short hair?" or "Would blonde become me?" My father never committed himself to an opinion. He had learned from long experience that no response he made could turn out well; anything he said would be used against him, if not in the immediate circumstances, down the line, for my mother never forgot anything anyone ever said about her hair. My father's refusal to engage the "hair question" irritated her.

So too, I was puzzled to see that unmarried women washed their own hair, and married women, in my mother's circle at least, by some unwritten dictum never touched their own hair. I began studying before and after photographs of my mother's friends. These photographs were all the same. In the pre-married mode, their hair was soft and unformed. After the wedding, the women's hairstyles bore the stamp of property, looked constructed from grooming talents not their own, hairstyles I'd call produced, requiring constant upkeep and technique to sustain the considerable loft and rigidity—in short, the antithesis of anything I might naively call natural. This was hair no one touched, crushed, or ran fingers through. One poked and prodded various hair masses back into formation. This hair presented obstacles to embrace, the scent of the hair spray alone warded off man, child, and pests. I never saw my father stroke my mother's head. Children whimpered when my mother came home fresh from the salon with a potent do. Just when a woman's life was supposed to be opening out into daily affection, *the* sanctioned affection of husband and children, the women of my mother's circle encased themselves in a helmet of hair not unlike Medusa's.

In so-called middle age, my mother's hair never moved, never blew, never fell in her face: her hair became a museum piece. When she went to bed, she wore a blue net, and when she took short showers, short because, after all, she wasn't washing her hair and she was seldom dirty, she wore a blue plastic cap for the sake of preservation. From one appointment to the next, the only change her hair could be said to undergo was to become crestfallen. Taking extended vacations presented problems sufficiently troublesome to rule out countries where she feared no beauty parlors existed. In the beginning, my parents took overnighters, then week jaunts, and thereby avoided the whole hair dilemma. Extending their vacations to two weeks was eventually managed by my mother applying more hair spray and sleeping sitting up. But after the two week mark had been reached, she was forced to either return home or venture into an unfamiliar salon and subject herself to scrutiny, the kind of scrutiny that leaves no woman unscathed. Then she faced Julie's disapproval, for no matter how expensive and expert the salon, my mother's hair was to be lamented. Speaking just for myself, I had difficulty distinguishing Julie's cunning from the stranger's. In these years my mother's hair looked curled, teased, and sprayed into a waved tossed monument with holes poked through for glasses. She believed the damage done to her hair was tangible proof she had been somewhere, like stickers on her suitcases.

My older sisters have worked out their hair positions differently. My oldest sister's solution has been to fix upon one hairstyle and never change it. She wants to be thought of in a singular fashion. She may vary the length from long to longer, but that is the extent of her alteration. Once, after having her first baby, the "dangerous time" for women, she recklessly cut her hair to just below the ear. She immediately regretted the decision and began growing it back as she walked home from the salon, vowing not to repeat the mistake. Her signature is dark, straight hair pulled heavily off her face in a large silver clip, found at any Woolworth's. When one clip breaks, she buys another just like it. My mother hates the timelessness of my sister's hair. She equates it with a refusal to face growing old. My mother says, "It's immature to wear your hair the same way all your life."

My sister replies, "It's immature to never stop thinking about your hair. If this hairstyle was good enough when I was twenty, it's good enough when I'm forty, if not better."

"But what about change?" my mother asks.

"Change is overrated," my sister says flipping her long hair over her shoulder definitively. "I feel my hair."

My other sister was born with thin, lifeless, nondescript hair: a cross she has had to bear. Even in the baby pictures, the limp strands plastered on her forehead in question marks wear her down. Shame and self-effacement are especially plain in the pictures where she posed with our eldest sister, whose dark hair dominates the frame. She's spent her life attempting to disguise the real state of her hair. Some years she'd focus on style, pulling it back in ponytails so that from the front no one could see there wasn't much hair in the back. She tried artless, even messy styles — as if she had just tied it up any old way before taking a bath or bunched it to look deliberately snarled. There were the weird years punctuated by styles that looked as if she had taken sugar water and lemon juice and squeezed them onto her wet hair and then let them crystallize. The worst style was when she took her hair and piled it on the top of her head in a cone shape and then crimped the ponytail into a zigzag. Personally, I thought she had gone too far. No single approach solved the hair problem, and so now, in maturity, she combines the various phases of attack in hope something will work. She frosts both the grey strands and the pale brown, and then perms for added body and thickness. She's forced to keep her hair short because chemicals do tend to destroy. My mother admires my sister's determination to transform herself, and never more than in my sister's latest assault upon middle age. No one has known for many years nor does anyone remember what the untreated color or texture of either my mother's or my sister's hair might be.

As the youngest by twelve years, there was little to distract Mother's considerable attention from the problem of my hair. I had cowlicks, a remarkable number of them, which like little arrows shot across my scalp. They refused to be trained, to lie down quietly in the same direction as the rest of my hair. One at the front insisted on sticking straight up while two on either side of my ears jutted out seeking sun. The lack of uniformity, the fact that my hair had a mind of its own, infuriated my mother and she saw to it that Julie cut my hair as short as possible in order to curtail its wanton expression. Sitting in the swivel chair before the mirror while Julie snipped, I felt invisible, as if I was unattached to my hair.

Just when I started to menstruate, my mother decided the battle plan needed a change, and presto, the page boy replaced the pixie. Having not outgrown the thicket of cowlicks, Mother bought a spectrum of brightly colored stretch bands to hold my hair back off my face. Then she attached thin pink plastic curlers with snap on lids to the ends of my hair to make them flip up or under, depending on her mood. The stretch bands pressed my hair flat until the very bottom, at which point the ends formed a tunnel with ridges from the roller caps — a point of emphasis, she called it. Coupled with the aquamarine eyeglasses, newly acquired, I looked like an overgrown insect that had none of its kind to bond with.

However, I was not alone. Unless you were the last in a long line of sisters, chances were good that your hair would not go unnoticed by your mother. Each of my best friends was subjected to her mother's hair dictatorship, although with entirely different results. Perry Jensen's mother insisted that all five of her daughters peroxide their hair blonde and pull it back into high ponytails. All the girls' hair turned green in the summer from chlorine. Melissa Matson underwent a look-alike "home perm" with her mother, an experience she never did recover from. She developed a phobic reaction to anything synthetic, which made life very expensive. Not only did mother and daughter have identical tight curls and wear mother-daughter outfits, later they had look-alike nose jobs.

In my generation, many women who survived hair bondage to their mothers now experiment with hairstyles as one would test a new design: to see how it works, what it will withstand, and how it can be improved. Testing requires boldness, for often the style fails dramatically, as when I had my hair cut about a half inch long at the top, and it stood straight up like a tacky shag carpet. I had to live with the results, bear daily witness to the kinks in its design for nine months until strategies of damage control could be deployed. But sometimes women I know create a look that startles in its originality and suggests a future not yet realized.

The women in my family divide into two general groups: those who fasten upon one style, become identified with a look, and are impervious to change, weathering the years steadfastly, and those who, for a variety of reasons, are in the business of transforming themselves. In my sister's case, the quest for perfect hair originates in a need to mask her own appearance; in my mother's case, she wants to achieve a beauty of person unavailable in her own life story. Some women seek transformation, not out of dissatisfaction with themselves, but because hair change is a means of moving along in their lives. These women create portraits of themselves that won't last forever, a new hairstyle will write over the last.

Since my mother dictated my hair, I never took a stand on the hair issue. In maturity, I'm incapable of assuming a coherent or consistent philosophy. I have wayward hair: it's always becoming something else. The moment it arrives at a recognizable style, it begins to undo itself, it grows, the sun colors it, it waves. When one hair pin goes in, another seems to come out. Sometimes I think

I should follow my oldest sister — she claims to never give more than a passing thought to her hair and can't see what all the angst is about. She asks, "Don't women have better things to think about than their hair?"

I bite back: "But don't you think hair should reflect who you are?"

"To be honest, I've never thought about it. I don't think so. Cut your hair the same way, and lose your self in something else. You're distracted from the real action."

I want to do what my sister says, but when I walk out into shop-lined streets, I automatically study women's hair and always with the same question: How did they arrive at their hair? Lately, I've been feeling more and more like my mother. I hadn't known how to resolve the dilemma until I found Rhonda. I don't know if I found Rhonda or made her up. She is not a normally trained hair-dresser: she has a different set of eyes, unaffected. One day while out driving around to no place in particular, at the bottom of a hill, I found: "Rhonda's Hair Salon — Don't Look Back" written on a life-size cardboard image of Rhonda. Her shop was on the top of this steep orchard planted hill, on a plateau with a great view that opened out and went on forever. I parked my car at the bottom and walked up. Zigzagging all the way up the hill, leaning against or sticking out from behind the apple trees were more life-sized cardboard likenesses of Rhonda. Except for the explosive sun-bursts in her hair, no two signs were the same. At the bottom, she wore long red hair falling below her knees and covering her entire body like a shawl. As I climbed the hill, Rhonda's hair gradually became shorter and shorter, and each length was cut differently, until when I reached the top, her head was shaved and glistening in the sun. I found Rhonda herself out under one of the apple trees wearing running shoes. Her hair was long and red and looked as if it had never been cut. She told me she had no aspira-tions to be a hairdresser, "she just fell into it." "I see hair," she con-tinued, "as an extension of the head and therefore I try to do hair with a lot of thought." Inside there were no mirrors, no swivel chairs, no machines of torture with their accompanying stink. She said, "Nothing is permanent, nothing is forever. Don't feel ham-pered or hemmed in by the shape of your face or the shape of your past. Hair is vital, sustains mistakes, can be born again. You don't have to marry it. Now tip back and put your head into my hands."

Reflections and Responses

---

1. Consider how Aldrich invites you to see hairstyles in terms of personal identity. Compare the different female members of her family. How does each reflect a different philosophical attitude through her hairstyle? What are they? Why do you think Aldrich left her father out of these reflections?

2. How does Aldrich establish a relationship between hairstyle and writing style? For Aldrich, what do the two have in common? In going through her essay, identify some features of her writing style that also reflect her attitude toward her hair.

3. Reread Aldrich's final paragraph carefully. It's tricky. What do you think is happening? Is "Rhonda" real or fictitious? What makes you think she is real? Alternatively, what makes you think Aldrich made her up? Why do you think Aldrich concluded her essay with this visit to Rhonda's Hair Salon?

LYNDA BARRY

Two Questions

Anyone who follows cartoons and comic art knows that the personal essay, journalism, biography, and autobiography can take visual as well as verbal forms. Readers today who enjoy the work of Robert Crumb, Art Spiegelman, Joe Sacco, Chris Ware, Harvey Pekar, Marjane Satrapi, Ho Che Anderson, and many others well know that comics are not all about fictional superheroes. Over the past few decades, comics have gradually developed an artistic and literary reputation that is becoming increasingly recognized by critics, publishers, and booksellers. One indication of this aesthetic trend is that a number of prestigious literary periodicals that once featured only poetry, fiction, essays, and reviews now regularly include the work of graphic and comic artists, sometimes in collaboration with prominent writers. Furthermore, the New York Times, *which does not contain so-called funny pages, now features comic artists among its opinions and editorials (called "Op-Art") and has recently introduced comic strips in its weekly Sunday magazine. Many of the new comic artists are playfully enjoying the dissolution of conventional verbal and visual boundaries—like Lynda Barry does in "Two Questions"—as they continue to explore the ways comic art can expand the genres of essay, memoir, literary journalism, and creative nonfiction.*

Linda Barry's comic strips appear in more than fifty newspapers nationwide. Her now well-known Ernie Pook's Comeek *strips were first published by a classmate while Barry was a student at Evergreen State College in Olympia, Washington; the classmate was Matt Groening, the creator of* The Simpsons. *Among her many cartoon strip publications are* Girls & Boys (*1981*), My Perfect Life (*1992*), The Freddie Stories (*1999*), *and* One! Hundred! Demons! *(2002). She is also the author of two* novels. The Good Times Are Killing Me *(1988) and* Cruddy *(1999).* *"Two Questions" originally appeared in an issue of* McSweeney's Quarterly *(no. 13, 2004) devoted to comic strip art and edited by Chris* Ware. *It was selected by Harvey Pekar for* The Best American Comics 2006 *(edited by Anne Elizabeth Moore).*

© Lynda Barry

© Lynda Barry

BEFORE the TWO QUESTIONS, PICTURES AND STORIES HAPPENED IN A WAY THAT DIDN'T INVOLVE MUCH THINKING. ONE LINE LED TO ANOTHER UNTIL THEY SOMEHOW FINISHED. I NEVER FELT LIKE I WAS TRYING, AND THE DRAWING ITSELF DIDN'T MATTER TO ME MUCH AFTER-WARD.

WHY DON'T YOU COME WITH ME LITTLE GIRL ON A MAGIC CARPET RIDE

BUT THE TWO QUESTIONS FIND EVERYBODY

Where is She?

Where is SHE?!

LET'S SEE THAT PICTURE-STORY!!

SHOW ME!

SHOW ME!

SO TRUE

ESS SUCK! RAWK

© Lynda Barry

© Lynda Barry

© Lynda Barry

© Lynda Barry

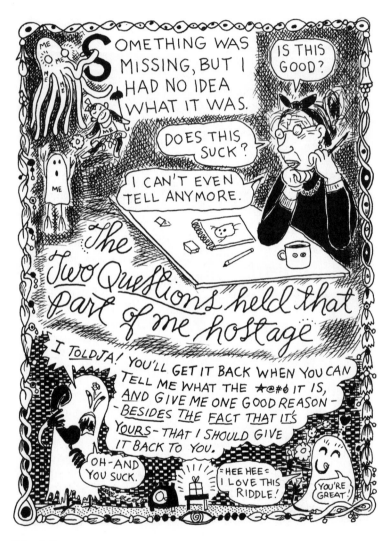

© Lynda Barry

© Lynda Barry

66

© Lynda Barry

© Lynda Barry

Reflections and Responses

1. What does Lynda Barry's comic strip suggest about children and drawing? What do they enjoy about it? Why might they suddenly stop drawing? What does Barry seem to be saying about the creative process in general?

2. What are the "two questions," and how are they visualized throughout the comic strip? What does their appearance suggest about them? What is their connection to "good" drawings and "bad" drawings? What do you think the octopus-like creature is meant to suggest? What is the significance of the repeated phrase "don't know"?

3. Consider "Two Questions" not as an illustrated personal essay but as an amalgam of verbal and visual craft intended as a unified creative process. Explain how Barry achieves this integration of word, image, and concept. How does she go about making the drawing inseparable from its language?

JUDITH ORTIZ COFER

Silent Dancing

Nothing rekindles childhood memories better than old photographs or home movies. In this vivid essay, a grainy and poorly focused five-minute home movie of a New Year's Eve party helps a writer capture the spirit of a Puerto Rican community in Paterson, New Jersey. That the movie is fragmented and silent adds to its documentary value and, for a lyrical essayist, it evokes much more than it can possibly reveal. "Even the home movie," Cofer writes, "cannot fill in the sensory details such a gathering left imprinted in a child's brain." Those sensory details — "the flavor of Puerto Rico"—must be supplied through the art of writing.

A professor of English and creative writing at the University of Georgia, Judith Ortiz Cofer has published prize-winning books in a number of genres: a novel, The Line of the Sun *(1989); two poetry collections,* Terms of Survival *(1987) and* Reaching for the Mainland *(1986); two autobiographical books combining prose and poetry,* Silent Dancing *(1990) and* The Latin Deli *(1993); and* An Island Like You: Stories of the Barrio *(1995). She has recently published* The Year of Our Revolution: New and Selected Stories and Poems *(1998),* Sleeping with One Eye Open: Women Writers and the Art of Survival *(1999),* Women in Front of the Sun: On Becoming a Writer *(2000), and* The Meaning of Consuelo: A Novel *(2003). Cofer has received many prestigious awards, including fellowships from the National Endowment for the Arts, the Witter Bynner Foundation for Poetry, and the Bread Loaf Writers' Conference. "Silent Dancing" originally appeared in* The Georgia Review *(1990) and was selected by Joyce Carol Oates for* The Best American Essays 1991. *Ms. Cofer courteously supplied the notes to this selection.*

We have a home movie of this party. Several times my mother and I have watched it together, and I have asked questions about the silent revelers coming in and out of focus. It is grainy and of short duration, but it's a great visual aid to my memory of life at that time. And it is in color — the only complete scene in color I can recall from those years.

We lived in Puerto Rico until my brother was born in 1954. Soon after, because of economic pressures on our growing family, my father joined the United States Navy. He was assigned to duty on a ship in Brooklyn Yard — a place of cement and steel that was to be his home base in the States until his retirement more than twenty years later. He left the Island first, alone, going to New York City and tracking down his uncle who lived with his family across the Hudson River in Paterson, New Jersey. There my father found a tiny apartment in a huge tenement that had once housed Jewish families but was just being taken over and transformed by Puerto Ricans, overflowing from New York City. In 1955 he sent for us. My mother was only twenty years old, I was not quite three, and my brother was a toddler when we arrived at *El Building*, as the place had been christened by its newest residents.

My memories of life in Paterson during those first few years are all in shades of gray. Maybe I was too young to absorb vivid colors and details, or to discriminate between the slate blue of the winter sky and the darker hues of the snow-bearing clouds, but that single color washes over the whole period. The building we lived in was gray, as were the streets, filled with slush the first few months of my life there. The coat my father had bought for me was similar in color and too big; it sat heavily on my thin frame.

I do remember the way the heater pipes banged and rattled, startling all of us out of sleep until we got so used to the sound that we automatically shut it out or raised our voices above the racket. The hiss from the valve punctuated my sleep (which has always been fitful) like a nonhuman presence in the room — a dragon sleeping at the entrance of my childhood. But the pipes were also a connection to all the other lives being lived around us. Having come from a house designed for a single family back in Puerto Rico — my mother's extended-family home — it was curious to know that strangers lived under our floor and above our heads, and that the heater pipe went through everyone's apartments. (My first spanking in Paterson came as a result of playing tunes on the pipes in my room to see if there would be an answer.) My mother was as new to this concept of beehive life as I was, but she had been given strict orders by my father to keep the doors locked, the noise down, ourselves to ourselves.

It seems that Father had learned some painful lessons about prejudice while searching for an apartment in Paterson. Not until years later did I hear how much resistance he had encountered with landlords who were panicking at the influx of Latinos into a neighborhood that had been Jewish for a couple of generations. It made no difference that it was the American phenomenon of ethnic turnover which was changing the urban core of Paterson, and that the human flood could not be held back with an accusing finger.

"You Cuban?" one man had asked my father, pointing at his name tag on the Navy uniform — even though my father had the fair skin and light-brown hair of his northern Spanish background, and the name Ortiz is as common in Puerto Rico as Johnson is in the U.S.

"No," my father had answered, looking past the finger into his adversary's angry eyes. "I'm Puerto Rican."

"Same shit." And the door closed.

My father could have passed as European, but we couldn't. My brother and I both have our mother's black hair and olive skin, and so we lived in El Building and visited our great-uncle and his fair children on the next block. It was their private joke that they were the German branch of the family. Not many years later that area too would be mainly Puerto Rican. It was as if the heart of the city map were being gradually colored brown —*café con leche* brown. Our color.

The movie opens with a sweep of the living room. It is "typical" immigrant Puerto Rican decor for the time: the sofa and chairs are square and hard-looking, upholstered in bright colors (blue and yellow in this instance), and covered with the transparent plastic that furniture salesmen then were so adept at convincing women to buy. The linoleum on the floor is light blue; if it had been subjected to spike heels (as it was in most places), there were dime-sized indentations all over it that cannot be seen in this movie. The room is full of people dressed up: dark suits for the men, red dresses for the women. When I have asked my mother why most of the women are in red that night, she has shrugged, "I don't remember. Just a coincidence." She doesn't have my obsession for assigning symbolism to everything.

The three women in red sitting on the couch are my mother, my eighteen-year-old cousin, and her brother's girlfriend. The novia *is just up from the Island, which is apparent in her body language. She sits up formally, her dress pulled over her knees. She is a pretty girl, but her posture makes her look insecure, lost in her full-skirted dress, which she has carefully tucked around her to make room for my gorgeous cousin, her future sister-in-law. My cousin has grown up in Paterson and is in her last year of high school. She doesn't have a trace of what Puerto Ricans call* la mancha *(literally, the stain: the mark of the new immigrant — something about the posture, the voice, or the humble demeanor that makes it obvious to everyone the person has just arrived on the mainland). My cousin is wearing a tight, sequined cocktail dress. Her brown hair has been lightened with peroxide around the bangs, and she is holding a cigarette expertly between her fingers, bringing it up to her mouth in a sensuous arc of her arm as she talks animatedly. My mother, who has come up to sit between the two women, both only a few years younger than herself, is somewhere between the poles they represent in our culture.*

It became my father's obsession to get out of the barrio, and thus we were never permitted to form bonds with the place or with the people who lived there. Yet El Building was a comfort to my mother, who never got over yearning for *la isla*. She felt surrounded by her language: the walls were thin, and voices speaking and arguing in Spanish could be heard all day. *Salsas* blasted out of radios, turned on early in the morning and left on for company. Women seemed to cook rice and beans perpetually — the strong aroma of boiling red kidney beans permeated the hallways.

Though Father preferred that we do our grocery shopping at the supermarket when he came home on weekend leaves, my mother insisted that she could cook only with products whose labels she could read. Consequently, during the week I accompanied her and my little brother to *La Bodega* — a hole-in-the-wall grocery store across the street from El Building. There we squeezed down three narrow aisles jammed with various products. Goya's and Libby's — those were the trademarks that were trusted by *her mamá*, so my mother bought many cans of Goya beans, soups, and condiments, as well as little cans of Libby's fruit juices for us. And she also bought Colgate toothpaste and Palmolive soap. (The final *e* is pronounced in both these products in Spanish, so for many years I believed that they were manufactured on the Island. I remember my surprise at first hearing a commercial on television in which Colgate rhymed with "ate.") We always lingered at La Bodega, for it was there that Mother breathed best, taking in the familiar aromas of the foods she knew from Mamá's kitchen. It was also there that she got to speak to the other women of El Building without violating outright Father's dictates against fraternizing with our neighbors.

Yet Father did his best to make our "assimilation" painless. I can still see him carrying a real Christmas tree up several flights of stairs to our apartment, leaving a trail of aromatic pine. He carried it formally, as if it were a flag in a parade. We were the only ones in El Building that I knew of who got presents on both Christmas day AND *día de Reyes*, the day when the Three Kings brought gifts to Christ and to Hispanic children.

Our supreme luxury in El Building was having our own television set. It must have been a result of Father's guilt feelings over the isolation he had imposed on us, but we were among the first in the barrio to have one. My brother quickly became an avid watcher of Captain Kangaroo and Jungle Jim, while I loved all the series showing families. By the time I started first grade, I could have drawn a map of Middle America as exemplified by the lives of characters in *Father Knows Best, The Donna Reed Show, Leave It to Beaver, My Three Sons,* and (my favorite) *Bachelor Father,* where John Forsythe treated his adopted teenage daughter like a princess because he was rich and had a Chinese houseboy to do everything for him. In truth, compared to our neighbors in El Building, *we* were rich. My father's Navy check provided us with financial security and a standard of life that the factory workers envied. The only thing his money could not buy us was a place to live away from the barrio — his greatest wish, Mother's greatest fear.

In the home movie the men are shown next, sitting around a card table set up in one corner of the living room, playing dominoes. The clack of the ivory pieces was a familiar sound. I heard it in many houses on the Island and in many apartments in Paterson. In Leave to Beaver, *the Cleavers played bridge in every other episode; in my childhood, the men started every social occasion with a hotly debated round of dominoes. The women would sit around and watch, but they never participated in the games.*

Here and there you can see a small child. Children were always brought to parties and, whenever they got sleepy, were put to bed in the host's bedroom.

Babysitting was a concept unrecognized by the Puerto Rican women I knew: a responsible mother did not leave her children with any stranger. And in a culture where children are not considered intrusive, there was no need to leave the children at home. We went where our mother went.

Of my preschool years I have only impressions: the sharp bite of the wind in December as we walked with our parents towards the brightly lit stores downtown; how I felt like a stuffed doll in my heavy coat, boots, and mittens; how good it was to walk into the five-and-dime and sit at the counter drinking hot chocolate. On Saturdays our whole family would walk downtown to shop at the big department stores on Broadway. Mother bought all our clothes at Penney's and Sears, and she liked to buy her dresses at the women's specialty shops like Lerner's and Diana's. At some point we'd go into Woolworth's and sit at the soda fountain to eat.

We never ran into other Latinos at these stores or when eating out, and it became clear to me only years later that the women from El Building shopped mainly in other places — stores owned by other Puerto Ricans or by Jewish merchants who had philo- sophically accepted our presence in the city and decided to make us their good customers, if not real neighbors and friends. These establishments were located not downtown but in the blocks around our street, and they were referred to generically as *La Tienda, El Bazar, La Bodega, La Botánica.* Everyone knew what was meant. These were the stores where your face did not turn a clerk to stone, where your money was as green as anyone else's.

One New Year's Eve we were dressed up like child models in the Sears catalogue: my brother in a miniature man's suit and bow tie, and I in black patent-leather shoes and a frilly dress with several layers of crinoline underneath. My mother wore a bright-red dress that night, I remember, and spike heels; her long black hair hung to her waist. Father, who usually wore his Navy uniform during his short visits home, had put on a dark civilian suit for the occasion: we had been invited to his uncle's house for a big celebration. Everyone was excited because my mother's brother Hernan — a bachelor who could indulge himself with luxuries — had bought a home movie camera, which he would be trying out that night.

Even the home movie cannot fill in the sensory details such a gathering left imprinted in a child's brain. The thick sweetness of women's perfumes mixing with the ever-present smells of food cooking in the kitchen: meat and plantain *pasteles*, as well as the ubiquitous rice dish made special with pigeon peas —*gandules*— and seasoned with precious *sofrito** sent up from the Island by somebody's mother or smuggled in by a recent traveler. *Sofrito* was one of the items that women hoarded, since it was hardly ever in stock at La Bodega. It was the flavor of Puerto Rico.

The men drank Palo Viejo rum, and some of the younger ones got weepy. The first time I saw a grown man cry was at a New Year's Eve party: he had been reminded of his mother by the smells in the kitchen. But what I remember most were the boiled *pasteles*— plantain or yucca rectangles stuffed with corned beef or other meats, olives, and many other savory ingredients, all wrapped in banana leaves. Everybody had to fish one out with a fork. There was always a "trick" pastel — one without stuffing — and whoever got that one was the "New Year's Fool."

There was also the music. Long-playing albums were treated like precious china in these homes. Mexican recordings were popular, but the songs that brought tears to my mother's eyes were sung by the melancholy Daniel Santos, whose life as a drug addict was the stuff of legend. Felipe Rodríguez was a particular favorite of couples, since he sang about faithless women and brokenhearted men. There is a snatch of one lyric that has stuck in my mind like a needle on a worn groove: *De piedra ha de ser mi cama, de piedra la cabezera . . . la mujer que a mi me quiera . . . ha de quererme de veras. Ay, Ay, Ay, corazón, porque no amas*[†]. . . . I must have heard it a thousand times since the idea of a bed made of stone, and its connection to love, first troubled me with its disturbing images.

The five-minute home movie ends with people dancing in a circle — the creative filmmaker must have set it up, so that all of

---

Author's note —*sofrito:** A cooked condiment. A sauce composed of a mixture of fatback, ham, tomatoes, and many island spices and herbs. It is added to many typical Puerto Rican dishes for a distinctive flavor.

Author's note —[†]**De piedra ha de ser . . . "** Lyrics from a popular romantic ballad (called a *bolero* in Puerto Rico). Freely translated: "My bed will be made of stone, of stone also my headrest (or pillow), the woman who (dares to) loves me, will have to love me for real. *Ay, Ay, Ay*, my heart, why can't you (let me) love. . . . "

them could file past him. It is both comical and sad to watch silent dancing. Since there is no justification for the absurd movements that music provides for some of us, people appear frantic, their faces embarrassingly intense. It's as if you were watching sex. Yet for years, I've had dreams in the form of this home movie. In a recurring scene, familiar faces push themselves forward into my mind's eye, plastering their features into distorted close-ups. And I'm asking them: "Who is she? Who is the old woman I don't recognize? Is she an aunt? Somebody's wife? Tell me who she is."

"See the beauty mark on her cheek as big as a hill on the lunar landscape of her face — well, that runs in the family. The women on your father's side of the family wrinkle early; it's the price they pay for that fair skin. The young girl with the green stain on her wedding dress is *La Novia* — just up from the Island. See, she lowers her eyes when she approaches the camera, as she's supposed to. Decent girls never look at you directly in the face. *Humilde*, humble, a girl should express humility in all her actions. She will make a good wife for your cousin. He should consider himself lucky to have met her only weeks after she arrived here. If he marries her quickly, she will make him a good Puerto Rican–style wife; but if he waits too long, she will be corrupted by the city — just like your cousin there."

"She means me. I do what I want. This is not some primitive island I live on. Do they expect me to wear a black mantilla on my head and go to mass every day? Not me. I'm an American woman, and I will do as I please. I can type faster than anyone in my senior class at Central High, and I'm going to be a secretary to a lawyer when I graduate. I can pass for an American girl anywhere — I've tried it. At least for Italian, anyway — I never speak Spanish in public. I hate these parties, but I wanted the dress. I look better than any of these *humildes* here. *My* life is going to be different. I have an American boyfriend. He is older and has a car. My parents don't know it, but I sneak out of the house late at night sometimes to be with him. If I marry him, even my name will be American. I hate rice and beans — that's what makes these women fat."

"Your *prima** is pregnant by that man she's been sneaking around with. Would I lie to you? I'm your *Tiá Política,*† your great-uncle's common-law

Author's note —*prima: Female cousin.

Author's note —†tía política: Aunt by marriage.

wife — the one he abandoned on the Island to go marry your cousin's mother. *I was not invited to this party, of course, but I came anyway. I came to tell you that story about your cousin that you've always wanted to hear.* Do you remember the comment your mother made to a neighbor that has always haunted you? The only thing you heard was your cousin's name, and then you saw your mother pick up your doll from the couch and say: 'It was as big as this doll when they flushed it down the toilet.' This image has bothered you for years, hasn't it? You had nightmares about babies being flushed down the toilet, and you wondered why anyone would do such a horrible thing. You didn't dare ask your mother about it. She would only tell you that you had not heard her right, and yell at you for listening to adult conversations. But later, when you were old enough to know about abortions, you suspected.

I am here to tell you that you were right. Your cousin was growing an *Americanito* in her belly when this movie was made. Soon after she put something long and pointy into her pretty self, thinking maybe she could get rid of the problem before breakfast and still make it to her first class at the high school. Well, *Niña,*[*] her screams could be heard downtown. Your aunt, her mamá, who had been a midwife on the Island, managed to pull the little thing out. Yes, they probably flushed it down the toilet. What else could they do with it — give it a Christian burial in a little white casket with blue bows and ribbons? Nobody wanted that baby — least of all the father, a teacher at her school with a house in West Paterson that he was filling with real children, and a wife who was a natural blond.

Girl, the scandal sent your uncle back to the bottle. And guess where your cousin ended up? Irony of ironies. She was sent to a village in Puerto Rico to live with a relative on her mother's side: a place so far away from civilization that you have to ride a mule to reach it. A real change in scenery. She found a man there — women like that cannot live without male company — but believe me, the men in Puerto Rico know how to put a saddle on a woman like her. *La Gringa,*[†] they call her. Ha, ha, ha. *La Gringa* is what she always wanted to be. . . . "

The old woman's mouth becomes a cavernous black hole I fall into. And as I fall, I can feel the reverberations of her laughter. I hear the echoes of her last mocking words: *La Gringa, La Gringa!*

Author's note —[*]**niña:** Girl.

Author's note —[†]**La gringa:** Derogatory epithet used here to ridicule a Puerto Rican girl who wants to look like a blonde North American.

And the conga line keeps moving silently past me. There is no music in my dream for the dancers.

When Odysseus visits Hades to see the spirit of his mother, he makes an offering of sacrificial blood, but since all the souls crave an audience with the living, he has to listen to many of them before he can ask questions. I, too, have to hear the dead and the forgotten speak in my dream. Those who are still part of my life remain silent, going around and around in their dance. The others keep pressing their faces forward to say things about the past.

My father's uncle is last in line. He is dying of alcoholism, shrunken and shriveled like a monkey, his face a mass of wrinkles and broken arteries. As he comes closer I realize that in his features I can see my whole family. If you were to stretch that rubbery flesh, you could find my father's face, and deep within *that* face — my own. I don't want to look into those eyes ringed in purple. In a few years he will retreat into silence, and take a long, long time to die. *Move back, Tío,* I tell him. *I don't want to hear what you have to say. Give the dancers room to move. Soon it will be midnight. Who is the New Year's Fool this time?*

Reflections and Responses

1. Consider the idea of "silence" in the essay. Why is it significant that the home movie has no soundtrack? What does Cofer do with that missing element? How does silence contribute to the theme of the essay?

2. What connections does Cofer make between the home movie and her dreams? In what ways is the movie dreamlike? In what ways does the essay become more nightmarish as it proceeds?

3. Consider Cofer's final paragraph. How does it pull together the various strands of the essay?

EDWIDGE DANTICAT

Westbury Court

What do we remember from our childhood? And why do we remember some things vividly, some things not at all, and yet others in some fuzzy in-between? In "Westbury Court," Edwidge Danticat examines the inner workings of memory, as she describes a deadly fire that took the lives of two children who lived next door to her in a New York apartment building when she was fourteen. Though vivid in many ways, the memory still leaves her wondering if she recalls the most significant details correctly: "Even now, I question what I remember about the children. Did they really die? Or did their mother simply move away with them after the fire?" She wonders if she is really "struggling to phase them out of [her] memory altogether."

Born in Port-au-Prince, Haiti, in 1969, Edwidge Danticat settled with her family in New York at age twelve. She began writing stories as a child and at fourteen she published a short essay about her experiences as a Haitian immigrant in New York. After graduating from Barnard College in Manhattan, she went on to earn an M.F.A. from Brown University. Her books include the novels Breath, Eyes, Memory *(1994),* The Farming of Bones *(1998), and* The Dew Breaker *(2004); a collection of short stories,* Krik? Krak! *(1995);* After the Dance *(2002), and several compilations of essays. "Westbury Court" originally appeared in* New Letters *and was selected by Alan Lightman for* The Best American Essays 2000.

When I was fourteen years old, we lived in a six-story brick building in a cul-de-sac off of Flatbush Avenue, in Brooklyn, called Westbury Court. Beneath the building ran a subway station through which rattled the D, M, and Q trains every fifteen minutes or so. Though there was graffiti on most of the walls of Westbury Court, and hills of trash piled up outside, and though the elevator wasn't always there when we opened the door to step inside and the heat and hot water weren't always on, I never dreamed of leaving Westbury Court until the year of the fire.

I was watching television one afternoon when the fire began. I loved television then, especially the afternoon soap operas, my favorite of which was *General Hospital*. I would bolt out of my last high school class every day, pick up my youngest brother, Karl, from day care, and watch *General Hospital* with him on my lap while doing my homework during the commercials. My other two brothers, André and Kelly, would later join us in the apartment, but they preferred to watch cartoons in the back bedroom.

One afternoon while *General Hospital* and afternoon cartoons were on, a fire started in apartment 6E, across the hall. There in that apartment lived our new neighbors, an African-American mother and her two boys. We didn't know the name of the mother, or the names and ages of her boys, but I venture to guess that they were around five and ten years old.

I didn't know a fire had started until two masked, burly firemen came knocking on our door. My brothers and I rushed out into the hallway filled with smoke and were quickly escorted down to the first floor by some other firemen already on our floor. While we ran by, the door to apartment 6E had already been knocked over by the fire squad and inside was filled with bright flames and murky smoke.

All of the tenants of the building who were home at that time were crowded on the sidewalk outside. My brothers and I, it seemed, were the last to be evacuated. Clutching my brothers' hands, I wondered if I had remembered to lock our apartment door. Was there anything valuable we could have taken?

An ambulance screeched to a stop in front of the building, and the two firemen who had knocked on our door came out carrying the pliant and lifeless bodies of the two children from across the hall. Their mother jumped out of the crowd and ran toward them, screaming, "My babies — not my babies," as the children were lowered into the back of the ambulance and transferred into the arms of the emergency medical personnel. The fire was started by the two boys, after their mother had stepped out to pick up some

groceries at the supermarket down the street. They had been playing with matches.

(Later my mother would tell us, "See, this is what happens to
children who play with matches. Sometimes it is too late to say,
'I shouldn't have.'" My brother Kelly, who was fascinated with fire
and liked to hold up a match to the middle of his palm until the
light fizzled out, gave up this party trick after the fire.)

We were quiet that afternoon when both our parents came
home. We were the closest to the fire in the building, and the most
religious of our parents' friends saw it as a miracle that we had
escaped safe and sound. When my mother asked how come I, the
oldest one, hadn't heard the children scream or hadn't smelled
the smoke coming from across the hall, I confessed that I had
been watching *General Hospital* and was too consumed in the intricate plot.

(After the fire, my mother had us stay with a family on the second floor for a few months, after school. I felt better not having to
be wholly responsible for myself and my brothers, in case something like that fire should ever happen again.)

The apartment across the hall stayed empty for a long time, and
whenever I walked past it, a piece of its inner skeleton would
squeak, and occasionally burnt wood that might have been hanging
by a fragile singed thread would crash down and cause a domino
effect of further ruptures, unleashed like those children's last cries,
which I had not heard because I had been so wrapped up in the
made-up drama of a world where, even though the adults' lives
were often in turmoil, the children came home to the welcoming
arms of waiting mommies and nannies who served them freshly
baked cookies on porcelain plates and helped them to remove
their mud-soaked boots, if it was raining, lest they soil the lily-white
carpets. But should their boots accidentally sully the carpet, or
should their bright yellow raincoats inadvertently drip on the
sparkling linoleum, there would be a remedy for that as well. And if
their house should ever catch fire, a smart dog or a good neighbor
would rescue them just in time, and the fire trucks would come
right quick because some attentive neighbor would call them.

Through the trail of voices that came up to comfort us, I heard
that the children's mother would be prosecuted for negligence
and child abandonment. I couldn't help but wonder, would our

parents have suffered the same fate had it been my brothers and me who were killed in the fire?

When they began to repair the apartment across the hall, I would occasionally sneak out to watch the workmen. They were shelling the inside of the apartment and replacing everything from the bedroom closets to the kitchen floors. I never saw the mother of the dead boys again and never heard anything of her fate.

A year later, after the apartment was well polished and painted, two blind Haitian brothers and their sister moved in. They were all musicians and were part of a group called les Frères Parent, the Parent Brothers. Once my parents allowed my brothers and me to come home from school to our apartment, I would always listen carefully for our new tenants, so I'd be the first to know if anything went awry.

What I heard coming from the apartment soon after they moved in was music, "engagé" music, which the brothers were composing to protest against the dictatorship in Haiti, from which they had fled. The Parent Brothers and their sister, Lydie, did nothing but rehearse a cappella most days when they were not receiving religious and political leaders from Haiti and from the Haitian community in New York.

The same year after the fire, a cabdriver who lived down the hall in 6J was killed on a night shift in Manhattan; a good friend of my father's, a man who gave great Sunday afternoon parties in 6F, died of cirrhosis of the liver. One day while my brothers and I were at school and my parents were at work, someone came into our apartment through our fire escape and stole my father's expensive camera. That same year a Nigerian immigrant was shot and killed in front of the building across the street. To appease us, my mother said, "Nothing like that ever happens out of the blue. He was in a fight with someone." It was too troublesome for her to acknowledge that people could die randomly, senselessly, at Westbury Court or anywhere else.

Every day on my way back from school, I hurried past the flowers and candles piled in front of the spot where the Nigerian, whose name I didn't know, had been murdered. Still I never thought I was living in a violent place. It was an elevated castle above a clattering train tunnel, a blind alley where children from our building and the building across the street had erected a common basketball court for hot summer afternoon games, an urban yellow brick road where hopscotch squares dotted the sidewalk next to burned-out, abandoned cars. It was home.

My family and I moved out of Westbury Court three years after the fire. Every once in a while, though, the place came up in conversation, linked to either a joyous or a painful memory. One of the girls who had scalded her legs while boiling a pot of water for her bath during one of those no-heat days got married last year. After the burglar had broken into the house and taken my father's camera, my father — an amateur photography buff — never took another picture.

My family and I often reminisce about the Parent Brothers when we see them in Haitian newspapers or on television; we brag that we knew them when, before one of the brothers became a senator in Haiti and the sister, Lydie, became mayor of one of the better-off Haitian suburbs, Pétion-Ville. We never talk about the lost children.

Even now, I question what I remember about the children. Did they really die? Or did their mother simply move away with them after the fire? Maybe they were not even boys at all. Maybe they were two girls. Or one boy and one girl. Or maybe I am struggling to phase them out of my memory altogether. Not just them, but the fear that their destiny could have so easily been mine and my brothers'.

A few months ago, I asked my mother, "Do you remember the children and the fire at Westbury Court?"

Without missing a flutter of my breath, my mother replied, "Oh those children, those poor children, their poor mother. Sometimes it is too late to say, 'I shouldn't have.'"

Reflections and Responses

1. Consider the way Danticat narrates her essay. What information does she introduce that she would not have known during the incident of the fire? What other methods of telling the story might she have chosen?

2. Why does Danticat emphasize her mother's response to the fire, referring to it at the time and then repeating it later? In what sense

is her mother's comment a warning? How do you think Danticat wants us to interpret her mother's comment in the final paragraph?

3. Why do you think that after vividly describing the firefighters carrying out the "lifeless bodies of the two children," Danticat toward the end of the essay wonders whether the children actually did die? What effect does her wondering about this produce? Do you think it leaves the issue open-ended? In light of her questions, how are we to understand the final paragraph?

YUSEF KOMUNYAKAA

The Blue Machinery of Summer

The central purpose behind an autobiographical essay can sometimes remain obscure, never explicitly stated by the writer, who may be more interested in self-exploration than full disclosure, more concerned with raising questions than with answering them. Essayists are under no obligation to write only about personal experiences they fully understand. In "The Blue Machinery of Summer," an essay full of questions and "maybes," one of America's foremost poets describes his successes and failures years ago at a summer factory job that forced him to realize the difficulties his education would bring.

Yusef Komunyakaa, who has received numerous honors and awards, including a 1994 Pulitzer Prize for Neon Vernacular, *the 2001 Ruth Lilly Poetry Prize, and a Bronze Star for service as a journalist in Vietnam, was born in Bogalusa, Louisiana, in 1947. His first book of poetry,* Dedications & Other Darkhorses, *appeared in 1977, and subsequent volumes include* Copacetic *(1984);* I Apologize for the Eyes in My Head *(1986);* Dien Cai Dau *(1988);* Magic City *(1992);* Thieves of Paradise *(1998);* Talking Dirty to the Gods *(2000);* Pleasure Dome: New & Collected Poems, 1975–1999 *(2001);* and Taboo: The Wishbone Trilogy, Part I *(2004). He has written extensively on jazz and in 1999 was elected a Chancellor of the Academy of American Poets. He lives in New York City and is a professor in the Council of Humanities and Creative Writing Program at Princeton University. "The Blue Machinery of Summer" first appeared in* The Washington Post Magazine *and was selected by Kathleen Norris for* The Best American Essays 2001.

"I feel like I'm part of this damn thing," Frank said. He carried himself like a large man even though he was short. A dead cigarette dangled from his half-grin. "I've worked on this machine for twenty-odd years, and now it's almost me."

It was my first day on a summer job at ITT Cannon in Phoenix in 1979. This factory manufactured parts for electronic systems — units that fit into larger, more complex ones. My job was to operate an air-powered punch press. Depending on each item formed, certain dies or templates were used to cut and shape metal plates into designs the engineers wanted.

"I know all the tricks of the trade, big and small, especially when it comes to these punch presses. It seems like I was born riding this hunk of steel."

Frank had a gift for gab, but when the foreman entered, he grew silent and meditative, bent over the machine, lost in his job. The whole day turned into one big, rambunctious dance of raw metal, hiss of steam, and sparks. Foremen strutted about like banty roosters. Women tucked falling curls back into hair nets, glancing at themselves in anything chrome.

This job reminded me of the one I'd had in 1971 at McGraw Edison, also in Phoenix, a year after I returned from Vietnam. Back then, I had said to myself, this is the right setting for a soap opera. Muscle and sex changed the rhythm of this place. We'd call the show "The Line."

I'd move up and down the line, shooting screws into metal cabinets of coolers and air conditioners — one hour for Montgomery Ward or Sears, and the next two hours for a long line of cabinets stamped McGraw Edison. The designs differed only slightly, but made a difference in the selling price later on. The days seemed endless, and it got to where I could do the job with my eyes closed.

In retrospect, I believe I was hyper from the war. I couldn't lay back; I was driven to do twice the work expected — sometimes taking on both sides of the line, giving other workers a hand. I worked overtime two hours before 7 A.M. and one hour after 4 P.M. I learned every thing about coolers and air conditioners, and rectified problem units that didn't pass inspection.

At lunch, rather than sitting among other workers, I chose a secluded spot near the mountain of boxed-up coolers to eat my homemade sandwiches and sip iced tea or lemonade. I always had a paperback book in my back pocket: Richard Wright's *Black Boy*,

Albert Camus' *The Fall,* Frantz Fanon's *The Wretched of the Earth,* or C. W. E. Bigsby's *The Black American Writer.* I wrote notes in the margins with a ballpoint. I was falling in love with language and ideas. All my attention went to reading.

When I left the gaze of Arizona's Superstition Mountain and headed for the Colorado Rockies, I wasn't thinking about higher education. Once I was in college, I vowed never to take another job like this, and yet here I was, eight years later, a first-year graduate student at the University of California at Irvine, and working another factory job in Phoenix, hypnotized by the incessant clang of machinery.

Frank schooled me in the tricks of the trade. He took pride in his job and practiced a work ethic similar to the one that had shaped my life early on even though I had wanted to rebel against it. Frank was from Little Rock: in Phoenix, everyone seemed to be from somewhere else except the indigenous Americans and Mexicans.

"If there's one thing I know, it's this damn machine," Frank said. "Sometimes it wants to act like it has a brain of its own, as if it owns me, but I know better."

"Iron can wear any man out," I said.

"Not this hunk of junk. It was new when I came here."

"But it'll still be here when you're long gone."

"Says who?"

"Says iron against flesh."

"They will scrap this big, ugly bastard when I'm gone."

"They'll bring in a new man."

"Are you the new man, whippersnapper? They better hire two of you to replace one of me."

"Men will be men."

"And boys will be boys."

The hard dance held us in its grip.

I spotted Lily Huong the second day in a corner of the wiring department. The women there moved their hands in practiced synchrony, looping and winding color-coded wires with such graceful dexterity and professionalism. Some chewed gum and blew bubbles, others smiled to themselves as if they were reliving the weekend. And a good number talked about the soap operas, naming off the characters as if they were family members or close friends.

Lily was in her own world. Petite, with long black hair grabbed up, stuffed beneath a net and baseball cap, her body was one fluid motion, as if it knew what it was doing and why.

"Yeah, boys will be boys," Frank said.

"What you mean?"

"You're looking at trouble, my friend."

"Maybe trouble is looking for me. And if it is, I'm not running."

"She is nothing but bona fide trouble."

I wonder if she was thinking of Vietnam while she sat bent over the table, or when she glided across the concrete floor as if she were moving through lush grass. Lily? It made me think of waterlily, lotus — how shoots and blooms were eaten in that faraway land. The lotus grows out of decay, in lagoons dark with sediment and rot.

Mornings arrived with the taste of sweet nighttime still in our mouths, when the factory smelled like the deepest ore, and the syncopation of the great heaving presses fascinated me.

The nylon and leather safety straps fit our hands like fingerless gloves and sometimes seemed as if they'd pull us into the thunderous pneumatic vacuum faster than an eye blink. These beasts pulsed hypnotically; they reminded everyone within earshot of terrifying and sobering accidents. The machinery's dance of smooth heft seemed extraordinary, a masterpiece of give-and-take precision. If a foolhardy novice wrestled with one of these metal contraptions, it would suck up the hapless soul. The trick was to give and pull back with a timing that meant the difference between life and death.

"Always use a safety block, one of these chunks of wood. Don't get careless," Frank said. "Forget the idea you can second-guess this monster. Two months ago we had a guy in here named Leo on that hunk of junk over there, the one that Chico is now riding."

"Yeah, and?"

"I don't believe it. It's crazy. I didn't know Leo was a fool. The machine got stuck, he bent down, looked underneath, and never knew his last breath. That monster flattened his head like a pancake."

One morning, I stood at the checkout counter signing out my tools for the day's work and caught a glimpse of Lily out of the corner of my eye. She stopped. Our eyes locked for a moment, and then she glided on toward her department. Did she know I had been in 'Nam? Had there been a look in my eyes that had given me away?

"You can't be interested in her," Paula said. She pushed her hair away from her face in what seemed like an assured gesture.

"Why not?" I said.

"She's nothing, nothing but trouble."

"Oh?"

"Anyway, you ain't nobody's foreman."

I took my toolbox and walked over to the punch press. The buzzer sounded. The gears kicked in. The day started.

After three weeks, I discovered certain social mechanisms ran the place. The grapevine, long, tangled, and thorny, was merciless. After a month on the job I had been wondering why Frank disappeared at lunchtime but always made it back just minutes before the buzzer.

"I bet Frank tells you why he comes back here with a smile on his mug?" Maria coaxed. She worked as a spot-welder, with most of her day spent behind heavy black goggles as the sparks danced around her.

"No."

"Why don't you ask Paula one of these mornings when you're signing out tools?"

"I don't think so," I said.

"She's the one who puts that grin on his face. They've been tearing up that rooming house over on Sycamore for years."

"Good for them," I said.

"Not if that cop husband of hers come to his senses."

It would have been cruel irony for Frank to work more than twenty years on the monster and lose his life at the hands of a mere mortal.

The grapevine also revealed that Lily had gotten on the payroll because of Rico, who was a foreman on the swing shift. They had been lovers and he had put in a good word for her. Rico was built like a lightweight boxer, his eyes bright and alert, always able to look over the whole room in a single glance. The next news said Lily was sleeping with Steve, the shipping foreman, who wore western shirts, a silver and turquoise belt buckle, and cowboy boots. His red Chevy pickup had a steer's horn on the hood. He was tall and lanky and had been in the Marines, stationed at Khe Sanh.

I wondered about Lily. What village or city had she come from — Chu Chi or Danang, Saigon or Hue? What was her story?

Did she still hear the war during sleepless nights? Maybe she had had an American boyfriend, maybe she was in love with a Vietnamese once, a student, and they had intimate moments besides the Perfume River as boats with green and red lanterns passed at dusk. Or maybe she met him on the edge of a rice paddy, or in some half-lit place in Danang a few doors down from the Blue Dahlia.

She looked like so many who tried to outrun past lovers, history. *"She's nothing but trouble . . . "* Had she become a scapegoat? Had she tried to play a game that wasn't hers to play? Didn't anyone notice her black eye one week, the corner of her lip split the next?

I told myself I would speak to her. I didn't know when, but I would.

The women were bowed over their piecework.

As a boy I'd make bets with myself, and as a man I was still making bets, and sometimes they left me in some strange situations.

"In New Guinea those Fuzzy Wuzzies saved our asses," Frank said. "They're the smartest people I've ever seen. One moment almost in the Stone Age, and the next they're zooming around in our jeeps and firing automatic weapons like nobody's business. They gave the Japanese hell. They were so outrageously brave it still hurts to think about it."

I wanted to tell him about Vietnam, a few of the things I'd witnessed, but I couldn't. I could've told him about the South Vietnamese soldiers who were opposites of Frank's heroes.

I gazed over toward Lily.

Holding up one of the doodads — we were stamping out hundreds hourly — I said to Frank, "Do you know what this is used for?"

"No. Never crossed my mind."

"You don't know? How many do you think you've made?"

"God only knows."

"And you don't know what they're used for?"

"No."

"How much does each sell for?"

"Your guess is as good as mine. I make 'em. I don't sell 'em."

He's right, I thought. Knowing wouldn't change these workers' lives. This great symphony of sweat, oil, steel, rhythm, it all made a strange kind of sense.

"These are used in the firing mechanisms of grenade launchers," I said as I scooped up a handful. "And each costs the government almost eighty-five dollars."

The buzzer sounded.

In the cafeteria, most everybody sat in their usual clusters. A few of the women read magazines — *True Romance, Tan, TV Guide, Reader's Digest* — as they nibbled at sandwiches and sipped Cokes. One woman was reading her Bible. I felt like the odd man out as I took my paperback from my lunch pail: a Great Books Foundation volume, with blue-white-black cover and a circle around *GB*. My coworkers probably thought I was reading the same book all summer long, or that it was a religious text. I read Voltaire, Hegel, and Darwin.

Voltaire spoke to me about Equality:

> All the poor are not unhappy. The greater number are born in that state, and constant labor prevents them from too sensibly feeling their situation; but when they do strongly feel it, then follow wars such as these of the popular party against the Senate at Rome, and those of the peasantry in Germany, England and France. All these wars ended sooner or later in the subjection of the people, because the great have money, and money in a state commands every thing: I say in a state, for the case is different between nation and nation. The nation that makes the best use of iron will always subjugate another that has more gold but less courage.

Maybe I didn't want to deal with those images of 'Nam still in my psyche, ones that Lily had rekindled.

"You catch on real fast, friend," Frank said. "It is hard to teach a man how to make love to a machine. It's almost got to be in your blood. If you don't watch out, you'll be doing twenty in this sweatbox too. Now mark my word."

I wanted to tell him about school. About some of the ideas filling my head. Lily would smile, but she looked as if she were gazing through me.

One morning in early August, a foreman said they needed me to work on a special unit. I was led through the security doors. The room was huge, and the man working on the big, circular-dome object seemed small and insignificant in the voluminous space. Then I was shaking hands with the guy they called Dave the Lathe.

Almost everyone had a nickname here, as in the Deep South, where, it turned out, many of the workers were from. The nicknames came from the almost instinctual impulse to make language a game of insinuation.

Dave was from Paradise, California. He showed me how to polish each part, every fixture and pin. The work led to painstaking tedium. Had I posed too many questions? Was that why I was working this job?

Here everything was done by hand, with patience and silence. The room was air-conditioned. Now the clang of machines and whine of metal being cut retreated into memory. Behind this door Dave the Lathe was a master at shaping metals, alloyed with secrets, a metal that could be smoothed but wouldn't shine, take friction and heat out of this world. In fact, it looked like a fine piece of sculpture designed aeronautically, that approached perfection. Dave the Lathe had been working on this nose cone for a spacecraft for more than five months.

Dave and I seldom talked. Lily's face receded from my thoughts. Now I stood across from Dave the Lathe, thinking about two women in my class back at the University of California with the same first name. One was from New York. She had two reproductions of French nudes over her bed and was in love with Colette, the writer. The other woman was part Okinawan from Honolulu. If we found ourselves in a room alone, she always managed to disengage herself. We had never had a discussion, but here she was, undressing in my mind. At that moment, standing a few feet from Dave the Lathe, I felt that she and I were made for each other but she didn't know it yet.

I told Dave that within two weeks I'd return to graduate school. He wished me luck in a tone that suggested he knew what I'd planned to say before I said it.

"Hey, college boy!" Maria shouted across the cafeteria. "Are you in college or did you do time like Frank says?" I wanted the impossible, to disappear.

Lily's eyes caught mine. I still hadn't told her I felt I'd left part of myself in her country. Maria sat down beside me. I fished out the ham sandwich, but left Darwin in the lunch box. She said, "You gonna just soft-shoe in here and then disappear, right?"

"No. Not really."

"*Not really*, he says," she mocked.

"Well."

"Like a lousy lover who doesn't tell you every thing. Doesn't tell the fine print."

"Well."

"Cat got your tongue, college boy?"

"Are you talking to me or somebody else?"

"Yeah, you! Walk into somebody's life and then turn into a ghost. A one-night stand."

"I didn't think anyone needed to know."

"I suppose you're too damn good to tell us the truth."

She stood up, took her lunch over to another table, sat down, and continued to eat. I didn't know what to say. I was still learning.

There's good silence. There's bad silence. Growing up in rural Louisiana, along with four brothers and one sister, I began to cultivate a life of the imagination. I traveled to Mexico, Africa, and the Far East. When I was in elementary school and junior high, sometimes I knew the answers to questions, but I didn't dare raise my hand. Boys and girls danced up and down, waving their arms, with right and wrong answers. It was hard for me to chance being wrong. Also, I found it difficult to share my feelings; but I always broke the silence and stepped in if someone was being mistreated.

Now, as I sat alone, looking out the window of a Greyhound bus at 1 A.M., I felt like an initiate who had gotten cold feet and was hightailing it back to some privileged safety zone. I began to count the figures sprawled on the concrete still warm from the sun's weight on the city. There seemed to be an uneasy equality among destitutes: indigenous Americans, Mexicans, a few blacks and whites. Eleven. Twelve. I thought, a massacre of the spirit.

The sounds of the machines were still inside my head. The clanging punctuated by Frank's voice: "Are you ready to will your body to this damn beast, my friend?"

"No, Frank. I never told you I am going to college," I heard myself saying. Did education mean moving from one class to the next? My grandmothers told me again and again that one could scale a mountain with a good education. But could I still talk to them, to my parents, my siblings? I would try to live in two worlds — at the very least. That was now my task. I never wanted again to feel that my dreams had betrayed me.

Maybe the reason I hadn't spoken to Lily was I didn't want to talk about the war. I hadn't even acknowledged to my friends that I'd been there.

The bus pulled out, headed for L.A. with its headlights sweeping like slow yellow flares across drunken faces, as if images of the dead had followed Lily and me from a distant land only the heart could bridge.

Reflections and Responses

1. What images does Komunyakaa use early in his essay to link the assembly-line work, the machinery, and sexuality? Why do you think he wants to establish these links?

2. Why do you think Komunyakaa informs us about his reading? What kind of books does he seem to prefer? Why do you think he includes a long quotation from Voltaire in an essay that is almost entirely personal?

3. How does Komunyakaa present himself in this essay? How does he portray the way his fellow workers relate to him? How does he relate to his fellow workers? What role does Lily Huong play in the essay? What sense do you make of his final conversation with Maria toward the end of the essay? What is she saying about him? How do her comments link up with the sexual themes introduced early in the essay?

DAVID MASELLO

My Friend Lodovico

Habitual readers of literature often feel as if they get to know a character in a novel as well—or perhaps even better—than they know actual friends and relatives. This odd feeling of relationship can be partly attributed to a great writer's ability to portray a complex character with convincing psychological depth. But there's another possible explanation: In a novel we can know what a character is thinking, and we can immerse ourselves in his or her consciousness. In actual life, of course, we can never truly know another person's thoughts—we can only infer them. Can a similar relationship be formed between a viewer and a portrait painting? Is it possible to feel so intimate with a portrait that we start to think of the subject as a good friend? In "My Friend Lodovico," David Masello describes the "odd relationship" he has maintained with one Lodovico Capponi, the young subject of a masterpiece painted in the mid-sixteenth century by Agnolo Bronzino. Friendship has traditionally been among the essayist's most common themes, yet rarely has anyone written so sensitively about an intimate relationship with a work of art.

David Masello is an editor at Country Living *magazine and the long time New York editor of* Art & Antiques. *His essays have appeared in the* New York Times, *the* Boston Globe, Newsweek, *the* San Francisco Chronicle, *and* The Massachusetts Review, *among other periodicals. His work has also been included in several anthologies, including* The Man I Might Become, Wonderlands, *and* New York Stories. *He is the author of two books,* Architecture Without Rules: The Houses of Marcel Breuer and Herbert Beckhard *and* Art in Public Places. *"My Friend Lodovico" originally appeared in the* New York Times *and was selected by Susan Orlean for* The Best American Essays 2005.

The portrait of Lodovico Capponi by Agnolo Bronzino. Painted with oil on panel between 1550 and 1555, the imposing four-foot high portrait can be seen at the Frick Museum in New York City. Full color representations can easily be found on the Internet by searching "Lodovico Capponi." © The Frick Collection, New York

Ten years ago, upon breaking up with someone after an embarrassing public argument in Central Park, I went to see Lodovico Capponi. I needed his approval and reassurance. He was also one of the first people I visited a few days after September 11. Whenever friends are in from out of town, I often take them to meet him, and if I find myself in his Upper East Side neighborhood, I can rarely resist dropping by.

Lodovico lives in the Frick Collection, the mansion-museum on Fifth Avenue. He is a portrait, painted in the 1550s by Agnolo Bronzino, the celebrated Florentine artist employed as a court painter to the Medicis; the 500th anniversary of Bronzino's birth is being celebration this year [2004]. In this four-foot-high oil, Lodovico is shown with wavy, red-brown hair, flawless complexion, and a wandering left eye.

I have known Lodovico for twenty-three years, as long as I have lived in New York. And after all these years, I keep asking myself the same questions: Why do I continue to visit this mute, over-dressed, imperious young man? Many people to whom I introduce him find him austere, even humorless. Others consider another Bronzino young man, who hangs on a well at the Metropolitan Museum of Art, handsomer and more engaging.

When I was close to Lodovico's age, about twenty-two, some people said I resembled him; my right eye wanders lazily in the way his left does; his nose appears to be equally ample and Italian. I suppose it's natural that we are attracted to those who remind us of ourselves. Years ago, after I sent a postcard of the portrait to my father in Florida, he called to mention that he had taped Lodovico to his refrigerator as a remider of me. "He looks like you, only without your eyeglasses," my father said. "And get a haircut — you could be as clean-cut as this kid."

Lodovico was a constant in my early years in New York. I knew always where to find him, in the West Gallery of the Frick. Being a painting, he would never change or age. At a time when I still had few friends and a fragile self-confidence as a young man in a new city working in an office job for a book publisher, I admired Lodovico's regal bearing, his unblinking confidence, and his solid ownership of a defined station in life.

Much has changed since we met. I am now twice as old as he is in the painting; I've had careers and I've been happily involved with a partner for years. Yet I need the unspoken advice that Lodovico still supplies. When I visit the Frick, his portrait is what I go to first, striding purposefully to the work, and leaving the museum after only several minutes, sometimes even before the coat checker has hung up my garment. I have never visited the Frick without spending some time with Lodovico.

He wears a high-collared, velvet-striped taffeta jacket over a white satin shirt, sleeves embellished with fisheye cutouts. A long swag of luxurious black velvet swoops from his right shoulder down to his billowing breeches, which seem fashioned from shimmering ribbons. In his right hand he pinches a cameo with the mysterious inscription "*Sorte*" (fate, or fortune, in Italian), and in his left he clasps neatly folded brown gloves, which I had long mistaken for a wallet until the audio-guide narrator enlightened me one day.

The space where he dwells is a retreat not only from Manhattan streets but from all concerns in life, although every passion, from lust and jealousy to murder and love, is on display. Even before reaching the galleries, some visitors are seduced by the trickling fountain in the interior courtyard, where they wind up spending contemplative hours listening to the water instead of looking at the art works. This is where I sat those many years ago after my romantic breakup; rather than confront Lodovico in tears, I collected myself beside the waters before presenting myself to him for consolation.

Despite his calm demeanor, Lodovico was living through trying times when his portrait was being painted. While on the job as a court page, he fell in love with a young girl, Maddalena Vettori, whom his employer, Duck Cosimo I de' Medici, had chosen as a bride for one of his cousins. Upon learning of their courtship, the duke forbade the couple to meet. The duke's wife, Eleonara of Toledo, empathized with the young couple and lobbied on their behalf. After three years the duke acquiesced, but stipulated that unless the couple married within twenty-four hours, they would be forever separated. They wed immediately and produced eight children.

One reason I go to see Lodovico is because he is an expect creation. I marvel at the folds in the fabric and the resulting shadows, the shimmer of material, the smoothness of skin, and the absence of brush strokes, an almost photographically flawless application of color. I love the literal cloak of mystery created by the green material. I can imagine a marble palazzo just behind the folds, corridos bustling with court pages, ladies-in-waiting lifting skirts as they walk, busybody Eleonara passing messages between Lodovico and Maddalena.

Lodovico and I have maintained an odd relationship. We don't speak, and when together, we stare each other down. Yet I can look at him indefinitely. And I miss him indefinitely. And I miss him quickly if too many weeks go by without a visit. I break my gaze only when another visitor approaches.

He neither smiles nor frowns, seems judging or indifferent, appears happy or sad, Lodovico is just he is. There is nothing else in the painting but him; no alluring snippets of late Renaissance cityscapes, beloved pets, fanciful furniture. He is simply a young, well-dressed, attractive man who has taken the time to stand for us over what must have been many weeks.

Lodovico is my Dorian Gray.* Because he will never age or fade, neither will my memories of life in New York in my early twenties, when Lodovico was one of the first figures I met and came to know.

If he could see me, he would have discerned over the years a portrait of me standing before him, alone, with various mates, as they entered and left my life, with friends (some of whom died in the eighties during our version of the black plague), and with strangers who share their thoughts about the painting. He would have seen me wearing ties as wide as napkins, later ones ruler-narrow, glasses in every style from granny to aviator.

I can't claim that an image in a painting became one of my first real friends in New York, but I can say that I visited the painting so often when I was new to the city that, as an object, it became friendly and familiar. The painting and the room where it hangs become, and remain, constants in my life.

Lodovico and I are equally removed from each other's time, and I worry increasingly about the growing gulf in our ages. Will his youth eventually intimidate me? Yet I know that if he came to life somehow, we would eagerly teach each other the ways of our time. I wouldn't know how to negotiate the intrigues of Renaissance Florentine court life, and he wouldn't understand whole-wheat pasta. But I'm sure our friendship would be an easy one. We would be, as they say in Italian, simpatico.

Dorian Gray: The central character of Oscar Wilde's sensational 1891 novel, *The Picture of Dorian Gray,* the story of a young man who is the subject of a portrait that takes on supernatural properties.

Reflections and Responses

---

1. Examine David Masello's opening paragraph. What key detail does he omit in his account of Lodovico? If you didn't learn that detail subsequently, what would you conclude from the first paragraph? What do you think Masello's intended effect is in opening the essay in this fashion? How exactly does his choice of words help him accomplish that effect?

2. Masello does not describe the first time that he saw Bronzino's portrait. What do you think the first encounter was like? What qualities of the portrait have attracted Masello? How does Masello use the portrait to tell us about himself? In what ways does Masello himself become like a "portrait"?

3. Is the thought of forming a friendship with a portrait preposterous? Does Masello offer any suggestions that it is? What aspects of his essay persuade you most that he has indeed cemented a deep friendship with Lodovico? Is there anything in the essay that you believe calls into question the very possibility of such a friendship? Do you think Masello uses the word *friendship* in a literal way, or do you think he uses it as a figure of speech?

REBECCA MCCLANAHAN

Book Marks

Anyone who's ever bought a used book (perhaps eventually this one) has found traces of a previous reader who marked up the volume in various ways — through marginal comments, underlining, doodles, and even an occasional personal note. Sometimes the presence of the other reader still lingers in food or beverage stains, handy bookmarks such as a fast-food receipt, or even forgotten letters or photographs that once marked a pause in the reading. In "Book Marks," Rebecca McClanahan contemplates the presence of someone whose life is suggested by marginal notes scribbled in a library book. As she plays detective and tries to imagine the person who previously borrowed the book, she recollects various stages of her own life as it moved in and out of books that became closely associated with relatives, schoolmates, husbands, and lovers. McClanahan weaves these episodes together, revealing how arbitrary the lines can be that we conventionally draw between life and literature.

Rebecca McClanahan lives in New York City and has published four books of poetry (most recently Naked as Eve *) and two books on writing:* Word Painting: A Guide to Writing More Descriptively *(1999) and* Write Your Heart Out *(2001). She has received the Carter Prize for the essay from* Shenandoah, *a Pushcart award in fiction, and the Wood Prize from* Poetry *magazine. A collection of personal essays,* The Riddle Song and Other Mysteries, *appeared in 2002. Her work is included in* The Best American Poetry 1998. *First published in* Southern Review, *"Book Marks" was selected by Kathleen Norris for* The Best American Essays 2001.

I am worried about the woman. I am afraid she might hurt herself, perhaps has already hurt herself — there's no way to know which of the return dates stamped on the book of poetry was hers. The book, Denise Levertov's *Evening Train*, belongs to the New York City Public Library. I checked it out yesterday and can keep it for three weeks. Ever since my husband and I moved to the city several months ago, I've been homesick for my books, the hundreds of volumes stored in my brother's basement. I miss having them near me, running my hands over their spines, recalling when and where I acquired each one, and out of what need.

There's no way to know for certain that the phantom library patron is a woman, but all signs point in that direction. On one page is a red smear that looks like lipstick, and between two other pages, lying like a bookmark, is a long, graying hair. The underlinings, which may or may not have been made by the woman, are in pencil — pale, tentative marks I study carefully, reverently, the way an archaeologist traces a fossil's delicate imprint. The rest is dream, conjecture, the making of *my* story. It's a weird obsession, I know, studying other readers' leavings and guessing the lives lived beneath. Even as my reasonable mind is having its say (*This makes no sense. How can you assume? The marks could have been made by anyone, for any reason, over any period of time . . .*), my other self is leaving on its own journey. I've always been a hungry reader, what one friend calls a "selfish reader." But is there any other kind? Don't we all read to answer our own needs, to complete the lives we've begun, to point us toward some light?

Some of the underlinings in *Evening Train* have been partially erased (eraser crumbles have gathered in the center seams), as if the woman reconsidered her first responses or tried to cover her tracks. The markings do not strike me as those of a defiant woman but rather of one who has not only taken her blows but feels she might deserve them. She has underlined "serviceable heart" in one poem; in another, "Grey-haired, I have not grown wiser." If she exists, I would like to sit down with this woman. We seem to have a lot in common. We chose the same book, we both wear red lipstick, and though I am not so honest (the gray in my hair is hidden beneath an auburn rinse), I am probably her age or thereabouts.

And from what she has left behind on the pages of Levertov's poems, it appears that our hearts have worn down in the same places. This is the part that worries me. Though my heart has mended, for the time being at least, hers seems to be in the very act of breaking. A present-tense pain pulses through each marked-up poem, and the further I read, the clearer it becomes what she is considering. I want to reach through the pages and lead her out.

My interest in marginalia, reading between the lines, began when I was an evening student at a college in California, still living with my parents but working days to help pay my expenses. It was a lonely time. Untethered from the rock-hard rituals of high school, I'd been set adrift, floating between adolescence and Real Life, a place I'd heard about that both terrified and seduced me. As a toddler, I'd been one of those milkily content clingers who must be pulled away from the nipple; eighteen years later I was still reluctant to leave my mother's side.

My siblings had no such trouble. An older sister had married and left home, a brother was away at college, and my younger siblings, in various stages of adolescent rebellion, had struck out on their own. As for my friends, most had left to study at faraway colleges; the few who stayed, taking jobs at the local bank or training to be dental assistants, seemed even more remote than those who had left. Whatever had held us together in high school — intramural sports, glee club, the senior-class play — was light-years away. As was the boy who'd promised to marry me someday. He'd found someone else, and though part of me had always known that's how that book would end (we'd never progressed beyond kissing), nevertheless his leaving was the first hairline crack in my serviceable heart.

My only strike at independence was the paycheck I earned typing invoices at a printing shop. Though I reluctantly accepted my father's offer to pay tuition costs, I insisted on buying my own textbooks. I could afford only used ones, and the more *used* the book, the cheaper it was. Some had passed through several hands; the multiple marked-through names and phone numbers on the flyleaves bore witness to this fact. At first I was put off by the previous owners' underlinings, marginal comments, bright yellow highlighted sections, sophomoric doodlings and obscenities. Worse still were the unintentional markings — coffee stains, dried pizza sauce, cigarette burns.

After a while, however, I became accustomed to the markings. I even began to welcome them. Since I didn't live on campus or have college buddies — I worked all day, then went straight home after class — I appreciated the company the used books offered. I imagined the boy who had splattered pizza sauce across the map of South America. Was he lonely too? Had he eaten the pizza alone, in his tiny dorm room, while memorizing Bolivia's chief exports? What about the girl who had misspelled *orgasm* (using two *s*'s) in the margins of John Donne's "The Canonization"? Had she ever said the word aloud? Was she a virgin like me?

The used texts served practical purposes as well. In the case of difficult subject matter (which, for me, meant political science, chemistry, and botany), it was as though I had engaged a private tutor, someone to sit at my elbow and guide me through each lesson, pointing out important concepts, underlining the principles that would show up on next week's exam. The marked-up textbook was my portable roommate, someone to sit up nights with me, to quiz me with questions I didn't know enough to ask.

Not since I was a child sharing a room with Great-Aunt Bessie, an inveterate reader, had I had a reading partner. Bessie and I would sit up late in our double bed and read mysteries and westerns aloud. We'd take turns, each reading a chapter a night, and at the end, right before Bessie removed her dentures and switched off the light (she was a disciplined reader, always stopping at the end of a chapter), right before she slipped her embroidered handkerchief into the book to mark our place, we would discuss our reactions to what we had read and make predictions about how the story would turn. Because of Aunt Bessie, I never saw books as dead, finished texts. They were living, breathing entities, unexplored territories into which we would venture the next night, and the next. Anything could happen, and we would be present when it did.

Years later, carrying this lesson into my first college class, I was amazed at what I encountered: rows of bleary-eyed students slumped around me, their limp hands spread across Norton anthologies. Most never ventured into the territory Bessie and I had explored. This stymied me, that people could read a poem by Shelley or Keats or Sylvia Plath and not want to live inside it, not want to add their words to the ones on the page. Looking back on my college literature texts, I can trace the journey of those years. In the margins of Wordsworth's sonnets, beside the lines

"The world is too much with us; late and soon, / Getting and spending, we lay waste our powers," I can chart my decision to quit my day job and pursue my studies full-time, even if it meant borrowing from the savings account I'd been feeding each payday. "I am done with this," I wrote in blue ink, meaning the commerce of getting and spending, the laying waste of powers I'd yet to discover.

And in the underlined sections of Gerard Manley Hopkins's poems, I can trace the ecstasy of my first spiritual awakening ("I caught this morning morning's minion"), made all the more ecstatic since, because I was unable to understand his elliptical syntax with my *mind*, I was forced to take it in through the rhythms of my body. This was a new music for me. My heart was no longer metaphorical. It beat rapidly in my chest, my temples, in my pale, veined wrists. Suddenly, within Hopkins's lines, I was breaking in new places: "here / Buckle! And the fire that breaks from thee then, a billion / Times told lovelier, more dangerous."

At the time I encountered those lines, I had no knowledge of the fire that awaited me in the eyes of a young man I'd yet to meet. I saw myself vaguely, like a character in one of the books I fell asleep with each night. In dreams I drank black coffee at street cafés, lay beneath the branches of the campus oaks, or wandered late at night, as Whitman's narrator had wandered, looking up "in perfect silence at the stars." In daylight, I pulled another used book from the shelf and fell into its pages. Could it be that Rilke's injunction, "You must change your life," was aimed at me? I highlighted it in yellow, then wrote in the margin, in bright blue indelible ink, "THIS MEANS *YOU!*"

Had I chosen to resell these books to the campus bookstore (I didn't; they had become part of me), their new owners might one day have read my underlinings, my marginal scribblings, and wondered at the person who left such a trail. "She needs to get more sun," they might have thought, if they could deduce I was a *she.* Maybe they would have worried about me the way I now worry about the gray-haired woman. They might even have responded, as I sometimes do, with an answering note. It might have gone on and on like that, a serial installment of marginalia, each new reader adding his own twist to Hopkins or Wordsworth — or to me, the phantom whose pages they were turning.

When life interrupts, you close the book. Or perhaps you leave it open, facedown on the bed or table, to mark your place. Aunt Bessie taught me never to do this. "You'll break its spine," she said, running her age-spotted hands across the book's cover, and the tenderness in her gesture made me ashamed that I'd ever considered such violence. After that I took to dog-earing pages, but after a while even that seemed too violent. Now, whenever I encounter a dog-eared page, I smooth its wounded edge.

Aunt Bessie used embroidered handkerchiefs to mark her place, though to me they seemed unnecessary since she always stopped at the end of a chapter. Some readers are like that. They regulate their reading, fitting books neatly into their lives the way some people schedule exercise or sex: five poems, twenty laps. One of my friends always stops after twenty-five pages so she can easily remember where she left off. Though I admire such discipline, I've never been able to accomplish it. I fall into books the way I fall into lust — wholly, hungrily. Often the book disappoints, or I disappoint. The first flush cools and the words grow tired and dull, or I grow tired and dull and slam the book shut. Occasionally, though, I keep reading, and lust ripens slowly into love, and I want to stay right there, at the lamplit table or in the soft, worn chair, until the last page is turned.

Then suddenly, always unexpectedly, life interferes; it is what life does best. It usually happens in mid-paragraph, sometimes even mid-sentence — a kind of biblio-interruptus — and I grab something to mark my place. Though I own many beautiful bookmarks, they are never there when I need them. So I reach for whatever is close at hand. A newspaper clipping, the phone bill, my bourbon-fossiled cocktail napkin, a note from a friend, the grocery list. Once I plucked a protruding feather from the sofa cushion where I rested my head, once I used a maple leaf that had blown in through the patio door, once I even pulled a hair from my head.

Looking back on my nineteenth year, I am amazed at how easily I closed the books I'd been living inside. What replaced them were the poems the young man handed me across a restaurant table. "Pretty Brown-Haired Girl" was the title of one; "Monday Rain" another. Some were written in German, and I used my secondhand Cassell's dictionary to translate them. The poems were not good — I remember thinking this even then — but they were the first love poems anyone had ever written for me. I ran my fingers across the words. I folded the papers, put them into my pocket, and later that night unfolded them on my bedside table. Already the poems were in my head, every ragged line break and rhyme.

At twenty-one he had one of those faces that might have looked old all along. His hair was retreating prematurely, exposing a forehead with furrows already deeply plowed. But his eyes were bright blue, center-of-a-flame blue, simultaneously cool and hot. He wore faded jeans and a rugged woolen jacket and drove a motorcycle; his mouth tasted of cigarettes. Plus he could quote Wordsworth, which weakened me even more. He was independently brilliant, a part-time student with no declared major, taking classes in subjects like German and astronomy and horticulture — nothing that fit together to form anything like a formal degree. "Come into the light of things," he teased. "Let nature be your teacher."

Nature taught me so much over the next year that it was all I could do to attend classes, let alone sit up nights with pencil in hand, scribbling notes in the margins of textbooks. He'd moved into his own apartment, and his marks were all over me — his mouth on my forehead, his tongue on my neck, my belly, the smell of his cigarettes in my hair. All else fell away. When an occasional misgiving surfaced I pushed it down. I had reason to doubt that I was his only brown-haired girl, the only one to whom he wrote poems. But I hushed the voice of reason, even when it spoke directly into my ear.

My parents disapproved of him, and though Aunt Bessie had moved back to her Midwest childhood home, I was certain she would have disapproved too. I *knew* Carolyn did. She'd told me so, in the same loving yet blatantly forthright tone she'd used on me since I was small. Carolyn was my mother's best friend, and had served as a kind of alternate mother for me as long as I could remember. Perhaps *mother* is the wrong word; *mentor* may come closer. She was a librarian who not only loved books but believed in them, even more so than Aunt Bessie. Carolyn believed that books could change our lives, could save us from ourselves.

My mother also loved books, but while she was raising her six children — sometimes single-handedly, when my pilot father was overseas — she put reading aside. I cannot recall, during those years, ever seeing my mother sit down, except to play a game of Monopoly or Old Maid, or to sew our Halloween costumes or

Easter dresses. Certainly not to read. Late at night, when my
father was away and she couldn't sleep, perhaps she switched on the
light beside their double bed and opened a book, probably her
Bible, a beautiful burgundy-leather King James my father had given
her early in their marriage and that she kept close at hand. I loved
to feel the cover and the onionskin pages that were tipped in gold
and totally free of marginalia. The only mark I could find was a
handwritten notation on the flyleaf. "Deuteronomy 29:29. The
secret things belong unto the Lord our God: but those things
which are revealed belong unto us and to our children for ever."

Over the years Carolyn gave me many books that she felt I needed
to read at particular stages of my life. Some she'd bought on her travels; some had belonged to her mother; some had been gifts. She
shared my passion for hand-me-downs, and never apologized for giving me used books. "Words don't go bad," she'd say, "like cheese. Read
every thing you can get your hands on. Live inside them." On the subject of my newfound love, she was adamant: "You're too young to give
it all up for a man." Carolyn had married an older, stable, kind man
who adored her yet allowed the space her inquiring mind demanded.
"I'm afraid you're going to lose yourself," she told me. "Besides," she
added, almost as an afterthought, "I don't trust him."

"You won't be able to put it down," booksellers claim as they ring
up your purchase. But of course you do, you must. The oven timer
goes off, the children come in from school, your plane lands, the
nurse calls your name, your lover kisses the back of your neck,
your heavy eyes close in sleep. By the time you return to the
book — if you return — you will be changed, will not be the same
person you were ten days, or ten years, before. Life is a river, and
you can't step into the same book twice.

One night after we'd made love, he lit a cigarette and leaned
back onto the pillows. "I'm in trouble," he said. "There's this girl."
Smoke floated around his eyes; he blinked, fanned the air. "*Was*
this girl. It's over, but she's been calling. She says she's pregnant."
Something hot flashed through my head, then was gone. All
I could think was *He will marry her, and I will lose him.*

"There's this place in Mexico City," he continued. "It's nine hundred dollars for every thing, to fly her there and back. I have two
hundred."

I had seen the word *abortion* in biology textbooks, but I had never uttered it. In 1969, even at the crest of the free-love movement, it was not a legal option. I had fourteen hundred dollars in my savings account, all that was left of nearly two years of typing invoices at the print shop. Each Friday I had taken the little vinyl passbook to the bank window, where the cashier recorded the deposit, half of my paycheck.

"I'll get the rest," I said, surprising even myself.

"I can't ask you to do that."

My next line was from a movie. Something out of the forties. I should have been wearing a hat with a feather. We should have been in a French café: "You're not asking. I'm offering."

"I'll make it up to you," he said.

To this day I can't recall if he repaid me. The passbook shows no record of the money being replaced. Within a year we were married, and what was left of my savings was pooled into a joint account. There was little money and much to buy — a dinette table, a TV stand, a couch. One night he suddenly sat straight up on that couch. "I'll bet she was lying all along," he said, as though continuing a conversation started just seconds before. "Maybe she just wanted a trip to Mexico. She probably spent the whole time on the beach." I wanted to believe him. I hoped the girl *had* spent the weekend on the sand. I hoped she'd gotten a tan. But I knew she hadn't lied. I knew because of what had been set into motion since I'd handed over the money. The shadow over our marriage had first approached in the bank's parking lot, had lengthened and darkened with each month, and has never completely lifted.

The girl's name is Barbara. She had blue eyes and long brown hair, and she lived in Garden Grove with her parents. She had a lisp. That's all he ever told me. The rest has been written in daylight imaginings and in dreams: Barbara and I are sitting beneath a beach umbrella reading books and sipping tall, cool drinks. The ocean is crashing in the distance, and the child crawling the space between our knees is a girl. She is a harlequin, seamed down the center. Not one eyelash, one fingernail, one cell of the child is his. She is the two best halves of Barbara and me, sewn with perfectly spaced stitches: this is the story I write.

*   *   *

Studying the markings in *Evening Train,* I surmise that the gray-haired woman is an honest reader, unashamed to admit her ignorance. She has drawn boxes around difficult words — *epiphanies, antiphonal, tessellations, serrations* — and placed a question mark above each box. Maybe she's merely an eager learner, the kind who sets small tasks for herself; she will go directly to the dictionary and find these words. Or maybe someone — her husband, her lover, whoever broke her serviceable heart — also criticized her vocabulary. It was too small or too large. She asked too many questions.

In the poem about the breaking heart, she has underlined "in surface fissures" and "a web / of hairline fractures." She probably didn't even notice the fissures at first. Maybe, she guessed, this webbing is the necessary landscape of every marriage, each act of love. But reading on, I sense that more has been broken than a metaphorical heart. She has circled the entire poem "The Batterers," about a man who, after beating a woman, dresses her wounds and, in so doing, begins to love her again. "Why had he never / seen, before, what she was? / What if she stops breathing?" I tell myself *I* wouldn't have stayed in that kind of situation. As it is, I'll never know. He never hit me, though one night, desperate for attention, I begged him to. (How do we live with the knowledge of our past selves?) He'd come home late, at two or three o'clock, with no explanation. Earlier in the evening, returning from a night class and looking for clues to his absence, I'd found a woman's jacket behind a chair. It smelled foreign yet familiar — her musky perfume mingled with the memory of his cigarettes. They had been here together, in our apartment. He had not touched me in weeks.

When his fist finally flew, it landed on the door of the filing cabinet where I kept my class notes, term papers, and poetry drafts. This should not have surprised me. For months he'd been angry that I'd returned to school. "What are you trying to prove?" he'd ask. "Where do you think this is going to get you? Just listen to yourself, can't you just hear yourself?" Though I still worked part-time at the print shop, he spent whole days on the assembly line, drilling holes into bowling balls. Anything to make ends meet. He was hoping, beyond logic, that as a married man with a full-time job, he would be saved from Vietnam. He was terrified; his draft number was low.

The force of the blow was audible: a thud, a crack. Loose sheets flew from the top of the cabinet. He cried out, then brought the fist to his mouth. Surely it was broken, I thought. I rushed toward him, but he held up his other hand to block me. Time slowed. White paper fluttered around me like birds. I stared at his hand, and something went out of me, I could feel it, a sucking force, tidal, pulling me out of myself. Then the moment was over. He turned and walked away, his wounded fist still pressed to his mouth, his blue eyes filling. I knelt on the floor and began to gather the papers. My eyes were dry, my vision clear. This is what hurt the most: the clarity of the moment, its sharp focus. Each black word, on each scattered page, distinct and singular.

Two years ago, when Carolyn was dying, when she could count the remaining months on her fingers, she wrote from her home in Virginia, asking me to come as soon as possible to help her sort through her books. "You can have whatever you want," she said. "The only thing I ask is that you don't cry. Just pretend it's a book sale. Come early, stay late. And go home with your arms full."

It took two full afternoons. Too weak to stand, Carolyn sat on a little stool, pointing and nodding, directing me shelf by shelf. Each row called forth a memory. Her life's story unfolded book by book. She told me she was glad she'd lived long enough to see a grandchild safely into the world. She was glad I had found a husband who was good to me, this time, and she wished me all the happiness she had known. When my car could hold no more books, she handed me a large envelope and explained that one of her jobs as assistant librarian had been to check the returned books before reshelving them. The envelope was labeled in Carolyn's scrawl: *Woodrow Wilson Public Library, Things Found in Books.* "You'd be surprised at what people use as bookmarks," she said.

When I got home, I emptied the envelope onto the floor, amazed at what spilled out. Bits and pieces of strangers' lives, hundreds of markers of personal histories. Love letters, folded placemats, envelopes, sympathy cards, valentines, handwritten recipes, train tickets, report cards, newspaper clippings, certificates of achievement, bills, receipts, religious tracts, swimming-pool passes, scratch-and-sniff perfume ads, canceled tickets for the bullfight, bar coasters, rice paper, happy money. Studying the bookmarks, I slid into each stranger's life, wondering which book he had checked out and whether he had finished it. What calls us away from books, then back to them?

When I am in pain, I *devour* books, often stripping the words of conceptual and metaphorical context and digging straight for the meat. The gray-haired woman seems to be doing the same thing, taking each word personally, *too* personally, as if Levertov had written them just for her, to guide her toward some terrible action. Certainly this wasn't the poet's intention, yet the more I study the markings, the more I fear what the woman is considering. In "Dream Instruction" she has underlined, twice, "gradual stillness," but appears to have missed entirely the "blessing" in the line that follows. The marks in "Contraband" are even more alarming. I want to take the woman by the hand and remind her of the poem's symbolic level, a level that's nearly impossible to see when you are in pain. Contraband, I would tell her, represents the Tree of Knowledge, the tree of reason, and the fruit is the words we stuff into our mouths, and yes, that fruit might indeed be "toxic in large quantities; fumes / swirled in our heads and around us," but those lines are not a prescription for suicide. There are other ways to live with knowledge.

For instance, you can leave, gather up what remains of yourself and set off on a journey much like the journey of faith Levertov writes of. Or, if that proves too difficult, you can send your self off on its own, wave goodbye, step back into childhood's shoes and refuse to go one step further. You can cut off your hair, take the pills the doctors prescribe and beg for more, then lose yourself daily in a gauzy sleep, surrounded by the books that have become your only food. His deferment dream did not materialize, so you have followed him to a military base where you know no one. Vietnam is still a possibility. Your heart is divided: you dread the orders yet pray for them. If they come, you will be able to retreat honorably to your parents' home. In the meantime, you have the pills and the books and the bed grown huge by his nightly absence — he is sleeping elsewhere now, with someone else, and he no longer even tries to hide it.

If you're lucky, one night your hand will find the phone, and if you are doubly lucky and have a mother like mine, she will arrive early the next day, having driven hundreds of miles alone in a car large enough to hold several children. Though she is a quiet woman who rarely interferes, in this case she will make an exception.

She will locate your husband, demand that he come home, now, and when he does (this is where the details get fuzzy, you have sent yourself off somewhere), together they will lift you into the backseat of her big car and rush you to the emergency room, where the attending physician will immediately direct you to the psychiatric wing.

I would remember none of this part, which is a blessing. Had I recalled the details of the breakdown, I might have felt compelled to tell the story too soon, to anyone who would listen: strangers on buses, prospective employers, longtime family friends, men I met in bars or churches (for months I would search both places, equally, for comfort). "There's no need to tell," my mother said after my release, and she would repeat this many times, long after I was out of danger. Though I've finally decided, after nearly thirty years, to tell, I still hear her words in my head: "You don't need any more hurt. It's no one's business but yours."

This is my mother's way. Though she freely gives to anyone in need — food, comfort, time, love — there is a part of herself, the heart's most enclosed, tender core, that she guards like a secret. In this way, and others, I would like to be more like her. Less needy, more protective of private fears and desires. Less prone to look back, more single-minded in forward resolve. Though I had rehearsed his leaving for months, when he finally went, for good this time (isn't it strange how we use *good* to mean *final?*), I was devastated, terrified to imagine my future. "What should I do," I begged my mother. "What would you do?" I don't know what I expected her to say. My mother has never been one to give advice. Experience, in her view, is not transferable. It is not an inheritance you pass on to your children, no matter how much you wish you could.

If her words held no answer, I decided, then I would read her life. Certainly there were worlds it could teach me. She had left her parents and the family farm to follow her husband from one military base to the next; waited out his long absences; buried one child and raised six others; watched as loved ones suffered divorces, financial ruin, alcoholism, depression, life-threatening illnesses and accidents; nursed them through their last years. "Take me with you," I begged, meaning back home, to *her* home, to the nest she and my father had made.

My mother remembers this as one of the painful moments of her life. "I wanted more than anything to say yes," she recalls. "But

I knew if I did, you'd never find your way. It was time you found your own way." So she took my face in her hands and said *no*. No, I could not follow her, I could not come back home. Then she helped me pack my suitcase, and, so I would not be alone, so I would be safe if worse once again came to worst, she made me a plane reservation to my brother's town in South Carolina. Half a world away, or so it seemed to me.

The narrator of Levertov's *Evening Train* sets off on a journey too, and though I suspect that the luggage and racks of the book's title poem are intended to be metaphorical, I cannot help but feel the heft of the bags, the steel slickness of the racks. And as I study the phantom woman's markings, it seems clear that, like mine, her journey required a real ticket on a real train or plane, and that by the time she arrived at the poem called "Arrived," she had already sat alone in a room with "Chairs, / sofa, table, a cup —" and begun the inventory of her life. Was she, like the poem's narrator, unable to call forth the face of the one she had left, who had left her? Why else mark these lines: "the shape / of his head, or / color of his eyes appear / at moments, but I can't / assemble feature with feature"?

In my pain, I prayed for such moments of forgetfulness. How pleasant it would be not to recall his hands, his tanned, furrowed forehead, the flame-cool blue of his eyes. My only release was to stuff my brain with cotton. That's how it felt when I took the pills. Though they no longer had the power to put me to sleep, they lifted me to a place of soundlessness and ether. I thought of T. S. Eliot's hollow men, their heads filled with straw. The image of scarecrows was comforting, as were thoughts of helium balloons, slow-floating dirigibles, and anything submerged in water. I was an aquarium, enclosed. Amniotic silence surrounded me hour after hour, and then suddenly —*What's that noise?*, I'd think, startled, amazed to discover it was my own breath in my lungs, my heart thumping, the blood thrumming in my ears.

When this happened, when I was brought back to myself, I'd think, *No, please not that.* I had forgotten for a while that I was alive, that there were hands at the ends of my arms, fingers that could burn themselves on the gas stove, the iron, the teakettle's steam. The world was too much with me. Why bother? (*This is the way the world ends . . .*) I fell back into bed, finding comfort in Eliot, and later in Job. The New Testament was stuffed too full of promise and light, but Old Testament sufferings were redemptive, though not in the traditional sense of the word. I was long past questioning why a loving God would destroy Job's house and cattle, afflict him with boils all over his body, and kill his children. The worst is yet to come, I thought — and almost said, aloud, to Job. Happiness is what you should be fearing. Why waste your breath talking back to God, calling out for salvation? The cure might be worse than the disease. If God answers, out of the whirlwind and the chaos of destruction, beware of what will be given: healing, forgiveness, six thousand camels, a thousand she-asses, seven sons and three daughters, each fairer than the next, your life overflowing, another high place from which to fall.

I didn't want to live, but I couldn't imagine dying. How to gather the energy? I didn't own a gun and could see no way to get one. I had no courage for knives. Pills seemed an easy way out; I tried, but my stomach refused to accept them. Over the next weeks I started taking long drives on country roads, staring at the yellow lines and thinking how easy it would be to pull the wheel to the left, into the oncoming truck, which was heavy enough, I was sure, to bear the impact without killing its driver. (I didn't want to kill anyone, not even myself. I just wanted not to live. There's a difference.) Or better yet, pull the wheel to the right, into that stand of pine trees.

What terrified me was not the thought of the mangled metal, the row of wounded trunks, or even of the sheet pulled over me — a gesture that seemed almost a kindness, something a loved one would do. What terrified me that late summer day was the sudden greenness of the trees, the way their beauty insinuated itself into my vision — peripherally at first, vaguely, and without my consent. I blinked to stop what felt like tears, which I hadn't tasted for so long I'd forgotten that they were made of salt, that they were something my body was producing on its own, long after I thought I had shut down. O.K., I said to the steering wheel, the padded dashboard, the pines. If I can think of five reasons not to die, I won't.

When I got back to my room, I pulled from the pages of Eliot a blank prescription refill form I'd been using as a bookmark.

I found a pencil in the nightstand, one without an eraser, I recall. I remember thinking that I couldn't go back on what I'd written, couldn't retrace my steps if I made a mistake. I turned the form over and numbered the blank side —1, 2, 3, 4, 5 — with a black period after each, as if preparing to take a spelling test. It was the first time I'd put pencil to paper since I'd left California. I thought for a while, then wrote beside number one, "My parents," immediately wishing I'd split them into "Mother" and "Dad" so that I could have filled two lines. Then to my surprise the next four blanks filled quickly, and my hand was adding numbers and more numbers to accommodate the names of my siblings, my nieces and nephews, the handful of friends I still claimed and even the ones who were gone. I filled the back of the form and probably could have filled another, but I didn't want to try, I couldn't bear any more just yet — the stab of joy, the possibility.

As months passed, the world slowly continued to make itself known, appearing in small, merciful gestures, as if not wishing to startle: voices, a pair of hands, golden leaf-shadow, a suggestion of sky. Then one morning, for no reason I can recall, the world lifted her veil and showed her whole self. She looked strangely familiar — yes, I thought, it's all coming back. Put on shoes, brush teeth, smile into the mirror, pour orange juice into a glass. *This is the way the world begins. This is the way the world begins. This is the way.*

I smooth the center seam of *Evening Train* and run my hands over the marked-up lines. Poems can be dangerous places in which to venture, alone, and I'm not sure the woman is ready for "After Mindwalk." She has underlined "panic's black cloth falling / over our faces, over our breath." Please don't, I want to say. Don't do it, don't drink it, don't eat that apple. I want to tell her about the pine trees, the list, Mother and Bessie and Carolyn and Wordsworth and Hopkins and Job. Look, I'd say, pointing to the footnote. See, *Mindwalk* was a film by Bernt Capra, it's not a real place; don't worry. It's about Pascal and the Void. It doesn't have to be about you. But it is, of course. That's why she is not only reading the book but writing one of her own as well, with each scratch of the pencil. The printed words are Levertov's, but the other poem is the woman's — written in the margins, in the small boxes that cage the words she cannot pronounce, in the crumbled erasures, in the question marks floating above the lines. Wait up, I want to say — a crazy thought, but I can't help myself. Wait up; I want to tell you something.

Reflections and Responses

1. How do the marginal notes of others that McClanahan finds in various books affect her? What general responses do they provoke in her? What connection do they have with loneliness and the need for companionship? How are markings connected with love and sexuality?

2. "I never saw books as dead, finished texts," McClanahan writes. "They were living breathing, entities. . . ." How does she throughout the essay blur the boundaries between books and people, herself included? How are books like people, and people like books? How do lines from poems intersect with her own life? What does she find so intriguing about *Evening Train*, the volume of Denise Levertov's poetry she borrowed from the library?

3. Consider the way McClanahan shapes her essay. Although it tells the story of her life, it does not proceed in an orderly chronological fashion. Go back through the essay and try putting events into a narrative timeline, starting with the earliest episodes and ending with her present time. How different does the essay seem when reassembled? Why do you think McClanahan chose to structure the essay in just the way she did?

JOHN MCPHEE

Silk Parachute

Personal memoirs can be hundreds of pages long or—like this one—very short. Whether long or short, they are fueled by the writer's recollection of evocative details. In "Silk Parachute," John McPhee constructs a complex miniature memoir around a number of details concerning his relationship with his mother; some of the details he claims he cannot vouch for and others he alleges he can. The reader is invited to wonder why he vividly recalls certain moments and denies any recollection of others: "The assertion is absolutely false that when I came home from high school with an A-minus she demanded an explanation for the minus."

One of America's most celebrated nonfiction writers, John McPhee was born in Princeton, New Jersey, in 1931 and is the author of numerous award-winning books. His first book, A Sense of Where You Are, *is a profile of basketball star Bill Bradley and appeared in 1965. He has published nearly a book every year since then, all of them with the same publisher, Farrar, Straus & Giroux. Although his subjects range from sports to science, McPhee has written extensively in the fields of nature and geology. Three of McPhee's recent books are* Annals of the Former World *(2000),* The Founding Fish *(2002), and* Uncommon Carriers *(2006). He has been a staff writer for* The New Yorker *magazine since 1965 and a professor of journalism at Princeton University since 1975. "Silk Parachute" originally appeared in* The New Yorker *and was selected by Cynthia Ozick for* The Best American Essays 1998.

When your mother is ninety-nine years old, you have so many memories of her that they tend to overlap, intermingle, and blur. It is extremely difficult to single out one or two, impossible to remember any that exemplify the whole.

It has been alleged that when I was in college she heard that I had stayed up all night playing poker and wrote me a letter that used the word "shame" forty-two times. I do not recall this.

I do not recall being pulled out of my college room and into the church next door.

It has been alleged that on December 24, 1936, when I was five years old, she sent me to my room at or close to 7 P.M. for using four-letter words while trimming the Christmas tree. I do not recall that.

The assertion is absolutely false that when I came home from high school with an A-minus she demanded an explanation for the minus.

It has been alleged that she spoiled me with protectionism, because I was the youngest child and therefore the most vulnerable to attack from overhead — an assertion that I cannot confirm or confute, except to say that facts don't lie.

We lived only a few blocks from the elementary school and routinely ate lunch at home. It is reported that the following dialogue and ensuing action occurred on January 22, 1941:

"Eat your sandwich."

"I don't want to eat my sandwich."

"I made that sandwich, and you are going to eat it, Mister Man. You filled yourself up on penny candy on the way home, and now you're not hungry."

"I'm late. I have to go. I'll eat the sandwich on the way back to school."

"Promise?"

"Promise."

Allegedly, I went up the street with sandwich in my hand and buried it in a snowbank in front of Dr. Wright's house. My mother, holding back the curtain in the window of the side door, was watching. She came out in the bitter cold, wearing only a light dress, ran to the snowbank, dug out the sandwich, chased me up Nassau Street,* and rammed the sandwich down my throat, snow and all. I do not recall any detail of that story. I believe it to be a total fabrication.

*__Nassau Street:__ Princeton's main street.

There was the case of the missing Cracker Jack at Lindel's corner store. Flimsy evidence pointed to Mrs. McPhee's smallest child. It has been averred that she laid the guilt on with the following words: "'Like mother, like son' is a saying so true, the world will judge largely of mother by you." It has been asserted that she immediately repeated that proverb three times, and also recited it on other occasions too numerous to count. I have absolutely no recollection of her saying that about the Cracker Jack or any other controlled substance.

We have now covered every thing even faintly unsavory that has been reported about this person in ninety-nine years, and even those items are a collection of rumors, half-truths, prevarications, false allegations, inaccuracies, innuendos, and canards.

This is the mother who — when Alfred Knopf* wrote her twenty-two-year-old son a letter saying, "The readers' report in the case of your manuscript would not be very helpful, and I think might discourage you completely"— said, "Don't listen to Alfred Knopf. Who does Alfred Knopf think he is, anyway? Someone should go in there and k-nock his block off." To the best of my recollection, that is what she said.

I also recall her taking me, on or about March 8, my birthday, to the theater in New York every year, beginning in childhood. I remember those journeys as if they were today. I remember *A Connecticut Yankee.* Wednesday, March 8, 1944. Evidently, my father had written for the tickets, because she and I sat in the last row of the second balcony. Mother knew what to do about that. She gave me for my birthday an elegant spyglass, sufficient in power to bring the Connecticut Yankee back from Vermont. I sat there watching the play through my telescope, drawing as many guffaws from the surrounding audience as the comedy on the stage.

On one of those theater days — when I was eleven or twelve — I asked her if we could start for the city early and go out to La Guardia Field to see the comings and goings of airplanes. The temperature was well below the freeze point and the March winds were so blustery that the wind-chill factor was forty below zero. Or seemed to be. My mother figured out how to take the subway to a

---

*__Alfred Knopf:__ founder of the prominent New York publishing house that bears his name; the "K" is sounded. — Ed.

stop in Jackson Heights and a bus from there — a feat I am unable
to duplicate to this day. At La Guardia, she accompanied me to the
observation deck and stood there in the icy wind for at least an
hour, maybe two, while I, spellbound, watched the DC-3s coming
in on final, their wings flapping in the gusts. When we at last left
the observation deck, we went downstairs into the terminal, where
she bought me what appeared to be a black rubber ball but on
closer inspection was a pair of hollow hemispheres hinged on one
side and folded together. They contained a silk parachute. Opposite the hinge, each hemisphere had a small nib. A piece of string
wrapped round and round the two nibs kept the ball closed. If you
threw it high into the air, the string unwound and the parachute
blossomed. If you sent it up with a tennis racket, you could put it
into the clouds. Not until the development of the ten-megabyte
hard disk would the world ever know such a fabulous toy. Folded
just so, the parachute never failed. Always, it floated back to you —
silkily, beautifully — to start over and float back again. Even if you
abused it, whacked it really hard — gracefully, lightly, it floated
back to you.

Reflections and Responses

1. Note the style of McPhee's opening paragraphs. Why do you
think he repeats the phrase "It has been alleged . . . "? What does
the tone of the phrase suggest, along with such words as *reported,
assertion,* and *averred?* Who do you imagine has made the assertions
and allegations?

2. Why is McPhee careful to say that he can't recall some details
and events yet specifically remembers others? Can you detect any
differences between what he recalls and what he doesn't?

3. Given its title role and its final emphasis, the silk parachute
McPhee's mother bought for him at La Guardia Airport is clearly
the essay's dominant image. How does McPhee enlarge its significance? What do you think the parachute represents?

ROBERT POLITO

Shame

What family secrets might be locked inside a small metal box kept hidden by a parent in a dresser drawer? In "Shame," Robert Polito recalls how as a young child he caught a glimpse of several old photographs his father kept inside a locked box. However, over the years when asked about the photos, his father "always denied their existence." One photo was a "tintype" (an inexpensive form of photography made popular in the early twentieth century by street vendors) of a "dark, curly-haired woman" artificially posed on a little bridge holding a flower. "Shame" tells the story behind that mysterious picture—a photograph the author would see once and never again.

Robert Polito is the author of Savage Art: A Biography of Jim Thompson, A Reader's Guide to James Merrill's The Changing Light at Sandover, *and* Doubles, *among other books. He also edited* The selected Poems of Kenneth Fearing, Crime Novels: American Noir of the 1930s and 1940s, *and* Crime Novels: American Noir of the 1950s, *all for the library of America. He writes regularly for* Bookforum *and directs the Graduate Writing Program at The New School. "Shame" first appeared in* Black Clock *and was selected by Lauren Slater for* The Best American Essays 2006.

This all started with a photograph I saw perhaps once and never again. We were packing up our old house in Dorchester — the first-floor flat of a classic Boston three-decker that Nana, my mother's mother, owned on Semont Road — for our move to Quincy. I had been taken by my father on a Saturday afternoon nor long before to look over the new house, our first single family home, on Hillside Avenue, appropriately near the summit of a minor hill. (The next street up was Summit Avenue). The place was a wreck, the

A representative sample of an old tintype. Note the staged pose and artificial background. Courtesy San Francisco Memories

living-room ceiling cracked and at the center dipping perilously, holes as though punched in the walls, bathtub dripping mold. But there were fine compensatory curiosities: a clapboard tool shed out back, a huge skull-shaped rock next to a stone fireplace for burning leaves, oak and fir trees, domed bushes for hiding. Inside off the front entrance hall was the smallest bathroom I've ever seen — even at age seven I could barely sit down without my knees hitting the pipes under the tiny sink. And I would finally have my own room — no longer sharing with Nana, as in Dorchester, the original master bedroom over the street, sleeping side by side in twin beds like a couple from a 1940s Hollywood movie. Whenever I was angry at my parents I would find the printed cardboard sign we used to signal that we needed heating oil and shove it in our bedroom bay window for the silver trucks that prowled the neighborhood, confusion and shouts at the door after a delivery man refilled our tank in summer or topped us off for the third time that winter week

This would have been late in 1960 — my first Quincy memory is watching the Kennedy inauguration on a TV that my father set up for us in the basement while workers plastered and painted upstairs. But while moving from Dorchester I was helping my father empty his dresser into cartons for the movers — his white work shirts and sleeveless t-shirts, his black box, his boxer shorts — saving the top drawer, his junk drawer, for last.

I always liked to look through his dresser if there was no one home, or just me and my younger sister and brother. All sorts of objects might spill out of the cigar boxes and trays in his junk drawer. Old coins, some inserted into blue folders, lots of stamps (he worked for the Post Office), his World War 11 medals and pins, a few $25 US Savings Bonds with my name on them — for college, he said — and lots of shiny silver shoe horns (weekends he moonlighted downtown at a woman's shoe store). Mornings after he took my mother out for dinner and dancing — maybe once every other month on a Friday night, occasionally to Boston nightclubs with names like the High Hat, more often to VFW posts and church functions — there would be a fresh pack of smokes in his top drawer, always filtered, mostly Kents, with just two or three cigarettes missing. As far as I could see he never retrieved the old pack the next time they went out. So the Kents tended to pile up, and my parents must have smoked as they drank, taking years to drain the bottle of Seagram's 7 that they stored in a dining room hutch for guests.

In his junk drawer my father kept a locked metal box, though "locked" and "metal" significantly embellish its dime-store, chipped and battered flimsiness. Still, it resisted all my attempts to pick it with a screwdriver and tweezers. But on this day that we were moving, he opened the box right up with a little key that apparently was inside the drawer all along, undetected by me, and out came everything you'd expect someone like my father should considerable valuable or at risk — his service discharge papers, his and my mother's Social Security cards, their marriage license, our birth certificates, a red bank book from a decade earlier, and the ring he fashioned during the war for my mother out of a sea shell and a New Guinea coin. I can recall all of this because the box came to me, contents more or less intact, after my father died. I keep the mother-of-pearl ring in a dish on a windowsill with both of my parents' wedding rings.

On this day there were photos in the box too, my parents seated by themselves at a table in a dining room I didn't recognize, some soldiers in uniform, young and smiling, my father among them, then what looked like two really ancient photos made — it seemed to me — from the same black metal as the box that held them, individual photos of a man with a mustache and a woman. Though the woman's picture was on top, my father quickly slipped it under the other one of the man like he was shuffling cards, and said that's your grandfather. Since I found out later that my grandfather died when I was four, less than three years before, presumably I met him. This is the only likeness I have of him. That thin mustache. A dark man in a dark suit and dark hat. Looking incredibly uncomfortable, like he never wore suits, or just didn't want to be there.

Of course my Irish grandmother, Nana, was still alive, and there were photographs of her family everywhere in the Dorchester house — her parents, sisters and brothers, her dead husband, her two other children, my Aunt Mary and Uncle John, both also dead, from cancer before they turned forty. But this Italian grandfather doesn't turn up even among the hundreds of snapshots in my parents' wedding album. I must have asked my father about the woman in the first photo, the dark girl who looked to be (I would say now) in her teens. I understood right away without being told or knowing why, beyond their same beak-like nose and large black eyes, that she was connected to my father, the way you usually know when someone is about to betray you or hurt you, even though there aren't any obvious signs and warnings, you feel it along your skin. Orphans fascinated me and part of my Dad's particular fascination for me was that he had lost his mother when he was my age, was on his own from the age of five, his father always away working. He said he had only one memory of his mother: one day he was playing in the kitchen, swinging on the door of their icebox, when the whole thing toppled over on him. His mother called out the window for help, and when no one came she lifted off the icebox herself, even though she was a small woman and frail, perhaps already dying. He told me just one story about his father too, laughing and shaking his head as he talked: he said that my dockworker grandfather, Luigi Polito, was among the thousands of stupid

---

*__Charles Ponzi__ (1882–1949) was an Italian immigrant who started a fraudulent "get rich quick" business in Boston in 1920 and swindled thousands of people out of their money as he made millions himself. Since then, such fraudulent enterprises are commonly known as *Ponzi schemes*. For a full account of this fascinating story, see Mitchell Zuckoff, *Ponzi's Scheme: The Story of a Financial Legend* (Random House, 2005).

Bostonians who in 1920 rushed down to 27 School Street to invest their wages in Charles Ponzi's* Securities Exchange Company.

I can't remember what I thought my father meant by a Ponzi "scheme," or even if he told me about Ponzi then or later. I'm guessing that he was trying to district me from the photograph of the woman — distract me as people will do when they're agitated, as my father visibly was then — by discussing *technique.* We discussed technique a lot. Does that mean we were often agitated? For most of my childhood my father was in my closest friend. A friendship of common interests, like science, rockets, UFOs and gadgets. Then we got very competitive. He told me that long ago photographs were first made of glass and then they were made of tin. His information mostly was wrong of course — or I got it wrong: daguerreotypes aren't printed on glass; the glass only protects the fragile plates. Tintypes aren't tin at all but thin iron sheets. But tintypes were popular with street photographers into the 1930s, for neighborhood fairs and carnivals. Did my father's tintypes come from one of the Italian summer street fairs — the St. Anthony Festival? St. Rocco? — in Boston's North End?

In the tintype the woman I've always assumed is my grandmother stands on the arc of a little bridge, holding a flower. There was no water under the bridge, so this must have been a set in an impromptu photography studio. A curtain backdrop. I think, also provided trees, plus the moon and the outline of a distant river. The woman wore an elaborate dress imprinted with leaves and flowers, and a kind of cape of over the dress. There were also flowers and leaves in her hair, which appeared black and curly like my father's and flowed along her shoulders into the swirls of her cape and dress. Her mouth open, smiling almost, she gazes at the camera, or the cameraman, or someone standing behind him, or whoever happens to be looking back at her image.

Later over the years when I mentioned these photos, my father always denied their existence. He said that he had no photographs of his mother, and that his sister, my Aunt Ann, kept the few pictures there were of my grandfather. My grandfather was an Italian peasant, he said, who didn't like cameras and photographs. He unloaded fish from ships in Boston harbor for the big seafood restaurants. He even tried to force my father to leave school and join him on the docks. He was a laborer. He never wore a suit.

My mentioning the photographs became a funny family story, something like the time I went on a deep-sea fishing trip with my father and supposedly caught thirty-six fish. To my eventual humiliation it actually was the charter boat captain who caught all the fish; he just handed me the fishing rod whenever he felt a tug on the line. Or the time that my fever spiked to a hundred five degrees and, as my father recalled. I went off my rocker, babbling delirious about God knows what. These photos were yet another instance of me going off my rocker.

I never saw that photograph of my grandmother again. No tintypes at all were in the metal box by the next time my sister and I opened it some thirty-five years later, after my mother died and more than a decade after the death of my father. But as I say, nearly everything else was there, all the papers, the shell ring, the other snapshots — though, oddly, the photograph of my grandfather wasn't a tintype either but a photographic postcard. Still, my father told me about tintypes that day we moved, so the photo of the dark, curly-haired woman must have been a tintype. From other tintypes and cabinet cards I've seen since, I realize the woman looked like, or was trying to look like, an opera singer, or an actress.

Once my mother died, I learned more from my sister about my grandmother. This was the way my father apparently told it to my mother who then told it to her. Around 1914 my grandfather arrived in the United States from Naples with his wife and their two children, George and Ann. His wife soon after was very ill and returned to Italy, taking the children home with her. A few years later she died, and George and Ann started to grow up with relatives on a vineyard near Bari. My father meanwhile was born in Boston in 1915, to a woman who appears as "Angela DiRuggiero" on his birth certificate and as "Mary Ruggiero" on his wedding license. There's no evidence that she and my grandfather were married then, or any time later. Angela, or Mary, didn't die when my father was five; instead she left my grandfather, my father and Boston for New York City. My grandfather summoned George and Ann from Italy, and Ann raised my father, who never saw his mother again.

Because this was a mother abandoning a child, I've always assumed there must have been another man involved. But who knows? Apparently my grandfather was a drunk, and so abusive and violent that he wasn't allowed to attend my parents' wedding. After I got to high school, my father and I fought about the war in Vietnam, Nixon, rock music, and my wanting to be an English professor and not an engineer. Nights when I came in the back door and passed him on the porch with is bound books of *New York Times* crossword puzzles, I thought he looked like the unhappiest person I'd ever met.

Now I don't think *unhappy* so much as ashamed. Something of the world my father must have lived inside, on the porch with his puzzles, hit me the one time I attempted to find out what happened to my grandmother from my Auntie Ann. "Your father was a good man, Bobby," she snapped back, as though this was the only possible answer to my question, and shut the subject down.

I've looked for that tintype ever since, and nearly any weekend in upstate New York I will find one at some antique store, usually for a few dollars, but occasionally a lot more if it's tinted or the store is posh. One of the dealers who gets them for me says that locals will sell old photographs to him even when they know the portraits are from their own family, and he offers practically nothing for them. I never met these people, they tell him. So sometimes I can buy multiple pictures of the same person, and groups who are clearly related, the tintypes still tucked into their original books, though damaged by water and insects.

I make my living writing about art, and have friends who collect what they call vernacular photography. But this has nothing to do with art. More like I'm assembling an alternate family, the way a childless couple might gather cats and dogs around them. I have stacks of the tintypes now, all over the place. When I see a photograph of a young woman with dark hair who would have been alive in 1915, posed against some fantastic contrived scene, I pay whatever it costs. Then I start looking for her all over again.

Reflections and Responses

1. Essays that depend on recollections from very early childhood might be judged skeptically by some readers who doubt that such memories are trustworthy. How does Polito anticipate this response? For example, how does he persuade his readers that the contents of

his father's little locked box are accurately recalled? Why does he introduce the word *perhaps* in the essay's opening sentence?

2. What do you think Polito is getting at when he says (in paragraph 7) that when agitated, people will try to distract others "by discussing *technique*." How does "technique" come into play in this instance with his father? How do you understand Polito's statement as a generalization?

3. Take a careful look at Polito's two concluding paragraphs. Do you find these to be a successful or satisfying conclusion to the essay? Why or why not? Why do you think he says, "But this has nothing to do with art"? What role has "art" played in the essay?

SCOTT RUSSELL SANDERS

The Inheritance of Tools

A heritage is not only ethnic or cultural; it can also be a code of behavior, a system of manners, or even the practical skills that grandparents and parents often pass along to their children. In this widely reprinted personal essay, a writer, upon hearing of his father's sudden death, is reminded of the tools and techniques he inherited from his grandfather and father, which he in turn is now passing along to his own children. Though these tools and techniques have literally to do with carpentry, they take on extra duty in this finely crafted essay in which the hand tools themselves become equivalent to works of art: "I look at my claw hammer, the distillation of a hundred generations of carpenters, and consider that it holds up well beside those other classics—Greek vases, Gregorian chants, Don Quixote, barbed fish hooks, candles, spoons."

Scott Russell Sanders is the author of more than a dozen books of fiction, science fiction, essays, and nonfiction; these include Stone Country *(1985),* The Paradise of Bombs *(1987),* Secrets of the Universe *(1991),* Staying Put *(1993),* Hunting for Hope: A Father's Journeys *(1998),* The Force of Spirit *(2001) and* A Private History of Awe *(2006).* Writing from the Center *(1994) is a volume of essays about living and working in the Midwest. The recipient of many prestigious writing awards and fellowships, Sanders is a professor of English at Indiana University. "The Inheritance of Tools" originally appeared in* The North American Review *(1986) and was selected by Gay Talese for* The Best American Essays 1987.

At just about the hour when my father died, soon after dawn one February morning when ice coated the windows like cataracts, I banged my thumb with a hammer. Naturally I swore at the hammer, the reckless thing, and in the moment of swearing I thought of what my father would say: "If you'd try hitting the nail it would go in a whole lot faster. Don't you know your thumb's not as hard as that hammer?" We both were doing carpentry that day, but far apart. He was building cupboards at my brother's place in Oklahoma; I was at home in Indiana, putting up a wall in the basement to make a bedroom for my daughter. By the time my mother called with news of his death — the long distance wires whittling her voice until it seemed too thin to bear the weight of what she had to say — my thumb was swollen. A week or so later a white scar in the shape of a crescent moon began to show above the cuticle, and month by month it rose across the pink sky of my thumbnail. It took the better part of a year for the scar to disappear, and every time I noticed it I thought of my father.

The hammer had belonged to him, and to his father before him. The three of us have used it to build houses and barns and chicken coops, to upholster chairs and crack walnuts, to make doll furniture and bookshelves and jewelry boxes. The head is scratched and pockmarked, like an old plowshare that has been working rocky fields, and it gives off the sort of dull sheen you see on fast creek water in the shade. It is a finishing hammer, about the weight of a bread loaf, too light, really, for framing walls, too heavy for cabinet work, with a curved claw for pulling nails, a rounded head for pounding, a fluted neck for looks, and a hickory handle for strength.

The present handle is my third one, bought from a lumberyard in Tennessee, down the road from where my brother and I were helping my father build his retirement house. I broke the previous one by trying to pull sixteen-penny nails out of floor joists — a foolish thing to do with a finishing hammer, as my father pointed out. "You ever hear of a crowbar?" he said. No telling how many handles he and my grandfather had gone through before me. My grandfather used to cut down hickory trees on his farm, saw them into slabs, cure the planks in his hayloft, and carve handles with a drawknife. The grain in hickory is crooked and knotty, and therefore tough, hard to split, like the grain in the two men who owned this hammer before me.

After proposing marriage to a neighbor girl, my grandfather used this hammer to build a house for his bride on a stretch of river bottom in northern Mississippi. The lumber for the place, like the hickory for the handle, was cut on his own land. By the day of the wedding he had not quite finished the house, and so right after the ceremony he took his wife home and put her to work. My grandmother had worn her Sunday dress for the wedding, with a fringe of lace tacked on around the hem in honor of the occasion. She removed this lace and folded it away before going out to help my grandfather nail siding on the house. "There she was in her good dress," he told me some fifty-odd years after that wedding day, "holding up them long pieces of clapboard while I hammered, and together we got the place covered up before dark." As the family grew to four, six, eight, and eventually thirteen, my grandfather used this hammer to enlarge his house room by room, like a chambered nautilus expanding its shell.

By and by the hammer was passed along to my father. One day he was up on the roof of our pony barn nailing shingles with it, when I stepped out the kitchen door to call him for supper. Before I could yell, something about the sight of him straddling the spine of that roof and swinging the hammer caught my eye and made me hold my tongue. I was five or six years old, and the world's commonplaces were still news to me. He would pull a nail from the pouch at his waist, bring the hammer down, and a moment later the *thunk* of the blow would reach my ears. And that is what had stopped me in my tracks and stilled my tongue, that momentary gap between seeing and hearing the blow. Instead of yelling from the kitchen door, I ran to the barn and climbed two rungs up the ladder — as far as I was allowed to go — and spoke quietly to my father. On our walk to the house he explained that sound takes time to make its way through air. Suddenly the world seemed larger, the air more dense, if sound could be held back like any ordinary traveler.

By the time I started using this hammer, at about the age when I discovered the speed of sound, it already contained houses and mysteries for me. The smooth handle was one my grandfather had made. In those days I needed both hands to swing it. My father would start a nail in a scrap of wood, and I would pound away until I bent it over.

"Looks like you got ahold of some of those rubber nails," he would tell me. "Here, let me see if I can find you some stiff ones." And he would rummage in a drawer until he came up with a fistful of more cooperative nails. "Look at the head," he would tell me. "Don't look at your hands, don't look at the hammer. Just look at the head of that nail and pretty soon you'll learn to hit it square."

Pretty soon I did learn. While he worked in the garage cutting dovetail joints for a drawer or skinning a deer or tuning an engine, I would hammer nails. I made innocent blocks of wood look like porcupines. He did not talk much in the midst of his tools, but he kept up a nearly ceaseless humming, slipping in and out of a dozen tunes in an afternoon, often running back over the same stretch of melody again and again, as if searching for a way out. When the humming did cease, I knew he was faced with a task requiring great delicacy or concentration, and I took care not to distract him.

He kept scraps of wood in a cardboard box — the ends of two-by-fours, slabs of shelving and plywood, odd pieces of molding — and everything in it was fair game. I nailed scraps together to fashion what I called boats or houses, but the results usually bore only faint resemblance to the visions I carried in my head. I would hold up these constructions to show my father, and he would turn them over in his hands admiringly, speculating about what they might be. My cobbled-together guitars might have been alien spaceships, my barns might have been models of Aztec temples, each wooden contraption might have been anything but what I had set out to make.

Now and again I would feel the need to have a chunk of wood shaped or shortened before I riddled it with nails, and I would clamp it in a vise and scrape at it with a handsaw. My father would let me lacerate the board until my arm gave out, and then he would wrap his hand around mine and help me finish the cut, showing me how to use my thumb to guide the blade, how to pull back on the saw to keep it from binding, how to let my shoulder do the work.

"Don't force it," he would say, "just drag it easy and give the teeth a chance to bite."

As the saw teeth bit down, the wood released its smell, each kind with its own fragrance, oak or walnut or cherry or pine — usually pine because it was the softest, easiest for a child to work. No matter how weathered or gray the board, no matter how warped and cracked, inside there was this smell waiting, as of something freshly baked. I gathered every smidgen of sawdust and stored it away in coffee cans, which I kept in a drawer of the workbench. When I did not feel like hammering nails, I would dump my sawdust on the concrete floor of the garage and landscape it into highways and farms and towns, running miniature cars and trucks along miniature roads. Looming as huge as a colossus, my father worked over and around me, now and again bending down to inspect my work, careful not to trample my creations. It was a landscape that smelled dizzyingly of wood. Even after a bath my skin would carry the smell, and so would my father's hair, when he lifted me for a bedtime hug.

I tell these things not only from memory but also from recent observation, because my own son now turns blocks of wood into nailed porcupines, dumps cans full of sawdust at my feet and sculpts highways on the floor. He learns how to swing a hammer from the elbow instead of the wrist, how to lay his thumb beside the blade to guide a saw, how to tap a chisel with a wooden mallet, how to mark a hole with an awl before starting a drill bit. My daughter did the same before him, and even now, on the brink of teenage aloofness, she will occasionally drag out my box of wood scraps and carpenter something. So I have seen my apprenticeship to wood and tools reenacted in each of my children, as my father saw his own apprenticeship renewed in me.

The saw I use belonged to him, as did my level and both of my squares, and all four tools had belonged to his father. The blade of the saw is the bluish color of gun barrels, and the maple handle, dark from the sweat of hands, is inscribed with curving leaf designs. The level is a shaft of walnut two feet long, edged with brass and pierced by three round windows in which air bubbles float in oil-filled tubes of glass. The middle window serves for testing if a surface is horizontal, the others for testing if a surface is plumb or vertical. My grandfather used to carry this level on the gun rack behind the seat in his pickup, and when I rode with him I would turn around to watch the bubbles dance. The larger of the two squares is called a framing square, a flat steel elbow, so beat up and tarnished you can barely make out the rows of numbers that show how to figure the cuts on rafters. The smaller one is called a try square, for marking right angles, with a blued steel blade for the shank and a brass-faced block of cherry for the head.

I was taught early on that a saw is not to be used apart from a square: "If you're going to cut a piece of wood," my father insisted, "you owe it to the tree to cut it straight."

Long before studying geometry, I learned there is a mystical virtue in right angles. There is an unspoken morality in seeking the level and the plumb. A house will stand, a table will bear weight, the sides of a box will hold together, only if the joints are square and the members upright. When the bubble is lined up between two marks etched in the glass tube of a level, you have aligned yourself with the forces that hold the universe together. When you miter the corners of a picture frame, each angle must be exactly forty-five degrees, as they are in the perfect triangles of Pythagoras, not a degree more or less. Otherwise the frame will hang crookedly, as if ashamed of itself and of its maker. No matter if the joints you are cutting do not show. Even if you are butting two pieces of wood together inside a cabinet, where no one except a wrecking crew will ever see them, you must take pains to ensure that the ends are square and the studs are plumb.

I took pains over the wall I was building on the day my father died. Not long after that wall was finished — paneled with tongue-and-groove boards of yellow pine, the nail holes filled with putty and the wood all stained and sealed — I came close to wrecking it one afternoon when my daughter ran howling up the stairs to announce that her gerbils had escaped from their cage and were hiding in my brand new wall. She could hear them scratching and squeaking behind her bed. Impossible! I said. How on earth could they get inside my drum-tight wall? Through the heating vent, she answered. I went downstairs, pressed my ear to the honey-colored wood, and heard the *scritch scritch* of tiny feet.

"What can we do?" my daughter wailed. "They'll starve to death, they'll die of thirst, they'll suffocate."

"Hold on," I soothed. "I'll think of something."

While I thought and she fretted, the radio on her bedside table delivered us the headlines: Several thousand people had died in a city in India from a poisonous cloud that had leaked overnight from a chemical plant. A nuclear-powered submarine had been launched. Rioting continued in South Africa. An airplane had been hijacked in the Mediterranean. Authorities calculated that several thousand homeless people slept on the streets within sight of the Washington

Monument. I felt my usual helplessness in the face of all these calamities. But here was my daughter, weeping because her gerbils were holed up in a wall. This calamity I could handle.

"Don't worry," I told her. "We'll set food and water by the heating vent and lure them out. And if that doesn't do the trick, I'll tear the wall apart until we find them."

She stopped crying and gazed at me. "You'd really tear it apart? Just for my gerbils? The wall?" Astonishment slowed her down only for a second, however, before she ran to the workbench and began tugging at drawers, saying, "Let's see, what'll we need? Crowbar. Hammer. Chisels. I hope we don't have to use them — but just in case."

We didn't need the wrecking tools. I never had to assault my handsome wall, because the gerbils eventually came out to nibble at a dish of popcorn. But for several hours I studied the tongue-and-groove skin I had nailed up on the day of my father's death, considering where to begin prying. There were no gaps in that wall, no crooked joints.

I had botched a great many pieces of wood before I mastered the right angle with a saw, botched even more before I learned to miter a joint. The knowledge of these things resides in my hands and eyes and the webwork of muscles, not in the tools. There are machines for sale — powered miter boxes and radial arm saws, for instance — that will enable any casual soul to cut proper angles in boards. The skill is invested in the gadget instead of the person who uses it, and this is what distinguishes a machine from a tool. If I had to earn my keep by making furniture or building houses, I suppose I would buy powered saws and pneumatic nailers; the need for speed would drive me to it. But since I carpenter only for my own pleasure or to help neighbors or to remake the house around the ears of my family, I stick with hand tools. Most of the ones I own were given to me by my father, who also taught me how to wield them. The tools in my workbench are a double inheritance, for each hammer and level and saw is wrapped in a cloud of knowing.

All of these tools are a pleasure to look at and to hold. Merchants would never paste NEW NEW NEW! signs of them in stores. Their designs are old because they work, because they serve their purpose well. Like folk songs and aphorisms and the grainy bits of language, these tools have been pared down to essentials. I look at my claw hammer, the distillation of a hundred generations of carpenters, and consider that it holds up well beside those other classics — Greek vases, Gregorian chants, *Don Quixote*, barbed fish hooks, candles, spoons. Knowledge of hammering stretches back to the earliest humans who squatted beside fires, chipping flints. Anthropologists have a lovely name for those unworked rocks that served as the earliest hammers. "Dawn stones," they are called. Their only qualification for the work, aside from hardness, is that they fit the hand. Our ancestors used them for grinding corn, tapping awls, smashing bones. From dawn stones to this claw hammer is a great leap in time, but no great distance in design or imagination.

On that iced-over February morning when I smashed my thumb with the hammer, I was down in the basement framing the wall that my daughter's gerbils would later hide in. I was thinking of my father, as I always did whenever I built anything, thinking how he would have gone about the work, hearing in memory what he would have said about the wisdom of hitting the nail instead of my thumb. I had the studs and plates nailed together all square and trim, and was lifting the wall into place when the phone rang upstairs. My wife answered, and in a moment she came to the basement door and called down softly to me. The stillness in her voice made me drop the framed wall and hurry upstairs. She told me my father was dead. Then I heard the details over the phone from my mother. Building a set of cupboards for my brother in Oklahoma, he had knocked off work early the previous afternoon because of cramps in his stomach. Early this morning, on his way into the kitchen of my brother's trailer, maybe going for a glass of water, so early that no one else was awake, he slumped down on the linoleum and his heart quit.

For several hours I paced around inside my house, upstairs and down, in and out of every room, looking for the right door to open and knowing there was no such door. My wife and children followed me and wrapped me in arms and backed away again, circling and staring as if I were on fire. Where was the door, the door, the door? I kept wondering. My smashed thumb turned purple and throbbed, making me furious. I wanted to cut it off and rush outside and scrape away the snow and hack a hole in the frozen earth and bury the shameful thing.

I went down into the basement, opened a drawer in my workbench, and stared at the ranks of chisels and knives. Oiled and sharp, as my father would have kept them, they gleamed at me like teeth. I took up a clasp knife, pried out the longest blade, and tested the edge on the hair of my forearm. A tuft came away cleanly, and I saw my father testing the sharpness of tools on his own skin, the blades of axes and knives and gouges and hoes, saw the red hair shaved off in patches from his arms and the backs of his hands. "That will cut bear," he would say. He never cut a bear with his blades, now my blades, but he cut deer, dirt, wood. I closed the knife and put it away. Then I took up the hammer and went back to work on my daughter's wall, snugging the bottom plate against a chalk line on the floor, shimming the top plate against the joists overhead, plumbing the studs with my level, making sure before I drove the first nail that every line was square and true.

Reflections and Responses

1. Consider the way Sanders opens the essay. Given the significance of his father's death, why does he mention his injured thumb in the same sentence? Why is this a relevant detail? How does it figure later in the essay?

2. Note the many concrete references to carpentry in the essay. In what ways is the language of tools and carpentry related to other aspects of life? Why is there "a mystical virtue in right angles"?

3. In rereading the essay, try to reconstruct the chronology of the February day that Sanders's father died. First, consider how Sanders constructs his narrative. Why does he deviate from a straightforward, hour-by-hour account? Why, for example, does he introduce the story about his daughter's gerbils? In what ways does that anecdote deepen the essay's theme?

LAUREN SLATER

Black Swans

Survival has become one of the dominant literary themes of our times.
Today's essayists seem to be especially candid about personal pain and suf-
fering and more willing to disclose the details of illnesses and injuries than
essayists were in the past. This literary phenomenon may be stimulated by
the public's vast interest in authentic medical case histories, an interest
more popularly manifested in the growing number of online support groups
and televised depictions of actual cases. A large number of contemporary
memoirs have focused on the transformative power of debilitating illnesses.
Some of the finest writing in this genre has come from a younger author,
Lauren Slater, whose essay "Black Swans" unforgettably documents the
severe mental discomfiture of an acute obsessive-compulsive disorder.

Lauren Slater holds a master's degree in psychology from Harvard Uni-
versity and a doctorate from Boston University. She has written articles and
contributed pieces to numerous periodicals, including the New York
Times, Harper's, Elle, *and* Nerve. *Her books include* Welcome to
My Country: A Therapist's Memoir of Madness *(1996)*, Prozac
Diary *(1998)*, Lying: A Metaphorical Memoir *(2000)*, Love Works
Like This: Travels through a Pregnant Year *(2003)*. Opening Skin-
ner's Box: Great Psychological Experiments of the Twentieth Cen-
tury *(2004)*, *and* Blue Beyond Blue: Extraordlnary Tales for
Ordinary Dilemmas *(2005)*. *"Black Swans" originally appeared in*
The Missouri Review *and was selected by Ian Frazier for* The Best
American Essays 1997.

There is something satisfying and scary about making an angel, lowering your bulky body into the drowning fluff, stray flakes landing
on your face. I am seven or eight and the sky looms above me, gray

and dead. I move my arms and legs — expanding, contracting — sculpting snow before it can swallow me up. I feel the cold filter into my head, seep through the wool of my mittens. I swish wider, faster, then roll out of my mold to inspect its form. There is the imprint of my head, my arms which have swelled into white wings. I step back, step forward, pause and peer. Am I dead or alive down there? Is this a picture of heaven or hell? I am worried about where I will go when I die, that each time I swallow, an invisible stone will get caught in my throat. I worry that when I eat a plum, a tree will grow in my belly, its branches twining around my bones, choking. When I walk through a door, I must tap the frame three times. Between each nighttime prayer to Yahweh I close my eyes and count to ten and a half.

And now I look down at myself sketched in the snow. A familiar anxiety chews at the edges of my heart, even while I notice the beauty of the white fur on all the trees, the reverent silence of this season. I register a mistake on my angel, what looks like a thumbprint on its left wing. I reach down to erase it, but unable to smooth the snow perfectly, I start again on another angel, lowering myself, swishing and sweeping, rolling over — no. Yet another mistake, this time the symmetry in the wingspan wrong. A compulsion comes over me. I do it again, and again. In my memory hours go by. My fingers inside my mittens get wrinkled and raw. My breath comes heavily and the snow begins to blue. A moon rises, a perfect crescent pearl whose precise shape I will never be able to re-create. I ache for something I cannot name. Someone calls me, a mother or a father. *Come in now, come in now.* Very early the next morning I awaken, look out my bedroom window, and see the yard covered with my frantic forms — hundreds of angels, none of them quite right. The forms twist and strain, the wings seeming to struggle up in the winter sun, as if each angel were longing for escape, for a free flight that might crack the crystal and ice of her still, stiff world.

Looking back on it now, I think maybe those moments in the snow were when my OCD began, although it didn't come to me full-fledged until my mid-twenties. OCD stands for obsessive-compulsive disorder, and some studies say more than three million Americans suffer from it. The "it" is not the commonplace rituals that weave throughout so many of our lives — the woman who checks the stove a few times before she leaves for work, or the man who combs his bangs back, and then again, seeking symmetry. Obsessive-compulsive disorder is pervasive and extreme, inundating the person's life to the point where normal functioning becomes difficult, maybe even impossible.

For a long time my life was difficult but not impossible. Both in my childhood and my adulthood I'd suffered from various psychiatric ailments — depressions especially — but none of these were as surreal and absurd as the obsessive-compulsive disorder that one day presented itself. Until I was twenty-five or so, I don't think I could have been really diagnosed with OCD, although my memory of the angels indicates I had tendencies in that direction. I was a child at once nervous and bold, a child who loved trees that trickled sap, the Vermont fields where grass grew the color of deep-throated rust. I was a child who gathered earthworms, the surprising pulse of pink on my fingers, and yet these same fingers, later in the evening, came to prayer points, searching for safety in the folds of my sheets, in the quick counting rituals.

Some mental health professionals claim that the onset of obsession is a response to an underlying fear, a recent trauma, say, or a loss. I don't believe that is always true because, no matter how hard I think about it, I remember nothing unusual or disorienting before my first attack, three years out of college. I don't know exactly why at two o'clock one Saturday afternoon what felt like a seizure shook me. I recall lying in my apartment in Cambridge. The floors were painted blue, the curtains a sleepy white. They bellied in and out with the breezes. I was immersed in a book, *The Seven Storey Mountain,** walking my way through the tale's church, dabbing holy water on my forehead. A priest was crooning. A monk moaned. And suddenly this: a thought careening across my cortex. I CAN'T CONCENTRATE. Of course the thought disturbed my concentration, and the monk's moan turned into a whisper, disappeared.

I blinked, looked up. I was back in Cambridge on a blue floor. The blue floor suddenly frightened me; between the planks

---

*The Seven Storey Mountain (1948) is a best-selling autobiography by Thomas Merton (1915–1969). It tells the story of Merton's conversion to Catholicism, his ordination into the priesthood, and his commitment to the life of a Trappist monk in a religious order known for its vow of silence. He was not silent as a writer, however, publishing more than fifty volumes of poetry, philosophy, memoir, and devotional writing in his relatively brief lifetime.

I could see lines of dark dirt and the sway of a spider crawling. Let me get back, I thought, into the world of the book. I lowered my eyes to the page, but instead of being able to see the print, there was the thought blocking out all else: I CAN'T CONCENTRATE. Now I started to panic. Each time I tried to get back to the book the words crumbled, lost their sensible shapes. I said to myself, *I must not allow that thought about concentration to come into my mind anymore,* but, of course, the more I tried to suppress it, the louder it jangled. I looked at my hand. I ached for its familiar skin, the paleness of its palm and the three threaded lines that had been with me since birth, but as I held it out before my eyes, the phrase I CAN'T CONCENTRATE ON MY HAND blocked out my hand, so all I saw was a blur of flesh giving way to the bones beneath, and inside the bones the grimy marrow, and in the grimy marrow the individual cells, all disconnected. Shattered skin.

My throat closed up with terror. For surely if I'd lost the book, lost language, lost flesh, I was well on my way to losing the rest of the world. And all because of a tiny phrase that forced me into a searing self-consciousness, that plucked me from the moment into the meta-moment, so I was doomed to think about thinking instead of thinking other thoughts. My mind devouring my mind.

I tried to force my brain onto other topics, but with each mental dodge I became aware that I was dodging, and each time I itched I became aware that I was itching, and with each inhalation I became aware that I was inhaling, and I thought, *If I think too much about breathing, will I forget how to breathe?*

I ran into the bathroom. There was a strange pounding in my head, and then a sensation I can only describe as a hiccup of the brain. My brain seemed to be seizing as the phrase about concentration jerked across it. I delved into the medicine cabinet, found a bottle of aspirin, took three, stood by the sink for five minutes. No go. Delved again, pulled out another bottle —Ativan, a Valium-like medication belonging to my housemate, Adam. Another five minutes, my brain still squirting. One more Ativan, a tiny white triangle that would put me to sleep. I would sleep this strange spell off, wake up me again, sane again. I went back to my bed. The day darkened. The Ativan spread through my system. Lights in a neighboring window seemed lonely and sweet. I saw the shadow of

a bird in a tree, and it had angel wings, and it soared me someplace else, its call a pure cry.

"What's wrong with you?" he said, shaking my shoulder. Adam
stood over me, his face a blur. Through cracked eyelids I saw a
wavering world, none of its outlines resolved: the latticed shadow
of a tree on a white wall, my friend's face a streak of pink. I am
O.K., I thought, for this was what waking up was always like, the
gentle resurfacing. I sat up, looked around.

"You've been sleeping for hours and hours," he said. "You slept
from yesterday afternoon until now."

I reached up, gently touched a temple. I felt the faraway nip of
my pulse. My pulse was there. I was here.

"Weird day yesterday," I said. I spoke slowly, listening to my
words, testing them on my tongue. So far so good.

I stood up. "You look weird," he said, "unsteady."

"I'm O.K.," I said, and then, in that instant, a surge of anxiety.
I had lied. I had not been O.K. *Say "God I'm sorry" fourteen times,*
I ordered myself. *This is crazy,* I said to myself. *Fifteen times,* a voice
from somewhere else seemed to command. "You really all right?"
Adam asked. I closed my eyes, counted, blinked back open.

"O.K.," I said. "I'm going to shower."

But it wasn't O.K. As soon as I was awake, obsessive thoughts
returned. What before had been inconsequential behaviors, such
as counting to three before I went through a doorway or checking
the stove several times before bed, now became imperatives. There
were a thousand and one of them to follow: rules about how to
step, what it meant to touch my mouth, a hot consuming urge to
fix the crooked angles of the universe. It was constant, a cruel nat-
tering. *There, that tilted picture on the wall. Scratch your head with your
left hand only.* It was noise, the beak of a woodpecker in the soft
bark of my brain. But the worst by far were the dread thoughts
about concentrating. I picked up a book but couldn't read, so
aware was I of myself reading, and the fear of that awareness, for it
meant a cold disconnection from this world.

I began to avoid written language because of the anxiety associated with words. I stopped reading. Every sentence I wrote came out
only half coherent. I became afraid of pens and paper, the red felt
tip bleeding into white, a wound. What was it? What was I? I could

not recognize myself spending hours counting, checking, avoiding. Gods seemed to hover in their air, inhabit me, blowing me full of their strange stellar breaths. I wanted my body back. Instead, I pulsed and stuttered and sparked with a glow not my own.

I spent the next several weeks mostly in my bedroom, door closed, shades drawn. I didn't want to go out because any movement might set off a cycle of obsessions. I sat hunched and lost weight. My friend Adam, who had some anxiety problems of his own and was a real pooh-pooher of "talk therapy," found me a behaviorist at McLean.

"These sorts of conditions," the behavioral psychologist, Dr. Lipman, told me as I sat one day in his office, "are associated with people who have depressive temperaments, but unlike depression, they do not yield particularly well to more traditional modes of psychotherapy. We have, however, had some real success with cognitive/behavioral treatments."

Outside it was a shining summer day. His office was dim, though, his blinds adjusted so only tiny gold chinks of light sprinkled through, illuminating him in patches. He was older, maybe fifty, and pudgy, and had tufts of hair in all the wrong places, in the whorls of his ears and his nostrils. I had a bad feeling about him.

Nevertheless, he was all I had right now. "What is this sort of condition exactly?" I asked. My voice, whenever I spoke these days, seemed slowed, stuck, words caught in my throat. I had to keep touching my throat, four times, five times, six times, or I would be punished by losing the power of speech altogether.

"Obsessive-compulsive disorder," he announced. "Only you," he said, and lifted his chin a little proudly, "have an especially difficult case of it."

This, of course, was not what I wanted to hear. "What's so especially difficult about my case?" I asked.

He tapped his chin with the eraser end of his pencil. He sat back in his leather seat. When the wind outside blew, the gold chinks scattered across his face and desk. Suddenly the world cleared a bit. The papers on his desk seemed animated, rustling, sheaves full of wings, books full of birds. I felt creepy, despondent, and excited all at once. Maybe he could help me. Maybe he had some special knowledge.

He then went on to explain to me how most people with obsessive thoughts — *my hands are filthy,* for instance — always follow those thoughts with a compulsive behavior, like hand washing. And while I did have some compulsive behaviors, Dr. Lipman explained, I had also reported that my most distressing obsession had to do with concentration, and that the concentration obsession had no clear-cut compulsion following in its wake.

"Therefore," he said. His eyes sparkled as he spoke. He seemed excited by my case. He seemed so sure of himself that for a moment I was back with language again, only this time it was his language, his words forming me. "Therefore, you are what we call a primary ruminator!"*

A cow, I thought, chewing and chewing on the floppy scum of its cud. I lowered my head.

He went on to tell me about treatment obstacles. Supposedly, primary ruminators are especially challenging because, while you can train people to cease compulsive behaviors, you can't train them nearly as easily to tether their thoughts. His method, he told me, would be to use a certain instrument to desensitize me to the obsessive thought, to teach me not to be afraid of it, so when it entered my mind, I wouldn't panic and thereby set off a whole cycle of anxiety and its partner, avoidance.

"How will we do it?" I asked.

And that is when he pulled "the instrument" from his desk drawer, a Walkman with a tiny tape in it. He told me he'd used it with people who were similar to me. He told me I was to record my voice saying "I can't concentrate I can't concentrate" and then wear the Walkman playing my own voice back to me for at least two hours a day. Soon, he said, I'd become so used to the thought it would no longer bother me.

He looked over at the clock. About half the session had gone by. "We still have twenty more minutes," he said, pressing the red Record button, holding the miniature microphone up to my mouth. "Why don't you start speaking now."

I paid Dr. Lipman for the session, borrowed the Walkman and the tape, and left, stepping into the summer light. McLean is a

---

***Ruminator:** Slater is playing on the dual meaning of the word, which can refer to the eating process of a cow, which regurgitates partially chewed food and then chews it again, as well as to the mental process of thinking or mulling things over. Note that the essay form is commonly considered "ruminative."

huge, stately hospital, buildings with pillars, yawning lawns. The world outside looked lazy in the sweet heat of June. Tulips in the garden lapped at the pollen-rich air with black tongues. A squirrel chirped high in the tuft of a tree. For a moment the world seemed lovely. Then, from far across the lawn, I saw a shadow in a window. Drawn to it for a reason I could not articulate, I stepped closer, and closer still. The shadow resolved itself into lines — two dark brows, a nose. A girl, pressed against glass on a top-floor ward. Her hands were fisted on either side of her face, her curls in a ratty tangle. Her mouth was open, and though I could not hear her, I saw the red splash of her scream.

Behavior therapy is in some ways the antithesis of psychoanalysis. Psychoanalysis focuses on cause, behavior therapy on consequence. Although I've always been a critic of old-style psychoanalysis with its fetish for the past, I don't completely discount the importance of origins. And I have always believed in the mind as an entity that at once subsumes the body and radiates beyond it, and therefore in need of interventions surpassing the mere technical — interventions that whisper to mystery, stroke the soul.

The Walkman, however, was a purely technical intervention. It had little red studs for buttons. The tape whirred efficiently in its center like a slick dark heart. My own voice echoed back to me, all blips and snaky static. I wondered what the obsession with concentration meant. Surely it had some significance beyond the quirks in my neuronal wiring. Surely the neuron itself — that tiny pulse of life embedded in the brain's lush banks — was a Godgiven charge. When I was a girl, I had seen stalks of wheat filled with a strange red light. When I was a girl, I once peeled back the corn's green clasps to find yellow pearls. With the Walkman on, I closed my eyes, saw again the prongs of corn, the wide world, and myself floating out of that world, in a place above all planets, severed even from my own mind. And I knew the obsession had something to do with deep disconnection and too much awe.

"There may be no real reasons," Dr. Lipman repeated to me during my next visit. "OCD could well be the result of a nervous system that's too sensitive. If the right medication is ever developed, we would use that."

Because the right medication had not yet been found, I wore the Walkman. The earplugs felt spongy. Sometimes I wore it to bed, listening to my own voice repeat the obsessive fear. When I took the earphones off, the silence was complete. My sheets were damp from sweat. I waited. Shadows whirled around. Planets sent down their lights, laying them across the blue floor. Blue. Silver. Space. *I can't concentrate.*

I did very little for the next year. Dr. Lipman kept insisting I wear the Walkman, turning up the volume, keeping it on for three, now four hours at a time. Fear and grief prevented me from eating much. When I was too terrified to get out of bed, Dr. Lipman checked me into the local hospital, where I lay amidst IV drips, bags of blood, murmuring heart machines that let me know someone somewhere near was still alive.

It was in the hospital that I was first introduced to psychiatric medications, which the doctors tried out on me, to no avail. The medications had poetic names and frequently rhymed with one another — nortriptyline, desipramine, amitriptyline. Nurses brought me capsules in miniature paper cups or oblong shapes of white that left a salty tingle on my tongue. None of them worked, except to make me drowsy and dull.

And then one day Dr. Lipman said to me, "There's a new medication called Prozac, still in its trial period, but it's seventy percent effective with OCD. I want to send you to a Dr. Stanley, here at McLean. He's one of the physicians doing trial runs."

I shrugged, willing to try. I'd tried so much, surely this couldn't hurt. I didn't expect much though. I certainly didn't expect what I finally got.

In my memory, Stanley is the Prozac Doctor. He has an office high in the eaves of McLean. His desk gleams. His children smile out from frames lined up behind him. In the corner is a computer with a screen saver of hypnotic swirling stars. I watch the stars die and swell. I watch the simple gold band on Stanley's hand. For a moment I think that maybe in here I'll finally be able to escape the infected repetitions of my own mind. And then I hear a clock tick-tick-ticking. The sound begins to bother me; I cannot tune it out. *The clock is ruining my concentration,* I think, and turn toward it. The numbers on its face are not numbers but tiny painted pills, green and white.

A chime hangs down, with another capsule, probably a plastic replica, swinging from the end of it. Back. Forth. Back. Back.

The pads of paper on Stanley's desk are all edged in green and white, with the word "Prozac" scripted across the bottom. The pen has "Prozac" embossed in tiny letters. He asks me about my symptoms for a few minutes, and then uses the Prozac pen to write out a prescription.

"What about side effects?" I ask.

"Very few," the Prozac Doctor answers. He smiles. "Maybe some queasiness. A headache in the beginning. Some short-term insomnia. All in all it's a very good medication. The safest we have."

"Behavior therapy hasn't helped," I say. I feel I'm speaking slowly, for the sound of that clock is consuming me. I put my hands over my ears.

"What is it?" he asks.

"Your — clock."

He looks toward it.

"Would you mind putting it away?"

"Then I would be colluding with your disease," he says. "If I put the clock away, you'll just fixate on something else."

"Disease," I repeat. "I have a disease."

"Without doubt," he says. "OCD can be a crippling disease, but now, for the first time, we have the drugs to combat it."

I take the prescription and leave. I will see him in one month for a follow-up. Disease. Combat. Collusions. My mind, it seems, is my enemy, my illness an absurdity that has to be exterminated. I believe this. The treatment I'm receiving, with its insistence upon cure — which means the abolition of hurt instead of its transformation — helps me to believe this. I have, indeed, been invaded by a virus, a germ I need to rid myself of.

Looking back on it now, I see this belief only added to my panic, shrunk my world still smaller.

On the first day of Prozac I felt nothing, on the second and third I felt nauseated, and for the rest of that week I had headaches so intense I wanted to groan and lower my face into a bowl of crushed ice. I had never had migraines before. In their own way they are beautiful, all pulsing suns and squeezing colors. When I closed my eyes, pink shapes flapped and angels' halos spun. I was a girl again, lying in the snow. Slowly, one by one, the frozen forms lifted toward the light.

And then there really was an angel over me, pressing a cool cloth to my forehead. He held two snowy tablets out to me, and in a haze of pain I took them.

"You'll be all right," Adam said to me. When I cried it was a creek coming from my eyes.

I rubbed my eyes. The headache ebbed.

"How are you?" he asked.

"O.K.," I said. And waited for a command. *Touch your nose, blink twelve times, try not to think about think about concentrating.*

The imperatives came — I could hear them — but from far far away, like birds beyond a mountain, a sound nearly silent and easy to ignore.

"I'm . . . O.K.," I repeated. I went out into the kitchen. The clock on the stove ticked. I pressed my ear against it and heard, this time, a steady, almost soothing pulse.

Most things, I think, diminish over time, rock and mountain, glacier and bone. But this wasn't the nature of Prozac, or me on Prozac. One day I was ill, cramped up with fears, and the next day the ghosts were gone. Imagine having for years a raging fever, and then one day someone hands you a new kind of pill, and within a matter of hours sweat dries, the scarlet swellings go down, your eyes no longer burn. The grass appears green again, the sky a gentle blue. *Hello hello. Remember me?* the planet whispers.

But to say I returned to the world is even a bit misleading, for all my life the world has seemed off-kilter. On Prozac, not only did the acute obsessions dissolve; so too did the blander depression that had been with me since my earliest memories. A sense of immense calm flooded me. Colors came out, yellow leaping from the light where it had long lain trapped, greens unwinding from the grass, dusk letting loose its lavender.

By the fourth day I still felt so shockingly fine that I called the Prozac Doctor. I pictured him in his office, high in the eaves of McLean. I believed he had saved me. He loomed large.

"I'm well," I told him.

"Not yet. It takes at least a month to build up a therapeutic blood level."

"No," I said. "It doesn't." I felt a rushing joy. "The medicine you gave me has made me well. I've — I've actually never felt better." A pause on the line. "I suppose it could be possible." "Yes," I said. "It's happened."

I became a "happening" kind of person. Peter Kramer, the author of *Listening to Prozac,* has written extensively on the drug's ability to galvanize personality change as well as to soothe fears or elevate mood. Kramer calls Prozac a cosmetic medication, for it seems to reshape the psyche, lift the face of the soul.

One night, soon after the medication had kicked in, I sat at the kitchen table with Adam. He was stuck in the muck of his master's thesis, fearful of failure.

"It's easy," I said. "Break the project down into bits. A page a day. Six days, one chapter. Twelve days, two. One month, presto." I snapped my fingers. "You're finished."

Adam looked at me, said nothing. The kitchen grew quiet, a deliberate sort of silence he seemed to be purposefully manufacturing so I could hear the echo of my own voice. Bugs thumped on the screen. I heard the high happy pitch of a cheerleader, the sensible voice of a vocational counselor. In a matter of moments I had gone from a fumbling, unsure person to this — all pragmatism, all sure solutions. For the first time on Prozac I felt afraid.

I lay in bed that night. From the next room I heard the patter of Adam's typewriter keys. He was stuck in the mire, inching forward and falling back. Where was I? Who was I? I lifted my hand to my face, the same motion as before, when the full force of obsession had struck me. The hand was still unfamiliar, but wonderfully so now, the three threaded lines seams of silver, the lights from passing cars rotating on my walls like the swish of a spaceship softly landing.

In space I was then, wondering. How could a drug change my mind so abruptly? How could it bring forth buried or new parts of my personality? The oldest questions, I know. My brain wasn't wet clay and paste, as all good brains should be, but a glinting thing crossed with wires. I wasn't human but machine. No, I wasn't machine but animal, linked to my electrified biology more completely than I could have imagined. We have lately come to think of machines and animals, of machines and nature, as occupying opposite sides of the spectrum — there is IBM and then there's the lake — but really they are so similar. A computer goes on when you push its button. A gazelle goes on when it sees a lynx. Only humans are supposedly different, above the pure cause and effect of the hard-wired primitive world. Free will and all.

But no, maybe not. For I had swallowed a pill designed through technology, and in doing so, I was discovering myself embedded in an animal world. I was a purely chemical being, mood and personality seeping through serotonin. We are all taught to believe it's true, but how strange to feel that supposed truth bubbling right in your own tweaked brainpan. Who was I, all skin and worm, all herd? For the next few weeks, amidst feelings of joy and deep relief, these thoughts accompanied me, these slow, simmering misgivings. In dreams, beasts roamed the rafters of my bones, and my bones were twined with wire, teeth tiny silicon chips.

I went to Drumlin Farm one afternoon to see the animals. A goose ate grass in an imperturbable rhythm. Sheep brayed robotically, their noses pointing toward the sky. I reached out to touch their fur. Simmering misgivings, yes, but my fingers alive, feeling clumps of cream, of wool.

Every noon I took my pill. Instead of just placing it on my tongue and swallowing with water, I unscrewed the capsule. White powder poured into my hands. I tossed the plastic husk away, cradled the healing talc. I tasted it, a burst of bitterness, a gagging. I took it that way every day, the silky slide of Prozac powder, the harshness in my mouth.

Mornings now, I got up early to jog, showered efficiently, then strode off to the library. I was able to go back to work, cutting deli part-time at Formaggio* while I prepared myself for divinity school the next year by reading. I read with an appetite, hungry from all the time I'd lost to illness. The pages of the books seemed very white; the words were easy, black beads shining, ebony in my quieted mind.

I found a book in the library's medical section about obsessive-compulsive disorder. I sat in a corner, on a corduroy cushion, to read it. And there, surrounded by pages and pages on the nature of God and mystery, on Job who cried out at his unfathomable pain, I read about my disorder from a medical perspective, followed

---

*Formaggio:** A popular Cambridge, Massachusetts, shop specializing in cheese and gourmet foods.

the charts and graphs and correlation coefficients. The author proposed that OCD was solely physical in origin, and had the same neurological etiology as Tourette's. Obsessive symptoms, the author suggested, are atavistic responses left over from primitive grooming behaviors. We still have the ape in us; a bird flies in our blood. The obsessive person, linked to her reptilian roots, her mammalian ancestors, cannot stop picking parasites off her brother's back, combing her hair with her tongue, or doing the human equivalent of nest building, picking up stick after stick, leaf after leaf, until her bloated home sits ridiculously unstable in the crotch of an old oak tree.

Keel keel, the crow in me cries. The pig grunts. The screen of myself blinks on. Blinks off. Darkens.

Still, I was mostly peaceful, wonderfully organized. My mind felt lubed, thoughts slipping through so easily, words bursting into bloom. I was reminded of being a girl on the island of Barbados, where we once vacationed. My father took me to a banquet beneath a tropical sky. Greased black men slithered under low poles, their liquid bodies bending to meet the world. Torches flared, and on a long table before me steamed food of every variety. *A feast,* my father said, *all the good things in life.* Yes, that was what Prozac was first like for me, all the good things in life: roasted ham, delicate grilled fish, lemon halves wrapped in yellow waxed paper, fat plums floating in jars.

I could, I thought, do anything in this state of mind. I put my misgivings aside — how fast they would soon come back! how hard they would hit! — and ate into my days, a long banquet. I did things I'd never done before: swimming at dawn in Walden Pond, writing poetry I knew was bad and loving it anyway.

I applied for and was awarded a three-month grant to go to Appalachia, where I wanted to collect oral histories of mountain women. I could swagger anywhere on the Zack, on Vitamin P. Never mind that even before I'd ever come down with OCD I'd been the anxious, tentative sort. Never mind that unnamed trepidations, for all of my life, had prevented me from taking a trip to New Hampshire for more than a few days. Now that I'd taken the cure, I really could go anywhere, even off to the rippling blue mountains of poverty, far from a phone or a friend.

A gun hung over the door. In the oven I saw a roasted bird covered with flies. In the bathroom, a fat girl stooped over herself, without bothering to shut the door, and pulled a red rag from between her legs.

Her name was Kim, her sister's name was Bridget, and their mother and father were Kat and Lonny. All the females were huge and doughy, while Lonny was a single strand of muscle tanned to the color of tobacco. He said very little, and the mother and daughters chattered on, offering me Cokes and Cheerios, showing me to my room, where I sat on a lumpy mattress and stared at the white walls.

And then a moon rose. A storm of hurricane force plowed through fields and sky. I didn't feel myself here. The sound of the storm, battering just above my head, seemed far far away. There was a whispering in my mind, a noise like silk being split. Next to me, on the night table, my sturdy bottle of Prozac. I was fine. So long as I had that, I would be fine.

I pretended I was fine for the next couple of days, racing around with manic intensity. I sat heavy Kat in one of her oversized chairs and insisted she tell me everything about her life in the Blue Ridge Mountains, scribbling madly as she talked. *I am happy happy happy,* I sang to myself. I tried to ignore the strange sounds building in my brain, kindling that crackles, a flame getting hot.

And then I was taking a break out in the sandy yard. It was near one hundred degrees. The sun was tiny in a bleary sky. Chickens screamed and pecked.

In one swift and seamless move, Lonny reached down to grab a bird. His fist closed in on its throat while all the crows cawed and the beasts in my bones brayed away. He laid the chicken down on a stump, raised an ax, and cut. The body did its dance. I watched the severing, how swiftly connections melt, how deep and black is space. Blood spilled.

I ran inside. I was far from a phone or a friend. Maybe I was reminded of some pre-verbal terror: the surgeon's knife, the violet umbilical cord. Or maybe the mountain altitudes had thrown my chemistry off. I don't really know why, or how. But as though I'd never swallowed a Prozac pill, my mind seized and clamped and the obsessions were back.

I took a step forward and then said to myself, *Don't take another step until you count to twenty-five.* After I'd satisfied that imperative, I had to count to twenty-five again, and then halve twenty-five, and then quarter it, before I felt safe enough to walk out the door. By the end of the day, each step took over ten minutes to complete. I stopped taking steps. I sat on my bed.

"What's wrong with you?" Kat said. "Come out here and talk with us."

I tried, but I got stuck in the doorway. There was a point above the doorway I just had to see, and then see again, and inside of me something screamed *back again back again,* and the grief was very large.

For I had experienced the world free and taken in colors and tasted grilled fish and moon. I had left one illness like a too tight snakeskin, and here I was, thrust back. What's worse than illness is to think you're cured — partake of cure in almost complete belief — and then with no warning to be dashed on a dock, moored.

Here's what they don't tell you about Prozac. The drug, for many obsessives who take it, is known to have wonderfully powerful effects in the first few months when it's new to the body. When I called the Prozac Doctor from Kentucky that evening, he explained to me how the drug, when used to treat OCD as opposed to depression, peaks at about six months and then loses some of its oomph. "Someday we'll develop a more robust pill," Dr. Stanley said. "In the meantime, up your dose."

I upped my dose. No relief. Why not? Please. Over the months I had come to need Prozac in a complicated way, had come to see it as my savior, half hating it, half loving it. I unscrewed the capsules and poured their contents over my fingers. Healing talc, gone. Dead sand. I fingered the empty husks.

"You'll feel better if you come to church with us," Kat said to me that Sunday morning. She peered into my face, which must have been white and drawn. "Are you suffering from some city sickness?"

I shrugged. My eyes hurt from crying. I couldn't read or write; I could only add, subtract, divide, divide again.

"Come to church," Kat said. "We can ask the preacher to pray for you."

But I didn't believe in prayers where my illness was concerned. I had come to think, through my reading and the words of doctors, and especially through my brain's rapid response to a drug, that whatever was wrong with me had a simplistic chemical cause. Such a belief can be devastating to sick people, for on top of their illness they must struggle with the sense that illness lacks any creative possibilities.

I think these beliefs, so common in today's high-tech biomedical era in which the focus is relentlessly reductionistic, rob illness of its potential dignity. Illness can be dignified; we can conceive of pain as a kind of complex answer from an elegant system, an arrow pointing inward, a message from soil or sky.

Not so for me. I wouldn't go to church or temple. I wouldn't talk or ask or wonder, for these are distinctly human activities, and I'd come to view myself as less than human.

An anger rose up in me then, a rage. I woke late one night, hands fisted. It took me an hour to get out of bed, so many numbers I had to do, but I was determined.

And then I was walking outside, pushing past the need to count before every step. The night air was muggy, and insects raised a chorus.

I passed midnight fields, a single shack with lighted windows. Cows slept in a pasture.

I rounded the pasture, walked up a hill. And then, before me, spreading out in moonglow, a lake. I stood by its lip. My mind was buzzing and jerking. I don't know at what point the swans appeared — white swans, they must have been, but in silhouette they looked black. They seemed to materialize straight out of the slumbering water. They rose to the surface of the water as memories rise to the surface of consciousness. Hundreds of black swans suddenly, floating absolutely silent, and as I stood there the counting ceased, my mind became silent, and I watched. The swans drifted until it seemed, for a few moments, that they were inside of me, seven dark, silent birds, fourteen princesses, a single self swimming in a tepid sea.

I don't know how long I stood there, or when, exactly, I left. The swans disappeared eventually. The counting ticking talking of my mind resumed.

Still, even in chattering illness I had been quieted for a bit; doors in me had opened; elegance had entered.

This thought calmed me. I was not completely claimed by illness, nor a prisoner of Prozac, entirely dependent on the medication to function. Part of me was still free, a private space not absolutely permeated by pain. A space I could learn to cultivate.

Over the next few days, I noticed that even in the thicket of obsessions my mind sometimes swam into the world, if only for brief forays. There, while I struggled to take a step, was the sun on a green plate. *Remember that,* I said to myself. And here, while I stood fixated in a doorway, was a beetle with a purplish shell, like eggplants growing in wet soil. *Appreciate this,* I told myself, and I can say I did, those slivers of seconds when I returned to the world. I loved the beetle, ached for the eggplant, paddled in a lake with black swans.

And so a part of me began to learn about living outside the disease, cultivating appreciation for a few free moments. It was nothing I would have wished for myself, nothing to noisily celebrate. But it was something, and I could choose it, even while mourning the paralyzed parts of me, the pill that had failed me.

A long time ago, Freud coined the term "superego." A direct translation from German is "over I." Maybe what Freud meant, or should have meant, was not a punitive voice but the angel in the self who rises above an ego under siege, or a medicated mind, to experience the world from a narrow but occasionally gratifying ledge.

I am thirty-one now, and I know that ledge well. It is a smaller space than I would have wished for myself — I who would like to possess a mind free and flexible. I don't. Even after I raised my dose, the Prozac never worked as well as it once had, and years later I am sometimes sad about that, other times strangely relieved, even though my brain is hounded. I must check my keys, the stove; I must pause many times as I write this and do a ritual count to thirty. It's distracting, to say the least, but still I write this. I can walk and talk and play. I've come to live my life in those brief stretches of silence that arrive throughout the day, working at what I know is an admirable speed, accomplishing all I can in clear pauses, knowing those pauses may be short-lived. I am learning something about the single moment, how rife with potential it is, how truly loud its tick. I have heard clocks and clocks. Time shines, sad and good.

And what of the unclear, mind-cluttered stretches? These, as well, I have bent to. I read books now, even when my brain has real difficulty taking in words. Half a word, or a word blurred by static, is better than nothing at all. There is also a kind of stance I've developed, detaching my mind from my mind, letting the static sizzle on while I walk, talk, read, while the obsessive cycles continue and I, stepping aside, try to link my life to something else. It is a meditative exercise of a high order, and one I'm getting better at. Compensations can be gritty gifts.

Is this adaptation a spiritual thing? When I'm living in moments of clarity, have I transcended disease, or has disease transformed me, taught me how to live in secret niches? I don't know.

A few nights ago, a man at a party, a psychologist, talked about the brain. "The amazing thing," he said, "is that if you cut the corpus callosum of small children, they learn without the aid of medication or reparative surgery how to transfer information from the left to the right hemisphere. And because we know cerebral neurons never rejuvenate, that's evidence," he said, "for a mind that lives beyond the brain, a mind outside of our biologies."

Perhaps. Or perhaps our biologies are broader than we ever thought. Perhaps the brain, because of its wound, has been forced into some kink of creativity we can neither see nor explain. This is what the doctors didn't tell me about illness: that an answer to illness is not necessarily cure, but an ambivalent compensation. Disease, for sure, is disorganization, but cure is not necessarily the synthetic, pill-swallowing righting of the mess. To believe this is to define brain function in rigid terms of "normal" and "abnormal," a devastating definition for many. And to believe this, especially where the psyche is concerned, may also mean dependence on psychotropic drugs, and the risk of grave disappointment if the drugs stop working.

I think of those children, their heads on white sheets, their corpus callosa exposed and cut. I wonder who did that to them, and why. I'm sure there is some compelling medical explanation — wracking seizures that need to be stopped — but still, the image disturbs me. I think more, though, of the children's brains once sewn back inside the bony pockets of skull. There, in the secret dark, between wrenched hemispheres, I imagine tiny tendrils growing, so small and so deep not even the strongest machines can see them. They are real but not real, biological but spiritual. They wind in and out, joining left to right, building webbed wings and rickety bridges, sending out messengers with critical information, like the earliest angels who descended from the sky with news and challenge, wrestling with us in nighttime deserts, straining our thighs, stretching our bodies in pain, no doubt, until our skin took on new shapes.

Reflections and Responses

1. Although most of "Black Swans" covers the author's experiences as a young woman, Lauren Slater begins the essay with a moment from her childhood. Why do you think she does this? What is the relevance of her childhood experience to her essay as a whole? How does she carry the imagery of the opening paragraphs into the rest of the essay? What significance do you see in that imagery?

2. In what sense could you call Slater's personal memoir a "nature essay"? What role does nature play in her thinking from the essay's opening to its conclusion? Locate a few moments in the essay when the natural world surfaces. Do these moments have anything in common?

3. What lesson does Slater learn when her Prozac prescription begins to fail her? Why does the psychologist's remark about children whose brain hemispheres have been severed have such an impact on Slater that she uses it to conclude her essay? How does the imagery in the final paragraph reinforce the lesson she has learned about diseases and their cures?

AMY TAN

Mother Tongue

*For many American students, the language spoken at home is far different
from the one spoken in school. For that reason, many students learn to
switch back and forth between two languages, the one they use with their
family and the one required for their education. Such switching, however,
need not be confining or demoralizing. Rather, it can enhance one's sensitivity to language and can even be creatively enabling, as the Chinese
American novelist Amy Tan suggests in this charming personal essay.
"Language is the tool of my trade," Tan writes. "And I use them all—all
the Englishes I grew up with."*

*Born into a Chinese family that had recently arrived in California, Amy
Tan began writing as a child and after graduation from college worked for
several years as a freelance business writer. In the mideighties, she began
writing fiction, basing much of her work on family stories. She is the author
of several best-selling novels:* The Joy Luck Club *(1989), which was a
finalist for both the National Book Award and National Book Critics Circle
Award and was made into a motion picture directed by Wayne Wang;*
The Kitchen God's Wife *(1991);* The Hundred Secret Senses
(1995); The Bonesetter's Daughter *(2000); and* Saving Fish from
Drowning *(2005). In 1992, she published a popular children's book,* The
Moon Lady, *and in 2003, a collection of essays,* The Opposite of Faith:
Memories of a Writing Life. *"Mother Tongue" originally appeared in the*
Threepenny Review *(1990) and was selected by Joyce Carol Oates for*
The Best American Essays 1991.

I am not a scholar of English or literature. I cannot give you much
more than personal opinions on the English language and its variations in this country or others.

I am a writer. And by that definition, I am someone who has always loved language. I am fascinated by language in daily life. I spend a great deal of my time thinking about the power of language — the way it can evoke an emotion, a visual image, a complex idea, or a simple truth. Language is the tool of my trade. And I use them all — all the Englishes I grew up with.

Recently, I was made keenly aware of the different Englishes I do use. I was giving a talk to a large group of people, the same talk I had already given to half a dozen other groups. The nature of the talk was about my writing, my life, and my book, *The Joy Luck Club*. The talk was going along well enough, until I remembered one major difference that made the whole talk sound wrong. My mother was in the room. And it was perhaps the first time she had heard me give a lengthy speech, using the kind of English I have never used with her. I was saying things like, "The intersection of memory upon imagination" and "There is an aspect of my fiction that relates to thus-and-thus"— a speech filled with carefully wrought grammatical phrases, burdened, it suddenly seemed to me, with nominalized forms, past perfect tenses, conditional phrases, all the forms of standard English that I had learned in school and through books, the forms of English I did not use at home with my mother.

Just last week, I was walking down the street with my mother, and I again found myself conscious of the English I was using, the English I do use with her. We were talking about the price of new and used furniture and I heard myself saying this: "Not waste money that way." My husband was with us as well, and he didn't notice any switch in my English. And then I realized why. It's because over the twenty years we've been together I've often used that same kind of English with him, and sometimes he even uses it with me. It has become our language of intimacy, a different sort of English that relates to family talk, the language I grew up with.

So you'll have some idea of what this family talk I heard sounds like, I'll quote what my mother said during a recent conversation which I videotaped and then transcribed. During this conversation, my mother was talking about a political gangster in Shanghai who had the same last name as her family's, Du, and how the gangster in his early years wanted to be adopted by her family, which was rich by comparison. Later, the gangster became more powerful, far richer than my mother's family, and one day showed up at my mother's wedding to pay his respects. Here's what she said in part:

"Du Yusong having business like fruit stand. Like off the street kind. He is Du like Du Zong — but not Tsung-ming Island people. The local people call putong, the river east side, he belong to that side local people. That man want to ask Du Zong father take him in like become own family. Du Zong father wasn't look down on him, but didn't take seriously, until that man big like become a mafia. Now important person, very hard to inviting him. Chinese way, came only to show respect, don't stay for dinner. Respect for making big celebration, he shows up. Mean gives lots of respect. Chinese custom. Chinese social life that way. If too important won't have to stay too long. He come to my wedding. I didn't see, I heard it. I gone to boy's side, they have YMCA dinner. Chinese age I was nineteen."

You should know that my mother's expressive command of English belies how much she actually understands. She reads the *Forbes* report, listens to *Wall Street Week*, converses daily with her stockbroker, reads all of Shirley MacLaine's books with ease — all kinds of things I can't begin to understand. Yet some of my friends tell me they understand 50 percent of what my mother says. Some say they understand 80 to 90 percent. Some say they understand none of it, as if she were speaking pure Chinese. But to me, my mother's English is perfectly clear, perfectly natural. It's my mother tongue. Her language, as I hear it, is vivid, direct, full of observation and imagery. That was the language that helped shape the way I saw things, expressed things, made sense of the world.

Lately, I've been giving more thought to the kind of English my mother speaks. Like others, I have described it to people as "broken" or "fractured" English. But I wince when I say that. It has always bothered me that I can think of no way to describe it other than "broken," as if it were damaged and needed to be fixed, as if it lacked a certain wholeness and soundness. I've heard other terms used, "limited English," for example. But they seem just as bad, as if everything is limited, including people's perceptions of the limited English speaker.

I know this for a fact, because when I was growing up, my mother's "limited" English limited *my* perception of her. I was ashamed of her English. I believed that her English reflected the quality of what she had to say. That is, because she expressed them imperfectly her thoughts were imperfect. And I had plenty of empirical evidence to support me: the fact that people in department stores, at banks, and at restaurants did not take her seriously, did not give her good service, pretended not to understand her, or even acted as if they did not hear her.

My mother has long realized the limitations of her English as well. When I was fifteen, she used to have me call people on the phone to pretend I was she. In this guise, I was forced to ask for information or even to complain and yell at people who had been rude to her. One time it was a call to her stockbroker in New York. She had cashed out her small portfolio and it just so happened we were going to go to New York the next week, our very first trip outside California. I had to get on the phone and say in an adolescent voice that was not very convincing, "This is Mrs. Tan."

And my mother was standing in the back whispering loudly, "Why he don't send me check, already two weeks late. So mad he lie to me, losing me money."

And then I said in perfect English, "Yes, I'm getting rather concerned. You had agreed to send the check two weeks ago, but it hasn't arrived."

Then she began to talk more loudly. "What he want, I come to New York tell him front of his boss, you cheating me?" And I was trying to calm her down, make her be quiet, while telling the stockbroker, "I can't tolerate any more excuses. If I don't receive the check immediately, I am going to have to speak to your manager when I'm in New York next week." And sure enough, the following week there we were in front of this astonished stockbroker, and I was sitting there red-faced and quiet, and my mother, the real Mrs. Tan, was shouting at his boss in her impeccable broken English.

We used a similar routine just five days ago, for a situation that was far less humorous. My mother had gone to the hospital for an appointment, to find out about a benign brain tumor a CAT scan had revealed a month ago. She said she had spoken very good English, her best English, no mistakes. Still, she said, the hospital did not apologize when they said they had lost the CAT scan and she had come for nothing. She said they did not seem to have any sympathy when she told them she was anxious to know the exact diagnosis, since her husband and son had both died of brain tumors. She said they would not give her any more information until the next time and she would have to make another appointment for that. So she said she would not leave until the doctor called her daughter. She wouldn't budge. And when the doctor finally called her daughter, me, who spoke in perfect English — lo and behold — we had assurances the CAT scan would be found, promises that a conference call on Monday would be held, and apologies for any suffering my mother had gone through for a most regrettable mistake.

I think my mother's English almost had an effect on limiting my possibilities in life as well. Sociologists and linguists probably will tell you that a person's developing language skills are more influenced by peers. But I do think that the language spoken in the family, especially in immigrant families which are more insular, plays a large role in shaping the language of the child. And I believe that it affected my results on achievement tests, IQ tests, and the SAT. While my English skills were never judged as poor, compared to math, English could not be considered my strong suit. In grade school I did moderately well, getting perhaps B's, sometimes B-pluses, in English and scoring perhaps in the sixtieth or seventieth percentile on achievement tests. But those scores were not good enough to override the opinion that my true abilities lay in math and science, because in those areas I achieved A's and scored in the ninetieth percentile or higher.

This was understandable. Math is precise; there is only one correct answer. Whereas, for me at least, the answers on English tests were always a judgment call, a matter of opinion and personal experience. Those tests were constructed around items like fill-in-the-blank sentence completion, such as, "Even though Tom was ———, Mary thought he was ———." And the correct answer always seemed to be the most bland combinations of thoughts, for example, "Even though Tom was shy, Mary thought he was charming," with the grammatical structure "even though" limiting the correct answer to some sort of semantic opposites, so you wouldn't get answers like, "Even though Tom was foolish, Mary thought he was ridiculous." Well, according to my mother, there were very few limitations as to what Tom could have been and what Mary might have thought of him. So I never did well on tests like that.

The same was true with word analogies, pairs of words in which you were supposed to find some sort of logical, semantic relationship — for example, "*Sunset* is to *nightfall* as ——— is to ———." And here you would be presented with a list of four possible pairs, one of which showed the same kind of relationship: *red* is to *stoplight*, *bus* is to *arrival*, *chills* is to *fever*, *yawn* is to *boring*. Well, I could never think that way. I knew what the tests were asking, but I could not block out of my mind the images already created by the first pair, "*sunset* is to *nightfall*"— and I would see a burst of colors against a darkening sky, the moon rising, the lowering of a curtain of stars. And all the other pairs of words — red, bus, stoplight, boring — just threw up a mass of confusing images, making it impossible for me to sort out something as logical as saying: "A sunset precedes nightfall" is the same as "a chill precedes a fever." The only way I would have gotten that answer right would have been to imagine an associative situation, for example, my being disobedient and staying out past sunset, catching a chill at night, which turns into feverish pneumonia as punishment, which indeed did happen to me.

I have been thinking about all this lately, about my mother's English, about achievement tests. Because lately I've been asked, as a writer, why there are not more Asian Americans represented in American literature. Why are there few Asian Americans enrolled in creative writing programs? Why do so many Chinese students go into engineering? Well, these are broad sociological questions I can't begin to answer. But I have noticed in surveys — in fact, just last week — that Asian students, as a whole, always do significantly better on math achievement tests than in English. And this makes me think that there are other Asian-American students whose English spoken in the home might also be described as "broken" or "limited." And perhaps they also have teachers who are steering them away from writing and into math and science, which is what happened to me.

Fortunately, I happen to be rebellious in nature and enjoy the challenge of disproving assumptions made about me. I became an English major my first year in college, after being enrolled as premed. I started writing nonfiction as a freelancer the week after

I was told by my former boss that writing was my worst skill and I should hone my talents toward account management.

But it wasn't until 1985 that I finally began to write fiction. And at first I wrote using what I thought to be wittily crafted sentences, sentences that would finally prove I had mastery over the English language. Here's an example from the first draft of a story that later made its way into *The Joy Luck Club*, but without this line: "That was my mental quandary in its nascent state." A terrible line, which I can barely pronounce.

Fortunately, for reasons I won't get into today, I later decided I should envision a reader for the stories I would write. And the reader I decided upon was my mother, because these were stories about mothers. So with this reader in mind — and in fact she did read my early drafts — I began to write stories using all the Englishes I grew up with: the English I spoke to my mother, which for lack of a better term might be described as "simple"; the English she used with me, which for lack of a better term might be described as "broken"; my translation of her Chinese, which could certainly be described as "watered down"; and what I imagined to be her translation of her Chinese if she could speak in perfect English, her internal language, and for that I sought to preserve the essence, but neither an English nor a Chinese structure. I wanted to capture what language ability tests can never reveal: her intent, her passion, her imagery, the rhythms of her speech and the nature of her thoughts.

Apart from what any critic had to say about my writing, I knew I had succeeded where it counted when my mother finished reading my book and gave me her verdict: "So easy to read."

Reflections and Responses

1. What "Englishes" did Amy Tan grow up with? Why does she feel uncomfortable with the term "broken English"? Why do you think she still uses that term toward the end of her essay?

2. What point is Tan making about language tests? Why did she perform less well on them than she did on math and science tests?

In her opinion, what aspects of language do the tests fail to take into account?

3. Tan cites a sentence — "That was my mental quandary in its nascent state"— that she deleted from *The Joy Luck Club*. What do you think she dislikes about that sentence? What kind of English does it represent? Does it or does it not demonstrate a "mastery" of the English language?

2

The Attentive Mind: Observation, Reflection, Insight

RUDOLPH CHELMINSKI

Turning Point

Warning: As you read this essay, your palms may begin to sweat and your stomach tighten, for it contains a breathtaking account of one of the most astonishing acrobatic feats ever performed. Few people today remember the name of Philippe Petit, the daring, enigmatic character who at the age of twenty-five mesmerized New Yorkers early one August morning by walking and dancing on a high wire he had secretly strung across the tops of the twin towers of the World Trade Center. In "Turning Point," Rudolph Chelminski recounts his visit with Petit at the top of the 1,360-foot-high South Tower just a few weeks before it would be destroyed by the 9/11 attacks. As Chelminski observes, Petit's feat was far more than a stunt or daredevil routine but instead represented "a creative statement of true theater, as valid as ballet or modern dance."

Rudolph Chelminski is a freelance writer living in France. Formerly a Life *magazine staff correspondent in Paris and Moscow, he has written for numerous major American and French publications, including* Life, Time, Fortune, People, Money, Playboy, Geo, Town & Country, Reader's Digest, Smithsonian, Signature, Saturday Review, Wired, Reporter, France Today, Le Monde, *and others. He is the author of four books— most recently a biography,* The Perfectionist: Life and Death in Haute Cuisine *(2005)—and has never won a single prize. Except, Chelminski says, the best one of all: having managed for more than thirty years to support himself and family as a freelancer. "Turning Point" first appeared in* Smithsonian *and was selected by Stephen Jay Gould for* The Best American Essays *2002.*

Was it only twenty-seven years ago? It seems a lifetime, or two, has passed since that August morning in 1974 when Philippe Petit,

Philippe Petit high wire walking between the 1,360-foot-tall towers of the World Trade Center on August 7, 1974. © AP/Wide World Photos

a slim, young Frenchman, upstaged Richard Nixon by performing one of the few acts more sensational — in those faraway times — than resigning the presidency of the United States.

A week before his twenty-sixth birthday, the nimble Petit clandestinely strung a cable between the not-yet-completed Twin Towers, already dominating lower Manhattan's skyline, and for the better part of an hour walked back and forth over the void, demonstrating his astonishing obsession to one hundred thousand or so wide-eyed gawkers gathered so far below.

I missed that performance, but last summer, just two weeks before the 1,360-foot-tall towers would come to symbolize a ghastly new reality, I persuaded Petit to accompany me to the top and show me how he did it and, perhaps, explain why. I was driven by a long-standing curiosity. Ever since reading about his exploit in New York, I had felt a kind of familiarity with this remarkable fellow. Years before, I had watched him at close range and much lower altitude, in another city on the other side of the pond.

In the 1960s, the Montparnasse area of Paris was animated by a colorful fauna of celebrities, eccentrics, and artistic characters. On any given day, you might run into Giacometti walking bent forward like one of his skinny statues, Raymond Duncan (Isadora's brother) in his goofy sandals and Roman toga, or Jean-Paul Sartre morosely seeking the decline of capitalism in the Communist daily, *L'Humanité*. And after nightfall, if you hung around long enough, you were almost certain to see Philippe Petit.

When he might appear was anyone's guess, but his hangouts were pretty well known: the corner of Rue de Buci and Boulevard St. Germain; the sidewalk outside Les Deux Magots, or directly under the terrace windows of La Coupole. Silent and mysterious, this skinny, pasty-faced kid dressed in black would materialize unannounced on his unicycle, a shock of pale blond hair escaping from under a battered top hat. He would draw a circle of white chalk on the sidewalk, string a rope between two trees, hop up onto it, and, impassive and mute as a carp, go into an improvised show that combined mime, juggling, prestidigitation, and the precarious balancing act of loose-rope walking. After an hour or so he would pass the hat and, as wordlessly as he had arrived, disappear into the night.

Then, on a drizzly morning in June 1971, the kid in black suddenly showed up dancing on a barely perceptible wire between the massive towers of Notre Dame Cathedral. For nearly three hours, he walked back and forth, mugged, saluted, and juggled Indian clubs while angry gendarmes waited for him to come down. When he finally did, they arrested him for disturbing the peace.

Disturbing the peace was a good part of what it was all about, of course, because Petit was out to prove something. Notre Dame was his first great coup, the sensational stunt that was to become his trademark. It was also his first declaration of status: he was not a mere street entertainer but a performer, an artiste. Ever since that June morning, he has dedicated himself to demonstrating his passionate belief that the high wire — his approach to the high wire, that is — transcends the cheap hype of circus "daredevil" routines to become a creative statement of true theater, as valid as ballet or modern dance.

Getting that point across has never been easy. After gratifying Petit with a few front-page pictures, the French establishment gave a Gallic shrug, dismissed him as a youthful crank, and returned to more serious matters — like having lunch and talking politics. There was a very interesting story to be told about this young loner who had learned the art of the *funambule* (literally, "rope walker") all by himself as a teenager, but the Parisian press ignored it. Within a couple of days, his Notre Dame stunt was largely forgotten.

Stung, Petit resolved to take his art elsewhere and began a long vagabondage around the world, returning to Paris for brief spells before setting off again. Traveling as light as a medieval minstrel and living hand to mouth, he carried his mute personage from city to city, juggling for his supper. None of his onlookers could know that back in his tiny Parisian studio — a rented broom closet he had somehow converted into a dwelling — he had a folder marked "projects."

Two years after the Notre Dame caper, the skinny figure in black appeared with his balancing pole between the gigantic northern pylons of the Sydney Harbour Bridge in Australia. Petit had strung his cable there just as furtively as he had done at Notre Dame, but this time the police reacted with brainless if predictable fury, attempting to force him down by cutting one of his cavalettis, the lateral guy ropes that hold a sky walker's cable steady. Flung a foot up in the air when the cavaletti sprang free, Petit managed to land square on the cable and keep his balance. He came in and was manacled, led to court, and found guilty of the usual crimes. The owner of a Sydney circus offered to pay his $250 fine in return for a tightrope walk two days later over the lions' cage.

And then came the World Trade Center. Petit had been planning it ever since he was nineteen when, in a dentist's waiting room, he saw an article with an artist's rendering of the gigantic towers planned for New York's financial district. ("When I see three oranges I juggle," he once said, "and when I see two towers I walk.") He ripped the article from the magazine and slipped it into his projects file.

The World Trade Center would be the ultimate test of Petit's fanatically meticulous planning. For Notre Dame and Sydney, he had copied keys to open certain locks, picked others, and hacksawed his way through still others in order to sneak his heavy material up into place for the sky walk. But New York presented a much more complicated challenge. The World Trade Center buildings were fearfully higher than anything he had ever tackled, making it impossible to set up conventional cavalettis. And how to get a cable across the 140-foot gap between the South and North Towers, anyway, in the face of omnipresent security crews?

There was one factor in Petit's favor: the buildings were still in the final stages of construction, and trucks were regularly delivering all sorts of material to the basement docks, to be transferred to a freight elevator and brought up to the floors by workers of all descriptions. Wearing hard hats, Petit and an accomplice hauled his gear to the top of the South Tower (his walking cable passed off as antenna equipment) while two other friends similarly made their way to the roof of the North Tower, armed with a bow and arrow and a spool of stout fishing line. Come nightfall, they shot the arrow and line across the 140-foot gap between the towers. Petit retrieved the line, pulled it over until he was in possession of the stronger nylon cord attached to it, then tied on the heavy rope that would be used to carry his steel walking cable over to the other side.

As Petit paid out the rope and then the cable, gravity took over. The cable ran wild, shooting uncontrollably through his hands and snaking down the side of the giant building before coming up short with a titanic *thwonk!* at the steel beam to which Petit had anchored it. On the North Tower, holding fast to the other end of the heavy rope, his friends were pulled perilously close to the roof's edge. Gradually, the four regained control and spent the rest of the night hours pulling the cable up, double-cinching the anchor points, getting it nearly level, tensioning it to three tons with a ratchet, and finally attaching a set of nearly horizontal cavalettis to the buildings.

At a few minutes past seven A.M., August 7, 1974, just as the first construction workers were arriving on the rooftop, Petit seized his balancing pole and stepped out over the void.

The conditions weren't exactly ideal. Petit had not slept for
forty-eight hours, and now he saw that the hurry-up rigging job he
had carried out in the dark had resulted in a cable that zigzagged
where the improvised cavalettis joined it. Sensitive to wind, temperature, and any sway of the buildings, it was so alive — swooping,
rolling, and twisting. At slightly more than twenty-six feet, his balancing pole was longer and heavier — fifty-five pounds — than any
he had ever used before. Greater weight meant greater stability,
but such a heavy load is hard enough to tote around on terra
firma, let alone on a thin wire in midair at an insane altitude. It
would require an uncommon debauch of nervous energy, but energy was the one thing Petit had plenty of.

With his eyes riveted to the edge of the far tower — wire walkers
aren't supposed to look down —Petit glided his buffalo-hide slippers along the cable, feeling his way until he was halfway across.
He knelt, put his weight on one knee, and swung his right arm
free. This was his "salute," the signature gesture of the high-wire
artist. Each has his own, and each is an individual trademark creation. Arising, he continued to the North Tower, hopped off the
wire, double-checked the cable's anchoring points, made a few adjustments, and hopped back on.

By now traffic had stopped in the environs of Wall Street, and
Petit could already hear the first police and ambulance sirens as he
nimbly set forth again. Off he went, humming and mumbling to
himself, puffing grunts of concentration at tricky moments.
Halfway across, he steadied, halted, then knelt again. And then,
God in heaven, he lay down, placing his spine directly atop the
cable and resting the balancing pole on his stomach. Breathless,
in Zen-like calm, he lay there for a long moment, contemplating
the red-eyed seabird hovering motionless above him.

Time to get up. But how do you do it, I asked Petit as we stood
together on the roof of the South Tower, when the only thing between you and certain death is a cable under your body and fifty-
five extra pounds lying on your belly?

"All the weight on the right foot," he replied with a shrug. "I draw
my right foot back along the cable and move the balancing bar

lower down below my belt. I get a little lift from the wire, because it is moving up and down. Then I do a sit-up and rise to a standing position, with all the weight on my right foot. It takes some practice."

He got up. Unable to resist the pleasure of seeing New York at his feet, he caressed the side of the building with a glance and slowly panned his eyes all the way down to the gridlocked traffic below. Then he flowed back to the South Tower. "I could hear the horns of cars below me," he recalled, relishing the memory. "I could hear the applause too. The *rumeur* [clamor] of the crowd rose up to me from four hundred meters below. No other show person has ever heard a sound like that."

Now, as he glided along north to south, a clutch of police officers, rescue crews, and security men hovered with arms outstretched to pull him in. But Petit hadn't finished. Inches from their grasp, he did a wire walker's turnaround, slipping his feet 180 degrees and swinging his balancing bar around to face in the other direction. He did his elegant "torero's" walk and his "promenader's" walk; he knelt; he did another salute; he sat in casual repose, lord of his domain; he stood and balanced on one foot.

After seven crossings and forty-five minutes of air dancing, it began to rain. For his finale he ran along the cable to give himself up. "Running, ah! ah!" he had written in one of his early books. "That's the laughter of the wire walker." Then he ran into the arms of waiting police.

Petit's astonishing star turn created a sensation the likes of which few New Yorkers had ever seen. Years later, the art critic Calvin Tompkins was still so impressed by what Petit had done that he wrote in *The New Yorker:* "He achieved the almost unimaginable feat of investing the World Trade Center . . . with a thrilling and terrible beauty."

Ever resourceful, Petit worked out a deal with the Manhattan district attorney. In lieu of punishment or fine, and as penance for his artistic crime, he agreed to give a free performance in Central Park. The following week he strung a 600-foot wire across Turtle Pond, from a tree on one side to Belvedere Castle on the other. And this time he nearly fell. He was wearing the same walking slippers and using the same balancing pole, but security was relaxed among the fifteen thousand people who had come to watch him perform, and kids began climbing and jumping on his cavalettis.

The wire twitched, and suddenly he felt himself going beyond the point of return.

But he didn't go all the way down. Instinctively squirming as he dropped, he hooked a leg over the wire. Somehow, he managed to swing himself back up, get vertical, and carry on with the performance. The crowd applauded warmly, assuming it was all part of the act, but Petit doesn't enjoy the memory. Falling is the wire walker's shame, he says, and due only to a lack of concentration.

In the years since his World Trade Center triumph, Petit has disdainfully turned away all offers to profit from it. "I could have become a millionaire," he told me. "Everyone was after me to endorse their products, but I was not going to walk a wire dressed in a hamburger suit, and I was not going to say I succeeded because I was wearing such and such a shirt." Continuing to operate as a stubbornly independent freelance artist, he has organized and starred in more than seventy performances around the world, all without safety nets. They have included choreographed strolls across the Louisiana Superdome in New Orleans, between the towers of the Laon Cathedral in France, and a "Peace Walk" between the Jewish and Arab quarters of Jerusalem. In 1989, on the bicentennial of the French Revolution, he took center stage in Paris — legally and officially this time — by walking the 2,300-foot gap between the Trocadéro esplanade on the Right Bank, over the Seine, and up to the second tier of the Eiffel Tower.

Today, at fifty-two, Petit is somewhat heavier than in his busking days in Paris, and his hair has turned a reddish blond, but neither his energy nor his overpowering self-confidence has waned in the least. He shares a pleasantly rustic farmhouse at the edge of the Catskills near Woodstock, New York, with his longtime companion, Kathy O'Donnell, daughter of a former Manhattan publishing executive. She handles the planning, producing, problem-solving, and money-raising aspects of Petit's enterprises while they both think up new high-wire projects and he painstakingly prepares them. Petit supplements his income from performances with, among other things, book royalties and fees from giving lectures and workshops.

His preferred place of study is his New York City office. Knowing what an artiste he is, you would not expect to find him in an ordinary building, and you would be right. Petit hangs out at the Cathedral of St. John the Divine, the world's biggest Gothic cathedral, at Amsterdam Avenue and 112th Street. His office is a balustraded aerie in the cathedral's triforium, the narrow gallery high above the vast nave. Behind a locked entryway, up a suitably medieval spiral staircase and then down a stone passageway, the rare visitor to his domain comes upon a sturdy door bearing a small framed sign: *Philippe Petit, Artist in Residence.* Behind that door, stowed as neatly as a yacht's navigational gear, lie his treasures: thousands of feet of rope coiled just so, all manner of rigging and tensioning equipment, floor-to-ceiling archives, maps and models of past and future walk projects, and shelves upon shelves of technical and reference books.

It was another of his coups that got him there. In 1980 he offered to walk the length of the nave to raise funds for the cathedral's building program. He was sure he had the perfect occasion for it: Ascension Day. The cathedral's then dean, the ebullient James Parks Morton, famous for his support of the arts, was enthusiastic, but his board of trustees vetoed the idea as too dangerous. Petit sneaked a cable crosswise over the nave and did his walk anyway. Once again the police came to arrest him, but Morton spoiled their day by announcing that Petit was artist in residence and the cathedral was his workplace. And so he came to be.

Over the years, taking his title seriously, Petit reciprocated by carrying out a dozen wire walks inside and outside the cathedral. He figures that by now he has raised half a million dollars for the still uncompleted cathedral's building program, and enjoys pointing out the small stone carving of a wire walker niched in among the saints in the main portal. "It is high art," Morton says of Petit's work. "There is a documented history of wire walkers in cathedrals and churches. It's not a new idea, but his walk here was his first in an American cathedral."

Sometimes after six P.M., when the lights go out, the big front door slams shut, and the cathedral closes down for the night, Petit is left alone in the mineral gloom of St. John with his writing, sketches, calculations, chess problems, poetry, and reveries. The comparison to Quasimodo is immediate and obvious, of course, but unlike Notre Dame's famous hunchback, Petit wants nothing more than to be seen, in the ever greater, more ambitious, and spectacular shows that fill his dreams. One night after he took me up to his cathedral office, he gazed longingly at a print of the Brooklyn Bridge — what a walk that could be! But there is, he assured me, plenty more in his projects file. A walk on Easter Island, from the famous carved heads to the volcano. Or the half-mile stretch over open water between the Sydney Harbour Bridge and the celebrated Opera House.

Even more than all these, though, there is one walk — *the* walk, the ultimate, the masterpiece — that has filled his dreams for more than a decade. It's the Grand Canyon. Prospecting in the heart of the Navajo nation by air in 1988, Petit discovered the ideal spot for crowning his career: a ruggedly beautiful landscape off the road from Flagstaff to Grand Canyon Village, where a noble mesa soars at the far end of a 1,200-foot gap from the canyon's edge. The gap is deeper than it is wide, 1,600 feet straight down to the Little Colorado River.

Petit's eyes glowed as he went through the mass of blueprints, maps, drawings, and models he has produced over all the years of planning the Canyon Walk. Only one thing is missing: money. Twice now, the money people have backed out at the last minute.

But none of that seemed to matter when I spoke to Petit a few days after the September 11 catastrophe struck. He could scarcely find words for his sorrow at the loss of so many lives, among them people he knew well — elevator operators, tour guides, mainte-nance workers. "I feel my house has been destroyed," he said. "Very often I would take family and friends there. It was my pride as a poet and a lover of beautiful things to show as many people as possible the audacity of those impossible monoliths."

Haunted, as we all are, by the images of the towers in their final moments, Petit told me it was his hope that they would be remem-bered not as they appeared then but as they were on that magical August day more than a generation ago, when he danced between them on a wire and made an entire city look up in awe. "In a very small way I helped frame them with glory," he said, "and I want to remember them in their glory."

Reflections and Responses

1. Chelminski begins his essay by setting the context for an interview with Petit. He says that he persuaded Petit "to accompany me to the

top and show me how he did it and, perhaps, explain why." What does Chelminski learn from Petit? Why do you think he places so little of the interview in dialogue format? How does he use the information he receives from Petit? In your opinion, does Petit give him an explanation of *why* he did what he did?

2. Chelminski had clearly begun to work on this essay and interview before the surprise attack on the World Trade Center. How do you think the devastation of the towers affected Chelminski's essay? How different would it be had the attacks never occurred? What connection does Chelminski see between Petit's feat and the Twin Towers? How is that connection supported by the way he concludes his essay?

3. Compare "Turning Point" with the next essay in this section, Annie Dillard's "The Stunt Pilot." In what ways are the two essays similar? How does each author construct a profile? How does each author use terms from art to describe the subject's exploits?

ANNIE DILLARD

The Stunt Pilot

Creative expression can take many forms; it need not refer only to literature, painting, or music. We can find creativity in craft and design, in the movements of dancers and athletes, and even—as the following essay reveals— in the aerobatics of a stunt pilot. Observing the breathtaking dives and spins, the "loops and arabesques" of a celebrated pilot, Annie Dillard is struck by their resemblance to artistic expression. She finds in the pilot's use of space a new kind of beauty, one that seems to encompass all the arts— poetry, painting, music, sculpture: "The black plane dropped spinning, and flattened out spinning the other way; it began to carve the air into forms that built wildly and musically on each other and never ended."

Annie Dillard is one of America's preeminent essayists, someone for whom, as she puts it, the essay is not an occasional piece but her "real work." Her many award-winning books of essays and nonfiction include Pilgrim at Tinker Creek, *which won the Pulitzer Prize for General Nonfiction in 1975;* Holy the Firm *(1977);* Living by Fiction *(1982);* Teaching a Stone to Talk *(1982);* An American Childhood *(1987);* The Writing Life *(1989); and* For the Time Being *(1999). Dillard has taught creative writing at Wesleyan University in Middletown, Connecticut, and currently lives in Key West, Florida. In 1992, she published her first novel,* The Living. *"The Stunt Pilot" originally appeared in* Esquire *(1989) and was selected by Justin Kaplan for* The Best American Essays 1990.

Dave Rahm lived in Bellingham, Washington, north of Seattle. Bellingham, a harbor town, lies between the alpine North Cascade Mountains and the San Juan Islands in Haro Strait above Puget Sound. The latitude is that of Newfoundland. Dave Rahm was a stunt pilot, the air's own genius.

In 1975, with a newcomer's willingness to try anything once, I attended the Bellingham Air Show. The Bellingham airport was a wide clearing in a forest of tall Douglas firs; its runways suited small planes. It was June. People wearing blue or tan zipped jackets stood loosely on the concrete walkways and runways outside the coffee shop. At that latitude in June, you stayed outside because you could, even most of the night, if you could think up something to do. The sky did not darken until ten o'clock or so, and it never got very dark. Your life parted and opened in the sunlight. You tossed your dark winter routines, thought up mad projects, and improvised everything from hour to hour. Being a stunt pilot seemed the most reasonable thing in the world; you could wave your arms in the air all day and night, and sleep next winter.

I saw from the ground a dozen stunt pilots; the air show scheduled them one after the other, for an hour of aerobatics. Each pilot took up his or her plane and performed a batch of tricks. They were precise and impressive. They flew upside down, and straightened out; they did barrel rolls, and straightened out; they drilled through dives and spins, and landed gently on a far runway.

For the end of the day, separated from all other performances of every sort, the air show director had scheduled a program titled "Dave Rahm." The leaflet said that Rahm was a geologist who taught at Western Washington University. He had flown for King Hussein in Jordan. A tall man in the crowd told me Hussein had seen Rahm fly on a visit the king made to the United States; he had invited him to Jordan to perform at ceremonies. Hussein was a pilot, too. "Hussein thought he was the greatest thing in the world."

Idly, paying scant attention, I saw a medium-sized, rugged man dressed in brown leather, all begoggled, climb in a black biplane's open cockpit. The plane was a Bücker Jungman, built in the thirties. I saw a tall, dark-haired woman seize a propeller tip at the plane's nose and yank it down till the engine caught. He was off; he climbed high over the airport in his biplane, very high until he was barely visible as a mote, and then seemed to fall down the air, diving headlong, and streaming beauty in spirals behind him.

The black plane dropped spinning, and flattened out spinning the other way; it began to carve the air into forms that built wildly and musically on each other and never ended. Reluctantly, I started paying attention. Rahm drew high above the world an inexhaustibly glorious line; it piled over our heads in loops and arabesques. It was like a Saul Steinberg[*] fantasy; the plane was the pen. Like Steinberg's contracting and billowing pen line, the line Rahm spun moved to form new, punning shapes from the edges of the old. Like a Klee[†] line, it smattered the sky with landscapes and systems.

The air show announcer hushed. He had been squawking all day, and now he quit. The crowd stilled. Even the children watched dumbstruck as the slow, black biplane buzzed its way around the air. Rahm made beauty with his whole body; it was pure pattern, and you could watch it happen. The plane moved every way a line can move, and it controlled three dimensions, so the line carved massive and subtle slits in the air like sculptures. The plane looped the loop, seeming to arch its back like a gymnast; it stalled, dropped, and spun out of it climbing; it spiraled and knifed west on one side's wings and back east on another; it turned cartwheels, which must be physically impossible; it played with its own line like a cat with yarn. How did the pilot know where in the air he was? If he got lost, the ground would swat him.

Rahm did everything his plane could do: tailspins, four-point rolls, flat spins, figure eights, snap rolls, and hammerheads. He did pirouettes on the plane's tail. The other pilots could do these stunts too, skillfully, one at a time. But Rahm used the plane inexhaustibly, like a brush marking thin air.

His was pure energy and naked spirit. I have thought about it for years. Rahm's line unrolled in time. Like music, it split the bulging rim of the future along its seam. It pried out the present. We watchers waited for the split-second curve of beauty in the present to reveal itself. The human pilot, Dave Rahm, worked in the cockpit right at the plane's nose; his very body tore into the future for us and reeled it down upon us like a curling peel.

Like any fine artist, he controlled the tension of the audience's longing. You desired, unwittingly, a certain kind of roll or climb,

[*]**Saul Steinberg:** Contemporary artist (1914–1999) who also created numerous covers for *The New Yorker* magazine. — Ed.

[†]**Klee:** Paul Klee (1879–1940), a Swiss artist known for his highly distinctive abstract paintings. — Ed.

or a return to a certain portion of the air, and he fulfilled your hope slantingly, like a poet, or evaded it until you thought you would burst, and then fulfilled it surprisingly, so you gasped and cried out.

The oddest, most exhilarating and exhausting thing was this: he never quit. The music had no periods, no rests or endings; the poetry's beautiful sentence never ended; the line had no finish; the sculptured forms piled overhead, one into another without surcease. Who could breathe, in a world where rhythm itself had no periods?

It had taken me several minutes to understand what an extraordinary thing I was seeing. Rahm kept all that embellished space in mind at once. For another twenty minutes I watched the beauty unroll and grow more fantastic and unlikely before my eyes. Now Rahm brought the plane down slidingly, and just in time, for I thought I would snap from the effort to compass and remember the line's long intelligence; I could not add another curve. He brought the plane down on a far runway. After a pause, I saw him step out, an ordinary man, and make his way back to the terminal.

The show was over. It was late. Just as I turned from the runway, something caught my eye and made me laugh. It was a swallow, a blue-green swallow, having its own air show, apparently inspired by Rahm. The swallow climbed high over the runway, held its wings oddly, tipped them, and rolled down the air in loops. The inspired swallow. I always want to paint, too, after I see the Rembrandts. The blue-green swallow tumbled precisely, and caught itself and flew up again as if excited, and looped down again, the way swallows do, but tensely, holding its body carefully still. It was a stunt swallow.

I went home and thought about Rahm's performance that night, and the next day, and the next.

I had thought I knew my way around beauty a little bit. I knew I had devoted a good part of my life to it, memorizing poetry and focusing my attention on complexity of rhythm in particular, on force, movement, repetition, and surprise, in both poetry and prose. Now I had stood among dandelions between two asphalt runways in Bellingham, Washington, and begun learning about beauty. Even the Boston Museum of Fine Arts was never more inspiriting than

this small northwestern airport on this time-killing Sunday afternoon in June. Nothing on earth is more gladdening than knowing
we must roll up our sleeves and move back the boundaries of the
humanly possible once more.

Later I flew with Dave Rahm; he took me up. A generous geographer, Dick Smith, at Western Washington University, arranged it,
and came along. Rahm and Dick Smith were colleagues at the
university. In geology, Rahm had published two books and many
articles. Rahm was handsome in a dull sort of way, blunt-featured,
wide-jawed, wind-burned, keen-eyed, and taciturn. As anyone would
expect. He was forty. He wanted to show me the Cascade Mountains; these enormous peaks, only fifty miles from the coast, rise
over nine thousand feet; they are heavily glaciated. Whatcom
County has more glaciers than the lower forty-eight states combined; the Cascades make the Rocky Mountains look like hills.
Mount Baker is volcanic, like most Cascade peaks. That year,
Mount Baker was acting up. Even from my house at the shore I
could see, early in the morning on clear days, volcanic vapor rise
near its peak. Often the vapor made a cloud that swelled all morning and hid the snows. Every day the newspapers reported on Baker's activity: Would it blow? (A few years later, Mount St. Helens
did blow.)

Rahm was not flying his trick biplane that day, but a faster enclosed plane, a single-engine Cessna. We flew from a bumpy grass
airstrip near my house, out over the coast and inland. There was
coastal plain down there, but we could not see it for clouds. We
were over the clouds at five hundred feet and inside them too,
heading for an abrupt line of peaks we could not see. I gave up on
everything, the way you do in airplanes; it was out of my hands.
Every once in a while Rahm saw a peephole in the clouds and
buzzed over for a look. "That's Larsen's pea farm," he said, or
"That's Nooksack Road," and he changed our course with a heave.

When we got to the mountains, he slid us along Mount Baker's
flanks sideways.

Our plane swiped at the mountain with a roar. I glimpsed a
windshield view of dirty snow traveling fast. Our shaking, swooping belly seemed to graze the snow. The wings shuddered; we
peeled away and the mountain fell back and the engines whined.

We felt flung, because we were in fact flung; parts of our faces and internal organs trailed pressingly behind on the curves. We came back for another pass at the mountain, and another. We dove at the snow headlong like suicides; we jerked up, down, or away at the last second, so late we left our hearts, stomachs, and lungs behind. If I forced myself to hold my heavy head up against the G's,* and to raise my eyelids, heavy as barbells, and to notice what I saw, I could see the wrinkled green crevasses cracking the glaciers' snow.

Pitching snow filled all the windows, and shapes of dark rock. I had no notion which way was up. Everything was black or gray or white except the fatal crevasses; everything made noise and shook. I felt my face smashed sideways and saw rushing abstractions of snow in the windshield. Patches of cloud obscured the snow fleetingly. We straightened out, turned, and dashed at the mountainside for another pass, which we made, apparently, on our ear, an inch or two away from the slope. Icefalls and cornices jumbled and fell away. If a commercial plane's black box, such as the FAA painstakingly recovers from crash sites, could store videotapes as well as pilots' last words, some videotapes would look like this: a mountainside coming up at the windows from all directions, ice and snow and rock filling the screen up close and screaming by.

Rahm was just being polite. His geographer colleague wanted to see the fissure on Mount Baker from which steam escaped. Everybody in Bellingham wanted to see that sooty fissure, as did every geologist in the country; no one on earth could fly so close to it as Rahm. He knew the mountain by familiar love and feel, like a face; he knew what the plane could do and what he dared to do.

When Mount Baker inexplicably let us go, he jammed us into cloud again and soon tilted. "The Sisters!" someone shouted, and I saw the windshield fill with red rock. This mountain looked infernal, a drear and sheer plane of lifeless rock. It was red and sharp; its gritty blades cut through the clouds at random. The mountain was quiet. It was in shade. Careening, we made sideways passes at these brittle peaks too steep for snow. Their rock was full of iron, somebody shouted at me then or later; the iron had rusted, so they were red. Later, when I was back on the ground, I recalled that,

---

*G's: A measure of gravitational force. — Ed.

from a distance, the two jagged peaks called the Twin Sisters looked translucent against the sky; they were sharp, tapered, and fragile as arrowheads.

I talked to Rahm. He was flying us out to the islands now. The islands were fifty or sixty miles away. Like many other people, I had picked Bellingham, Washington, by looking at an atlas. It was clear from the atlas that you could row in the salt water and see snow-covered mountains; you could scale a glaciated mountainside with an ice ax in August, skirting green crevasses two hundred feet deep, and look out on the islands in the sea. Now, in the air, the clouds had risen over us; dark forms lay on the glinting water. There was almost no color to the day, just blackened green and some yellow. I knew the islands were forested in dark Douglas firs the size of skyscrapers. Bald eagles scavenged on the beaches; robins the size of herring gulls sang in the clearings. We made our way out to the islands through the layer of air between the curving planet and its held, thick clouds.

"When I started trying to figure out what I was going to do with my life, I decided to become an expert on mountains. It wasn't much to be, it wasn't everything, but it was something. I was going to know everything about mountains from every point of view. So I started out in geography." Geography proved too pedestrian for Rahm, too concerned with "how many bushels of wheat an acre." So he ended up in geology. Smith had told me that geology departments throughout the country used Rahm's photographic slides — close-ups of geologic features from the air.

"I used to climb mountains. But you know, you can get a better feel for a mountain's power flying around it, flying all around it, than you can from climbing it tied to its side like a flea."

He talked about his flying performances. He thought of the air as a line, he said. "This end of the line, that end of the line — like a rope." He improvised. "I get a rhythm going and stick with it." While he was performing in a show, he paid attention, he said, to the lighting. He didn't play against the sun. That was all he said about what he did.

In aerobatic maneuvers, pilots pull about seven positive G's on some stunts and six negative G's on others. Some gyrations push; others pull. Pilots alternate the pressures carefully, so they do not gray out or black out.

Later I learned that some stunt pilots tune up by wearing gravity boots. These are boots made to hook over a doorway; wearing them, you hang in the doorway upside down. It must startle a pilot's children to run into their father or mother in the course of their home wanderings — the parents hanging wide-eyed, upside down in the doorway like a bat.

We were landing; here was the airstrip on Stuart Island — that island to which Ferrar Burn was dragged by the tide. We put down, climbed out of the plane, and walked. We wandered a dirt track through fields to a lee shore where yellow sandstone ledges slid into the sea. The salt chuck, people there called salt water. The sun came out. I caught a snake in the salt chuck; the snake, eighteen inches long, was swimming in the green shallows.

I had a survivor's elation. Rahm had found Mount Baker in the clouds before Mount Baker found the plane. He had wiped it with the fast plane like a cloth and we had lived. When we took off from Stuart Island and gained altitude, I asked if we could turn over — could we do a barrel roll? The plane was making a lot of noise, and Dick Smith did not hear any of this, I learned later. "Why not?" Rahm said, and added surprisingly, "It won't hurt the plane." Without ado he leaned on the wheel and the wing went down and we went somersaulting over it. We upended with a roar. We stuck to the plane's sides like flung paint. All the blood in my body bulged on my face; it piled between my skull and skin. Vaguely I could see the chrome sea twirling over Rahm's head like a baton, and the dark islands sliding down the skies like rain.

The G's slammed me into my seat like thugs and pinned me while my heart pounded and the plane turned over slowly and compacted each organ in turn. My eyeballs were newly spherical and full of heartbeats. I seemed to hear a crescendo; the wing rolled shuddering down the last 90 degrees and settled on the flat. There were the islands, admirably below us, and the clouds, admirably above. When I could breathe, I asked if we could do it again, and we did. He rolled the other way. The brilliant line of the sea slid up the side window bearing its heavy islands. Through the shriek of my blood and the plane's shakes I glimpsed the line of the sea over the windshield, thin as a spear. How in performance did Rahm keep track while his brain blurred and blood roared in his ears without ceasing? Every performance was a tour de force and a show of will, a *Machtspruch.*[*] I had seen the other stunt pilots straighten out after a trick or two; their blood could drop back and the planet simmer down. An Olympic gymnast, at peak form, strings out a line of spins ten stunts long across a mat, and is hard put to keep his footing at the end. Rahm endured much greater pressure on his faster spins using the plane's power, and he could spin in three dimensions and keep twirling till he ran out of sky room or luck.

When we straightened out, and had flown straightforwardly for ten minutes toward home, Dick Smith, clearing his throat, brought himself to speak. "What was that we did out there?"

"The barrel rolls?" Rahm said. "They were barrel rolls." He said nothing else. I looked at the back of his head; I could see the serious line of his cheek and jaw. He was in shirtsleeves, tanned, strong-wristed. I could not imagine loving him under any circumstance; he was alien to me, unfazed. He looked like GI Joe. He flew with that matter-of-fact, bored gesture pilots use. They click overhead switches and turn dials as if only their magnificent strength makes such dullness endurable. The half circle of wheel in their big hands looks like a toy they plan to crush in a minute; the wiggly stick the wheel mounts seems barely attached.

A crop-duster pilot in Wyoming told me the life expectancy of a crop-duster pilot is five years. They fly too low. They hit buildings and power lines. They have no space to fly out of trouble, and no space to recover from a stall. We were in Cody, Wyoming, out on the north fork of the Shoshone River. The crop duster had wakened me that morning flying over the ranch house and clearing my bedroom roof by half an inch. I saw the bolts on the wheel assembly a few feet from my face. He was spraying with pesticide the plain old grass. Over breakfast I asked him how long he had been dusting crops. "Four years," he said, and the figure stalled in the air between us for a moment. "You know you're going to die at it someday," he added. "We all know it. We accept that; it's part of it." I think now that, since the crop duster was in his twenties, he accepted only that he had to say such stuff; privately he counted on skewing the curve.

---

[*]***Machtspruch:*** German, meaning "power speech." — Ed.

I suppose Rahm knew the fact too. I do not know how he felt about it. "It's worth it," said the early French aviator Mermoz. He was Antoine de Saint-Exupéry's friend. "It's worth the final smashup."

Rahm smashed up in front of King Hussein, in Jordan, during a performance. The plane spun down and never came out of it; it nosedived into the ground and exploded. He bought the farm. I was living then with my husband out on that remote island in the San Juans, cut off from everything. Battery radios picked up the Canadian Broadcasting Company out of Toronto, half a continent away; island people would, in theory, learn if the United States blew up, but not much else. There were no newspapers. One friend got the Sunday *New York Times* by mail boat on the following Friday. He saved it until Sunday and had a party, every week; we all read the Sunday *Times* and no one mentioned that it was last week's.

One day, Paul Glenn's brother flew out from Bellingham to visit; he had a seaplane. He landed in the water in front of the cabin and tied up to our mooring. He came in for coffee, and he gave out news of this and that, and — Say, did we know that stunt pilot Dave Rahm had cracked up? In Jordan, during a performance: he never came out of a dive. He just dove right down into the ground, and his wife was there watching. "I saw it on CBS News last night." And then — with a sudden sharp look at my filling eyes — "What, did you know him?" But no, I did not know him. He took me up once. Several years ago. I admired his flying. I had thought that danger was the safest thing in the world, if you went about it right.

Later, I found a newspaper. Rahm was living in Jordan that year; King Hussein invited him to train the aerobatics team, the Royal Jordanian Falcons. He was also visiting professor of geology at the University of Jordan. In Amman that day he had been flying a Pitt Special, a plane he knew well. Katy Rahm, his wife of six months, was sitting beside Hussein in the viewing stands, with her daughter. Rahm died performing a Lomcevak combined with a tail slide and hammerhead. In a Lomcevak, the pilot brings the plane up on a slant and pirouettes. I had seen Rahm do this: the falling plane twirled slowly like a leaf. Like a ballerina, the plane seemed to hold its head back stiff in concentration at the music's slow, painful beauty. It was one of Rahm's favorite routines. Next the pilot flies straight up, stalls the plane, and slides down the air on his tail. He brings the nose down — the hammerhead — kicks the engine, and finishes with a low loop.

It is a dangerous maneuver at any altitude, and Rahm was doing it low. He hit the ground on the loop; the tail slide had left him no height. When Rahm went down, King Hussein dashed to the burning plane to pull him out, but he was already dead.

A few months after the air show, and a month after I had flown with Rahm, I was working at my desk near Bellingham, where I lived, when I heard a sound so odd it finally penetrated my concentration. It was the buzz of an airplane, but it rose and fell musically, and it never quit; the plane never flew out of earshot. I walked out on the porch and looked up: it was Rahm in the black and gold biplane, looping all over the air. I had been wondering about his performance flight: could it really have been so beautiful? It was, for here it was again. The little plane twisted all over the air like a vine. It trailed a line like a very long mathematical proof you could follow only so far, and then it lost you in its complexity. I saw Rahm flying high over the Douglas firs, and out over the water, and back over farms. The air was a fluid, and Rahm was an eel.

It was as if Mozart could move his body through his notes, and you could walk out on the porch, look up, and see him in periwig and breeches, flying around in the sky. You could hear the music as he dove through it; it streamed after him like a contrail.

I lost myself; standing on the firm porch, I lost my direction and reeled. My neck and spine rose and turned, so I followed the plane's line kinesthetically. In his open-cockpit black plane, Rahm demonstrated curved space. He slid down ramps of air, he vaulted and wheeled. He piled loops in heaps and praised height. He unrolled the scroll of air, extended it, and bent it into Möbius strips; he furled line in a thousand new ways, as if he were inventing a script and writing it in one infinitely recurring utterance until I thought the bounds of beauty must break.

From inside, the looping plane had sounded tinny, like a kazoo. Outside, the buzz rose and fell to the Doppler effect as the plane looped near or away. Rahm cleaved the sky like a prow and tossed out time left and right in his wake. He performed for forty minutes; then he headed the plane, as small as a wasp, back to the airport inland. Later I learned Rahm often practiced acrobatic flights over this shore. His idea was that if he lost control and was going to go down, he could ditch in the salt chuck, where no one else would get hurt.

If I had not turned two barrel rolls in an airplane, I might have fancied Rahm felt good up there, and playful. Maybe Jackson Pollock felt a sort of playfulness, in addition to the artist's usual deliberate and intelligent care. In my limited experience, painting, unlike writing, pleases the senses while you do it, and more while you do it than after it is done. Drawing lines with an airplane, unfortunately, tortures the senses. Jet bomber pilots black out. I knew Rahm felt as if his brain were bursting his eardrums, felt that if he let his jaws close as tight as centrifugal force pressed them, he would bite through his lungs.

"All virtue is a form of acting," Yeats said. Rahm deliberately turned himself into a figure. Sitting invisible at the controls of a distant airplane, he became the agent and the instrument of art and invention. He did not tell me how he felt when we spoke of his performance flying; he told me instead that he paid attention to how his plane and its line looked to the audience against the lighted sky. If he had noticed how he felt, he could not have done the work. Robed in his airplane, he was as featureless as a priest. He was lost in his figural aspect like an actor or a king. Of his flying, he had said only, "I get a rhythm and stick with it." In its reticence, this statement reminded me of Veronese's[*] "Given a large canvas, I enhanced it as I saw fit." But Veronese was ironic, and Rahm was not; he was as literal as an astronaut; the machine gave him tongue.

When Rahm flew, he sat down in the middle of art and strapped himself in. He spun it all around him. He could not see it himself. If he never saw it on film, he never saw it at all — as if Beethoven could not hear his final symphonies not because he was deaf but because he was inside the paper on which he wrote. Rahm must have felt it happen, that fusion of vision and metal, motion and idea. I think of this man as a figure, a college professor with a PhD upside down in the loud band of beauty. What are we here for? *Propter chorum*, the monks say: for the sake of the choir.

[*]**Veronese:** Paolo Veronese (1528–1588), famous Venetian painter. — Ed.

"Purity does not lie in separation from but in deeper penetration into the universe," Teilhard de Chardin* wrote. It is hard to imagine a deeper penetration into the universe than Rahm's last dive in his plane, or than his inexpressible wordless selfless line's inscribing the air and dissolving. Any other art may be permanent. I cannot recall one Rahm sequence. He improvised. If Christo† wraps a building or dyes a harbor, we join his poignant and fierce awareness that the work will be gone in days. Rahm's plane shed a ribbon in space, a ribbon whose end unraveled in memory while its beginning unfurled as surprise. He may have acknowledged that what he did could be called art, but it would have been, I think, only in the common misusage, which holds art to be the last extreme of skill. Rahm rode the point of the line to the possible; he discovered it and wound it down to show. He made his dazzling probe on the run. "The world is filled, and filled with the Absolute," Teilhard de Chardin wrote. "To see this is to be made free."

Reflections and Responses

1. How does Dillard establish a connection between stunt piloting and artistic performance? Identify the various moments in her essay when she makes such a connection. What do these moments have in common? What images do they share?

2. Note that Dillard doesn't wait until the very end of her essay to introduce Rahm's death. Why do you think she avoids this kind of climax? What advantage does this give her?

3. "The Stunt Pilot" also appears as an untitled chapter in Dillard's book *The Writing Life*. Why is this an appropriate context for the essay? What does the essay tell us about expression and composition?

*Teilhard de Chardin: Pierre Teilhard de Chardin (1881–1953), a noted paleontologist and Catholic priest whose most famous book, *The Phenomenon of Man*, attempts to bridge the gap between science and religion. — Ed.

†Christo: A contemporary Bulgarian artist known for staging spectacular environmental effects. — Ed.

BRIAN DOYLE

Joyas Voladoras

*Certain essays are composed like poetry, with a lyric intensity in which
every word, every phrase, and every image seems critical. Such essays are
usually quite short (often only a few paragraphs) since, for one thing, it is
extremely difficult to sustain such verbal intensity over many pages, and for
another, if extended too long, the style could become tiresome. Critics sometimes call such works "prose poems," suggesting that their prose style is en-
riched by such poetic characteristics as cadence and imagery. Attention to
the sound of the prose and its phrasal rhythms is crucial, as is metaphorical
originality. Suggestiveness of the theme is often favored over explicit statement. All of these literary characteristics can be seen in Brian Doyle's "Joyas
Voladoras" as he looks lyrically into matters of the heart ranging from hummingbirds to humans.*

Brian Doyle is the editor of Portland Magazine *at the University of Por-
tand, in Oregon. He is the author of five collections of essays, among them*
Spirited Men *(about writers and musicians, 2004) and* Leaping *(about
everything else, 2003). His most recent books are* The Wet Engine *(2005),
about the "muddle & music of hearts"; and* The Grail *(2006), about
a year in an Oregon vineyard. A collection of poems called* Epiphanies
& Elegies *was published in the fall of 2006 by Rowman and Littlefield.
"Joyas Voladoras"—which means "flying jewels," the name the first Spanish
explorers gave to hummingbirds—originally appeared in* The American
Scholar *and was selected by Susan Orlean for* The Best American
Essays 2005.

Consider the hummingbird for a long moment. A hummingbird's
heart beats ten times a second. A hummingbird's heart is the size of
a pencil eraser. A hummingbird's heart is a lot of the hummingbird.

Joyas voladoras, flying jewels, the first white explorers in the Americas called them, and the white men had never seen such creatures, for hummingbirds came into the world only in the Americas, nowhere else in the universe, more than three hundred species of them whirring and zooming and nectaring in hummer time zones nine times removed from ours, their hearts hammering faster than we could clearly hear if we pressed our elephantine ears to their infinitesimal chests.

Each one visits a thousand flowers a day. They can dive at sixty miles an hour. They can fly backward. They can fly more than five hundred miles without pausing to rest. But when they rest they come close to death: on frigid nights, or when they are starving, they retreat into torpor, their metabolic rate slowing to a fifteenth of their normal sleep rate, their hearts sludging nearly to a halt, barely beating, and if they are not soon warmed, if they do not soon find that which is sweet, their hearts grow cold, and they cease to be. Consider for a moment those hummingbirds who did not open their eyes again today, this very day, in the Americas: bearded helmetcrests and booted racket-tails, violet-tailed sylphs and violet-capped woodnymphs, crimson topazes and purple-crowned fairies, red-tailed comets and amethyst woodstars, rainbow-bearded thornbills and glittering-bellied emeralds, velvet-purple coronets and golden-bellied star-frontlets, fiery-tailed awlbills and Andean hillstars, spatuletails and pufflegs,* each the most amazing thing you have never seen, each thunderous wild heart the size of an infant's fingernail, each mad heart silent, a brilliant music stilled.

Hummingbirds, like all flying birds but more so, have incredible enormous immense ferocious metabolisms. To drive those metabolisms they have racecar hearts that eat oxygen at an eyepopping rate. Their hearts are built of thinner, leaner fibers than ours. Their arteries are stiffer and more taut. They have more mitochondria in their heart muscles — anything to gulp more oxygen. Their hearts are

---

*A list of some species of hummingbirds; the majority of hummingbirds are found in the tropics. Only one species is commonly seen in the eastern region of the United States: the ruby-throated hummingbird. — Ed.

stripped to the skin for the war against gravity and inertia, the mad search for food, the insane idea of flight. The price of their ambition is a life closer to death; they suffer more heart attacks and aneurysms and ruptures than any other living creature. It's expensive to fly. You burn out. You fry the machine. You melt the engine. Every creature on earth has approximately two billion heartbeats to spend in a lifetime. You can spend them slowly, like a tortoise, and live to be two hundred years old, or you can spend them fast, like a hummingbird, and live to be two years old.

The biggest heart in the world is inside the blue whale. It weighs more than seven tons. It's as big as a room. It *is* a room, with four chambers. A child could walk around in it, head high, bending only to step through the valves. The valves are as big as the swinging doors in a saloon. This house of a heart drives a creature a hundred feet long. When this creature is born it is twenty feet long and weighs four tons. It is waaaaay bigger than your car. It drinks a hundred gallons of milk from its mama every day and gains two hundred pounds a day, and when it is seven or eight years old it endures an unimaginable puberty and then it essentially disappears from human ken, for next to nothing is known of the mating habits, travel patterns, diet, social life, language, social structure, diseases, spirituality, wars, stories, despairs, and arts of the blue whale. There are perhaps ten thousand blue whales in the world, living in every ocean on earth, and of the largest mammal who ever lived we know nearly nothing. But we know this: the animals with the largest hearts in the world generally travel in pairs, and their penetrating moaning cries, their piercing yearning tongue, can be heard underwater for miles and miles.

Mammals and birds have hearts with four chambers. Reptiles and turtles have hearts with three chambers. Fish have hearts with two chambers. Insects and mollusks have hearts with one chamber. Worms have hearts with one chamber, although they may have as many as eleven single-chambered hearts. Unicellular bacteria have no hearts at all; but even they have fluid eternally in motion, washing from one side of the cell to the other, swirling and whirling. No living being is without interior liquid motion. We all churn inside.

So much held in a heart in a lifetime. So much held in a heart in a day, an hour, a moment. We are utterly open with no one, in the end — not mother and father, not wife or husband, not lover, not child, not friend. We open windows to each but we live alone in the house of the heart. Perhaps we must. Perhaps we could not bear to be so naked, for fear of a constantly harrowed heart. When young we think there will come one person who will savor and sustain us always; when we are older we know this is the dream of a child, that all hearts finally are bruised and scarred, scored and torn, repaired by time and will, patched by force of character, yet fragile and rickety forevermore, no matter how ferocious the defense and how many bricks you bring to the wall. You can brick up your heart as stout and tight and hard and cold and impregnable as you possibly can and down it comes in an instant, felled by a woman's second glance, a child's apple breath, the shatter of glass in the road, the words "I have something to tell you," a cat with a broken spine dragging itself into the forest to die, the brush of your mother's papery ancient hand in the thicket of your hair, the memory of your father's voice early in the morning echoing from the kitchen where he is making pancakes for his children.

Reflections and Responses

1. A common poetic device used often is prose is known as *anaphora.* In prose it is often seen as the repetition of the same words (sometimes with slight variations) at the start of a sentence or clause. Try underlining the use of anaphora in Doyle's short essay. How many examples do you find? Select one sequence of examples and try to explain the effect this device has on your response to the essay.

2. Why do you think Doyle contrasts the hearts of hummingbirds and blue whales? What physical details does he introduce to make you aware of their relative sizes? To what extent do his descriptive details of both creatures' hearts surprise you? What expressions do you find especially original or imaginative?

3. What happens when you reach the final paragraph? In what ways does an essay that at first appeared to be about creatures great and small suddenly turn into an essay about human nature? What has happened to the word *heart*? Do you think "Joyas Voladoras" could be considered a personal essay, even a private one? How would you account for all the specific details that the author introduces in the concluding paragraph apparently to support a generalization about the human heart?

MARSHALL JON FISHER

Memoria ex Machina

Why do we remember some things so vividly and completely forget others? And why is it that some of the things we recall in amazing detail played only a trivial role in our lives compared with others far more important that we only dimly recall? In "Memoria ex Machina," Marshall Jon Fisher examines the way his memory seems fixated on the material objects of his youth—a Seiko watch, a clock radio, a 1973 green Datsun, a Walkman headset. Why, he wonders in this nostalgic, reflective essay, does he picture these things in such detail? "What does it mean," he asks, "that some of my fondest memories are of technology? Have we begun our slide toward the ineluctable merging of man and machine?"

Marshall Jon Fisher has written on a wide range of topics for The Atlantic Monthly, *and his work has also appeared in* Double-Take, Harper's Magazine, Discover, *and other magazines. He is the coauthor (with David E. Fisher) of* Tube: The Invention of Television *(1996) and* Strangers in the Night: A Brief History of Life on Other Worlds *(1998). "Memoria ex Machina" first appeared in* DoubleTake *and was selected by Anne Fadiman for* The Best American Essays 2003.

It was a silver Seiko watch with a clasp that folded like a map and snapped shut. The stainless-steel casing was a three-dimensional octagon with distinct edges, too thick and ponderous, it seems now, for a thirteen-year-old. Four hands — hour, minute, second, and alarm — swept around a numberless metallic-blue face. I received it for my bar mitzvah; a quarter century later I can, in my mind, fingernail the button just one click to set the alarm hand — not too far, or I'll change the time — and pull out the other, obliquely positioned button to turn on the alarm. When the hour hand finally overcame the angle between itself and the alarm hand, a soft, deep mechanical buzzing would ensue — a pleasant hum long since obliterated by hordes of digital beeps. I haven't seen my watch for twenty years, but I can still hear that buzz, feel its vibrations in my wrist.

What I cannot remember is the timbre or inflection of my sister's voice from that time. She flitted in and out of view, appearing in the gaps between high school, club meetings, and dates. I can't even recall her at the dinner table with my parents, my brother, and me, though she must have been there most of the time.

After she and my brother left for college, when I was in high school, I spent countless hours lying in bed listening to my clock radio. I can still see the burnt-amber numerals and the way their discrete line segments would metamorphose each minute. The tuning knob on the right-hand side, and the way it resisted torque as you approached either end of the dial, remain as clear to me as the remote controls of my new DVD player. I was listening in the dark to a Monday-night Miami Dolphins game (home, against the New England Patriots) when the radio broadcast broke to the announcement that John Lennon had been shot. I heard Bruce Springsteen singing "Racing in the Street" for the first time on that radio, along with other songs I'd rather forget, like Queen's "We Are the Champions," dedicated one night by a local disc jockey to some high school basketball team. I remember the golden light from within illuminating the frequency band, and I remember tuning by sound for years after that light burned out.

Yet I can't remember what time I went to bed as an adolescent, or anything else about my nocturnal ritual. Did I say goodnight and then go off to my room, or did my parents come in to say goodnight after I was in bed? I don't know. But I do know, decades after it found oblivion, exactly how to set that radio to play for half an hour and then shut off.

The memory of my quotidian habits of those years has been washed away by a thousand new habits, just as my sister's teenage presence has given way to her succeeding selves. In his novel

Vertigo, W. G. Sebald[*] paraphrases Stendhal's[†] advice "not to purchase engravings of fine views and prospects seen on one's travels,
since before very long they will displace our memories completely,
indeed one might say they destroy them." "For instance," Sebald
continues, "[Stendhal] could no longer recall the wonderful *Sistine
Madonna* he had seen in Dresden, try as he might, because Müller's
engraving after it had become superimposed in his mind." In the
same way, as the people in our lives grow older, their new faces,
voices, and demeanors replace those of their former selves in our
memory. Yet the new technology that continually replaces old machines fails to have the same effect, because the individuals — the
radios, wristwatches, and automobiles that inhabited our lives —
never change. That chrome "sleep knob" on my clock radio still
looks exactly the same, wherever it may now rest in the center of
some unknowable mountainous landfill.

"The past," wrote Proust,[‡] "is hidden somewhere outside the
realm, beyond the reach, of intellect, in some material object (in
the sensation which that material object will give us) which we do
not suspect." And just as the taste of the famous *petite madeleine*
awakens in Proust's narrator an entire vanished world — the memories of his childhood vacations in Combray — the thought of my
old Walkman resurrects my postcollegiate existence. It was a red
and black 1985 model, and I've never seen another just like it. The
tendency of Sony to constantly bring out new designs lent an air of
individuality to one's Walkman, but it also caused successful designs to get lost in the shuffle. Mine was a particularly pleasing construction — sleek, rounded, with an analog radio dial and push

---

[*]**W. G. Sebald** (1944–2001). German novelist, essayist, and literary scholar who
came into prominence in the 1990s with the English translations of *The Emigrants*
(1996), *The Rings of Saturn* (1998), and *Vertigo* (1999). — Ed.

[†]**Stendhal** is the pen name of the French novelist Marie-Henri Beyle (1783–1842).
The author of a number of travel books, he is best known today for his classic novel
The Red and the Black (1830). — Ed.

[‡]**Marcel Proust** (1871–1922), one of the most influential novelists of the twentieth
century, is the author of the seven-volume series *Remembrance of Things Past* (also
known as *In Search of Last Time*). The reference here is to a famous moment of "involuntary memory" (Proust's term) that occurs in the opening chapter of the first
novel when the narrator's memories are vividly evoked by the odor of a certain
pastry (*petite madeleine*) that he loved as a boy. — Ed.

buttons that made you feel that you were *doing* something. Unlike many other models, it also worked properly for years, providing the soundtrack to a decade of my life. I can summon the physical memory of squeezing the Play button, the middle of three oblong pieces of silver metal, and suddenly I am back in Munich in 1986, listening to the new Bob Dylan album on a brown threadbare corduroy sofa in my Goethestrasse apartment. Or I'm driving eight hours down I-95 to visit a girlfriend, listening to tapes on the Walkman because my Rabbit's stereo has been stolen. Or I'm riding the Amtrak between New York and Boston, listening to Indigo Girls while the autumn leaves blow by the window. I can even tell you the album and track that unwound on the tape, visible through the tape player's window, in that specific recollection. I have no idea why that moment should survive in my mind, but the red and black Walkman is as much a part of that moment as the music itself, and the leaves, and the dark, sheltering train.

Another machine still lingering in the afterlife: the 1973 Datsun 1200 my dad handed down to me to run into the ground, which I eventually did. A bottom-of-the-line economy model, "the Green Machine," as my friends called it, looked like a vehicle out of Dr. Seuss, but it always started and got forty miles to the gallon — a cause for nostalgia, indeed, in these simmering, gas-guzzling days. I can still see the schematic four-gear diagram on the head of the stick shift and feel the knob — and the worn transmission of the gears — in my right hand. The radio had five black cuboid push buttons for preset stations: the two on the left each sported AM in white indentations, and the other three said FM. It took almost the entire ten-minute ride to school for the anemic defogger to rid the windshield of its early-morning dew. One day that teary outward view was replaced, at forty miles an hour, by green. A rusted latch had finally given out, and the wind had opened the hood and slapped it all the way back against the glass. Luckily, the glass didn't break, and I could see enough through the rust holes to avoid a collision as I braked. Whenever the friend I drove to school was not ready to go, her father would come out and wait with me, looking the Green Machine up and down and shaking his head.

What does it mean that some of my fondest memories are of technology? Have we begun our slide toward the ineluctable merging of man and machine? Are Walkman headphones in the ears the first step toward a computer chip implanted in the brain? Or is it merely that inanimate objects, whether Citizen Kane's wooden "Rosebud" or my handheld electronic circuitry, by virtue of their obliviousness to the passage of time, seize our longing? As photographs do, these objects capture particular periods of our lives. The sense memory of turning that clock-radio knob, or shifting that gear stick, fixes the moment in time as well as any photograph. Just as we painstakingly fit photos into albums or, in the new age, organize them into computer folders and make digital copies for safekeeping, so I hang on to the impression of a stainless-steel wristwatch that once applied a familiar force of weight to my left wrist.

(Where have they gone, these mechanisms of my youth? The Datsun was hauled off for parts. The clock radio and the Walkman no doubt were tossed without a second thought when they no longer functioned properly. But the Seiko? Who would throw out a fine watch that, to my recollection, never broke? My mother swears she wouldn't have. Spring cleaning is not exactly my father's pastime. Could a watch, along with its deep blue case with the silvery embossed square border, vanish into time itself?)

Of course, my memory of these objects may be inaccurate. Were I to come upon my old clock radio, wrapped in old T-shirts inside a threadbare leather overnight bag in the attic, the sensation might be like that felt on entering a high school reunion and being jolted by the discrepancy between the memory of old friends and their current reality. In this case the object has not aged, but the memory has. In his wonderful book-length essay *U and I*, Nicholson Baker* practices what he calls "memory criticism": he records his impressions of John Updike's works without allowing himself to reread them. When he does go back to the texts to check, Baker finds that his memories of many passages, so emblazoned upon his mind, are imperfect. He fashions an argument around a remembered line from a poem, discovers that the actual poem does not

---

Nicholson Baker: The award-winning contemporary novelist and essayist, whose *U and I: A True Story* (1991) — an experiment in literary criticism — is a personal account of the author's fascination with the works of the American novelist John Updike. — Ed.

support the argument, and finishes off the argument anyway. A story remembered fondly for its metaphor likening a character's sick stomach to "an unprepossessing tuber" turns out not to contain the treasured trope. Baker remembers Updike making a brilliant comparison between "a strange interruption in his act of signature, between the *p* and the *d*," and his verbal stuttering — a comparison that had never in fact been made.

Even Nabokov,* that grand master of recollection, with a self-ascribed "almost pathological keenness of the retrospective faculty," is fallible. In the first version of his autobiography, *Speak, Memory*, he describes his family coat of arms as depicting two bears holding up a chessboard. Later, the chess-loving author is chagrined to discover that the bears are lions, and that they support a knight's shield comprising "only one sixteenth of a checkerboard."

So perhaps the clock radio is better off in oblivion. Unearthed, it might strike me as simply a cheap J. C. Penney's item from the 1970s — hardly a golden age for design. Now, for better or worse, holding the object in my hands might remind me of the bored loneliness of the years I spent steering its tuning knob, just as Baker feared being "disappointed by the immediate context of a phrase [of Updike's he] loved, when the context was now hazy and irrelevant."

Once, these humanly flawed recollections were the only means we had of reconstructing the past. And even though our selective memory may have been salubrious, we yearned to possess the past more completely. Now we have created the technology to satisfy our longing. Only machines — tape recorders, cameras, video cameras — can accurately preserve the details of our former selves, of our loved ones' younger faces, of our long-gone possessions. Nostalgia, even for machines, is bolstered by machines of nostalgia.

I am typing this on a Macintosh G4 Powerbook. Will the thought of this laptop someday conjure up such piquant memories? As much as the recollection of my first computer, a 1985 Kaypro I received for

*Vladimir Nabokov (1899–1977): The world-acclaimed Russian novelist is best known in America for *Lolita* (1955); his autobiography, *Speak, Memory*, appeared in 1967. — Ed.

college graduation? It was the first "portable" computer — a thirty-pound metal box the size of a small suitcase, with a keyboard that detached from one end. I can still feel the power switch on the right side of the back, where I reached to flick it on thousands of times. The green glow of the characters on screen, the five-and-a-half-inch floppy disks that had to be inserted in order to boot up or run Wordstar, even the control-K commands that brought up various menus — they all seem like the markings of a bygone era, even as they retain an intimate immediacy.

Yet computers, while they have probably replaced the automobile and the television as the most dominating technological feature of our daily lives, seem to have reached a uniformity — as well as a dismayingly short lifespan — that may weaken their nostalgic potential. This laptop isn't very different from past laptops, and I've gone through a succession of desktop computers with almost identical exteriors. I feel little nostalgia for my PCs of the early 1990s. It's hard to get choked up about the fact that a particular box packed only twenty megabytes.

Perhaps, though, this very act of typing is what will linger one day in my mind's reliquary. Voice-recognition software is pounding at the gates; videomail seems every day more feasible. How much longer will our computers even have keyboards? Typing may someday survive only as another sense memory. A writer, while composing with his voice, will still tap his fingers on the desk like an amputee scratching a wooden leg. Rather than the ghost of a particular machine, it will be this metacarpal tapdance, an apparition of the way we used to express language, that will haunt him.

Reflections and Responses

1. What contrast in the essay's opening paragraphs does the author make between what he remembers and what he doesn't? Why is this contrast significant? How does it eventually tie in with a larger theme?

2. Note Fisher's references to quotations from the novelists W. G. Sebald, Marcel Proust, Nicholson Baker, and Vladimir Nabokov.

What do the citations all have in common? How do they each contribute to Fisher's essay?

3. The essay moves from Fisher's boyhood memories to a larger point about technology. Explain whether or not you think this movement is justified — that is, do you think Fisher persuades us that his personal experiences are common enough to warrant a generalization about human memory and technology?

KITTY BURNS FLOREY

Sister Bernadette's Barking Dog

It's said that we live in an increasingly visual culture, surrounded by imagery everywhere we turn. Our phones now have cameras; our computer screen is a collage of icons and flashing screen savers; our information often comes in colorful layouts and graphical formats. Yet one form of visualization has disappeared: We no longer picture sentences. The days are long gone, as Kitty Burns Florey reminds us in "Sister Bernadette's Barking Dog," when elementary school students learned the rules of grammar and parts of speech through the use of visual diagrams. "The diagram," Florey vividly remembers, "was a bit like art, a bit like mathematics. It was much more than words uttered or words written: it was a picture of language."

Kitty Burns Florey is the author of nine novels, most recently Solos *(2004) and* Souvenir of Cold Springs *(2001). Her short stories and essays have been published in the* New York Times, Harper's Magazine, The North American Review, The Greensboro Review, *and* House Beautiful. *"Sister Bernadette's Barking Dog" was reprinted from Harper's Magazine (a version also appeared in* The Vocabula Review*) and was selected by Susan Orlean for* The Best American Essays 2005.

Diagramming sentences is one of those lost skills, like darning socks or playing the sackbut, that no one seems to miss. Invented, or at least codified, in an 1877 text called *Higher Lessons in English,* by Alonzo Reed and Brainerd Kellogg, it swept through American public schools like the measles, and was embraced by teachers as the way to reform students who were engaged in "the cold-blooded murder of the English tongue" (to take Henry

Higgins* slightly out of context). By promoting the beautifully logical rules of syntax, diagramming would root out evils like "it's me" and "I ain't got none," until everyone wrote like Ralph Waldo Emerson, or at least James Fenimore Cooper.

In my own youth, many years after 1877, diagramming was still serious business. I learned it in the sixth grade from Sister Bernadette. I can still see her: a tiny nun with a sharp pink nose, confidently drawing a dead-straight horizontal line like a highway across the blackboard, flourishing her chalk in the air at the end of it, her veil flipping out behind her as she turned back to the class. "We begin," she said, "with a straight line." And then, in her firm and saintly script, she put words on the line, a noun and a verb — probably something like *dog barked*. Between the words she drew a short vertical slash, bisecting the line. Then she made a road that forked off at an angle — a short country lane under the word *dog*— and on it she wrote *The*.

That was it: subject, predicate, and the little modifying article that civilized the sentence — all of it made into a picture that was every bit as clear and informative as an actual portrait of a beagle in mid-woof. The thrilling part was that this was a picture not of the animal but of the words that stood for the animal and its noises. It was a representation of something both concrete and abstract. The diagram was a bit like art, a bit like mathematics. It was much more than words uttered or words written: it was a picture of language.

I was hooked. So, it seems, were many of my contemporaries. Among the myths that have attached themselves to memories of being educated in the fifties is the notion that activities like diagramming sentences (along with memorizing poems and adding long columns of figures without a calculator) were pointless and monotonous. I thought diagramming was fun, and most of my friends who were

---

*Henry Higgins is the leading character in George Bernard Shaw's famous play *Pygmalion* (1912), which was made into the popular musical comedy *My Fair Lady*. A phonetics professor, Higgins wins a bet that he can transform Liza Doolittle's accent into such perfect-sounding English that she could be mistaken for a duchess. — Ed.

subjected to it look back with varying degrees of delight. Some of us were better at it than others, but it was considered a kind of treat, a game that broke up the school day. You took a sentence, threw it against the wall, picked up the pieces, and put them together again, slotting each word into its pigeonhole. When you got it right, you made order and sense out of what we used all the time and took for granted: sentences.

Gertrude Stein,* of all people, was a great fan of diagramming. "I really do not know that anything has ever been more exciting than diagramming sentences," she wrote in the early 1930s. "I like the feeling the everlasting feeling of sentences as they diagram themselves."

In my experience they didn't exactly diagram themselves; they had to be coaxed, if not wrestled. But — the feeling the everlasting feeling: if Gertrude Stein wasn't just riffing on the words, the love-song sound of them, she must have meant the glorious definiteness of the process. I remember loving the look of the sentences, short or long, once they were tidied into diagrams — the curious maplike shapes they made, the way the words settled primly along their horizontals like houses on a road, the way some roads were culs-de-sac and some were long meandering interstates with many exit ramps and scenic lookouts. And the clarity of it all, the ease with which — once they were laid open, their secrets exposed — those sentences could be comprehended.

On a more trivial level, part of the fun was being summoned to the blackboard to show off. There you stood, chalk in hand, while, with a glint in her eye, Sister Bernadette read off an especially tricky sentence. Compact, fastidious handwriting was an asset. A good spatial sense helped you arrange things so that the diagram didn't end up with the words jammed together against the edge of the black-board like commuters in a subway car. The trick was to think fast, write fast, and not get rattled if you failed in the attempt.

As we became more proficient, the tasks got harder. There was great appeal in the Shaker-like simplicity of sentences like *The dog chased a rabbit* (subject, predicate, direct object), with their plain, no-nonsense diagrams:

*Gertrude Stein (1874–1946) was a prolific novelist and essayist known for her experimental and innovative prose. She wrote extensively on the subject of composition and today is perhaps best known for her best-selling book, *The Autobiography of Alice B. Toklas* (1933). — Ed.

But there were also lovable subtleties, like the way the line that set off a predicate adjective slanted back like a signpost toward the subject it modified:

Or the thorny rosebush created by diagramming a prepositional phrase modifying another prepositional phrase:

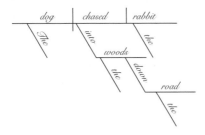

Or the elegant absence of the preposition when using an indirect object, indicated by a short road with no house on it:

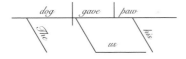

The missing preposition — in this case *to*— could also be placed on that road in parentheses, but this always seemed to me a clumsy solution, right up there with explaining a pun. In a related situation, however, the void where the subject of an imperative sentence would go was better filled, to my mind, with the graphic and slightly menacing parenthesized pronoun, as in:

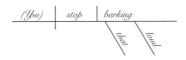

Questions were a special case. For diagramming, they had to be turned inside out, the way a sock has to be eased onto a foot: *What is the dog doing?* transformed into the more dramatic *The dog is doing what?*

Mostly we diagrammed sentences out of a grammar book, but sometimes we were assigned the task of making up our own, taking pleasure in coming up with wild Proustian* wanderings that — kicking and screaming — had to be corralled, harnessed, and made to trot into the barn in neat rows.

Part of the fun of diagramming sentences was that it didn't matter what they said. The dog could bark, chew gum, play chess — in the world of diagramming, sentences weren't about meaning so much as they were about subject, predicate, object, and their various dependents or modifiers. If they were diagrammed properly, they always illustrated correct syntax, no matter how silly their content. We hung those sentences out like a wash until we understood every piece of them. We could see for ourselves the difference between *who* and *whom.* We knew what an adverb was, and we knew where in a sentence it went, and why it went there. We were aware of dangling modifiers because we could see them, quite literally, dangle.

Today, diagramming is not exactly dead, but for many years it has been in sharp decline. This is partly because diagramming sentences seems to double the task of the student, who has to learn a whole new set of rules — where does that pesky line go, and which way does it slant?— in order to illustrate a set of rules that, in fact, has been learned pretty thoroughly simply by immersion in the

---

*Proustian: A reference to the prose style of the influential French novelist Marcel Proust (1871–1922), who was known for his fluid and meandering sentences. — Ed.

language from birth. It's only the subtleties that are difficult — *who* versus *whom*, adjective versus adverb, *it's I* versus *it's me* — and most of those come from the mostly doomed attempt, in the early days of English grammar, to stuff English into the well-made boxes of Latin and Greek, which is something like forcing a struggling cat into the carrier for a trip to the vet.

Another problem is that teachers — and certainly students — have become more willing to accept the idea that the sentences that can be popped into a diagram aren't always sentences anyone wants to write. One writer friend of mine says that she disliked diagramming because it meant "forcing sentences into conformity." And indeed language can be more supple and interesting than the patterns that perfect syntax forces on it. An attempt to diagram a sentence by James Joyce, or one by Henry James (whose style H. G. Wells compared so memorably to "a magnificent but painful hippopotamus resolved at any cost . . . upon picking up a pea"), will quickly demonstrate the limitations of Sister Bernadette's methods. Diagramming may have taught us to write more correctly — and maybe even to think more logically — but I don't think anyone would claim that it taught us to write well. And besides, any writer knows that the best way to learn to write good sentences is not to diagram them but to read them.

Still, like pocket watches and Gilbert and Sullivan operas, diagramming persists, alternately reviled and championed by linguists and grammarians. It can be found in university linguistics courses and on the Web sites of a few diehard enthusiasts. There are teachers' guides, should any teacher want one; it's taught in ESL courses and in progressive private schools. There's a video, *English Grammar: The Art of Diagramming Sentences*, that features a very 1950s-looking teacher named Miss Lamb working at a blackboard. There's even a computer program, apparently, that diagrams.

Sometimes, on a slow subway or a boring car trip, I mentally diagram a sentence, just as I occasionally try to remember the declension of *hic, haec, hoc* or the words to the second verse of "The Star-Spangled Banner." I have no illusions that diagramming sentences in my youth did anything for me, practically speaking. But in an occasional fit of nostalgia, I like to bring back those golden afternoons when

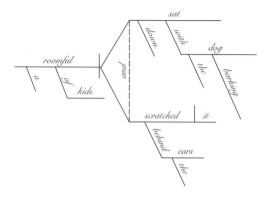

Reflections and Responses

1. Note the author's use of figurative language throughout the essay. For example, she recalls Sister Bernadete "confidently drawing a dead-straight horizontal line like a highway across the blackboard. . . ." Why is the horizontal line likened to a "highway"? Why is it an appropriate metaphor? How does the author continue this metaphor throughout the essay?

2. Besides the extensive use of figurative language, what other elements does Florey employ to emphasize the role of visualization? How does the idea of art and perception enter into her love of diagramming? How does it help her appreciate the architecture of a sentence?

3. After reading Kitty Burns Florey's nostalgic tribute to diagramming, do you think diagramming is an effective method for learning English grammar that ought to be restored? Why or why not? What advantages do you see in learning to diagram? What are the limitations of this method? In what ways does Florey cover both the advantages and the limitations in her essay? Can you restore her final sentence to the way it would have originally read had she not diagrammed it?

IAN FRAZIER

A Lovely Sort of Lower Purpose

In the middle of the eighteenth century, the great English essayist Samuel
Johnson regularly published a series of essays known as The Idler. *The*
title was carefully chosen; from Montaigne on, essayists have traditionally
cultivated a leisurely pace and written many pieces in praise of idleness or
what in today's terms would be called "hanging out" and "fooling
around." In "A Lovely Sort of Lower Purpose," Ian Frazier revisits this
time-tested topic and, in his inimitable fashion, celebrates the virtues of
doing nothing. Frazier warns us, however, that this virtue is rapidly declin-
ing as our restless society continually finds ways to make everything busy,
useful, and purposeful. As Frazier suggests, the terrible question grown-ups
often ask children, "What are you doing?" now haunts us all.

Besides several collections of humorous essays and two award-winning
books of nonfiction, Family *(1994) and* Great Plains *(1989), Ian Fra-*
zier has published On the Rez *(1999), a look at life on a reservation;*
The Fish's Eye *(2002), a collection of his fishing essays; and* Gone to
New York: Adventures in the City, *a collection of his essays on New*
York City and environs. *His writing has appeared in* The New Yorker,
Outside, The Atlantic Monthly, *and many other magazines. Frazier*
was the guest editor of The Best American Essays 1997. *"A Lovely Sort*
of Lower Purpose" originally appeared in Outside *magazine and was*
selected by Edward Hoagland for The Best American Essays 1999.

As kids, my friends and I spent a lot of time out in the woods. "The
woods" was our part-time address, destination, purpose, and excuse. If I went to a friend's house and found him not at home, his
mother might say, "Oh, he's out in the woods," with a tone of airy
acceptance. It's similar to the tone people sometimes use nowadays

to tell me that someone I'm looking for is on the golf course or at the hairdresser's or at the gym, or even "away from his desk." The combination of vagueness and specificity in the answer gives a sense of somewhere romantically incommunicado. I once attended an awards dinner at which Frank Sinatra was supposed to appear, and when he didn't, the master of ceremonies explained that Frank had called to say he was "filming on location." Ten-year-olds suffer from a scarcity of fancy-sounding excuses to do whatever they feel like for a while. For us, saying we were "out in the woods" worked just fine.

We sometimes told ourselves that what we were doing in the woods was exploring. Exploring was a more prominent idea back then than it is today. History, for example, seemed to be mostly about explorers, and the semirural part of Ohio where we lived still had a faint recollection of being part of the frontier. At the town's two high schools, the sports teams were the Explorers and the Pioneers. Our explorations, though, seemed to have less system than the historic kind: something usually came up along the way. Say we began to cross one of the little creeks plentiful in the second-growth forests we frequented and found that all the creek's moisture had somehow become a shell of milk-white ice about eight inches above the now-dry bed. No other kind of ice is as satisfying to break. The search for the true meridian would be postponed while we spent the afternoon breaking the ice, stomping it underfoot by the furlong, and throwing its bigger pieces like Frisbees to shatter in excellent, war-movie-type fragmentation among the higher branches of the trees.

Stuff like that — throwing rocks at a fresh mudflat to make craters, shooting frogs with slingshots, making forts, picking blackberries, digging in what we were briefly persuaded was an Indian burial mound — occupied much of our time in the woods. Our purpose there was a higher sort of un-purpose, a free-form aimlessness that would be beyond me now. Once as we tramped for miles along Tinker's Creek my friend Kent told me the entire plot of two Bob Hope movies, *The Paleface* and *Son of Paleface*, which he had just seen on a double bill. The joke-filled monotony of his synopsis went well with the soggy afternoon, the muddy water, the endless tangled brush. (Afterward, when I saw the movies themselves, I found a lot to prefer in Kent's version.) The woods were ideal for those trains of thought that involved tedium and brooding. Often when I went by myself I would climb a tree and just sit. I could list a hundred pointless things we did in the woods. Climbing trees, though, was a common one. Often we got "lost" and had to climb a tree to get our bearings. If you read a story in which someone does that successfully, be skeptical; the topmost branches are usually too skinny to hold weight, and we could never climb high enough to see anything except other trees. There were four or five trees that we visited regularly — tall beeches, easy to climb and comfortable to sit in. We spent hours at a time in trees, afflicting the best perches with so many carved-in names, hearts, arrows, and funny sayings from the comic strips that we ran out of room for more.

It was in a tree, too, that our days of fooling around in the woods came to an end. By then some of us had reached seventh grade and had begun the bumpy ride of adolescence. In March, the month when we usually took to the woods again after winter, two friends and I set out to go exploring. Right away, we climbed a tree, and soon were indulging in the spurious nostalgia of kids who have only short pasts to look back upon. The "remember whens" faltered, finally, and I think it occurred to all three of us at the same time that we really were rather big to be up in a tree. Some of us had started wearing unwoodsy outfits like short-sleeved madras shirts and penny loafers, even after school. Soon there would be the spring dances on Friday evenings in the high school cafeteria. We looked at the bare branches around us receding into obscurity, and suddenly there was nothing up there for us. Like Adam and Eve, we saw our own nakedness, and that terrible grown-up question "What are you *doing?*" made us ashamed.

We went back to the woods eventually — and when I say "we," I'm speaking demographically, not just of my friends and me. Millions of us went back, once the sexual and social business of early adulthood had been more or less sorted out. But significantly, we brought that same question with us. Now we had to be seriously doing — racing, strengthening, slimming, traversing, collecting, achieving, catching-and-releasing. A few parts per million of our concentrated purpose changed the chemistry of the whole outdoors. Even those rare interludes of actually doing nothing in the woods took on a certain fierceness as we reinforced them with personal dramas, usually of a social or sexual kind: the only way we could justify sitting motionless in an A-frame cabin in the north woods of Michigan, for example, was if we had just survived a really messy divorce.

"What are you *doing?*" The question pursues me still. When I go fishing and catch no fish, the idea that it's fun simply to be out on the river consoles me for not one second. I must catch fish; and if I do, I must then catch more and bigger fish. On a Sunday afternoon last summer I took my two young children fishing with me on a famous trout stream near my house. My son was four and my daughter was eight, and I kidded myself that in their company I would be able to fish with my usual single-minded mania. I suited up in my waders and tackle-shopful of gear and led my kids from the parking area down toward the water. On the way, however, we had to cross a narrow, shallow irrigation ditch dating from when this part of the valley had farms. Well, the kids saw that little ditch and immediately took off their shoes and waded in and splashed and floated pine cones. My son got an inexplicable joy from casting his little spinning rod far over the ditch into the woods and reeling the rubber casting weight back through the trees. My daughter observed many tent caterpillars — a curse of yard-owners that year — falling from bushes into the ditch and floating helplessly along, and she decided to rescue them. She kept watching the water carefully, and whenever she spotted a caterpillar she swooped down and plucked it out and put it carefully on the bank. I didn't have the heart to drag the kids away, and as I was sitting in all my fishing gear beside the unlikely trickle, a fly fisherman about my age and just as geared-up came along. He took me in at a glance, noticed my equipment and my idleness, and gave a small but unmistakable snort of derision. I was offended, but I understood how he felt as he and his purpose hurried on by.

Here, I'd like to consider a word whose meaning has begun to drift like a caterpillar on a stream. That word is *margin*. Originally its meaning — the blank space around a body of type or the border of a piece of ground — had neutral connotations. But its adjective form, *marginal*, now has a negative tinge. Marginal people or places or activities are ones that don't quite work out, don't sufficiently account of themselves in the economic world. From the adjective sprouted a far-fetched verb, *marginalize,* whose meaning is only bad. To be marginalized is to be a victim, and to marginalize someone else is an act of exclusion that can cost you tenure. Today's so-called marginal people are the exact equivalents, etymologically, of the old-time heathens. A heathen was a savage, wild, un-Christian person who lived out on a heath. The heath was the margin of Christendom. No one today would ever use the word *heathen* except ironically, but we call certain people and activities marginal without a hint of irony all the time.

I've never been on a heath, but to judge from accounts of coal-smogged London in the days when *heathen* was in vogue, a windswept place full of heather and salmon streams sounds like the better place to be. And if the modern version of the margin is somewhere in western Nebraska, and the un-margin, the coveted red-hot center, is a site like Rodeo Drive, I wouldn't know which to choose. We need both, but especially as the world gets more jammed up, we need margins. A book without margins is impossible to read. And marginal behavior can be the most important kind. Every purpose-filled activity we pursue in the woods began as just fooling around. The first person to ride his bicycle down a mountain trail was doing a decidedly marginal thing. The margin is where you can try out odd ideas that you might be afraid to admit to with people looking on. Scientists have a term for research carried on with no immediate prospects of economic gain: "blue-sky research." Marginal places are the blue-sky research zones of the outdoors.

Unfortunately, there are fewer and fewer of them every day. Now a common fate of a place on the margin is to have a convenience store or a windowless brick building belonging to a telephone company built on it. Across the country, endless miles of exurbia now overlap and spill into one another with hardly a margin at all. There's still a lot of open space out there, of course, but usually it's far enough from home that just getting to it requires purpose and premeditation. As the easy-to-wander-into hometown margins disappear, a certain kind of wandering becomes endangered too.

On the far west side of the small western city where I live, past the town-killer discount stores, is an open expanse of undeveloped

ground. Its many acres border the Bitterroot River, and its far end
abuts a fence surrounding a commercial gravel pit. It is a classic
marginal, anything-goes sort of place, and at the moment I prefer
it to just about anywhere I know.

Army reservists sometimes drive tanks there on weekends. The
camouflaged behemoths slithering across the ground would make
my skin crawl if I didn't suspect that the kids driving them were having such a good time. The dirt-bike guys certainly are, as they zip all
over, often dawn to dusk, exuberantly making a racket. Dads bring
their kids to this place to fly kites and model airplanes, people in a
converted school bus camp there for weeks on end, coin-shooters
cruise around with metal detectors, hunters just in off the river clean
game, college kids party and leave heaps of cigarette butts and beer
cans and occasionally pieces of underwear. I fish there, of course,
but remarkably I don't always feel I have to. Sometimes I also pick up
the trash, and I pull my kids around on a sled in the winter, and I
bring friends just off the plane to sit on the riverbank and drink wine
and watch the sunset.

Soon, I'm sure, Development will set its surveyor's tripod on
this ground and make it get with one program or another. Rum-
blings of this have already begun to sound in the local newspaper.
I foresee rows of condominiums, or an expansion of the gravel
pit, or a public park featuring hiking trails and grim pieces of exercise equipment every twenty yards. That last choice, in all its
worthy banality, somehow is the most disheartening of all. A plan
will claim the empty acres and erase the spotted knapweed and
the tank tracks and the beer-can heaps. The place's possibilities,
which at the moment are approximately infinite, will be reduced
to merely a few. And those of uncertain purpose will have to go
elsewhere when they feel like doing nothing in particular, just
fooling around.

Reflections and Responses

1. What do you think Frazier means by a "lower purpose"? What
would a higher purpose be? Give a few examples of lower-purpose
activities that appear in the essay.

2. What is Frazier opposed to in this essay? Do you think he opposes all kinds of purposeful activity? Explain in your own words what he objects to.

3. Why is the idea of margins important to the development of his essay? How has the term taken on negative meanings? Why does Frazier want to retain the word's other meanings? How do Frazier's final three paragraphs illustrate his use of the word *marginal*?

BARRY LOPEZ

The Stone Horse

*Great works of art do not always hang in museums, accessible to anyone
who cares to see them. When Barry Lopez wanted to see a mysterious stone
horse carved perhaps some four hundred years ago by the Quechan people,
his journey took him far off the beaten track. What he finds in the deserts of
southern California near the Mexican border is the kind of large ground
carving (an intaglio) that some think was intended as a sign to extraterres-
trials. But, upon seeing the horse, Lopez does not believe it was "meant to be
seen by gods in the sky above," nor does he think it can even be properly
appreciated in an aerial photograph. How we see this work of art, Lopez
suggests, is as important as what we see. And how we see it requires the journey to it.*

*One of America's most distinguished nonfiction writers, Lopez is the au-
thor of* Arctic Dreams, *which won the National Book Award in 1986,
and* Of Wolves and Men, *which won the John Burroughs Medal in
1979. His other publications include* Desert Notes *(1979),* River Notes
(1979), Winter Count *(1981),* Crossing Open Ground *(1988),*
Coyote Love *(1989),* The Rediscovery of North America *(1990),*
Field Notes *(1994), and* Lessons from the Wolverine *(1997). He has
also recently published* About This Life: Journeys on the Threshold of
Memory *(1998) and a work of fiction,* Resistance *(2004). He received
an award for fiction from the Friends of American Writers in 1982 and the
Award in Literature from the American Academy and Institute of Arts and
Letters in 1986. "The Stone Horse" originally appeared in* Antaeus
(1986) and was selected by Gay Talese for The Best American Essays
1987.

I

The deserts of southern California, the high, relatively cooler and wetter Mojave and the hotter, dryer Sonoran to the south of it, carry the signatures of many cultures. Prehistoric rock drawings in the Mojave's Coso Range, probably the greatest concentration of petroglyphs in North America, are at least three thousand years old. Big-game-hunting cultures that flourished six or seven thousand years before that are known from broken spear tips, choppers, and burins left scattered along the shores of great Pleistocene lakes, long since evaporated. Weapons and tools discovered at China Lake may be thirty thousand years old; and worked stone from a quarry in the Calico Mountains is, some argue, evidence that human beings were here more than 200,000 years ago.

Because of the long-term stability of such arid environments, much of this prehistoric stone evidence still lies exposed on the ground, accessible to anyone who passes by — the studious, the acquisitive, the indifferent, the merely curious. Archaeologists do not agree on the sequence of cultural history beyond about twelve thousand years ago, but it is clear that these broken bits of chalcedony, chert, and obsidian, like the animal drawings and geometric designs etched on walls of basalt throughout the desert, anchor the earliest threads of human history, the first record of human endeavor here.

Western man did not enter the California desert until the end of the eighteenth century, 250 years after Coronado brought his soldiers into the Zuni pueblos in a bewildered search for the cities of Cibola. The earliest appraisals of the land were cursory, hurried. People traveled *through* it, en route to Santa Fe or the California coastal settlements. Only miners tarried. In 1823 what had been Spain's became Mexico's, and in 1848 what had been Mexico's became America's; but the bare, jagged mountains and dry lake beds, the vast and uniform plains of creosote bush and yucca plants, remained as obscure as the northern Sudan until the end of the nineteenth century.

Before 1940 the tangible evidence of twentieth-century man's passage here consisted of very little — the hard tracery of travel corridors; the widely scattered, relatively insignificant evidence of mining operations; and the fair expanse of irrigated fields at the desert's periphery. In the space of a hundred years or so the wagon roads were paved, railroads were laid down, and canals and high-tension lines were built to bring water and electricity across the desert to Los Angeles from the Colorado River. The dark mouths of gold, talc, and tin mines yawned from the bony flanks of desert ranges. Dust-encrusted chemical plants stood at work on the lonely edges of dry lake beds. And crops of grapes, lettuce, dates, alfalfa, and cotton covered the Coachella and Imperial valleys, north and south of the Salton Sea, and the Palo Verde Valley along the Colorado.

These developments proceeded with little or no awareness of earlier human occupations by cultures that preceded those of the historic Indians — the Mojave, the Chemehuevi, the Quechan. (Extensive irrigation began actually to change the climate of the Sonoran Desert, and human settlements, the railroads, and farming introduced many new, successful plants into the region.)

During World War II, the American military moved into the desert in great force, to train troops and to test equipment. They found the clear weather conducive to year-round flying, the dry air and isolation very attractive. After the war, a complex of training grounds, storage facilities, and gunnery and test ranges was permanently settled on more than three million acres of military reservations. Few perceived the extent or significance of the destruction of the aboriginal sites that took place during tank maneuvers and bombing runs or in the laying out of highways, railroads, mining districts, and irrigated fields. The few who intuited that something like an American Dordogne Valley lay exposed here were (only) amateur archaeologists; even they reasoned that the desert was too vast for any of this to matter.

After World War II, people began moving out of the crowded Los Angeles basin into homes in Lucerne, Apple, and Antelope valleys in the western Mojave. They emigrated as well to a stretch of resort land at the foot of the San Jacinto Mountains that included Palm Springs, and farther out to old railroad and military towns like Twentynine Palms and Barstow. People also began exploring the desert, at first in military-surplus jeeps and then with a variety of all-terrain and off-road vehicles that became available in the 1960s. By the mid-1970s, the number of people using such vehicles for desert recreation had increased exponentially. Most came and went in innocent curiosity; the few who didn't wreaked a havoc all out of proportion to their numbers. The disturbance of previously isolated archaeological sites increased by an order of magnitude. Many sites were vandalized before archaeologists, themselves late to the desert, had any firm grasp of the bounds of human history in the desert. It was as though in the same moment an Aztec library had been discovered intact various lacunae had begun to appear.

The vandalism was of three sorts: the general disturbance usually caused by souvenir hunters and by the curious and the oblivious; the wholesale stripping of a place by professional thieves for black-market sale and trade; and outright destruction, in which vehicles were actually used to ram and trench an area. By 1980, the Bureau of Land Management estimated that probably 35 percent of the archaeological sites in the desert had been vandalized. The destruction at some places by rifles and shotguns, or by power winches mounted on vehicles, was, if one cared for history, demoralizing to behold.

In spite of public education, land closures, and stricter law enforcement in recent years, the BLM estimates that, annually, about 1 percent of the archaeological record in the desert continues to be destroyed or stolen.

II

A BLM archaeologist told me, with understandable reluctance, where to find the intaglio. I spread my Automobile Club of Southern California map of Imperial County out on his desk, and he traced the route with a pink felt-tip pen. The line crossed Interstate 8 and then turned west along the Mexican border.

"You can't drive any farther than about here," he said, marking a small X. "There's boulders in the wash. You walk up past them."

On a separate piece of paper he drew a route in a smaller scale that would take me up the arroyo to a certain point where I was to cross back east, to another arroyo. At its head, on higher ground just to the north, I would find the horse.

"It's tough to spot unless you know it's there. Once you pick it up . . ." He shook his head slowly, in a gesture of wonder at its existence.

I waited until I held his eye. I assured him I would not tell anyone else how to get there. He looked at me with stoical despair, like a man who had been robbed twice, whose belief in human beings was offered without conviction.

I did not go until the following day because I wanted to see it at dawn. I ate breakfast at four A.M. in El Centro and then drove south. The route was easy to follow, though the last section of road proved difficult, broken and drifted over with sand in some spots. I came to the barricade of boulders and parked. It was light enough by then to find my way over the ground with little trouble. The contours of the landscape were stark, without any masking vegetation. I worried only about rattlesnakes.

I traversed the stone plain as directed, but, in spite of the frankness of the land, I came on the horse unawares. In the first moment of recognition I was without feeling. I recalled later being startled, and that I held my breath. It was laid out on the ground with its head to the east, three times life size. As I took in its outline I felt a growing concentration of all my senses, as though my attentiveness to the pale rose color of the morning sky and other peripheral images had now ceased to be important. I was aware that I was straining for sound in the windless air, and I felt the uneven pressure of the earth hard against my feet. The horse, outlined in a standing profile on the dark ground, was as vivid before me as a bed of tulips.

I've come upon animals suddenly before, and felt a similar tension, a precipitate heightening of the senses. And I have felt the inexplicable but sharply boosted intensity of a wild moment in the bush, where it is not until some minutes later that you discover the source of electricity — the warm remains of a grizzly bear kill, or the still moist tracks of a wolverine.

But this was slightly different. I felt I had stepped into an unoccupied corridor. I had no familiar sense of history, the temporal structure in which to think: this horse was made by Quechan people three hundred years ago. I felt instead a headlong rush of images: people hunting wild horses with spears on the Pleistocene veld of southern California; Cortés riding across the causeway into Montezuma's Tenochtitlán; a short-legged Comanche, astride his horse like some sort of ferret, slashing through cavalry lines of young men who rode like farmers; a hoof exploding past my face one morning in a corral in Wyoming. These images had the weight and silence of stone.

When I released my breath, the images softened. My initial feeling, of facing a wild animal in a remote region, was replaced with a calm sense of antiquity. It was then that I became conscious, like an ordinary tourist, of what was before me, and thought: this horse was probably laid out by Quechan people. But when? I wondered. The first horses they saw, I knew, might have been those that came north from Mexico in 1692 with Father Eusebio Kino. But Cocopa people, I recalled, also came this far north on occasion, to fight with their neighbors, the Quechan. And *they* could have seen horses with Melchior Diaz, at the mouth of the Colorado River in the fall of 1540. So, it could be four hundred years old. (No one in fact knows.)

I still had not moved. I took my eyes off the horse for a moment to look south over the desert plain into Mexico, to look east past its head at the brightening sunrise, to situate myself. Then, finally, I brought my trailing foot slowly forward and stood erect. Sunlight was running like a thin sheet of water over the stony ground and it threw the horse into relief. It looked as though no hand had ever disturbed the stones that gave it its form.

The horse had been brought to life on ground called desert pavement, a tight, flat matrix of small cobbles blasted smooth by sand-laden winds. The uniform, monochromatic blackness of the stones, a patina of iron and magnesium oxides called desert varnish, is caused by long-term exposure to the sun. To make this type of low-relief ground glyph, or intaglio, the artist either selectively turns individual stones over to their lighter side or removes areas of stone to expose the lighter soil underneath, creating a negative image. This horse, about eighteen feet from brow to rump and eight feet from withers to hoof, had been made in the latter way, and its outline was bermed at certain points with low ridges of stone a few inches high to enhance its three-dimensional qualities. (The left side of the horse was in full profile; each leg was extended at 90 degrees to the body and fully visible, as though seen in three-quarter profile.)

I was not eager to move. The moment I did I would be back in the flow of time, the horse no longer quivering in the same way before me. I did not want to feel again the sequence of quotidian events — to be drawn off into deliberation and analysis. A human being, a four-footed animal, the open land. That was all that was present — and a "thoughtless" understanding of the very old desires bearing on this particular animal: to hunt it, to render it, to fathom it, to subjugate it, to honor it, to take it as a companion.

What finally made me move was the light. The sun now filled the shallow basin of the horse's body. The weighted line of the stone berm created the illusion of a mane and the distinctive roundness of an equine belly. The change in definition impelled me. I moved to the left, circling past its rump, to see how the light might flesh the horse out from various points of view. I circled it completely before squatting on my haunches. Ten or fifteen minutes later I chose another view. The third time I moved, to a point near the rear hooves, I spotted a stone tool at my feet. I stared at it a long while, more in awe than disbelief, before reaching out to pick it up. I turned it over in my left palm and took it between my fingers to feel its cutting edge. It is always difficult, especially with something so portable, to rechannel the desire to steal.

I spent several hours with the horse. As I changed positions and as the angle of the light continued to change I noticed a number of things. The angle at which the pastern carried the hoof away from the ankle was perfect. Also, stones had been placed within the image to suggest at precisely the right spot the left shoulder above the foreleg. The line that joined thigh and hock was similarly accurate. The muzzle alone seemed distorted — but perhaps these stones had been moved by a later hand. It was an admirably accurate representation, but not what a breeder would call perfect conformation. There was the suggestion of a bowed neck and an undershot jaw, and the tail, as full as a winter coyote's, did not appear to be precisely to scale.

The more I thought about it, the more I felt I was looking at an individual horse, a unique combination of generic and specific detail. It was easy to imagine one of Kino's horses as a model, or a horse that ran off from one of Coronado's columns. What kind of horses would these have been? I wondered. In the sixteenth century the most sought-after horses in Europe were Spanish, the offspring of Arabian stock and Barbary horses that the Moors brought to Iberia and bred to the older, eastern European strains brought in by the Romans. The model for this horse, I speculated, could easily have been a palomino, or a descendant of horses trained for lion hunting in North Africa.

A few generations ago, cowboys, cavalry quartermasters, and dray-men would have taken this horse before me under consideration and not let up their scrutiny until they had its heritage fixed to their satisfaction. Today, the distinction between draft and harness horses is arcane knowledge, and no image may come to mind for a blue roan or a claybank horse. The loss of such refinement in everyday conversation leaves me unsettled. People praise the Eskimo's ability to distinguish among forty types of snow but forget the skill of oth-ers who routinely differentiate between overo and tobiano pintos. Such distinctions are made for the same reason. You have to do it to be able to talk clearly about the world.

For parts of two years I worked as a horse wrangler and packer in Wyoming. It is dim knowledge now; I would have to think to re-member if a buckskin was a kind of dun horse. And I couldn't throw a double-diamond hitch over a set of panniers — the pack-er's basic tie-down — without guidance. As I squatted there in the desert, however, these more personal memories seemed tenuous in comparison with the sweep of this animal in human time. My memories had no depth. I thought of the Hittite cavalry riding against the Syrians 3,500 years ago. And the first of the Chinese emperors, Ch'in Shih Huang, buried in Shensi Province in 210 B.C. with thousands of life-size horses and soldiers, a terra-cotta guardian army. What could I know of what was in the mind of who-ever made this horse? Was there some racial memory of it as an animal that had once fed the artist's ancestors and then disappeared from North America? And then returned in this strange alliance with another race of men?

Certainly, whoever it was, the artist had observed the animal very closely. Certainly the animal's speed had impressed him. Among the first things the Quechan would have learned from an encounter with Kino's horses was that their own long-distance runners — men who could run down mule deer — were no match for this animal.

From where I squatted I could look far out over the Mexican plain. Juan Bautista de Anza passed this way in 1774, extending El Camino Real into Alta California from Sinaloa. He was followed by others, all of them astride the magical horse; *gente de razón,* the people of reason, coming into the country of *los primitivos.* The horse, like the stone animals of Egypt, urged these memories upon me. And as I drew them up from some forgotten corner of my mind — huge horses carved in the white chalk downs of southern England by an Iron Age people; Spanish horses rearing and wheeling in fear before alligators in Florida — the images seemed tethered before me. With this sense of proportion, a memory of my own — the morning I almost lost my face to a horse's hoof — now had somewhere to fit.

I rose up and began to walk slowly around the horse again. I had taken the first long measure of it and was now looking for a way to depart, a new angle of light, a fading of the image itself before the rising sun, that would break its hold on me. As I circled, feeling both heady and serene at the encounter, I realized again how strangely vivid it was. It had been created on a barren bajada between two arroyos, as nondescript a place as one could imagine. The only plant life here was a few wands of ocotillo cactus. The ground beneath my shoes was so hard it wouldn't take the print of a heavy animal even after a rain. The only sounds I heard here were the voices of quail.

The archaeologist had been correct. For all its forcefulness, the horse is inconspicuous. If you don't care to see it you can walk right past it. That pleases him, I think. Unmarked on this bleak shoulder of the plain, the site signals to no one; so he wants no protective fences here, no informative plaque, to act as beacons. He would rather take a chance that no motorcyclist, no aimless wanderer with a flair for violence and a depth of ignorance, will ever find his way here.

The archaeologist had given me something before I left his office that now seemed peculiar — an aerial photograph of the horse. It is widely believed that an aerial view of an intaglio provides a fair and accurate depiction. It does not. In the photograph the horse looks somewhat crudely constructed; from the ground it appears far more deftly rendered. The photograph is of a single moment, and in that split second the horse seems vaguely impotent. I watched light pool in the intaglio at dawn; I imagine you could watch it withdraw at dusk and sense the same animation I did. In those prolonged moments its shape and so, too, its general character changed — noticeably. The living quality of the image, its immediacy to the eye, was brought out by the light-in-time, not, at least here, in the camera's frozen instant.

Intaglios, I thought, were never meant to be seen by gods in the sky above. They were meant to be seen by people on the ground, over a long period of shifting light. This could even be true of the huge figures on the Plain of Nazca in Peru, where people could walk for the length of a day beside them. It is our own impatience that leads us to think otherwise.

This process of abstraction, almost unintentional, drew me gradually away from the horse. I came to a position of attention at the edge of the sphere of its influence. With a slight bow I paid my respects to the horse, its maker, and the history of us all, and departed.

III

A short distance away I stopped the car in the middle of the road to make a few notes. I could not write down what I was thinking when I was with the horse. It would have seemed disrespectful, and it would have required another kind of attention. So now I patiently drained my memory of the details it had fastened itself upon. The road I'd stopped on was adjacent to the All American Canal, the major source of water for the Imperial and Coachella valleys. The water flowed west placidly. A disjointed flock of coots, small, dark birds with white bills, was paddling against the current, foraging in the rushes.

I was peripherally aware of the birds as I wrote, the only movement in the desert, and of a series of sounds from a village a half-mile away. The first sounds from this collection of ramshackle houses in a grove of cottonwoods were the distracted dawn voices of dogs. I heard them intermingled with the cries of a rooster. Later, the high-pitched voices of children calling out to each other came disembodied through the dry desert air. Now, a little after seven, I could hear someone practicing on the trumpet, the same rough phrases played over and over. I suddenly remembered how as children we had tried to get the rhythm of a galloping horse with hands against our thighs, or by fluttering our tongues against the roofs of our mouths.

After the trumpet, the impatient calls of adults summoning children. Sunday morning. Wood smoke hung like a lens in the trees. The first car starts — a cold eight-cylinder engine, of Chrysler extraction perhaps, goosed to life, then throttled back to murmur through dual mufflers, the obbligato music of a shade-tree mechanic. The rote bark of mongrel dogs at dawn, the jagged outcries of men and women, an engine coming to life. Like a thousand villages from West Virginia to Guadalajara.

I finished my notes — where was I going to find a description of the horses that came north with the conquistadors? Did their manes come forward prominently over the brow, like this one's, like the forelocks of Blackfeet and Assiniboin men in nineteenth-century paintings? I set the notes on the seat beside me.

The road followed the canal for a while and then arced north, toward Interstate 8. It was slow driving and I fell to thinking how the desert had changed since Anza had come through. New plants and animals — the MacDougall cottonwood, the English house sparrow, the chukar from India — have about them now the air of the native-born. Of the native species, some — no one knows how many — are extinct. The populations of many others, especially the animals, have been sharply reduced. The idea of a desert impoverished by agricultural poisons and varmint hunters, by off-road vehicles and military operations, did not seem as disturbing to me, however, as this other horror, now that I had been those hours with the horse. The vandals, the few who crowbar rock art off the desert's walls, who dig up graves, who punish the ground that holds intaglios, are people who devour history. Their self-centered scorn, their disrespect for ideas and images beyond their ken, create the awful atmosphere of loose ends in which totalitarianism thrives, in which the past is merely curious or wrong.

I thought about the horse sitting out there on the unprotected plain. I enumerated its qualities in my mind until a sense of its vulnerability receded and it became an anchor for something else. I remembered that history, a history like this one, which ran deeper than Mexico, deeper than the Spanish, was a kind of medicine. It permitted the great breadth of human expression to reverberate, and it did not urge you to locate its apotheosis in the present.

Each of us, individuals and civilizations, has been held upside down like Achilles in the River Styx. The artist mixing his colors in the dim light of Altamira; an Egyptian ruler lying still now, wrapped in his byssus,* stored against time in a pyramid; the faded Dorset culture of the Arctic; the Hmong and Samburu and Walbiri of historic

---

*byssus: Ancient cloth. — Ed.

time; the modern nations. This great, imperfect stretch of human expression is the clarification and encouragement, the urging and the reminder, we call history. And it is inscribed everywhere in the face of the land, from the mountain passes of the Himalayas to a nameless bajada in the California desert.

Small birds rose up in the road ahead, startled, and flew off. I prayed no infidel would ever find that horse.

Reflections and Responses

1. Lopez divides his essay into three parts. How does each of these parts differ? What purpose does each serve?

2. Examine Lopez's choice of words. When does he introduce technical terms into the essay? Go through the essay and identify the various technical terms. From what diverse disciplines are they drawn? How do these terms affect your response to both the author and his subject?

3. When this essay originally appeared, it included no photographs of the carving. Why do you think that decision was made? What distortions would photography introduce? What would a photograph *not* be able to show us? What is Lopez's attitude toward photography in this instance?

KYOKO MORI

Yarn

Many fine essays deal with ordinary, routine matters. In fact, as a genre, the essay is usually more comfortable in our habitual worlds than it is in worlds we may imagine. Our hobbies, daily schedules, everyday interests and amusements, preoccupations (whether kayaking, knitting, or karate)— these will supply the building blocks that the essayist will assemble, disassemble, and reassemble. The trick of making our ordinary lives and concerns of interest to others, however, is what aspiring essayists must learn. In "Yarn," Kyoko Mori provides a solid demonstration of the way an experienced essayist can toggle between the micro and the macro, the personal and the historical. As she writes about her lifelong passion for knitting, Mori at the same time makes us aware of the way life and art are shaped by the pursuit, the improvisation, and the dissolution of patterns.

*Kyoko Mori is the author of two nonfiction books—*The Dream of Water: A Memoir *and* Polite Lies: On Being a Woman Caught Between Cultures— *as well as three novels, the most recent of which is* Stone Field, True Arrow. *Born in Kobe, Japan, Mori has lived in the American Midwest for most of her adult life. She has taught creative nonfiction at Harvard University and fiction in Lesley University's low-residency MFA program. Mori is currently on the MFA faculty at George Mason University. "Yarn" originally appeared in the* Harvard Review *and was selected by Louis Menand for* The Best American Essays 2004.

1

The yellow mittens I made in seventh-grade home economics proved that I dreamed in color. For the unit on knitting, we were supposed to turn in a pair of mittens. The two hands had to be precisely the same size so that when we held them together, palm to palm, no extra stitches would stick out from the thumb, the tips of the fingers, or the cuff. Somewhere between making the fourth and the fifth mitten to fulfill this requirement, I dreamed that the ball of yellow yarn in my bag had turned green. Chartreuse, leaf, Granny Smith, lime, neon, acid green. The brightness was electric. I woke up knowing that I was, once again, doomed for a D in home ec.

I don't remember what possessed me to choose yellow yarn for that assignment. Yellow was a color I never liked; perhaps I was conceding defeat before I started. Mittens, as it turns out, are just about the worst project possible for a beginner. Each hand has to be knitted as a very small tube, with the stitches divided among four pointed needles that twist and slip unless you are holding them with practiced confidence. The pair won't be the same size if you drop or pick up extra stitches along the way, skip a couple of decreases in shaping the top, or knit too tightly in your nervousness and then let up in relief as you approach the end. You might inadvertently make two right mittens or two lefts because you forgot that the thumb has to be started in a different position for each hand. I ended up with two right hands of roughly the same size and three left hands that could have been illustrations for a fairy tale. *Once upon a time there lived three brothers, each with only one hand — large, medium and very small — and, even though the villagers laughed at them and called them unkind names, the brothers, could do any thing when they put their three left hands together. . . .*

I didn't knit again until graduate school when I met a woman from Germany with a closetful of beautiful sweaters. Sabina came to our seminar wearing a soft angora cardigan one week, a sturdy fisherman's pullover the next.

"I make all my sweaters," she said. "I can teach you."

I told her about my mitten fiasco.

"Knitting is easy," Sabina insisted. "A sweater's bigger than a mitten but much simpler."

"The patterns will confuse me."

"You don't need patterns. You can make things up as you go."

Sabina took me to a local yarn store, where I bought skeins of red cotton yarn. Following her instructions, I first knit the body of the sweater: two flat pieces, front and back, with a few simple decreases to shape the shoulders and the neck. The pieces were surprisingly easy to sew together. Sabina showed me how to pick up the stitches along the arm opening, connect the new yarn, and knit the sleeves, going from the shoulder to the wrist. I finished the sweater in a month, The result was slightly lopsided — one sleeve was half an inch wider than the other around the elbow — but the arms looked more or less even once I put the sweater on. The small mistakes in a knitted garment disappear when the garment is on the body, where it belongs. That might have been the most important thing I learned from my first sweater.

In the twenty years since then, I've made sweaters, vests, hats, bedspreads, lap blankets, shawls, scarves, socks, and mittens. Like most people who knit, I have bags of yarn stashed in my closet for future projects. The bags are a record of the cities where I've wandered into yarn stores: Madison, Portland, Cambridge, New Orleans. Evanston, Washington, DC. Like hair salons, yarn stores have slightly witty names: Woolgathering, Woolworks, Woolcotts, the Knitting Tree, the Quarter Stitch (New Orleans), Fiber Space. Inside each store, the walls are lined with plastic crates bursting with color. My friend Yenkuei took up knitting because she fell in love with the fuchsia sleeveless sweater in the window of Woolcotts in Harvard Square, floating, she thought, and beckoning to her. Another friend, who doesn't knit, comes along just to touch. She goes from shelf to shelf fingering the rayon chenilles, angoras, alpacas, and silk-cotton blends while I'm trying to figure out how much yarn I need. When I was five, in kindergarten, I was horrified to see other kids stick their fingers in the library paste, scoop up the pale glop, and put it in their mouths, but I tried to eat the raspberry-colored crayon on my teacher's desk because it looked so delicious. Knitting is about that same hunger for color. I never again picked up yellow yarn.

2

Knitting is a young craft. The oldest surviving examples — blue and white cotton socks and fabric fragments discovered in an Egyptian tomb — are dated around A.D. 1200. Knitting probably originated in Egypt or another Arabic country around that time and reached Europe through Spain. Two knitted cushions, found in the tomb of a thirteenth-century Castilian prince and princess, are the oldest known European artifacts of knitring. Once it reached Europe, the craft spread quickly. By the fourteenth century, Italian and German artists were painting the Virgin Mary knitting in a domestic setting.

Most of the early knitting in Europe was for socks and stockings. Elizabeth I preferred the knitted silk stockings from France to the woven-and-sewn foot coverings made in England. Mary, Queen of Scots, wore two pairs of French stockings — one plain white and the other patterned with gold stitches — on the day of her execution; the stockings were held up with green garters. By the end of the sixteenth century, cheap metal needles became widely available, enabling the rural families throughout England to knit socks and stockings during the winter months to supplement their income.

In the cities, guilds controlled the licensing of knitting workshops. An apprentice would spend three years working under one master and three more traveling as a "journeyman," to learn new techniques from various masters, before he could submit samples of his work for the guild's approval. In Vienna at the beginning of the seventeenth century, the samples had to include a six-colored tablecloth, a beret, a pair of silk stockings, and a pair of gloves.

Sweaters are not on this list because in Vienna at that time, as in most of Europe, upper-body garments such as shirts, tunics, vests, and jackets were cut and sewn from woven fabrics only. The first knitted upper-body garments were made in the fifteenth century, in the Channel Islands of Guernsey and Jersey, where fishermen and sailors needed thick tunics made of wool to repel water and protect against the cold. Although these garments spread slowly across the rest of Europe among laborers, they did not become popular as "sweaters" until the 1890s when American athletes wore heavy, dark blue pullovers before and after contests to ward off the chills.

Knitting is an activity that can be performed anywhere, while weaving requires a loom, a complicated piece of equipment that takes up space and is difficult to move. Still, the earliest proof of woven cloth predates knitting by more than eight thousand years. Clay balls found in Iraq and dated around 7000 B.C. have clear impressions of woven textiles on them. Numerous images of weavers are preserved on papyruses and tomb paintings from ancient Egypt. In the *Odyssey*, Penelope weaves and unweaves a funeral cloth to ward off the suitors; in Greek mythology, Aracne is turned into a spider when she challenges Athena to a weaving contest and loses. The knitting Madonnas of the fourteenth century represent some of the earliest depictions of women knitting, and no Greek hero's wife or foolish mortal ever won praise or punishment for this simple activity.

3

As with people, so with garments: the strengths and the weaknesses are often one and the same. A knitted garment, whose loose construction traps air next to the body, is warmer but more fragile than a woven one, and the stretching property of yarn makes knitting a less precise but more forgiving craft than sewing. On a knitted fabric, one broken loop can release all the loops, causing the fabric to "run." This same quality allows a knitter to unravel the yarn on purpose, undo a few inches of work, and correct a mistake she has discovered. Even after the garment is finished, a knitter can snip one of the stitches, carefully unravel one round of knitting, put the loops back on a needle, and redo the bottom of the sweater or the sleeve to make it smaller, larger, or a different shape. Sewing doesn't allow the same flexibility.

My first home ec sewing project was no better than the mittens: an Oxford shirt with cuffs, buttonholes, darts along the bust line, and square collars; a pleated skirt with a zipper closure, I'm sure there are much easier things to sew. Still, in sewing, you can't get away from cutting, assembling, and fitting. If you cut the pieces wrong, you'll have to buy more cloth and lay out the pattern again. If the finished shirt is half an inch too small, it's not going to stretch the way a sweater will.

Even the words "thread" (the stringlike material we sew with) and "yarn" (the stringlike material we knit with) convey different degrees of flexibility. Thread holds together and restricts, while yarn stretches and gives. Thread is the overall theme that gives meaning to our words and thoughts — to lose the thread is to be incoherent or inattentive. A yarn is a long, pointless, but usually amusing story whose facts have been exaggerated. It is infinitely more relaxing to listen to a yarn than to a lecture whose thread we must follow.

In my first ten years of knitting, I took full advantage of the forgiving quality of yarn and made hats and scarves from patterns that had only five- to ten-sentence directions. For sweaters, I made three tubes (one big tube for the body, two smaller tubes for the sleeves) and then knitted them together at the yoke and shoulders so I didn't have to sew the pieces together at the end. If, halfway through the body or the sleeve, I noticed the piece getting wider faster than I'd expected, I simply stopped increasing stitches; if the piece looked too small, I increased more. It was just as Sabina had told me: I could make things up as I went along.

My favorite project was a hat from a pattern I found in a yarn store on a visit to Portland, Oregon. I bought the thick mohair yarn and extra needles so I could start knitting the first one in my hotel room. The hat, which I finished on the flight home the next day, looked more like a lampshade; the brim came down to my shoulders. At home, I threw this enormous hat in the washer, set it on hot wash and cold rinse, and ran the cycle twice. Just as the pattern promised, the hat came out shrunk and "felted"; the stitches had contracted till they were invisible, leaving a dense, fuzzy nap. I reshaped the hat on a mixing bowl about the size of my head, and by the time it dried, it looked like a professionally made bowler.

The washing-machine hat became a staple of my gift-giving. A few years later, I visited an antiques mall with a couple who had fallen in love with an oak dresser they though was too expensive. Every weekend for two months, they brought a different friend to look at the dresser, to ooh and aah over it, and help them work up the nerve to spend the money. The antiques mall was a huge place out in the country, and we had to walk what felt like three city blocks crammed with furniture and knickknacks. When we finally got to the right section, I failed my friends completely by not noticing the dresser because to the right of it, on a small table, was a wooden hat form. To an untrained eye, the hat form looks like a wooden head, but I knew what it was. Tired of reshaping hats over a bowl, I had been trying to order one (except all the modern hat forms were made of Styrofoam and I didn't think I could stand the squeaky noise they would make), I grabbed the wooden head and walked around with it tightly clutched under my arm while my friends showed me all the other oak dressers, every one of them inferior to the one they wanted. At the counter, I paid $12 for my find.

This fall, I brought the wooden head with me to Wisconsin because I still make those hats for gifts. But in the past five years, I've graduated to more complicated patterns. I had gotten tired of the rugged look of the make-it-as-you-go kind of sweater, but more than that, my reasons for knitting have changed. In my twenties and thirties, I wanted everything I did to express what I considered my essential nature: casual, relaxed, and intuitively creative, rather than formal, precise, and meticulous. That's why I chose knitting over sewing, running and cycling over tennis or golf. Now, in my mid-forties, I look instead for balance. If following step-by-step instructions doesn't come naturally to me, that is all the more reason for me to try it. I would rather knit from a complicated pattern and make a few mistakes than execute an easier one flawlessly.

The folklore among knitters is that everything handmade should have at least one mistake so an evil spirit will not become trapped in the maze of perfect stitches. A missed increase or decrease, a crooked seam, a place where the tension is uneven — the mistake is a crack left open to let in the light. The evil spirit I want to usher out of my knitting and my life is at once a spirit of laziness and of overachieving. It's that little voice in my head that says, I won't even try this because it doesn't come naturally to me and I won't be very good at it.

4

A friend of mine fell in love with a young man at college because he was knitting a sweater between classes the first time she saw him. She concluded that he must be an extraordinarily sensitive and creative man, though eventually she found out he was neither. This man, whom I never met, is the only contemporary male knitter I know of, besides Kaffe Fasset, the British sweater designer.

Knitting wasn't always a feminine craft. The knitting masters and apprentices of the medieval guilds were all men, since women were not admitted into guilds. Before the Industrial Revolution, both men and women, of all ages, knitted socks in the countryside. The fishermen and the sailors from the English Channel Islands made their own sweaters during their long sea voyages. In the late nineteenth century, the Japanese samurai whose clans were faltering tried to supplement their income by knitting *tabi*, split-toed Japanese socks (essentially, mittens for feet). Even so, knitting — like sewing, spinning, weaving, and embroidery — has been historically associated with women's household skills and marriageability. One of the most remarkable examples involves the mitten.

In Latvia, until the early twentieth century, every girl learned to knit by the age of six so she could get an early start on her dowry chest. A full dowry chest would decrease the number of cattle her family would have to pay the groom's family when it came time for her to marry. The main contents of the dowry chest were mittens with multicolored, geometrical designs. On the day of the wedding, these mittens were distributed to all the participants from the carriage driver to the minister, as well as to the numerous relatives, in-laws, and neighbors. At the feast after the ceremony, the bride and the groom ate with mittened hands to invite good luck. At the end of the day, the bride walked around the inside and outside of her new home, laying mittens (to be collected later by her mother-in-law) on all the important locations: the hearth, the doors, the windows, the cow barn, the sheep shed, the beehives, and the garden. To properly complete these marriage rites, a bride needed one to two hundred pairs of mittens. The mittens were treasured as heirlooms, and the complicated knitting patterns were meant to show off a young woman's patience — her ability to perform meticulous and repetitive work — as well as her skill.

When my Japanese home ec teacher decided to teach us how to knit mittens, the assignment was, in a sense, grimly appropriate, since the not-so-hidden purpose of home ec was also to give us skills that showed off our patience and meticulousness. After the semester of knitting and sewing, we were required to take several semesters of cooking) in which we made elaborate casseroles and soufflés and desserts, food to impress people, food for parties, not the kind of food I would cook for myself when I moved out to live on my own.

In most schools in the United States and Japan now, home ec is an elective, open to both girls and boys. Young women in Latvia no longer make two hundred pairs of mittens in order to get married. Of course I'm happy for these changes, though a part of me worries whether anyone will preserve these centuries-old crafts. I have not met one man who has ever knitted, sewn, or embroidered clothes for his partner or children — or a woman knitter, quilter, garment maker, or embroiderer who has not made something for the men and the children among her family and friends. I don't know what to do with the weight of history and the way it affects our daily lives.

At least on a purely personal level, I've reconciled myself to the mitten. Last year in Cambridge, I tackled the ultimate mitten. The pattern, marked for "experienced knitters." called them "flip-flop mittens" because the top half could be made to flip back like a hinged lid, exposing the fingers in a fingerless glove. I thought of them as cat mittens: at the necessary moment, the sheath pulled back and out came the claws. It was a slow and complicated project. To achieve the gauge for the pattern, I had to use number zero needles, which were thinner than satay sticks, The fuzzy mohair yarn made the stitches difficult to see, and each finger had to be knitted separately. It took me two months to make myself a pair. Then I started another pair for my friend Junko, whose hands are smaller than the smallest measurement in the directions. I was proud of having managed to follow the directions and, at the same time, make a few adjustments on my own, until I finished the second mitten and realized that — only on that hand — I had made the top flip forward instead of back. After thirty years, I was back where I'd started; I had been blown back into the mitten purgatory of mismatched hands.

The next morning, I sat down and thought of the various tricks I'd learned. I looked at knitting books, went over the notes I'd made in the margins of some patterns. Finally I figured out how to unravel just a few rows of stitches and detach the flip at the front, make a new edging for it, and graft the stitches to the back of the hand so that the flip now faced the right way. The procedure left a small scar, hardly noticeable in the fuzzy mohair. When I gave the mittens to Junko, I showed her my mistake. Across the back of her left hand stretched a faint broken line, like a rural road on a map of the desert, a path across unknown terrain.

Reflections and Responses

1. The essay begins with a reference to the author's inability to knit mittens properly when she was a young girl. How does Kyoko Mori continue this image through the essay? In what ways do mittens emerge as an important part of the essay's theme?

2. Why do you think Kyoko Mori weaves as much history as she does into her rather short essay? Why doesn't she concentrate entirely on

her own knitting and what it means to her? What do the historical details add to the essay?

3. In what ways does "Yarn" suggest matters larger than the enjoyment and satisfaction of knitting? What pun is intended in the essay's title? How does Mori connect knitting with art and life in general? Can you infer the author's attitude toward life and art from her account of knitting? For example, can you see any similarities between knitting mittens and writing an essay?

JOYCE CAROL OATES

They All Just Went Away

The essay has long been the perfect form for the reflective mind. In the hands of a great writer, the process of reflection can be stimulated by a single incident or image and then veer off in so many different directions that, by the end of the essay, the reader is amazed at how much ground has been covered. "They All Just Went Away" does everything a superb reflective essay can do because it moves from the personal eccentricities of a lonely young girl who finds herself drawn to abandoned houses and desolate families into a consideration of American art, class boundaries, sexual abuse, and strange erotic attachments. It is not a cheerful or placid piece of writing, however. "As I am not drawn to art that makes me feel good, comfortable, or at ease," Joyce Carol Oates writes, "so I am not drawn to essays that 'smile,' except in the context of larger, more complex ambitions."

One of the country's most distinguished authors, Joyce Carol Oates has published over two dozen novels and numerous collections of poems, plays, short stories, criticism, and essays. Equipped with her work alone, the scholar and essayist Henry Louis Gates Jr. claimed, a future archaeologist could "easily piece together the whole postwar America." The recipient of countless literary awards, she was at thirty-one the youngest writer ever to receive the prestigious National Book Award for fiction when her novel them *was chosen in 1969. She currently teaches writing at Princeton University. Among her most recent works of fiction are* Man Crazy *(1997),* The Collector of Hearts *(1998),* My Heart Laid Bare *(1998),* Broke Heart Blues *(1999),* Blonde *(2000),* I'll Take You There *(2002),* The Tattooed Girl *(2003),* The Falls *(2004) and* Missing Mom *(2005). "They All Just Went Away" originally appeared in* The New Yorker *(1995) and was selected by Geoffrey C. Ward for* The Best American Essays 1996.

I must have been a lonely child. Until the age of twelve or thirteen, my most intense, happiest hours were spent tramping desolate fields, woods, and creek banks near my family's farmhouse in Millersport, New York. No one knew where I went. My father, working most of the day at Harrison's, a division of General Motors in Lockport, and at other times preoccupied, would not have asked; if my mother asked, I might have answered in a way that would deflect curiosity. I was an articulate, verbal child. Yet I could not have explained what drew me to the abandoned houses, barns, silos, corncribs. A hike of miles through fields of spiky grass, across outcroppings of shale as steeply angled as stairs, was a lark if the reward was an empty house.

Some of these houses had been inhabited as "homes" fairly recently — they had not yet reverted to the wild. Others, abandoned during the Depression, had long since begun to rot and collapse, engulfed by vegetation (trumpet vine, wisteria, rose of Sharon, willow) that elsewhere, on our property for instance, was kept neatly trimmed. I was drawn to both kinds of houses, though the more recently inhabited were more forbidding and therefore more inviting.

To push open a door into such silence: the absolute emptiness of a house whose occupants have departed. Often, the crack of broken glass underfoot. A startled buzzing of flies, hornets. The slithering, ticklish sensation of a garter snake crawling across floorboards.

Left behind, as if in haste, were remnants of a lost household. A broken toy on the floor, a baby's bottle. A rain-soaked sofa, looking as if it has been gutted with a hunter's skilled knife. Strips of wallpaper like shredded skin. Smashed crockery, piles of tin cans; soda, beer, whiskey bottles. An icebox, its door yawning open. Once, on a counter, a dirt-stiffened rag that, unfolded like precious cloth, revealed itself to be a woman's cheaply glamorous "see-through" blouse, threaded with glitter-strips of gold.

This was a long time ago, yet it is more vivid to me than anything now.

This was when I was too young to think *the house is the mother's body, you have been expelled and are forbidden now to reenter.*

Always, I was prepared to see a face at a high, empty window. A woman's hand uplifted in greeting, or in warning. *Hello! Come in! Stay away! Run! Who are you?* A movement in the corner of my eye: the blurred motion of a person passing through a doorway, or glimpsed through a window. There might be a single shriek of laughter from a barn — piercing as a bird's cry. Murmurous, teasing voices confused with wind rippling through tall, coarse, gone-to-seed grass. Voices that, when you pause to listen, fade immediately and are gone.

The sky in such places of abandonment was always of the hue and brightness of tin, as if the melancholy rural poverty of tin roofs reflected upward.

A house: a structural arrangement of space, geometrically laid out to provide what are called rooms, these divided from one another by verticals and horizontals called walls, ceilings, floors. The house contains the home but is not identical with it. The house antici-pates the home and will very likely survive it, reverting again sim-ply to house when home (that is, life) departs. For only where there is life can there be home.

I have never found the visual equivalent of these abandoned farmhouses of upstate New York, of northern Erie County, in the area of the long, meandering Tonawanda Creek and the Barge Canal. You think most immediately of the canvases of Edward Hop-per: those dreamily stylized visions of a lost America, houses never depicted as homes, and human beings, if you look closer, never de-picted as other than mannequins. For Hopper is not a realist but a surrealist. His dreams are of the ordinary, as if, even in imagina-tion, the artist were trapped in an unyielding daylight conscious-ness. There seems almost a kind of rage, a revenge against such restraints, in Hopper's studied, endlessly repeated *simplicity*. By con-trast, Charles Burchfield, with his numerous oils and watercol-ors — frequently of upstate New York landscapes, houses, and farms — rendered the real as visionary and luminous, suffused with a Blakean rapture and a kind of radical simplicity, too. Then there are the shimmering New England barns, fields, and skies of our contemporary Wolf Kahn — images evoked by memory, almost on the verge of dissolution. But the "real" — what assaults the eye be-fore the eye begins its work of selection — is never on the verge of dissolution, still less of appropriation. The real is raw, jarring, un-expected, sometimes trashy, sometimes luminous. Above all, the real is arbitrary. For to be a realist (in art or in life) is to acknowl-edge that all things might be other than they are. That there is no design, no intention, no aesthetic or moral or teleological imprimatur but, rather, the equivalent of Darwin's great vision of a blind, purposeless, ceaseless evolutionary process that yields no "products" — only temporary strategies against extinction.

Yet, being human, we think, To what purpose these broken-off things, if not to be gathered up, at last, in a single ecstatic vision?

There is a strange and profound and unknowable reality to these abandoned houses where jealously guarded, even prized possessions have become mere trash: windowpanes long ago smashed, and the spaces where they had been festooned with cobwebs, and cobwebs brushing against your face, catching in your hair like caresses. The peculiar, dank smell of wood rot and mildew, in one of the houses I most recall that had partly burned down, the smell of smoke and scorch, in early summer pervading even the lyric smell of honeysuckle — these haunting smells, never, at the time of experiencing, given specific sources, names.

Where a house has been abandoned — unworthy of being sold to new tenants, very likely seized by the county for default on taxes and the property held in escrow — you can be sure there has been a sad story. There have been devastated lives. Lives to be spoken of pityingly. How they went wrong. Why did she marry him, why did she stay with him? Just desperate people. Ignorant. Poor white trash. Runs in the family. A wrong turn.

Shall I say for the record that ours was a happy, close-knit, and unextraordinary family for our time, place, and economic status? Yet what was vividly real in the solid-built old farmhouse that contained my home (my family consisted of my father, mother, younger brother, grandfather, and grandmother, who owned the property — a slow-failing farm whose principal crop had become Bartlett pears by the time I was a girl) was of far less significance to me than what was real elsewhere. A gone-to-seed landscape had an authority that seemed to me incontestable: the powerful authority of silence in houses from which the human voice had vanished. For the abandoned house contained the future of any house — the lilac tree pushing through the rotted veranda, hornets' nests beneath eaves, windows smashed by vandals, human excrement left to dry on a parlor floor once scrubbed on hands and knees.

The abandoned, the devastated, was the profound experience, whereas involvement in family life — the fever, the bliss, the abrasions, the infinite distractions of human love — was so clearly temporary. Like a television screen upon which antic images (at this time, in the fifties, minimally varying gradations of gray) appear fleetingly and are gone.

I have seemed to suggest that the abandoned houses were all distant from our house, but in fact the one that had been partly gutted by fire — which I will call the Weidel house — was perhaps a half mile away. If you drove, turning right off Transit Road, which was our road, onto the old Creek Road, it would have been a distance of a mile or more, but if you crossed through our back potato field and through the marshy woods which no one seemed to own, it was a quick walk.

The Weidels' dog, Slossie, a mixed breed with a stumpy, energetic tail and a sweet disposition, sand-colored, rheumy-eyed, as hungry for affection as for the scraps we sometimes fed her, trotted over frequently to play with my brother and me. Though, strictly speaking, Slossie was not wanted at our house. None of the Weidels were wanted.

The "Weidel house," it would be called for years. The "Weidel property." As if the very land — which the family had not owned in any case, but only rented, partly with county-welfare support — were somehow imprinted with that name, a man's identity. Or infamy.

For tales were told of the father who drank, beat and terrorized his family, "did things to" his daughters, and finally set the house on fire and fled and was arrested, disappearing forever from the proper, decent life of our community. There was no romance in Mr. Weidel, whom my father knew only slightly and despised as a drinker, and as a wife- and child-beater. Mr. Weidel was a railway worker in Lockport, or perhaps an ex-railway worker, for he seemed to work only sporadically, though he always wore a railway-man's cap. He and his elder sons were hunters, owning a shotgun among them and one or two deer rifles. His face was broad, fair, vein-swollen, with a look of flushed, alcoholic reproach. He was tall and heavyset, with graying black whiskers that sprouted like quills. His eyes had a way of swerving in their sockets, seeking you out when you could not slip away quickly enough. *H'lo there, little Joyce! Joycie! Joycie Oates, h'lo!* He wore rubber boots that flapped, unbuckled, about his feet.

Mrs. Weidel was a faded-pretty, apologetic woman with a body that seemed to have become bloated, as with a perpetual pregnancy. Her bosom had sunk to her waist. Her legs were encased, sausagelike, in flesh-colored support hose. *How can that woman live with him? That pig.* There was disdain, disgust, in this frequent refrain. *Why doesn't she leave him? Did you see that black eye? Did you hear them the other night? Take the girls away, at least.* It was thought that she could, for Mrs. Weidel was the only one in the family who seemed to work at all regularly. She was hired for seasonal canning in a tomato factory in lower Lockport and may have done housecleaning in the city.

A shifting household of relatives and rumored "boarders" lived in the Weidel house. There were six Weidel children, four sons and two daughters. Ruth was a year older than I, and Dorothy two years younger. There was an older brother of Mr. Weidel's, who walked with a cane and was said to be an ex-convict, from Attica. The eldest Weidel son, Roy, owned a motorcycle, and friends of his often visited, fellow bikers. There were loud parties, frequent disputes, and tales of Mr. Weidel's chasing his wife with a butcher knife, a claw hammer, the shotgun, threatening to "blow her head off." Mrs. Weidel and the younger children fled outdoors in terror and hid in the hayloft. Sheriff's deputies drove out to the house, but no charges were ever pressed against Mr. Weidel. Until the fire, which was so public that it couldn't be denied.

There was the summer day — I was eleven years old — that Mr. Weidel shot Slossie. We heard the poor creature yelping and whimpering for what seemed like hours. When my father came home from work, he went to speak to Mr. Weidel, though my mother begged him not to. By this time, the dog had dragged herself beneath the Weidels' house to die. Mr. Weidel was furious at the intrusion, drunk, defensive — Slossie was his goddam dog, he said, she'd been getting in the way, she was "old." But my father convinced him to put the poor dog out of her misery. So Mr. Weidel made one of his sons drag Slossie out from beneath the house, and he straddled her and shot her a second time, and a third, at close range. My father, who'd never hunted, who'd never owned a gun, backed off, a hand over his eyes.

Afterward, my father would say of that day that walking away from that drunken son of a bitch with a rifle in his hands was

about the hardest thing he'd ever done. He'd expected a shot between his shoulders.

The fire was the following year, around Thanksgiving.

After the Weidels were gone from Millersport and the house
stood empty, I discovered Slossie's grave. I'm sure it was Slossie's
grave. It was beyond the dog hutch, in the weedy back yard, a
sunken patch of earth measuring about three feet by four with one
of Mrs. Weidel's big whitewashed rocks at the head.

Morning glories grew in clusters on the posts of the front
porch. Mrs. Weidel had planted hollyhocks, sunflowers, and trumpet vine in the yard. Tough, weedlike flowers that would survive
for years.

It had been said of Ruth and her sister Dorothy that they were
"slow." Yet Ruth was never slow to fly into a rage when she was
teased by neighborhood boys or by her older brothers. She waved
her fists and stammered obscenities, words that stung like hail.
Her face darkened with blood, and her full, thick lips quivered
with a strange sort of pleasure. How you loved to see Ruth Weidel
fly into one of her rages; it was like holding a lighted match to
flammable material.

The Weidel house was like any other rundown woodframe
house, said by my grandfather to have been "thrown up" in the
1920s. It had no cellar, only a concrete-block foundation — an
emptiness that gradually filled with debris. It had an upstairs with
several small bedrooms. There was no attic. No insulation. Steep,
almost vertical stairs. The previous tenant had started to construct
a front porch of raw planks, never completed or painted. (Though
Mrs. Weidel added "touches" to the porch — chairs, a woven-rush
rug, geraniums in flowerpots.) The roof of the house was made of
sheets of tin, scarred and scabbed like skin, and the front was covered in simulated-brick asphalt siding pieced together from lumberyard scraps. All year round, a number of the windows were
covered in transparent duct tape and never opened. From a distance, the house was the fading dun color of a deer's winter coat.

Our house had an attic and a cellar and a deep well and a solid
cement foundation. My father did all the carpentry on our house,
most of the shingling, the painting, the masonry. I would not know
until I was an adult that he'd come from what's called a "broken
home" himself — what an image, luridly visual, of a house literally

broken, split in two, its secrets spilled out onto the ground for all to see, like entrails.

My mother, unlike Mrs. Weidel, had time to houseclean. It was a continuous task, a mother's responsibility. My mother planted vegetables, strawberries, beds of flowers. Petunias and pansies and zinnias. Crimson peonies that flowered for my birthday, in mid-June.

I remember the night of the fire vividly, as if it had been a festive affair to which I'd been invited.

There was the sound of a siren on the Creek Road. There were shouts, and an astonishing burst of flame in the night, in the direction of the Weidel house. The air was moist, and reflected and magnified the fire, surrounding it like a nimbus. My grandparents would claim there had never been such excitement in Millersport, and perhaps that was true. My father dressed hurriedly and went to help the firefighters, and my mother and the rest of us watched from upstairs windows. The fire began at about 1 A.M., and it would be past 4 A.M. before my seven-year-old brother and I got back to bed.

Yet what was so exciting an event was, in fact, an ending, with nothing to follow. Immediately afterward, the Weidels disappeared from Millersport and from our lives. It was said that Mr. Weidel fled "as a fugitive" but was captured and arrested the next day, in Buffalo. The family was broken up, scattered, the younger children placed in foster homes. That quickly, the Weidels were gone.

For a long time, the smell of wood smoke, scorch, pervaded the air of Millersport, the fresh, damp smell of earth sullied by its presence. Neighbors complained that the Weidel house should be razed at the county's expense, bulldozed over, and the property sold. But nothing was done for years. Who knows why? When I went away to college, the old falling-down house was still there.

How swiftly, in a single season, a human habitation can turn wild. The bumpy cinder driveway over which the eldest Weidel son had ridden his motorcycle was soon stippled with tall weeds.

What had happened to Roy Weidel? It was said he'd joined the navy. No, he had a police record and could not have joined the navy. He'd disappeared. Asked by the police to give a sworn statement about the night of his father's "arson," he'd panicked and fled.

Signs were posted —NO TRESPASSING, THIS PROPERTY CONDEMNED BY ERIE CO. — and they, too, over a period of months, became shabby and faded. My parents warned me never to wander onto the Weidel property. There was a well with a loose-fitting cover, among other dangers. As if *I* would fall into a well! I smiled to think how little my parents knew me. How little anyone knew me.

Have I said that my father never struck his children, as Mr. Weidel struck his? And did worse things to them, to the girls sometimes, it was whispered. Yes, and Mrs. Weidel, who seemed so soft and apologetic and sad, she too had beaten the younger children when she'd been drinking. County social workers came around to question neighbors, and spread the story of what they learned along the way.

In fact, I may have been disciplined, spanked, a few times. Like most children, I don't remember. I remember Mr. Weidel spanking his children until they screamed (though I wasn't a witness, was I?), but I don't remember being spanked by my parents, and in any case, if I was, it was no more than I deserved.

I'd seen Mr. Weidel urinating once at the roadside. The loose-flying skein of the kerosene he'd flung around the house before setting the fire must have resembled the stream of his urine, transparent and glittering. But they laughed, saying Mr. Weidel had been too drunk, or too careless, to have done an adequate job of sprinkling kerosene through the downstairs of the house. Wasn't it like him, such a slovenly job. Only part of the house had burned, a wall of the kitchen and an adjoining woodshed.

Had Mr. Weidel wanted to burn his family alive in their beds? Mrs. Weidel testified no, they'd all been awake, they'd run out into the yard before the fire began. They'd never been in any danger, she swore. But Mr. Weidel was indicted on several counts of attempted murder, along with other charges.

For so many years the Weidel house remained standing. There was something defiant about it, like someone who has been mortally wounded but will not die. In the weedy front yard, Mrs. Weidel's display of whitewashed rocks and plaster-of-Paris gnomes and the clay pedestal with the shiny blue glass ball disappeared from view within a year or so. Brambles grew everywhere. I forced myself to taste a small bitter red berry but spat it out, it made my mouth pucker so.

What did it mean that Erie County had "condemned" the Weidel property? The downstairs windows were carelessly boarded over, and both the front and rear doors were unlocked, collapsing on their hinges. Broken glass underfoot and a sickish stench of burn, mildew, decay. Yet there were "touches" — on what remained of a kitchen wall, a Holstein calendar from a local feed store, a child's crayon drawing. Upstairs, children's clothes, socks and old shoes heaped on the floor. I recognized with a thrill of repugnance an old red sweater of Ruth's, angora-fuzzy. There were broken Christmas tree ornaments, a naked pink plastic doll. Toppled bedsprings, filthy mattresses streaked with yellow and rust-colored stains. The mattresses looked as if they'd been gutted, their stuffing strewn about. The most terrible punishment, I thought, would be to be forced to lie down on such a mattress.

I thought of Mrs. Weidel, her swollen, blackened eyes, her bruised face. Shouts and sirens in the night, the sheriff's patrol car. But no charges filed. The social worker told my mother how Mrs. Weidel had screamed at the county people, insisting her husband hadn't done anything wrong and shouldn't go to jail. The names she'd called them! Unrepeatable.

She was the wife of that man, they'd had babies together. The law had no right to interfere. The law had nothing to do with them.

As a woman and as a writer, I have long wondered at the wellsprings of female masochism. Or what, in despair of a more subtle, less reductive phrase, we can call the congeries of predilections toward self-hurt, self-erasure, self-repudiation in women. These predilections are presumably "learned" — "acquired" — but perhaps also imprinted in our genes, of biological necessity, neurophysiological fate, predilections that predate culture. Indeed, may shape culture. Do not say, "Yes, but these are isolated, peripheral examples. These are marginal Americans, uneducated. They tell us nothing about ourselves." They tell us everything about ourselves, and even the telling, the exposure, is a kind of cutting, an inscription in the flesh.

Yet what could possibly be the evolutionary advantage of selfhurt in the female? Abnegation in the face of another's cruelty? Acquiescence to another's will? This loathsome secret that women do not care to speak of, or even acknowledge.

Two or three years later, in high school, twelve miles away in a consolidated district school to which, as a sophomore, I went by school bus, Ruth Weidel appeared. She was living now with relatives in

Lockport. She looked, at sixteen, like a woman in her twenties; big-breasted, with full, strong thighs and burnished-brown hair inex-pertly bleached. Ruth's homeroom was "special education," but she took some classes with the rest of us. If she recognized me, in our home economics class, she was careful to give no sign.

There was a tacit understanding that "something had happened" to Ruth Weidel, and her teachers treated her guardedly. Ruth was special, the way a handicapped person is special. She was with-drawn, quiet; if still prone to violent outbursts of rage, she might have been on medication to control it. Her eyes, like her father's, seemed always about to swerve in their sockets. Her face was round, fleshy, like a pudding, her nose oily-pored. Yet she wore lipstick, she was "glamorous" — almost. In gym class, Ruth's large breasts straining against her T-shirt and the shining rippled muscles and fatty flesh of her thighs were amazing to us; we were so much thin-ner and less female, so much younger.

I believed that I should protect Ruth Weidel, so I told none of the other students about her family. Even to Ruth, for a long time I pretended not to know who she was. I can't explain how Ruth could have possibly believed me, yet this seems to have been so. Quite purposefully, I befriended Ruth. I thought her face would lose its sallow hardness if she could be made to smile, and so it be-came a kind of challenge to me to induce Ruth Weidel to smile. She was lonely and miserable at school, and flattered by my atten-tion. For so few "normal" girls sought out "specialed" girls. At first she may have been suspicious, but by degrees she became trusting. I thought of Slossie: trust shows in the eyes.

I sat with Ruth at lunch in the school cafeteria and eventually I asked her about the house on the old Creek Road, and she lied bluntly, to my face, insisting that an uncle of hers had owned that house. She'd only visited a few times. She and her family. I asked, "How did the fire start?" and Ruth said, slowly, each word sucked like a pebble in the mouth, "Lightning. Lightning hit it. One night in a storm." I asked, "Are you living with your mother now, Ruth?" and Ruth shrugged, and made a face, and said, "She's OK. I see her sometimes." I asked about Dorothy. I asked where Mrs. Weidel was. I said that my mother had always liked her mother, and missed her when she went away. But Ruth seemed not to hear. Her gaze had drifted. I said, "Why did you all move away?" Ruth did not reply, though I could hear her breathing hard. "Why did you abandon your house? It could have been fixed. It's still there. Your mom's hollyhocks are still there. You should come out and see it sometime. You could visit me." Ruth shrugged, and laughed. She gave me a sidelong glance, almost flirtatiously. It was startling to see how good-looking she could be, how sullen-sexy; to know how men would stare at her who would never so much as glance at a girl like me. Ruth said slowly, as if she'd come to a final, adamant conclusion to a problem that had long vexed her, "They all just went away."

Another time, after lunch with Ruth. I left a plastic change purse with a few coins in it on the ledge in one of the girls' lavatories, where Ruth was washing her hands. I don't recall whether I left it on purpose or not. But when I returned, after waiting for Ruth to leave the lavatory, the change purse was gone.

Once or twice, I invited Ruth Weidel to come home with me on the school bus some afternoon, to Millersport, to have supper with my family and stay the night. I must not have truly believed she might accept, for my mother would have been horrified and would have forced me to rescind the invitation. Ruth had hesitated, as if she wanted to say yes, wanted very badly to say yes, but finally she said, "No. I guess I better not."

Reflections and Responses

1. How does Joyce Carol Oates introduce the issue of class into the essay? How does her background differ from Ruth Weidel's? How would you describe her attitude toward the Weidel family? Why is she drawn to them? What does she find attractive about them?

2. How can you account for the abrupt introduction in the ninth paragraph of houses as the subject for famous American painters? Why do you think the author suddenly interjected this information? What does it contribute to the essay as a whole?

3. Where does the essay's title come from? Why do you think Joyce Carol Oates used this expression as the title? What does it suggest about the overall experience of the essay?

SUSAN ORLEAN

Lifelike

*Although essays have been published in newspapers since the eighteenth cen-
tury and in magazines since the middle of the nineteenth, it wasn't until the
early twentieth century that the essay began to form a full partnership with
periodical journalism. American writers such as Stephen Crane and Jack
London were instrumental in taking the conventional essay out of the library and study, where it had been at ease for decades, and putting the form
to reportorial work as they covered shipwrecks, earthquakes, big-time sporting events, and life in America's squalid cities. By the 1920s, the reportorial
essay had become a staple of the American magazine and was in the process
of being brought to perfection in one new periodical,* The New Yorker,
*which had been founded in 1925. Since then, the magazine has become a
literary institution, featuring the essay and nonfiction of some of the nation's finest writers. One of these writers is Susan Orlean (pronounced with
two syllables: "Or-leen"), whose work regularly appears in current issues. In
"Lifelike" she demonstrates her mastery of the reportorial essay as she attends
a taxidermy championship and closely observes the meticulous skill and
weird dedication to craft that go into the "questionable enterprise of making
dead things look like live things."*

Susan Orlean has been a staff writer for The New Yorker *since 1992.
In addition, she has contributed to* Vogue, Outside, Rolling Stone,
and the New York Times Magazine. *Her books include* The Orchid
Thief, The Bullfighter Checks Her Makeup, Saturday Night, *and*
My Kind of Place. *In 2004, she was a fellow at the Nieman Foundation
for Journalism at Harvard University. She is currently at work on a biography of Rin Tin Tin. "Lifelike" originally appeared in* The New Yorker
and was selected by Louis Menand for The Best American Essays
2004.

As soon as the 2003 World Taxidermy Championships opened, the heads came rolling in the door. There were foxes and moose and freeze-dried wild turkeys; mallards and buffalo and chipmunks and wolves; weasels and buffleheads and bobcats and jackdaws; big fish and little fish and razor-backed boar. The deer came in herds, in carloads, and on pallets: dozens and dozens of whitetail and roe; half deer and whole deer and deer with deformities, sneezing and glowering and nuzzling and yawning; does chewing apples and bucks nibbling leaves. There were millions of eyes, boxes and bowls of them; some as small as a lentil and some as big as a poached egg. There were animal mannequins, blank-faced and brooding, earless and eyeless and utterly bald: ghostly gray duikers and spectral pine martens and black-bellied tree ducks from some other world. An entire exhibit hall was filled with equipment, all the gear required to bring something dead back to life: replacement noses for grizzlies, false teeth for beavers, fish-fin cream, casting clay, upholstery nails.

The championships were held in April at the Springfield, Illinois, Crowne Plaza hotel, the sort of nicely appointed place that seems more suited to regional sales conferences and rehearsal dinners than to having wolves in the corridors and people crossing the lobby shouting, "Heads up! Buffalo coming through!" A thousand taxidermists converged on Springfield to have their best pieces judged and to attend such seminars as "Mounting Flying Waterfowl," "Whitetail Deer — From a Master!," and "Using a Fleshing Machine." In the Crowne Plaza lobby, across from the concierge desk, a grooming area had been set up. The taxidermists were bent over their animals, holding flashlights to check problem areas like tear ducts and nostrils, and wielding toothbrushes to tidy flyaway fur. People milled around, greeting fellow taxidermists they hadn't seen since the last world championships, held in Springfield two years ago, and talking shop:

"Acetone rubbed on a squirrel tail will fluff it right back up."

"My feeling is that it's quite tough to do a good tongue."

"The toes on a real competitive piece are very important. I think Bondo works nicely, and so does Super Glue."

"I knew a fellow with cattle, and I told him, 'If you ever have one stillborn, I'd really like to have it.' I thought it would make a really nice mount."

That there is a taxidermy championship at all is something of an astonishment, not only to the people in the world who have no use for a Dan-D-Noser and Soft Touch Duck Degreaser but also to taxidermists themselves. For a long time, taxidermists kept their own counsel. Taxidermy, the three-dimensional representation of animals for permanent display, has been around since the eighteenth century, but it was first brought into popular regard by the Victorians, who thrilled to all tokens of exotic travel and especially to any domesticated representations of wilderness — the glassed-in miniature rain forest on the tea table, the mounted antelope by the front door. The original taxidermists were upholsterers who tanned the hides of hunting trophies and then plumped them up with rags and cotton, so that they reassumed their original shape and size; those early poses were stiff and simple, and the expressions fairly expressionless. The practice grew popular in this country, too: by 1882, there was a Society of American Taxidermists, which held annual meetings and published scholarly reports, especially on the matter of preparing animals for museum display. As long as taxidermy served to preserve wild animals and make them available for study, it was viewed as an honorable trade, but most people were still discomfited by it. How could you not be? It was the business of dealing with dead things, coupled with the questionable enterprise of making dead things look like live things. In spite of its scientific value, it was usually regarded as almost a black art, a wholly owned subsidiary of witchcraft and voodoo. By the early part of the twentieth century, taxidermists such as Carl E. Akeley, William T. Horneday, and Leon Pray had refined techniques and begun emphasizing artistry. But the more the techniques of taxidermy improved, the more it discomfited: instead of the lumpy moose head that was so artless that it looked fake, there were mounts of pouncing bobcats so immaculately and exactly preserved they made you flinch.

For the next several decades, taxidermy existed in the margins — a few practitioners here and there, often self-taught, and usually known only by word of mouth. Then, in the late 1960s, a sort of transformation began: the business started to seem cleaner and less creepy — or maybe, in that messy, morbid time, popular culture started to again appreciate the messy, morbid business of mounting animals for display. An ironic reinterpretation of cluttered, bourgeois Victoriana and its strained juxtapositions of the natural and the man-made was in full revival — what hippie outpost didn't have a stuffed owl or a moose head draped with a silk shawl?—so, once again, taxidermy found a place in the public eye. Supply houses concocted new solvents and better tanning compounds, came out with lightweight mannequins, produced modern formulations of resins and clays. Taxidermy schools opened; previously, any aspiring taxidermist could only hope to learn the trade by apprenticing or by taking one of a few correspondence courses available. In 1971, the National Taxidermy Association was formed (the old society had moldered long before). In 1974, a trade magazine called *Taxidermy Review* began sponsoring national competitions. For the first time, most taxidermists had a chance to meet one another and share advice on how to glue tongues into jaw sets or accurately measure the carcass of a squirrel.

The competitions were also the first time that taxidermists could compare their skills and see who in the business could sculpt the best moose septum or could most perfectly capture the look on a prowling coyote's face. Taxidermic skill is a function of how deft you are at skinning an animal and then stretching its hide over a mannequin and sewing it into place. Top-of-the-line taxidermists sculpt their own mannequins; otherwise they will buy a ready-made polyurethane-foam form and tailor the skin to fit. Body parts that can't be preserved (ears, eyes, noses, lips, tongues) can be either store-bought or handmade. How good the mount looks — that is, how alive it looks — is a function of how assiduously the taxidermist has studied reference material (photographs, drawings, and actual live animals) so that he or she knows the particular creature literally and figuratively inside out.

To be good at taxidermy, you have to be good at sewing, sculpting, painting, and hairdressing, and mostly you have to be a little bit of a zoology nerd. You have to love animals — love looking at them, taking photographs of them, hunting them, measuring them, casting them in plaster of Paris when they're dead so that you have a reference when you're, say, attaching ears or lips and want to get the angle and shape exactly right. Some taxidermists raise the animals they most often mount, so they can just step out in the back yard when they're trying to remember exactly how a deer looks when it's licking its nose, especially because modern taxidermy emphasizes mounts with interesting expressions, rather than the stunned-looking creations of the past. Taxidermists seem to make little distinction between loving animals that are alive and loving ones that are not. "I love deer," one of the champions in the Whitetail division said to me. "They're my babies."

Taxidermy is now estimated to be a $570-million annual business, made up of small operators around the country who mount animals for museums, for decorators, and mostly for the thirteen million or so Americans who are recreational hunters and on occasion want to preserve and display something they killed and who are willing to shell out anywhere from $200 to mount a pheasant to several thousand for a kudu or a grizzly bear. There are state and regional taxidermy competitions throughout the year and the world championships, which are held every other year; two trade magazines; a score of taxidermy schools; and three thousand visits to Taxidermy.net every day, where taxidermists can trade information and goods with as little self-consciousness as you would find on a knitting Web site:

"I am in need of several pair of frozen goat feet!"

"Hi! I have up to 300 sets of goat feet and up to 1000 set of sheep feet per month. Drop me an email at frozencritters.com . . . or give me a call and we can discuss your needs."

"I have a very nice small raccoon that is frozen whole. I forgot he was in the freezer. Without taking exact measurements I would guess he is about twelve inches or so — very cute little one. Will make a very nice mount."

"Can I rinse a boar hide good and freeze it?"

"Bob, if it's salted, don't worry about it!"

"Can someone please tell me the proper way to preserve turkey legs and spurs? Thanks!"

"Brian, I inject the feet with Preservz-It . . . Enjoy!"

The word in the grooming area was that the piece to beat was Chris Krueger's happy-looking otters swimming in a perpetual circle around a leopard frog. A posting on Taxidermy.net earlier in the week declared, "EVERYTHING about this mount KICKS BUTT!!" Kicking butt, in this era of taxidermy, requires having a mount that is not just lifelike but also artistic. It used to be enough to do what taxidermists call "fish on a stick" displays; now a serious competitor worries about things like flow and negative space and originality. One of this year's contenders, for instance, Ken Walker's giant panda, had artistry and accuracy going for it, along with the element of surprise. The thing looked 100 percent pure panda, but you can't go out and shoot a panda, and you aren't likely to get hold of a panda that has met a natural end, so everyone was dying to know how he had done it. The day the show opened, Walker was in the grooming area, gluing bamboo into place behind the animal's back paws, and a crowd had gathered around him. Walker works as a staff taxidermist for the Smithsonian. He is a breezy, shaggy-haired guy whose hands are always busy. One day, I saw him holding a piece of clay while waiting for a seminar to begin, and within thirty seconds or so, without actually paying much attention to it, he had molded the clay into a little minklike creature.

"The panda was actually pretty easy," he was saying. "I just took two black bears and bleached one of them — I think I used Clairol Basic. Then I sewed the two skins together into a panda pattern." He took out a toothbrush and fluffed the fur on the panda's face. "At the world championship two years ago, a guy came in with an extinct Labrador duck. I was in awe. I thought, What could beat that — an extinct duck? And I came up with this idea." He said he thought that the panda would get points for creativity alone. "You can score a ninety-eight with a squirrel, but it's still a squirrel," he said. "So that means I'm going with a panda."

"What did you do for toenails, Ken?" someone asked.

"I left the black bear's toenails in," he said. "They looked pretty good."

Another passerby stopped to admire the panda. He was carrying a grooming kit, which appeared to contain Elmer's glue, brown and black paint, a small tool set, and a bottle of Suave mousse. "I killed a blond bear once," he said to Ken. "A two-hundred-pound sow. Whew, she made a beautiful mount."

"I'll bet," Ken said. He stepped back to admire the panda. "I like doing re-creations of these endangered animals and extinct animals, since that's the only way anyone's going to have one. Two years ago, I did a saber-toothed cat. I got an old lioness from a zoo and bleached her."

The panda was entered in the Re-Creation (Mammal) division, one of the dozens of divisions and subdivisions and sub-subcategories, ranging from the super-specific (Whitetail Deer Long Hair, Open Mouth division) to the sweepingly colossal

(Best in World), that would share in $25,000 worth of prizes. (There is even a sub-sub-subspecialty known as "fish carving," which uses no natural fish parts at all; it is resin and wood sculpted into a fish form and then painted.) Nearly all the competitors are professionals, and they publicize their awards wherever possible. For instance, instead of ordering just any Boar Eye-Setting Reference Head out of a taxidermy catalogue, you can order the Noonkester's #NRB-ERH head sculpted by Bones Johnson, which was, as the catalogue notes, the 2000 National Taxidermy Association Champion Gamehead.

The taxidermists take the competition very seriously. During the time I was in Springfield, I heard conversations analyzing such arcane subjects as exactly how much a javelina's snout wrinkles when it snarls and which molars deer use to chew acorns as opposed to which ones they use to chew leaves. This is important because the ultimate goal of a taxidermist is to make the animal look as if it had never died, as if it were still in the middle of doing ordinary animal things like plucking berries off a bush or taking a nap. When I walked around with the judges one morning, I heard discussions that were practically Talmudic,* about whether the eyelids on a bison mount were overdetailed, and whether the nostrils on a springbok were too wide, and whether the placement of whiskers on an otter appeared too deliberate. "You do get compulsive," a taxidermist in the exhibit hall explained to me one afternoon. At the time, he was running a feather duster over his entry — a bobcat hanging off an icicle-covered rock — in the last moments before the judging would begin. "When you're working on a piece, you forget to eat, you forget to drink, you even forget to sleep. You get up in the middle of the night and go into the shop so you can keep working. You get completely caught up in it. You want it to be perfect. You're trying to make something come back to life."

I said that his bobcat was beautiful, and that even the icicles on the piece looked completely real. "I made them myself," he said. "I used clear acrylic toilet-plunger handles. The good Lord sent the

---

*Talmudic: Refers to the collection of ancient Jewish writings that form the basis of Judaic law; the adjective suggests a highly specified and hair-splitting system of rules and regulations. — Ed.

idea to me while I was in a hardware store. I just took the handles and put them in the oven at four hundred degrees." He tapped the icicles and then added, "My wife was pretty worried, but I did it on a nonstick cookie sheet."

So who wants to be a taxidermist? "I was a meat cutter for fifteen years," a taxidermist from Kentucky said to me. "That whole time, no one ever said to me, 'Boy, that was a wonderful steak you cut me.' Now I get told all the time what a great job I've done." Steve Faechner, who is the president and chairman of the Academy of Realistic Taxidermy, in Havre, Montana, started mounting animals in 1989, after years spent working on the railroad. "I had gotten hurt, and was looking for something to do," he said. "I was with a friend who did taxidermy and I thought to myself, I have got to get a life. And this was it." Larry Blomquist, who is the owner of the World Taxidermy Championships and of Breakthrough, the trade magazine that sponsors the competition, was a schoolteacher for three years before setting up his business. There are a number of women taxidermists (one was teaching this year's seminar on Problem Areas in Mammal Taxidermy), and there are budding junior taxidermists, who had their own competition division, for kids fourteen and younger, at the show.

The night the show opened, I went to dinner with three taxidermists who had driven in from Kentucky, Michigan, and Maryland. They were all married, and all had wives who complained when they found one too many antelope carcasses in the family freezer, and all worked full time mounting animals — mostly deer, for local hunters, but occasional safari work, for people who had shot something in Africa. When I mentioned that I had no idea that a person could make a living as a taxidermist, they burst out laughing, and the guy from Kentucky pointed out that he lived in a little town and there were two other full-time taxidermists in business right down the road.

"What's the big buzz this year?" the man from Michigan asked.

"I don't know. Probably something new with eyes," the guy from Maryland answered. "That's where you see the big advances. Remember at the last championship, those Russian eyes?" These were glass animal eyes that had a reflective paint embedded in them, so that if you shone a light they would shine back at you, sort of like the way real animals' eyes do. The men discussed those for a while, then talked about the new fish eyes being introduced this year, which have photographic transfers of actual fish eyes printed on plastic lenses. We happened to be in a restaurant with a sports theme, and there were about a hundred televisions on around the room, broadcasting dozens of different athletic events, but the men never glanced at them, and never stopped talking about their trade. We had all ordered barbecued ribs. When dinner was over, all three of them were fiddling around with the bones before the waitress came to clear our plates.

"Look at these," the man from Kentucky said, holding up a rib. "You could take these home and use them to make a skeleton."

In the seminars, the atmosphere was as sober and exacting as a tax-law colloquium. "Whiskers," one of the instructors said to the group, giving them a stern look. "I pull them out. I label them. There are left whiskers and there are right whiskers. If you want to get those top awards, you're going to have to think about whiskers." Everyone took notes. In the next room: "Folks, remember, your carcass is your key. The best thing you can do is to keep your carcass in the freezer. Freeze the head, cast it in plaster. It's going to really help if your head is perfect." During the breaks, the group made jokes about a T-shirt that had been seen at one of the regional competitions. The shirt said "PETA" in big letters, but when you got up close you saw that PETA didn't spell out People for the Ethical Treatment of Animals, the bane of all hunters and, by extension, all taxidermists; it spelled out People Eating Tasty Animals. Chuckles all around, then back to the solemn business of Mounting Flying Waterfowl: "People, follow what the bird is telling you. Study it, do your homework. When you've got it ready, fluff the head, shake it, and then get your eyes. There are a lot of good eyes out there on the market today. Do your legwork, and you can have a beautiful mount."

It was brisk and misty outside — the antler venders in the parking lot looked chilled and miserable — and the modest charms of Springfield, with its mall and the Oliver P. Parks Telephone Museum and Abraham Lincoln's tomb, couldn't compete with the strange and wondrous sights inside the hotel. The mere experience of waiting for the elevator — knowing that the doors would peel back to reveal maybe a man and a moose, or a bush pig, or a cougar — was much more exciting than the usual elevator wait in the usual Crowne Plaza hotel. The trade show was a sort of mad tea party of body parts and taxidermy supplies, things for pulling flesh off a carcass, for rinsing blood out of fur — a surreal carnality, but all conveyed with the usual trade-show earnestness and hucksterism, with no irony and no acknowledgment that having buckets of bear noses for sale was anything out of the ordinary. "Come take a look at our beautiful synthetic fur! We're the hair club for lions! If you happen to shoot a lion who is out of season or bald, we can provide you with a gorgeous replacement mane!" "Too many squirrels? Are they driving you nuts? Let us mount them for you!" "Divide and Conquer animal forms — an amazing advance in small-mammal mannequins, patent pending!"

The big winner at the show turned out to be a tiny thing — a mount of two tree sparrows, submitted by a strapping German named Uwe Bauch, who had grown up in the former East Germany dreaming of competing in an American taxidermy show. The piece was precise and lovely, almost haunting, since the more you looked at it the more certain you were that the birds would just stop building their nest, spread their wings, and fly away. Early one morning, before I left Springfield, I took a last walk around the competition hall. It was quiet and uncanny, with hundreds of mounts arranged on long tables throughout the room; the deer heads clustered together, each in a slightly different pose and angle, looked like a kind of animal Roman forum caught in mid-debate. A few of the mounts were a little gory — a deer with a mailbox impaled on an antler, another festooned with barbed wire, and one with an arrow stuck in its brisket — and one display, a coyote whose torso was split open to reveal a miniature scene of the destruction of the World Trade Center, complete with little firemen and rubble piles, was surpassingly weird. Otherwise, the room was biblically tranquil, the lion at last lying down with the Corsican lamb, the family of jackdaws in everlasting, unrequited pursuit of a big green beetle, and the stillborn Bengal tiger cub magically revived, its face in an eternal snarl, alive-looking although it had never lived.

Reflections and Responses

1. Every month in the United States there are perhaps a thousand professional conventions and trade shows that a reporter could cover. Why do you think Susan Orlean chose to attend a taxidermists' championship and convention? She doesn't acknowledge a prior interest or expertise in taxidermy, so what in particular do you think attracted her to this event? Why do you think *The New Yorker* would be interested in publishing this essay?

2. *The New Yorker* is an urban, liberal-oriented, sophisticated magazine that appeals to a like-minded readership. What attitude would you expect it to take toward nonurban Americans who enjoy hunting and displaying their stuffed trophies? Do you think Orlean brings any "attitude" or predisposition into her coverage? How would you summarize her general approach to the trade show? For example, do you find anything condescending in her report? After reading the essay, what image do you carry away of taxidermy? What do the details she introduces in her final paragraph suggest about Orlean's general attitude towards the taxidermists' exhibit?

3. Reporters can play a range of roles in their essays: They can be invisible, be constantly present, or move quietly in and out of the reader's attention. How would you describe Orlean's presence in her coverage? Does she provide any background identity for herself? What would we know about her from the essay alone? What appear to be the sources of her information? Examine her opening paragraphs: There is no "I" reporting, yet how do you feel her presence?

GAY TALESE

Ali in Havana

When one of America's leading journalists was assigned to profile one of the world's biggest celebrities on a humanitarian-aid visit to one of the world's most controversial political figures, the result was bound to be a fascinating piece of writing and disclosure. In "Ali in Havana," Gay Talese accompanies the great fighter Muhammad Ali as he travels with his wife and entourage, along with many other visitors, to a reception at Havana's Palace of the Revolution to meet aging communist leader Fidel Castro. What ensues is both comic and poignant, as the magical Ali, stricken with Parkinson's disease, leaves Castro — who has been struggling to keep the small talk flowing — with a very odd parting token. A connoisseur of the unnoticed detail, Talese captures all of the humor, tension, and awkwardness of this nearly surrealistic scene.

Gay Talese is one of the founders of the New Journalism, a literary movement that irrevocably altered both the art of reporting and the art of the essay. He is the best-selling author of books about the New York Times (The Kingdom and the Power), *the inside story of a Mafia family* (Honor Thy Father), *the changing moral values of America* (Thy Neighbor's Wife), *and a historical memoir* (Unto the Sons). *Other nonfiction books include* The Bridge, New York: A Serendipiter's Journey *and* Fame and Obscurity. *In 2006, he published a memoir,* A Writer's Life. *Talese served as guest editor of* The Best American Essays 1987. *"Ali in Havana" originally appeared in* Esquire *and was selected by Ian Frazier for the 1997 volume.*

It is a warm, breezy, palm-flapping winter evening in Havana, and the leading restaurants are crowded with tourists from Europe, Asia, and South America being serenaded by guitarists relentlessly singing *"Guan-tan-a-mera . . . guajira . . . Guan-tan-a-mera"*; and at the Café Cantante there are clamorous salsa dancers, mambo kings, grunting, bare-chested male performers lifting tables with their teeth, and turbaned women swathed in hip-hugging skirts, blowing whistles while gyrating their glistening bodies into an erotic frenzy. In the café's audience as well as in the restaurants, hotels, and other public places throughout the island, cigarettes and cigars are smoked without restraint or restriction. Two prostitutes are smoking and talking privately on the corner of a dimly lit street bordering the manicured lawns of Havana's five-star Hotel Nacional. They are copper-colored women in their early twenties wearing faded miniskirts and halters, and as they chat, they are watching attentively while two men — one white, the other black — huddle over the raised trunk of a parked red Toyota, arguing about the prices of the boxes of black-market Havana cigars that are stacked within.

The white man is a square-jawed Hungarian in his mid-thirties, wearing a beige tropical suit and a wide yellow tie, and he is one of Havana's leading entrepreneurs in the thriving illegal business of selling top-quality hand-rolled Cuban cigars below the local and international market price. The black man behind the car is a well-built, baldish, gray-bearded individual in his mid-fifties from Los Angeles named Howard Bingham; and no matter what price the Hungarian quotes, Bingham shakes his head and says, "No, no — that's too much!"

"You're crazy!" cries the Hungarian in slightly accented English, taking one of the boxes from the trunk and waving it in Howard Bingham's face. "These are Cohiba Esplendidos! The best in the world! You will pay one thousand dollars for a box like this in the States."

"Not me," says Bingham, who wears a Hawaiian shirt with a camera strapped around his neck. He is a professional photographer, and he is staying at the Hotel Nacional with his friend Muhammad Ali. "I wouldn't give you more than fifty dollars."

"You really are crazy," says the Hungarian, slicing through the box's paper seal with his fingernail, opening the lid to reveal a gleaming row of labeled Esplendidos.

"Fifty dollars," says Bingham.

"A hundred dollars," insists the Hungarian. "And hurry! The police could be driving around." The Hungarian straightens up and

stares over the car toward the palm-lined lawn and stanchioned
lights that glow in the distance along the road leading to the
hotel's ornate portico, which is now jammed with people and vehicles; then he turns and flings a glance back toward the nearby public street, where he notices that the prostitutes are now blowing
smoke in his direction. He frowns.

"Quick, quick," he says to Bingham, handing him the box. "One
hundred dollars."

Howard Bingham does not smoke. He and Muhammad Ali and
their traveling companions are leaving Havana tomorrow, after
participating in a five-day American humanitarian-aid mission that
brought a planeload of medical supplies to hospitals and clinics
depleted by the United States' embargo, and Bingham would like
to return home with some fine contraband cigars for his friends.
But, on the other hand, one hundred is still too much.

"Fifty dollars," says Bingham determinedly, looking at his watch.
He begins to walk away.

"O.K., O.K.," the Hungarian says petulantly. "Fifty."

Bingham reaches into his pocket for the money, and the Hungarian grabs it and gives him the Esplendidos before driving off in the
Toyota. One of the prostitutes takes a few steps toward Bingham,
but the photographer hurries on to the hotel. Fidel Castro is having a reception tonight for Muhammad Ali, and Bingham has only
a half hour to change and be at the portico to catch the chartered
bus that will take them to the government's headquarters. He will
be bringing one of his photographs to the Cuban leader: an en-
larged, framed portrait showing Muhammad Ali and Malcolm X
walking together along a Harlem sidewalk in 1963. Malcolm X was
thirty-seven at the time, two years away from an assassin's bullet; the
twenty-one-year-old Ali was about to win the heavyweight title in a
remarkable upset over Sonny Liston in Miami. Bingham's photograph is inscribed, TO PRESIDENT FIDEL CASTRO, FROM MUHAMMAD ALI.
Under his signature, the former champion has sketched a little
heart.

Although Muhammad Ali is now fifty-four and has been retired
from boxing for more than fifteen years, he is still one of the most
famous men in the world, being identifiable throughout five continents; and as he walks through the lobby of the Hotel Nacional

toward the bus, wearing a gray sharkskin suit and a white cotton shirt buttoned at the neck without a tie, several guests approach him and request his autograph. It takes him about thirty seconds to write "Muhammad Ali," so shaky are his hands from the effects of Parkinson's syndrome; and though he walks without support, his movements are quite slow, and Howard Bingham and Ali's fourth wife, Yolanda, are following nearby.

Bingham met Ali thirty-five years ago in Los Angeles, shortly after the fighter had turned professional and before he discarded his "slave name" (Cassius Marcellus Clay) and joined the Black Muslims. Bingham subsequently became his closest male friend and has photographed every aspect of Ali's life: his rise and fall three times as the heavyweight champion; his three-year expulsion from boxing, beginning in 1967, for refusing to serve in the American military during the Vietnam War ("I ain't got no quarrel with them Vietcong"); his four marriages; his fatherhood of nine children (one adopted, two out of wedlock); his endless public appearances in all parts of the world — Germany, England, Egypt (sailing on the Nile with a son of Elijah Muhammad's), Sweden, Libya, Pakistan (hugging refugees from Afghanistan), Japan, Indonesia, Ghana (wearing a dashiki and posing with President Kwame Nkrumah), Zaire (beating George Foreman), Manila (beating Joe Frazier) . . . and now, on the final night of his 1996 visit to Cuba, he is en route to a social encounter with an aging contender he has long admired — one who has survived at the top for nearly forty years despite the ill will of nine American presidents, the CIA, the Mafia, and various militant Cuban Americans.

Bingham waits for Ali near the open door of the charter bus that is blocking the hotel's entrance; but Ali lingers within the crowd in the lobby, and Yolanda steps aside to let some people get closer to her husband.

She is a large and pretty woman of thirty-eight, with a radiant smile and a freckled, fair complexion that reflects her interracial ancestry. A scarf is loosely draped over her head and shoulders, her arms are covered by long sleeves, and her well-designed dress in vivid hues hangs below her knees. She converted to Islam from Catholicism when she married Ali, a man sixteen years her senior but one with whom she shared a familial bond dating back to her girlhood in their native Louisville, where her mother and Ali's mother were sisterly soul mates who traveled together to attend his fights. Yolanda had occasionally joined Ali's entourage, becoming acquainted with not only the boxing element but with Ali's female contemporaries who were his lovers, his wives, the mothers of his children; and she remained in touch with Ali throughout the 1970s, while she majored in psychology at Vanderbilt and later earned her master's degree in business at UCLA. Then — with the end of Ali's boxing career, his third marriage, and his vibrant health — Yolanda intimately entered his life as casually and naturally as she now stands waiting to reclaim her place at his side.

She knows that he is enjoying himself. There is a slight twinkle in his eyes, not much expression on his face, and no words forthcoming from this once most talkative of champions. But the mind behind his Parkinson's mask is functioning normally, and he is characteristically committed to what he is doing: he is spelling out his full name on whatever cards or scraps of paper his admirers are handing him. "Muhammad Ali." He does not settle for a time-saving "Ali" or his mere initials. He has never shortchanged his audience.

And in this audience tonight are people from Latin America, Canada, Africa, Russia, China, Germany, France. There are two hundred French travel agents staying at the hotel in conjunction with the Cuban government's campaign to increase its growing tourist trade (which last year saw about 745,000 visitors spending an estimated one billion dollars on the island). There is also on hand an Italian movie producer and his lady friend from Rome and a onetime Japanese wrestler, Antonio Inoki, who injured Ali's legs during a 1976 exhibition in Tokyo (but who warmly embraced him two nights ago in the hotel's lounge as they sat listening to Cuban pianist Chucho Valdes playing jazz on a Russian-made Moskva baby grand); and there is also in the crowd, standing taller than the rest, the forty-three-year-old, six-foot five-inch Cuban heavyweight hero Teófilo Stevenson, who was a three-time Olympic gold medalist, in 1972, 1976 and 1980, and who, on this island at least, is every bit as renowned as Ali or Castro.

Though part of Stevenson's reputation derives from his erstwhile power and skill in the ring (although he never fought Ali), it is also attributable to his not having succumbed to the offers of professional boxing promoters, stubbornly resisting the Yankee dollar — although Stevenson hardly seems deprived. He dwells among his countrymen like a towering Cuban peacock, occupying high positions within the government's athletic programs and gaining sufficient attention from the island's women to have garnered four wives so far, who are testimony to his eclectic taste.

His first wife was a dance instructor. His second was an industrial engineer. His third was a medical doctor. His fourth and present wife is a criminal attorney. Her name is Fraymari, and she is a girlishly petite olive-skinned woman of twenty-three who, standing next to her husband in the lobby, rises barely higher than the midsection of his embroidered guayabera — a tightly tailored, short-sleeved shirt that accentuates his tapered torso, his broad shoulders, and the length of his dark, muscular arms, which once prevented his opponents from doing any injustice to his winning Latin looks.

Stevenson always fought from an upright position, and he maintains that posture today. When people talk to him, his eyes look downward, but his head remains high. The firm jaw of his oval-shaped head seems to be locked at a right angle to his straight-spined back. He is a proud man who exhibits all of his height. But he does listen, especially when the words being directed up at him are coming from the perky little attorney who is his wife. Fraymari is now reminding him that it is getting late — everyone should be on the bus; Fidel may be waiting.

Stevenson lowers his eyes toward her and winks. He has gotten the message. He has been Ali's principal escort throughout this visit. He was also Ali's guest in the United States during the fall of 1995; and though he knows only a few words of English, and Ali no Spanish, they are brotherly in their body language.

Stevenson edges himself into the crowd and gently places his right arm around the shoulders of his fellow champion. And then, slowly but firmly, he guides Ali toward the bus.

The road to Fidel Castro's Palace of the Revolution leads through a memory lane of old American automobiles chugging along at about twenty-five miles an hour — springless, pre-embargo Ford coupes and Plymouth sedans, DeSotos and LaSalles, Nashes and Studebakers, and various vehicular collages created out of Cadillac grilles and Oldsmobile axles and Buick fenders patched with pieces of oil-drum metal and powered by engines interlinked with kitchen utensils and pre-Batista lawn mowers and other gadgets that have elevated the craft of tinkering in Cuba to the status of high art.

The relatively newer forms of transportation seen on the road are, of course, non-American products — Polish Fiats, Russian Ladas, German motor scooters, Chinese bicycles, and the glistening, newly imported, air-conditioned Japanese bus from which Muhammad Ali is now gazing through a closed window out toward the street. At times, he raises a hand in response to one of the waving pedestrians or cyclists or motorists who recognize the bus, which has been shown repeatedly on the local TV news conveying Ali and his companions to the medical centers and tourist sites that have been part of the busy itinerary.

On the bus, as always, Ali is sitting alone, spread out across the two front seats in the left aisle directly behind the Cuban driver. Yolanda sits a few feet ahead of him to the right; she is adjacent to the driver and within inches of the windshield. The seats behind her are occupied by Teófilo Stevenson, Fraymari, and the photographer Bingham. Seated behind Ali, and also occupying two seats, is an American screenwriter named Greg Howard, who weighs more than three hundred pounds. Although he has traveled with Ali for only a few months while researching a film on the fighter's life, Greg Howard has firmly established himself as an intimate sidekick, and as such is among the very few on this trip who have heard Ali's voice. Ali speaks so softly that it is impossible to hear him in a crowd, and as a result whatever public comments or sentiments he is expected to, or chooses to, express are verbalized by Yolanda, or Bingham, or Teófilo Stevenson, or even at times by this stout young screenwriter.

"Ali is in his Zen period," Greg Howard has said more than once, in reference to Ali's quiescence. Like Ali, he admires what he has seen so far in Cuba — "There's no racism here" — and as a black man he has long identified with many of Ali's frustrations and confrontations. His student thesis at Princeton analyzed the Newark race riots of 1967, and the Hollywood script he most recently completed focuses on the Negro baseball leagues of the pre–World War II years. He envisions his new work on Ali in the genre of *Gandhi*.

*　*　*

The two-dozen bus seats behind those tacitly reserved for Ali's inner circle are occupied by the secretary-general of the Cuban Red Cross and the American humanitarian personnel who have entrusted him with $500,000 worth of donated medical supplies; and there are also the two Cuban interpreters and a dozen members of the American media, including the CBS-TV commentator Ed Bradley and his producers and camera crew from *60 Minutes.*

Ed Bradley is a gracious but reserved individualist who has appeared on television for a decade with his left earlobe pierced by a small circular ring — which, after some unfavorable comment initially expressed by his colleagues Mike Wallace and Andy Rooney, prompted Bradley's explanation: "It's *my* ear." Bradley also indulges in his identity as a cigar smoker; and as he sits in the midsection of the bus next to his Haitian lady friend, he is taking full advantage of the Communist regime's laissez-faire attitude toward tobacco, puffing away on a Cohiba Robusto, for which he paid full price at the Nacional's tobacco shop — and which now exudes a costly cloud of fragrance that appeals to his friend (who occasionally also smokes cigars) but is not appreciated by the two California women who are seated two rows back and are affiliated with a humanitarian-aid agency.

Indeed, the women have been commenting about the smoking habits of countless people they have encountered in Havana, being especially disappointed to discover earlier this very day that the pediatric hospital they visited (and to which they committed donations) is under the supervision of three tobacco-loving family physicians. When one of the American women, a blonde from Santa Barbara, reproached one of the cigarette-smoking doctors indirectly for setting such a poor example, she was told in effect that the island's health statistics regarding longevity, infant mortality, and general fitness compared favorably with those in the United States and were probably better than those of Americans residing in the capital city of Washington. On the other hand, the doctor made it clear that he did not believe that smoking was good for one's health — after all, Fidel himself had given it up; but unfortunately, the doctor added, in a classic understatement, "Some people have not followed him."

Nothing the doctor said appeased the woman from Santa Barbara. She did not, however, wish to appear confrontational at the hospital's news conference, which was covered by the press; nor during her many bus rides with Ed Bradley did she ever request that he discard his cigar. "Mr. Bradley intimidates me," she confided to her California coworker. But he was of course living within the law on this island that the doctor had called "the cradle of the best tobacco in the world." In Cuba, the most available American periodical on the newsstands is *Cigar Aficionado*.

The bus passes through the Plaza de la Revolución and comes to a halt at a security checkpoint near the large glass doors that open onto the marble-floored foyer of a 1950s modern building that is the center of communism's only stronghold in the Western Hemisphere.

As the bus door swings open, Greg Howard moves forward in his seat and grabs the 235-pound Muhammad Ali by the arms and shoulders and helps him to his feet; and after Ali has made his way down to the metal step, he turns and stretches back into the bus to take hold of the extended hands and forearms of the 300-pound screenwriter and pulls him to a standing position. This routine, repeated at each and every bus stop throughout the week, is never accompanied by either man's acknowledging that he had received any assistance, although Ali is aware that some passengers find the pas de deux quite amusing, and he is not reluctant to use his friend to further comic effect. After the bus had made an earlier stop in front of the sixteenth-century Morro Castle — where Ali had followed Teófilo Stevenson up a 117-step spiral staircase for a rooftop view of Havana Harbor — he spotted the solitary figure of Greg Howard standing below in the courtyard. Knowing that there was no way the narrow staircase could accommodate Howard's wide body, Ali suddenly began to wave his arms, summoning Howard to come up and join him.

Castro's security guards, who know in advance the names of all the bus passengers, guide Ali and the others through the glass doors and then into a pair of waiting elevators for a brief ride that is followed by a short walk through a corridor and finally into a large white-walled reception room, where it is announced that Fidel Castro will soon join them. The room has high ceilings and potted palms in every corner and is sparsely furnished with modern tan leather furniture. Next to a sofa is a table with two telephones, one gray and the other red. Overlooking the sofa is an oil painting of the Viñales valley, which lies west of Havana; and among the primitive art displayed on a circular table in front of the sofa is a grotesque tribal figure similar to the one Ali had examined earlier in the week at a trinket stand while touring with the group in Havana's Old Square. Ali had then whispered into the ear of Howard Bingham, and Bingham had repeated aloud what Ali had said: "Joe Frazier."

Ali now stands in the middle of the room, next to Bingham, who carries under his arm the framed photograph he plans to give Castro. Teófilo Stevenson and Fraymari stand facing them. The diminutive and delicate-boned Fraymari has painted her lips scarlet and has pulled back her hair in a matronly manner, hoping no doubt to appear more mature than her twenty-three years suggest, but standing next to the three much older and heavier and taller men transforms her image closer to that of an anorexic teenager. Ali's wife and Greg Howard are wandering about within the group that is exchanging comments in muted tones, either in English or Spanish, sometimes assisted by the interpreters. Ali's hands are shaking uncontrollably at his sides; but since his companions have witnessed this all week, the only people who are now paying attention are the security guards posted near the door.

Also waiting near the door for Castro is the four-man CBS camera team, and chatting with them and his two producers is Ed Bradley, without his cigar. There are no ashtrays in this room! This is a most uncommon sight in Cuba. Its implications might be political. Perhaps the sensibilities of the blond woman from Santa Barbara were taken into account by the doctors at the hospital and communicated to Castro's underlings, who are now making a conciliatory gesture toward their American benefactress.

Since the security guards have not invited the guests to be seated, everybody remains standing — for ten minutes, for twenty minutes, and then for a full half hour. Teófilo Stevenson shifts his weight from foot to foot and gazes over the heads of the crowd toward the upper level of the portal through which Castro is expected to enter — if he shows up. Stevenson knows from experience that Castro's schedule is unpredictable. There is always a crisis of some sort in Cuba, and it has long been rumored on the island that Castro constantly changes the location of where he sleeps. The identity of his bed partners is, of course, a state secret. Two nights ago, Stevenson and Ali and the rest were kept waiting until midnight for an expected meeting with Castro at the Hotel Biocaribe (to which Bingham had brought his gift photograph). But Castro never appeared. And no explanation was offered.

Now in this reception room, it is already 9 P.M. Ali continues to shake. No one has had dinner. The small talk is getting smaller: A few people would like to smoke. The regime is not assuaging anyone in this crowd with a bartender. It is a cocktail party without cocktails. There are not even canapés or soft drinks. Everyone is becoming increasingly restless — and then suddenly there is a collective sigh. The very familiar man with the beard strides into the room, dressed for guerrilla combat; and in a cheerful, high-pitched voice that soars beyond his whiskers, he announces, *"Buenas noches!"*

In an even higher tone, he repeats, *"Buenas noches,"* this time with a few waves to the group while hastening toward the guest of honor; and then, with his arms extended, the seventy-year-old Fidel Castro immediately obscures the lower half of Ali's expressionless face with a gentle embrace and his flowing gray beard.

"I am glad to see you," Castro says to Ali, via the interpreter who followed him into the room, a comely, fair-skinned woman with a refined English accent. "I am very, very glad to see you," Castro continues, backing up to look into Ali's eyes while holding on to his trembling arms, "and I am thankful for your visit." Castro then releases his grip and awaits a possible reply. Ali says nothing. His expression remains characteristically fixed and benign, and his eyes do not blink despite the flashbulbs of several surrounding photographers. As the silence persists, Castro turns toward his old friend Teófilo Stevenson, feigning a jab. The Cuban boxing champion lowers his eyes and, with widened lips and cheeks, registers a smile. Castro then notices the tiny brunette standing beside Stevenson.

"Stevenson, who is this young woman?" Castro asks aloud in a tone of obvious approval. But before Stevenson can reply, Fraymari steps forward with a hint of lawyerly indignation: "You mean you don't remember me?"

Castro seems stunned. He smiles feebly, trying to conceal his confusion. He turns inquiringly toward his boxing hero, but Stevenson's eyes only roll upward. Stevenson knows that Castro has met

Fraymari socially on earlier occasions, but unfortunately the Cuban leader has forgotten, and it is equally unfortunate that Fraymari is now behaving like a prosecutor.

"You held my son in your arms before he was one year old!" she reminds him while Castro continues to ponder. The crowd is attentive; the television cameras are rolling.

"At a volleyball game?" Castro asks tentatively.

"No, no," Stevenson interrupts, before Fraymari can say anything more, "that was my former wife. The doctor."

Castro slowly shakes his head in mock disapproval. Then he abruptly turns away from the couple, but not before reminding Stevenson, "You should get name tags."

Castro redirects his attention to Muhammad Ali. He studies Ali's face.

"Where is your wife?" he asks softly. Ali says nothing. There is more silence and turning of heads in the group until Howard Bingham spots Yolanda standing near the back and waves her to Castro's side.

Before she arrives, Bingham steps forward and presents Castro with the photograph of Ali and Malcolm X in Harlem in 1963. Castro holds it up level with his eyes and studies it silently for several seconds. When this picture was taken, Castro had been in control of Cuba for nearly four years. He was then thirty-seven. In 1959, he defeated the U.S.-backed dictator Fulgencio Batista, overcoming odds greater than Ali's subsequent victory over the supposedly unbeatable Sonny Liston. Batista had actually announced Castro's death back in 1956. Castro, then hiding in a secret outpost, thirty years old and beardless, was a disgruntled Jesuit-trained lawyer who was born into a landowning family and who craved Batista's job. At thirty-two, he had it. Batista was forced to flee to the Dominican Republic.

During this period, Muhammad Ali was only an amateur. His greatest achievement would come in 1960, when he received a gold medal in Rome as a member of the United States Olympic boxing team. But later in the sixties, he and Castro would share the world stage as figures moving against the American establishment — and now, in the twilight of their lives, on this winter's night in Havana, they meet for the first time: Ali silent and Castro isolated on his island.

"Que bien!" Castro says to Howard Bingham before showing the photograph to his interpreter. Then Castro is introduced by Bingham to Ali's wife. After they exchange greetings through the interpreter, he asks her, as if surprised, "You don't speak Spanish?"

"No," she says softly. She begins to caress her husband's left wrist, on which he wears a $250 silver Swiss Army watch she bought him. It is the only jewelry Ali wears.

"But I thought I saw you speaking Spanish on the TV news this week," Castro continues wonderingly before acknowledging that her voice had obviously been dubbed.

"Do you live in New York?"

"No, we live in Michigan."

"Cold," says Castro.

"Very cold," she repeats.

"In Michigan, don't you find many people that speak Spanish?"

"No, not many," she says. "Mostly in California, New York . . ." and, after a pause, "Florida."

Castro nods. It takes him a few seconds to think up another question. Small talk has never been the forte of this man who specializes in nonstop haranguing monologues that can last for hours; and yet here he is, in a room crowded with camera crews and news photographers — a talk-show host with a guest of honor who is speechless. But Fidel Castro plods on, asking Ali's wife if she has a favorite sport.

"I play a little tennis," Yolanda says, and then asks him, "Do you play tennis?"

"Ping-Pong," he replies, quickly adding that during his youth he had been active in the ring. "I spent hours boxing . . . " he begins to reminisce, but before he finishes his sentence, he sees the slowly rising right fist of Muhammad Ali moving toward his chin! Exuberant cheering and handclapping resound through the room, and Castro jumps sideways toward Stevenson, shouting, *"Asesorame!"* — "Help me!"

Stevenson's long arms land upon Ali's shoulders from behind, squeezing him gently; and then, after he releases him, the two ex-champions face each other and begin to act out in slow motion the postures of competing prizefighters — bobbing, weaving, swinging, ducking — all of it done without touching and all of it accompanied by three minutes of ongoing applause and the clicking of cameras, and also some feelings of relief from Ali's friends because, in his own way, he has decided to join them. Ali still says nothing, his face still inscrutable, but he is less remote, less alone, and he does not pull away from Stevenson's embrace as the latter eagerly tells Castro about a boxing exhibition that he and Ali had staged earlier in the week at the Balado gym, in front of hundreds of fans and some of the island's up-and-coming contenders.

Stevenson did not actually explain that it had been merely another photo opportunity, one in which they sparred openhanded in the ring, wearing their street clothes and barely touching each other's bodies and faces; but then Stevenson had climbed out of the ring, leaving Ali to the more taxing test of withstanding two abbreviated rounds against one and then another young bully of grade school age who clearly had not come to participate in a kiddie show. They had come to floor the champ. Their bellicose little bodies and hot-gloved hands and helmeted hell-bent heads were consumed with fury and ambition; and as they charged ahead, swinging wildly and swaggering to the roars of their teenage friends and relatives at ringside, one could imagine their future boastings to their grandchildren: On one fine day back in the winter of '96, I whacked Muhammad Ali! Except, in truth, on this particular day, Ali was still too fast for them. He backpedaled and shifted and swayed, stood on the toes of his black woven-leather pointed shoes, and showed that his body was made for motion — his Parkinson's problems were lost in his shuffle, in the thrusts of his butterfly sting that whistled two feet above the heads of his aspiring assailants, in the dazzling dips of his rope-a-dope that had confounded George Foreman in Zaire, in his ever-memorable style, which in this Cuban gym moistened the eyes of his ever-observant photographer friend and provoked the overweight screen writer to cry out in a voice that few in this noisy Spanish crowd could understand, "Ali's on a high! Ali's on a high!"

Teófilo Stevenson raises Ali's right arm above the head of Castro, and the news photographers spend several minutes posing the three of them together in flashing light. Castro then sees Fraymari watching alone at some distance. She is not smiling. Castro nods toward her. He summons a photographer to take a picture of Fraymari and himself. But she relaxes only after her husband comes over to join her in the conversation, which Castro immediately directs to the health and growth of their son, who is not yet two years old.

"Will he be as tall as his father?" Castro asks.

"I assume so," Fraymari says, glancing up toward her husband. She also has to look up when talking to Fidel Castro, for the Cuban leader is taller than six feet and his posture is nearly as erect as her husband's. Only the six-foot three-inch Muhammad Ali, who is standing with Bingham on the far side of her husband — and whose skin coloring, oval-shaped head, and burr-style haircut are very similar to her husband's — betrays his height with the slope-shouldered forward slouch he has developed since his illness.

"How much does your son weigh?" Castro continues.

"When he was one year old, he was already twenty-six pounds," Fraymari says. "This is three above normal. He was walking at nine months."

"She still breast-feeds him," Teófilo Stevenson says, seeming pleased.

"Oh, that's very nourishing," agrees Castro.

"Sometimes the kid becomes confused and thinks my chest is his mother's breast," Stevenson says, and he could have added that his son is also confused by Ali's sunglasses. The little boy engraved teeth marks all over the plastic frames while chewing on them during the days he accompanied his parents on Ali's bus tour.

As a CBS boom pole swoops down closer to catch the conversation, Castro reaches out to touch Stevenson's belly and asks, "How much do you weigh?"

"Two hundred thirty-eight pounds, more or less."

"That's thirty-eight more than me," Castro says, but he complains, "I eat very little. Very little. The diet advice I get is never accurate. I eat around fifteen hundred calories — less than thirty grams of protein, less than that."

Castro slaps a hand against his own midsection, which is relatively flat. If he does have a potbelly, it is concealed within his well-tailored uniform. Indeed, for a man of seventy, he seems in fine health. His facial skin is florid and unsagging, his dark eyes dart around the room with ever-alert intensity, and he has a full head of lustrous gray hair not thinning at the crown. The attention he pays to himself might be measured from his manicured fingernails down to his square-toed boots, which are unscuffed and smoothly buffed without the burnish of a lackey's spit shine. But his beard seems to belong to another man and another time. It is excessively long and scraggly. Wispy white hairs mix with the faded black and dangle down the front of his uniform like an old shroud, weather-worn and drying out. It is the beard from the hills. Castro strokes it constantly, as if trying to revive the vitality of its fiber.

Castro now looks at Ali.

"How's your appetite?" he asks, forgetting that Ali is not speaking.

"Where's your wife?" he then asks aloud, and Howard Bingham calls out to her. Yolanda has once more drifted back into the group.

When she arrives, Castro hesitates before speaking to her. It is as if he is not absolutely sure who she is. He has met so many people since arriving, and with the group rotating constantly due to the jostling of the photographers, Castro cannot be certain whether the woman at his side is Muhammad Ali's wife or Ed Bradley's friend or some other woman he has met moments ago who has left him with an unlasting impression. Having already committed a faux pas regarding one of the wives of the two multimarried ex-champions standing nearby, Castro waits for some hint from his interpreter. None is offered. Fortunately, he does not have to worry in this country about the women's vote — or any vote, for that matter — but he does sigh in mild relief when Yolanda reintroduces herself as Ali's wife and does so by name.

"Ah, Yolanda," Castro repeats, "what a beautiful name. That's the name of a queen somewhere."

"In our household," she says.

"And how is your husband's appetite?"

"Good, but he likes sweets."

"We can send you some of our ice cream to Michigan," Castro says. Without waiting for her to comment, he asks, "Michigan is very cold?"

"Oh, yes," she replies, not indicating that they had already discussed Michigan's winter weather.

"How much snow?"

"We didn't get hit with the blizzard," Yolanda says, referring to a storm in January, "but it can get three, four feet — "

Teófilo Stevenson interrupts to say that he had been in Michigan during the previous October.

"Oh," Castro says, raising an eyebrow. He mentions that during the same month he had also been in the United States (attending the United Nations' fiftieth-anniversary tribute). He asks Stevenson the length of his American visit.

"I was there for nineteen days," says Stevenson.

"Nineteen days!" Castro repeats. "Longer than I was."

Castro complains that he was limited to five days and prohibited from traveling beyond New York.

"Well, *comandante*," Stevenson responds offhandedly, in a slightly superior tone, "if you like, I will sometime show you my video."

Stevenson appears to be very comfortable in the presence of the Cuban leader, and perhaps the latter has habitually encouraged this; but at this moment, Castro may well be finding his boxing hero a bit condescending and worthy of a retaliatory jab. He knows how to deliver it.

"When you visited the United States," Castro asks pointedly, "did you bring your wife, the lawyer?"

Stevenson stiffens. He directs his eyes toward his wife. She turns away.

"No," Stevenson answers quietly. "I went alone."

Castro abruptly shifts his attention to the other side of the room, where the CBS camera crew is positioned, and he asks Ed Bradley, "What do you do?"

"We're making a documentary on Ali," Bradley explains, "and we followed him to Cuba to see what he was doing in Cuba and . . ."

Bradley's voice is suddenly overwhelmed by the sounds of laughter and handclapping. Bradley and Castro turn to discover that Muhammad Ali is now reclaiming everyone's attention. He is holding his shaky left fist in the air; but instead of assuming a boxer's pose, as he had done earlier, he is beginning to pull out from the top of his upraised fist, slowly and with dramatic delicacy, the tip of a red silk handkerchief that is pinched between his right index finger and thumb.

After he has pulled out the entire handkerchief, he dangles it in the air for a few seconds, waving it closer and closer to the forehead of the wide-eyed Fidel Castro. Ali seems bewitched. He continues to

stare stagnantly at Castro and the others, surrounded by applause
that he gives no indication he hears. Then he proceeds to place the
handkerchief back into the top of his cupped left hand — pecking
with the pinched fingers of his right — and then quickly opens his
palms toward his audience and reveals that the handkerchief has
disappeared.

"Where is it?" cries Castro, who seems to be genuinely surprised
and delighted. He approaches Ali and examines his hands, repeating, "Where is it? Where have you put it?"

Everyone who has traveled on Ali's bus during the week knows
where he has hidden it. They have seen him perform the trick repeatedly in front of some of the patients and doctors at the hospitals and clinics as well as before countless tourists who have
recognized him in his hotel lobby or during his strolls through the
town square. They have also seen him follow up each performance
with a demonstration that exposes his method. He keeps hidden
in his fist a flesh-colored rubber thumb that contains the handkerchief that he will eventually pull out with the fingers of his other
hand; and when he is reinserting the handkerchief, he is actually
shoving the material back into the concealed rubber thumb, into
which he then inserts his own right thumb. When he opens his
hands, the uninformed among his onlookers are seeing his empty
palms and missing the fact that the handkerchief is tucked within
the rubber thumb that is covering his outstretched right thumb.
Sharing with his audience the mystery of his magic always earns
him additional applause.

After Ali has performed and explained the trick to Castro, he
gives Castro the rubber thumb to examine — and, with more zest
than he has shown all evening, Castro says, "Oh, let me try it, I want
to try — it's the first time I have seen such a wonderful thing!" And
after a few minutes of coaching from Howard Bingham, who long
ago learned how to do it from Ali, the Cuban leader performs with
sufficient dexterity and panache to satisfy his magical ambitions
and to arouse another round of applause from the guests.

Meanwhile, more than ten minutes have passed since Ali began
his comic routine. It is already after 9:30 P.M., and the commentator Ed Bradley, whose conversation with Castro had been interrupted, is concerned that the Cuban leader might leave the room

without responding to the questions Bradley has prepared for his show. Bradley edges close to Castro's interpreter, saying in a voice that is sure to be heard, "Would you ask him if he followed . . . was able to follow Ali when he was boxing professionally?"

The question is relayed and repeated until Castro, facing the CBS cameras, replies, "Yes, I recall the days when they were discussing the possibilities of a match between the two of them" — he nods toward Stevenson and Ali — "and I remember when he went to Africa."

"In Zaire," Bradley clarifies, referring to Ali's victory in 1974 over George Foreman. And he follows up: "What kind of impact did he have in this country, because he was a revolutionary as well as . . . ?"

"It was great," Castro says. "He was very much admired as a sportsman, as a boxer, as a person. There was always a high opinion of him. But I never guessed one day we would meet here, with this kind gesture of bringing medicine, seeing our children, visiting our polyclinics. I am very glad, I am thrilled, to have the opportunity to meet him personally, to appreciate his kindness. I see he is strong. I see he has a very kind face."

Castro is speaking as if Ali were not in the room, standing a few feet away. Ali maintains his fixed façade even as Stevenson whispers into his ear, asking in English, "Muhammad, Muhammad, why you no speak?" Stevenson then turns to tell the journalist who stands behind him, "Muhammad does speak. He speaks to me." Stevenson says nothing more because Castro is now looking at him while continuing to tell Bradley, "I am very glad that he and Stevenson have met." After a pause, Castro adds, "And I am glad that they never fought."

"He's not so sure," Bradley interjects, smiling in the direction of Stevenson.

"I find in that friendship something beautiful," Castro insists softly.

"There is a tie between the two of them," Bradley says.

"Yes," says Castro. "It is true." He again looks at Ali, then at Stevenson, as if searching for something more profound to say.

"And how's the documentary?" he finally asks Bradley.

"It'll be on *60 Minutes.*"

"When?"

"Maybe one month," Bradley says, reminding Castro's interpreter, "This is the program on which the *comandante* has been interviewed by Dan Rather a number of times in the past, when Dan Rather was on *60 Minutes.*"

"And who's there now?" Castro wants to know.

"I am," Bradley answers.

"You," Castro repeats, with a quick glance at Bradley's earring. "So you are there — the boss now?"

Bradley responds as a media star without illusions: "I'm a worker."

Trays containing coffee, tea, and orange juice finally arrive, but only in amounts sufficient for Ali and Yolanda, Howard Bingham, Greg Howard, the Stevensons, and Castro — although Castro tells the waiters he wants nothing.

Castro motions for Ali and the others to join him across the room, around the circular table. The camera crews and the rest of the guests follow, standing as near to the principals as they can. But throughout the group there is a discernible restlessness. They have been standing for more than an hour and a half. It is now approaching 10 P.M. There has been no food. And for the vast majority, it is clear that there will also be nothing to drink. Even among the special guests, seated and sipping from chilled glasses or hot cups, there is a waning level of fascination with the evening. Indeed, Muhammad Ali's eyes are closed. He is sleeping.

Yolanda sits next to him on the sofa, pretending not to notice. Castro also ignores it, although he sits directly across the table, with the interpreter and the Stevensons.

"How large is Michigan?" Castro begins a new round of questioning with Yolanda, returning for the third time to a subject they had explored beyond the interest of anyone in the room except Castro himself.

"I don't know how big the state is as far as demographics," Yolanda says. "We live in a very small village [Barrien Springs] with about two thousand people."

"Are you going back to Michigan tomorrow?"

"Yes."

"What time?"

"Two-thirty."

"Via Miami?" Castro asks.

"Yes."

"From Miami, where do you fly?"

"We're flying to Michigan."

"How many hours' flight?"

"We have to change at Cincinnati — about two and a half hours."

"Flying time?" asks Castro.

Muhammad Ali opens his eyes, then closes them.

"Flying time," Yolanda repeats.

"From Miami to Michigan?" Castro continues.

"No," she again explains, but still with patience, "we have to go to Cincinnati. There are no direct flights."

"So you have to take two planes?" Castro asks.

"Yes," she says, adding for clarification, "Miami to Cincinnati — and then Cincinnati to South Bend, Indiana."

"From Cincinnati . . . ?"

"To South Bend," she says. "That's the closest airport."

"So," Fidel goes on, "it is on the outskirts of the city?"

"Yes."

"You have a farm?"

"No," Yolanda says, "just land. We let someone else do the growing."

She mentions that Teófilo Stevenson has traveled through this part of the Midwest. The mention of his name gains Stevenson's attention.

"I was in Chicago," Stevenson tells Castro.

"You were at their home?" Castro asks.

"No," Yolanda corrects Stevenson, "you were in Michigan."

"I was in the countryside," Stevenson says. Unable to resist, he adds, "I have a video of that visit. I'll show it to you sometime."

Castro seems not to hear him. He directs his attention back to Yolanda, asking her where she was born, where she was educated, when she became married, and how many years separate her age from that of her husband, Muhammad Ali.

After Yolanda acknowledges being sixteen years younger than Ali, Castro turns toward Fraymari and with affected sympathy says that she married a man who is twenty years her senior.

"*Comandante!*" Stevenson intercedes, "I am in shape. Sports keep you healthy. Sports add years to your life and life to your years!"

"Oh, what conflict she has," Castro goes on, ignoring Stevenson and catering to Fraymari — and to the CBS cameraman who steps forward for a closer view of Castro's face. "She is a lawyer, and she does not put this husband in jail." Castro is enjoying much more than Fraymari the attention this topic is now getting from the group. Castro had lost his audience and now has it back and seemingly wants to retain it, no matter at what cost to Stevenson's harmony with Fraymari. Yes, Castro continues, Fraymari had the misfortune to select a husband "who can never settle down. . . . Jail would be an appropriate place for him."

"*Comandante*," Stevenson interrupts in a jocular manner that seems intended to placate both the lawyer who is his spouse and the lawyer who rules the country, "I might as well be locked up!" He implies that should he deviate from marital fidelity, his lawyer wife "will surely put me in a place where she is the only woman who can visit me!"

Everyone around the table and within the circling group laughs. Ali is now awake. The banter between Castro and Stevenson resumes until Yolanda, all but rising in her chair, tells Castro, "We have to pack."

"You're going to have dinner now?" he asks.

"Yes, sir," she says. Ali stands, along with Howard Bingham. Yolanda thanks Castro's interpreter directly, saying, "Be sure to tell him, 'You're always welcome in our home.'" The interpreter quotes Castro as again complaining that when he visits America, he is usually restricted to New York, but he adds, "Things change."

The group watches as Yolanda and Ali pass through, and Castro follows them into the hallway. The elevator arrives, and its door is held open by a security guard. Castro extends his final farewell with handshakes — and only then does he discover that he holds Ali's rubber thumb in his hand. Apologizing, he tries to hand it back to Ali, but Bingham politely protests. "No, no," Bingham says, "Ali wants you to have it."

Castro's interpreter at first fails to understand what Bingham is saying.

"He wants you to keep it," Bingham repeats.

Bingham enters the elevator with Ali and Yolanda. Before the door closes, Castro smiles, waves goodbye, and stares with curiosity at the rubber thumb. Then he puts it in his pocket.

Reflections and Responses

1. Read Gay Talese's comments "On Certain Magazine Interviews" and "Listening to People Think" (pages 35–36). How do you think his journalistic procedures in this essay compare to his comments about the art of interviewing?

2. How would you describe Talese's role in the essay? Where does he seem visible? Where does he seem almost invisible? How does he fit himself as a participant or as an observer into different situations?

3. Consider how Talese sets up the drama at the palace reception. How does he build tension? How does he mix both the leading and minor roles? Why do you think he focuses so closely on the different conversations? What do you think he wants the conversations to convey in general about the overall event? Consider, too, the strange gift Ali leaves with Castro. Do you think the gift can have any larger significance? Do you think Talese finds it significant? What exactly is it, and what might it represent?

JOHN UPDIKE

The Disposable Rocket

In "The Disposable Rocket," John Updike, one of America's preeminent novelists, delivers his version of the male body. He states at the outset that it is quite different from the female body in that "it is a low-maintenance proposition." Men don't necessarily identify themselves with their bodies. In his characteristic metaphorical manner, Updike concludes, "A man and his body are like a boy and the buddy who has a driver's license and the use of his father's car for the evening; he goes along, gratefully, for the ride."

Updike was born in 1932 in Shillington, Pennsylvania. After gradua-tion from Harvard in 1954 and a year at an English art school, he worked for The New Yorker's *"Talk of the Town" department for two years. Since 1957 he has lived in Massachusetts as a freelance writer. A novelist, poet, essayist, and reviewer, Updike is one of the nation's most distinguished au-thors. His fiction has won the Pulitzer Prize, the National Book Award, the American Book Award, and the National Book Critics Circle Award. He has published numerous books and collections and is perhaps best known for a series of novels—*Rabbit, Run *(1960);* Rabbit Redux *(1971);* Rabbit Is Rich *(1981); and* Rabbit At Rest *(1990). His most recent novels are* Toward the End of Time *(1997),* Gertrude and Claudius *(2000),* Seek My Face *(2002),* Villages *(2004), and* Terrorist *(2006).* Still Looking: Essays on American Art *appeared in 2005. "The Disposable Rocket" originally appeared in* Michigan Quarterly Review *and was selected by Tracy Kidder for* The Best American Essays *1994.*

Inhabiting a male body is much like having a bank account; as long as it's healthy, you don't think much about it. Compared to the female body, it is a low-maintenance proposition: a shower now and then, trim the fingernails every ten days, a haircut once a month. Oh yes, shaving — scraping or buzzing away at your face every morning. Byron, in *Don Juan*, thought the repeated nuisance of shaving balanced out the periodic agony, for females, of child-birth. Women are, his lines tell us,

> Condemn'd to child-bed, as men for their sins
> Have shaving too entail'd upon their chins, —
>
> A daily plague, which in the aggregate
> May average on the whole with parturition.

From the standpoint of reproduction, the male body is a delivery system, as the female is a mazy device for retention. Once the delivery is made, men feel a faint but distinct falling-off of interest. Yet against the enduring female heroics of birth and nurture should be set the male's superhuman frenzy to deliver his goods: he vaults walls, skips sleep, risks wallet, health, and his political future all to ram home his seed into the gut of the chosen woman. The sense of the chase lives in him as the key to life. His body is, like a delivery rocket that falls away in space, a disposable means. Men put their bodies at risk to experience the release from gravity.

When my tenancy of a male body was fairly new — of six or so years' duration — I used to jump and fall just for the joy of it. Falling — backwards, downstairs — became a specialty of mine, an attention-getting stunt I was practicing into my thirties, at suburban parties. Falling is, after all, a kind of flying, though of briefer duration than would be ideal. My impulse to hurl myself from high windows and the edges of cliffs belongs to my body, not my mind, which resists the siren call of the chasm with all its might; the interior struggle knocks the wind from my lungs and tightens my scrotum and gives any trip to Europe, with its Alps, castle parapets, and gargoyled cathedral lookouts, a flavor of nightmare. Falling, strangely, no longer figures in my dreams, as it often did when I was a boy and my subconscious was more honest with me. An airplane, that necessary evil, turns the earth into a map so quickly the brain turns aloof and calm; still, I marvel that there is no end of young men willing to become jet pilots.

Any accounting of male-female differences must include the male's superior recklessness, a drive not, I think, toward death, as the darker feminist cosmogonies would have it, but to test the limits, to see what the traffic will bear — a kind of mechanic's curiosity. The number of men who do lasting damage to their young bodies is striking; war and car accidents aside, secondary-school sports, with the approval of parents and the encouragement of brutish coaches, take a fearful toll of skulls and knees. We were made for combat, back in the post-simian, East African days, and the bumping, the whacking, the breathlessness, the pain-smothering adrenaline rush, form a cumbersome and unfashionable bliss, but bliss nevertheless. Take your body to the edge, and see if it flies.

The male sense of space must differ from that of the female, who has such interesting, active, and significant inner space. The space that interests men is outer. The fly ball high against the sky, the long pass spiraling overhead, the jet fighter like a scarcely visible pinpoint nozzle laying down its vapor trail at forty thousand feet, the gazelle haunch flickering just beyond arrow-reach, the uncountable stars sprinkled on their great black wheel, the horizon, the mountaintop, the quasar — these bring portents with them, and awaken a sense of relation with the invisible, with the empty. The ideal male body is taut with lines of potential force, a diagram extending outward; the ideal female body curves around centers of repose. Of course, no one is ideal, and the sexes are somewhat androgynous subdivisions of a species: Diana the huntress is a more trendy body-type nowadays than languid, overweight Venus, and polymorphous Dionysus poses for more underwear ads than Mars. Relatively, though, men's bodies, however elegant, are designed for covering territory, for moving on.

An erection, too, defies gravity, flirts with it precariously. It extends the diagram of outward direction into downright detachability — objective in the case of the sperm, subjective in the case of the testicles and penis. Men's bodies, at this juncture, feel only partly theirs; a demon of sorts has been attached to their lower torsos, whose performance is erratic and whose errands seem, at times, ridiculous. It is like having a (much) smaller brother toward whom you feel both fond and impatient; if he is you, it is you in curiously simplified and ignoble form. This sense, of the male body being two of them, is acknowledged in verbal love play and erotic writing, where the penis is playfully given its own name, an individuation not even the rarest rapture grants a vagina. Here, where maleness gathers to a quintessence of itself, there can be no insincerity, there can be no hiding; for sheer nakedness, there is nothing like a hopeful phallus; its aggressive shape is indivisible from its tender-skinned vulnerability. The act of intercourse, from the point of view of a consenting female, has an element of mothering, of enwrapment, of merciful concealment, even. The male body, for this interval, is tucked out of harm's way.

To inhabit a male body, then, is to feel somewhat detached from it. It is not an enemy, but not entirely a friend. Our essence seems to lie not in cells and muscles but in the traces our thoughts and actions inscribe on the air. The male body skims the surface of nature's deep, wherein the blood and pain and mysterious cravings of women perpetuate the species. Participating less in nature's processes than the female body, the male body gives the impression — false — of being exempt from time. Its powers of strength and reach descend in early adolescence, along with acne and sweaty feet, and depart, in imperceptible increments, after thirty or so. It surprises me to discover, when I remove my shoes and socks, the same paper-white hairless ankles that struck me as pathetic when I observed them on my father. I felt betrayed when, in some tumble of touch football twenty years ago, I heard my tibia snap; and when, between two reading engagements in Cleveland, my appendix tried to burst; and when, the other day, not for the first time, there arose to my nostrils out of my own body the musty attic smell my grandfather's body had.

A man's body does not betray its tenant as rapidly as a woman's. Never as fine and lovely, it has less distance to fall; what rugged beauty it has is wrinkle-proof. It keeps its capability of procreation indecently long. Unless intense athletic demands are made on it, the thing serves well enough to sixty, which is my age now. From here on, it's chancy. There are no breasts or ovaries to admit cancer to the male body, but the prostate, that awkwardly located little source of seminal fluid, shows the strain of sexual function with fits of hysterical cell replication, and all that beer and potato chips add up in the coronary arteries. A writer, whose physical equipment can be minimal, as long as it gets him to the desk, the lectern, and New York City once in a while, cannot but be grateful to his body, especially to his eyes, those tender and intricate sites where the brain extrudes from the skull, and to his hands, which hold the pen or tap the keyboard. His body has been, not himself exactly, but a close pal, pot-bellied and balding like most of his other pals now. A man and his body are like a boy and the buddy who has a driver's license and the use of his father's car for the evening; he goes along, gratefully, for the ride.

Reflections and Responses

1. Updike's essay is constructed around numerous points of comparison between the male and the female body. What are the essential differences? Do you agree with Updike about the different ways men and women perceive their bodies? Are there points about which you disagree?

2. To what does the essay's title refer? Why do you think Updike chose this particular metaphor? Why is the rocket "disposable"? In what ways is the essay's central metaphor of a rocket reinforced by other imagery Updike uses in the essay?

3. Do you think Updike believes the male body is superior to the female — or vice versa? Can you detect any hints of preference for either one, or do you think he takes a neutral position?

3

The Public Sphere: Advocacy, Argument, Controversy

FRANK CONROY

Think About It

Though educators don't like to think so, education is often a mysterious process. How we come to understand something — both in and out of school — can be far less direct and systematic than methodically minded teachers might acknowledge. Illumination sometimes takes time: "The light bulb may appear over your head," Frank Conroy writes, "but it may be a while before it actually goes on." In this brief but deeply intriguing essay, Conroy explores several episodes from his younger years and shows how some puzzling things he couldn't quite understand at first finally revealed their meaning to him long afterward. But not every such illumination came with "a resolving kind of click." Conroy also recalls a series of enigmatic meetings with two of America's most famous legal minds and how they led to the strange satisfaction of an unresolved problem.

Conroy, who died in 2005, was director of the prestigious Iowa Writers' Workshop and wrote the highly influential memoir Stop-Time *(1967) and the short story collection* Midair *(1985). His stories and essays have appeared in* The New Yorker, Esquire, Harper's Magazine, GQ, *and many other publications. He worked as a jazz pianist and often wrote about American music. His other works include a novel,* Body & Soul *(1993); an essay collection,* Dogs Bark, But the Caravan Rolls On *(2002); and a travelogue,* Time and Tide: A Walk Through Nantucket *(2004). "Think About It" originally appeared in* Harper's Magazine *(1988) and was selected by Geoffrey Wolff for* The Best American Essays *1989.*

When I was sixteen I worked selling hot dogs at a stand in the Fourteenth Street subway station in New York City, one level above the trains and one below the street, where the crowds continually flowed back and forth. I worked with three Puerto Rican men who could not speak English. I had no Spanish, and although we understood each other well with regard to the tasks at hand, sensing and adjusting to each other's body movements in the extremely confined space in which we operated, I felt isolated with no one to talk to. On my break I came out from behind the counter and passed the time with two old black men who ran a shoeshine stand in a dark corner of the corridor. It was a poor location, half hidden by columns, and they didn't have much business. I would sit with my back against the wall while they stood or moved around their ancient elevated stand, talking to each other or to me, but always staring into the distance as they did so.

As the weeks went by I realized that they never looked at anything in their immediate vicinity — not at me or their stand or anybody who might come within ten or fifteen feet. They did not look at approaching customers once they were inside the perimeter. Save for the instant it took to discern the color of the shoes, they did not even look at what they were doing while they worked, but rubbed in polish, brushed, and buffed by feel while looking over their shoulders, into the distance, as if awaiting the arrival of an important person. Of course there wasn't all that much distance in the underground station, but their behavior was so focused and consistent they seemed somehow to transcend the physical. A powerful mood was created, and I came almost to believe that these men could see through walls, through girders, and around corners to whatever hyperspace it was where whoever it was they were waiting and watching for would finally emerge. Their scattered talk was hip, elliptical, and hinted at mysteries beyond my white boy's ken, but it was the staring off, the long, steady staring off, that had me hypnotized. I left for a better job, with handshakes from both of them, without understanding what I had seen.

Perhaps ten years later, after playing jazz with black musicians in various Harlem clubs, hanging out uptown with a few young artists and intellectuals, I began to learn from them something of the extraordinarily varied and complex riffs and rituals embraced by different people to help themselves get through life in the ghetto. Fantasy of all kinds — from playful to dangerous — was in the very air of Harlem. It was the spice of uptown life.

Only then did I understand the two shoeshine men. They were trapped in a demeaning situation in a dark corner in an underground corridor in a filthy subway system. Their continuous staring off was a kind of statement, a kind of dance. Our bodies are here, went the statement, but our souls are receiving nourishment from distant sources only we can see. They were powerful magic dancers, sorcerers almost, and thirty-five years later I can still feel the pressure of their spell.

The light bulb may appear over your head, is what I'm saying, but it may be a while before it actually goes on. Early in my attempts to learn jazz piano, I used to listen to recordings of a fine player named Red Garland, whose music I admired. I couldn't quite figure out what he was doing with his left hand, however; the chords eluded me. I went uptown to an obscure club where he was playing with his trio, caught him on his break, and simply asked him. "Sixths," he said cheerfully. And then he went away.

I didn't know what to make of it. The basic jazz chord is the seventh, which comes in various configurations, but it is what it is. I was a self-taught pianist, pretty shaky on theory and harmony, and when he said sixths I kept trying to fit the information into what I already knew, and it didn't fit. But it stuck in my mind — a tantalizing mystery.

A couple of years later, when I began playing with a bass player, I discovered more or less by accident that if the bass played the root and I played a sixth based on the fifth note of the scale, a very interesting chord involving both instruments emerged. Ordinarily, I suppose I would have skipped over the matter and not paid much attention, but I remembered Garland's remark and so I stopped and spent a week or two working out the voicings, and greatly strengthened my foundations as a player. I had remembered what I hadn't understood, you might say, until my life caught up with the information and the light bulb went on.

I remember another, more complicated example from my sophomore year at the small liberal-arts college outside Philadelphia. I seemed never to be able to get up in time for breakfast in the dining hall. I would get coffee and a doughnut in the Coop instead — a basement area with about a dozen small tables where students could get something to eat at odd hours. Several mornings in a row I noticed a strange man sitting by himself with a cup of coffee. He was in his sixties, perhaps, and sat straight in his chair with very little extraneous movement. I guessed he was some sort of distinguished visitor to the college who had decided to put in some time at a student hangout. But no one ever sat with him. One morning I approached his table and asked if I could join him. "Certainly," he said. "Please do." He had perhaps the clearest eyes I had ever seen, like blue ice, and to be held in their steady gaze was not, at first, an entirely comfortable experience. His eyes gave nothing away about himself while at the same time creating in me the eerie impression that he was looking directly into my soul. He asked a few quick questions, as if to put me at my ease, and we fell into conversation. He was William O. Douglas from the Supreme Court, and when he saw how startled I was he said, "Call me Bill. Now tell me what you're studying and why you get up so late in the morning." Thus began a series of talks that stretched over many weeks. The fact that I was an ignorant sophomore with literary pretensions who knew nothing about the law didn't seem to bother him. We talked about everything from Shakespeare to the possibility of life on other planets. One day I mentioned that I was going to have dinner with Judge Learned Hand. I explained that Hand was my girlfriend's grandfather. Douglas nodded, but I could tell he was surprised at the coincidence of my knowing the chief judge of the most important court in the country save the Supreme Court itself. After fifty years on the bench Judge Hand had become a famous man, both in and out of legal circles — a living legend, to his own dismay. "Tell him hello and give him my best regards," Douglas said.

Learned Hand, in his eighties, was a short, barrel-chested man with a large, square head, huge, thick, bristling eyebrows, and soft brown eyes. He radiated energy and would sometimes bark out remarks or questions in the living room as if he were in court. His humor was sharp, but often leavened with a touch of self-mockery. When something caught his funny bone he would burst out with explosive laughter — the laughter of a man who enjoyed laughing. He had a large repertoire of dramatic expressions involving the use of his eyebrows — very useful, he told me conspiratorially, when looking down on things from behind the bench. (The court stenographer could not record the movement of his eyebrows.) When I told him I'd been talking to William O. Douglas, they first shot up in exaggerated surprise, and then lowered and moved forward in a glower.

"*Justice* William O. Douglas, young man," he admonished. "Justice Douglas, if you please." About the Supreme Court in general, Hand insisted on a tone of profound respect. Little did I know that in private correspondence he had referred to the Court as "The Blessed Saints, Cherubim and Seraphim," "The Jolly Boys," "The Nine Tin Jesuses," "The Nine Blameless Ethiopians," and my particular favorite, "The Nine Blessed Chalices of the Sacred Effluvium."

Hand was badly stooped and had a lot of pain in his lower back. Martinis helped, but his strict Yankee wife approved of only one before dinner. It was my job to make the second and somehow slip it to him. If the pain was particularly acute he would get out of his chair and lie flat on the rug, still talking, and finish his point without missing a beat. He flattered me by asking for my impression of Justice Douglas, instructed me to convey his warmest regards, and then began talking about the Dennis case, which he described as a particularly tricky and difficult case involving the prosecution of eleven leaders of the Communist party. He had just started in on the First Amendment and free speech when we were called in to dinner.

William O. Douglas loved the outdoors with a passion, and we fell into the habit of having coffee in the Coop and then strolling under the trees down toward the duck pond. About the Dennis case, he said something to this effect: "Eleven Communists arrested by the government. Up to no good, said the government; dangerous people, violent overthrow, etc. First Amendment, said the defense, freedom of speech, etc." Douglas stopped walking. "Clear and present danger."

"What?" I asked. He often talked in a telegraphic manner, and one was expected to keep up with him. It was sometimes like listening to a man thinking out loud.

"Clear and present danger," he said. "That was the issue. Did they constitute a clear and present danger? I don't think so. I think everybody took the language pretty far in Dennis." He began walking, striding along quickly. Again, one was expected to keep up with him. "The FBI was all over them. Phones tapped, constant surveillance. How could it be clear and present danger with the FBI watching every move they made? That's a ginkgo," he said suddenly, pointing at a tree. "A beauty. You don't see those every day. Ask Hand about clear and present danger."

I was in fact reluctant to do so. Douglas's argument seemed to me to be crushing — the last word, really — and I didn't want to embarrass Judge Hand. But back in the living room, on the second martini, the old man asked about Douglas. I sort of scratched my nose and recapitulated the conversation by the ginkgo tree. "What?" Hand shouted. "Speak up, sir, for heaven's sake." "He said the FBI was watching them all the time so there couldn't be a clear and present danger," I blurted out, blushing as I said it. A terrible silence filled the room. Hand's eyebrows writhed on his face like two huge caterpillars. He leaned forward in the wing chair, his face settling, finally, into a grim expression. "I am astonished," he said softly, his eyes holding mine, "at Justice Douglas's newfound faith in the Federal Bureau of Investigation." His big, granite head moved even closer to mine, until I could smell the martini. "I had understood him to consider it a politically corrupt, incompetent organization, directed by a power-crazed lunatic." I realized I had been holding my breath throughout all of this, and as I relaxed, I saw the faintest trace of a smile cross Hand's face. Things are sometimes more complicated than they first appear, his smile seemed to say. The old man leaned back. "The proximity of the danger is something to think about. Ask him about that. See what he says."

I chewed the matter over as I returned to campus. Hand had pointed out some of Douglas's language about the FBI from other sources that seemed to bear out his point. I thought about the words "clear and present danger," and the fact that if you looked at them closely they might not be as simple as they had first appeared. What degree of danger? Did the word "present" allude to the proximity of the danger, or just the fact that the danger was there at all—that it wasn't an anticipated danger? Were there other hidden factors these great men were weighing of which I was unaware?

But Douglas was gone, back to Washington. (The writer in me is tempted to create a scene here—to invent one for dramatic purposes—but of course I can't do that.) My brief time as a messenger boy was over, and I felt a certain frustration, as if, with a few more exchanges, the matter of *Dennis* v. *United States* might have been resolved to my satisfaction. They'd left me high and dry. But, of course, it is precisely because the matter did not resolve that has caused me to think about it, off and on, all these years.

"The Constitution," Hand used to say to me flatly, "is a piece of paper. The Bill of Rights is a piece of paper." It was many years before I understood what he meant. Documents alone do not keep democracy alive, nor maintain the state of law. There is no particular safety in them. Living men and women, generation after generation, must continually remake democracy and the law, and that involves an ongoing state of tension between the past and the present which will never completely resolve.

Education doesn't end until life ends, because you never know when you're going to understand something you hadn't understood before. For me, the magic dance of the shoeshine men was the kind of experience in which understanding came with a kind of click, a resolving kind of click. The same with the experience at the piano. What happened with Justice Douglas and Judge Hand was different, and makes the point that understanding does not always mean resolution. Indeed, in our intellectual lives, our creative lives, it is perhaps those problems that will never resolve that rightly claim the lion's share of our energies. The physical body exists in a constant state of tension as it maintains homeostasis, and so too does the active mind embrace the tension of never being certain, never being absolutely sure, never being done, as it engages the world. That is our special fate, our inexpressibly valuable condition.

Reflections and Responses

1. How does Conroy finally come to understand why the two shoeshine men always seemed to be looking into the distance? What has Conroy learned that illuminates their behavior? Can you think of other explanations?

2. What connections can you see between Conroy's insight into the behavior of the shoeshine men and his later understanding of the elusive jazz chords? In what ways does the insight go beyond music?

3. Consider the conclusion of the episode involving William O. Douglas and Learned Hand. How does it end? Conroy says: "The writer in me is tempted to create a scene here — to invent one for dramatic purposes — but of course I can't do that." What do you think he means by the "writer in me"? Why is the refusal to "create a scene" significant to both Conroy's theme and his technique?

ALAN M. DERSHOWITZ

Shouting "Fire!"

Artists and performers are not the only ones who explore the boundaries of free expression. Lawyers and judges, too, frequently find themselves struggling to ascertain the limits of free speech. In the following essay, one of America's best-known trial lawyers, Alan M. Dershowitz, takes a close look at one of the most commonly used arguments against free speech, the idea that some speech should be suppressed because it is "just like" falsely shouting fire in a crowded theater. In his investigation into the source of this famous analogy, Dershowitz demonstrates how it has been widely misused and abused by proponents of censorship. Indeed, it was an "inapt analogy even in the context in which it was originally offered." As an expression to suppress expression, the "shouting fire" analogy, Dershowitz maintains, has been "invoked so often, by so many people, in such diverse contexts, that it has become part of our national folk language."

Alan M. Dershowitz is Felix Frankfurter professor of law at Harvard Law School. He is the author of many books, including The Best Defense *(1982),* Taking Liberties *(1988),* Chutzpah *(1991),* Contrary to Public Opinion *(1992),* The Abuse Excuse *(1994),* Reasonable Doubts *(1996), and* Sexual McCarthyism *(1998). His most recent books include* Supreme Injustice *(2001),* Letters to a Young Lawyer *(2001),* Why Terrorism Works *(2002),* America on Trial *(2004),* Rights from Wrongs *(2004), and* Preemption: A Knife That Cuts Both Ways *(2006). In addition to his teaching and writing, Professor Dershowitz is an active criminal defense and civil liberties lawyer. "Shouting 'Fire!'" originally appeared in* The Atlantic *(1989) and was selected by Justin Kaplan for* The Best American Essays *1990.*

When the Reverend Jerry Falwell learned that the Supreme Court had reversed his $200,000 judgment against *Hustler* magazine for the emotional distress that he had suffered from an outrageous parody, his response was typical of those who seek to censor speech: "Just as no person may scream 'Fire!' in a crowded theater when there is no fire, and find cover under the First Amendment, likewise, no sleazy merchant like Larry Flynt should be able to use the First Amendment as an excuse for maliciously and dishonestly attacking public figures, as he has so often done."

Justice Oliver Wendell Holmes's classic example of unprotected speech — falsely shouting "Fire!" in a crowded theater — has been invoked so often, by so many people, in such diverse contexts, that it has become part of our national folk language. It has even appeared — most appropriately — in the theater: in Tom Stoppard's play *Rosencrantz and Guildenstern Are Dead* a character shouts at the audience, "Fire!" He then quickly explains: "It's all right — I'm demonstrating the misuse of free speech." Shouting "Fire!" in the theater may well be the only jurisprudential analogy that has assumed the status of a folk argument. A prominent historian recently characterized it as "the most brilliantly persuasive expression that ever came from Holmes' pen." But in spite of its hallowed position in both the jurisprudence of the First Amendment and the arsenal of political discourse, it is and was an inapt analogy, even in the context in which it was originally offered. It has lately become — despite, perhaps even because of, the frequency and promiscuousness of its invocation — little more than a caricature of logical argumentation.

The case that gave rise to the "Fire!"-in-a-crowded-theater analogy, *Schenck* v. *United States*, involved the prosecution of Charles Schenck, who was the general secretary of the Socialist party in Philadelphia, and Elizabeth Baer, who was its recording secretary. In 1917 a jury found Schenck and Baer guilty of attempting to cause insubordination among soldiers who had been drafted to fight in the First World War. They and other party members had circulated leaflets urging draftees not to "submit to intimidation" by fighting in a war being conducted on behalf of "Wall Street's chosen few."

Schenck admitted, and the Court found, that the intent of the pamphlets' "impassioned language" was to "influence" draftees to resist the draft. Interestingly, however, Justice Holmes noted that unlawful or violent means to oppose conscription: "In form at least [the pamphlet] confined itself to peaceful measures, such as a petition for the repeal of the act" and an exhortation to exercise "your right to assert your opposition to the draft." Many of its most impassioned words were quoted directly from the Constitution.

Justice Holmes acknowledged that "in many places and in ordinary times the defendants, in saying all that was said in the circular, would have been within their constitutional rights." "But," he added, "the character of every act depends upon the circumstances in which it is done." And to illustrate that truism he went on to say:

> The most stringent protection of free speech would not protect a man in falsely shouting fire in a theater, and causing a panic. It does not even protect a man from an injunction against uttering words that may have all the effect of force.

Justice Holmes then upheld the convictions in the context of a wartime draft, holding that the pamphlet created "a clear and present danger" of hindering the war effort while our soldiers were fighting for their lives and our liberty.

The example of shouting "Fire!" obviously bore little relationship to the facts of the Schenck case. The Schenck pamphlet contained a substantive political message. It urged its draftee readers to *think* about the message and then — if they so chose — to act on it in a lawful and nonviolent way. The man who shouts "Fire!" in a crowded theater is neither sending a political message nor inviting his listener to think about what he has said and decide what to do in a rational, calculated manner. On the contrary, the message is designed to force action *without* contemplation. The message "Fire!" is directed not to the mind and the conscience of the listener but, rather, to his adrenaline and his feet. It is a stimulus to immediate *action*, not thoughtful reflection. It is — as Justice Holmes recognized in his follow-up sentence — the functional equivalent of "uttering words that may have all the effect of force."

Indeed, in that respect the shout of "Fire!" is not even speech, in any meaningful sense of that term. It is a *clang* sound, the equivalent of setting off a nonverbal alarm. Had Justice Holmes been more honest about his example, he would have said that freedom of speech does not protect a kid who pulls a fire alarm in the absence of a fire. But that obviously would have been irrelevant to the case at hand. The proposition that pulling an alarm is not protected speech certainly leads to the conclusion that shouting the word "fire" is also not protected. But the core analogy is the nonverbal alarm, and the derivative example is the verbal shout. By cleverly substituting the derivative shout for the core alarm, Holmes made it possible to analogize one set of words to another — as he could not have done if he had begun with the self-evident proposition that setting off an alarm bell is not free speech.

The analogy is thus not only inapt but also insulting. Most Americans do not respond to political rhetoric with the same kind of automatic acceptance expected of schoolchildren responding to a fire drill. Not a single recipient of the Schenck pamphlet is known to have changed his mind after reading it. Indeed, one draftee, who appeared as a prosecution witness, was asked whether reading the pamphlet asserting that the draft law was unjust would make him "immediately decide that you must erase that law." Not surprisingly, he replied, "I do my own thinking." A theatergoer would probably not respond similarly if asked how he would react to a shout of "Fire!"

Another important reason why the analogy is inapt is that Holmes emphasizes the factual falsity of the shout "Fire!" The Schenck pamphlet, however, was not factually false. It contained political opinions and ideas about the causes of the war and about appropriate and lawful responses to the draft. As the Supreme Court recently reaffirmed (in Falwell v. Hustler), "The First Amendment recognizes no such thing as a 'false' idea." Nor does it recognize false opinions about the causes of or cures for war.

A closer analogy to the facts of the Schenck case might have been provided by a person's standing outside a theater, offering the patrons a leaflet advising them that in his opinion the theater was structurally unsafe, and urging them not to enter but to complain to the building inspectors. That analogy, however, would not have served Holmes's argument for punishing Schenck. Holmes needed an analogy that would appear relevant to Schenck's political speech but that would invite the conclusion that censorship was appropriate.

Unsurprisingly, a war-weary nation — in the throes of a know-nothing hysteria over immigrant anarchists and socialists — welcomed the comparison between what was regarded as a seditious political pamphlet and a malicious shout of "Fire!" Ironically, the "Fire!" analogy is nearly all that survives from the Schenck case; the ruling itself is almost certainly not good law. Pamphlets of the kind that resulted in Schenck's imprisonment have been circulated with impunity during subsequent wars.

Over the past several years I have assembled a collection of instance[s] — cases, speeches, arguments — in which proponents of censorship have maintained that the expression at issue is "just like" or "equivalent to" falsely shouting "Fire!" in a crowded theater and ought to be banned, "just as" shouting "Fire!" ought to be banned. The analogy is generally invoked, often with self-satisfaction, as an absolute argument-stopper. It does, after all, claim the high authority of the great Justice Oliver Wendell Holmes. I have rarely heard it invoked in a convincing, or even particularly relevant, way. But that, too, can claim lineage from the great Holmes.

   Not unlike Falwell, with his silly comparison between shouting "Fire!" and publishing an offensive parody, courts and commentators have frequently invoked "Fire!" as an analogy to expression that is not an automatic stimulus to panic. A state supreme court held that "Holmes' aphorism . . . applies with equal force to pornography" — in particular to the exhibition of the movie *Carmen Baby* in a drive-in theater in close proximity to highways and homes. Another court analogized "picketing . . . in support of a secondary boycott" to shouting "Fire!" because in both instances "speech and conduct are brigaded." In the famous Skokie case one of the judges argued that allowing Nazis to march through a city where a large number of Holocaust survivors live "just might fall into the same category as one's 'right' to cry fire in a crowded theater."

   Outside court the analogies become even more badly stretched. A spokesperson for the New Jersey Sports and Exposition Authority complained that newspaper reports to the effect that a large number of football players had contracted cancer after playing in the Meadowlands — a stadium atop a landfill — were the "journalistic equivalent of shouting fire in a crowded theater." An insect researcher acknowledged that his prediction that a certain amusement park might become roach-infested "may be tantamount to shouting fire in a crowded theater." The philosopher Sidney Hook, in a letter to the *New York Times* bemoaning a Supreme Court decision that required a plaintiff in a defamation action to prove that the offending statement was actually false, argued that the First Amendment does not give the press carte blanche to accuse innocent persons "anymore than the First Amendment protects the right of someone falsely to shout fire in a crowded theater."

Some close analogies to shouting "Fire!" or setting off an alarm are, of course, available: calling in a false bomb threat; dialing 911 and falsely describing an emergency; making a loud, gunlike sound in the presence of the President; setting off a voice-activated sprinkler system by falsely shouting "Fire!" In one case in which the "Fire!" analogy was directly to the point, a creative defendant tried to get around it. The case involved a man who calmly advised an airline clerk that he was "only here to hijack the plane." He was charged, in effect, with shouting "Fire!" in a crowded theater, and his rejected defense — as quoted by the court — was as follows: "If we built fireproof theaters and let people know about this, then the shouting of 'Fire!' would not cause panic."

Here are some more-distant but still related examples: the recent incident of the police slaying in which some members of an onlooking crowd urged a mentally ill vagrant who had taken an officer's gun to shoot the officer; the screaming of racial epithets during a tense confrontation; shouting down a speaker and preventing him from continuing his speech.

Analogies are, by their nature, matters of degree. Some are closer to the core example than others. But any attempt to analogize political ideas in a pamphlet, ugly parody in a magazine, offensive movies in a theater, controversial newspaper articles, or any of the other expressions and actions catalogued above to the very different act of shouting "Fire!" in a crowded theater is either self-deceptive or self-serving.

The government does, of course, have some arguably legitimate bases for suppressing speech which bear no relationship to shouting "Fire!" It may ban the publication of nuclear-weapon codes, of information about troop movements, and of the identity of undercover agents. It may criminalize extortion threats and conspiratorial agreements. These expressions may lead directly to serious harm, but the mechanisms of causation are very different from that at work when an alarm is sounded. One may also argue — less persuasively, in my view — against protecting certain forms of public obscenity and defamatory statements. Here, too, the mechanisms of causation are very different. None of these exceptions to the First Amendment's exhortation that the government "shall make no law . . . abridging the freedom of speech, or of the press" is anything like falsely shouting "Fire!" in a crowded theater; they all must be justified on other grounds.

A comedian once told his audience, during the stand-up routine, about the time he was standing around a fire with a crowd of people and got in trouble for yelling "Theater, theater!" That, I think, is about as clever and productive a use as anyone has ever made of Holmes's flawed analogy.

Reflections and Responses

1. Consider Dershowitz's analysis of Justice Holmes's decision in the Schenck case. What does Dershowitz find wrong with Holmes's reasoning? In what ways is Holmes's analogy "flawed"?

2. To what kinds of expression does Dershowitz find Holmes's analogy applicable? Go through Dershowitz's examples of protected and unprotected speech. Why is the "falsely shouting fire" analogy appropriate in some instances and not in others?

3. Consider Dershowitz's anecdote in the last paragraph about the comedian who yells "Theater, theater!" What was the comedian expressing? Why does Dershowitz find this response to Holmes's analogy "clever and productive"?

ANNE FADIMAN

Mail

Anne Fadiman's "Mail" grows out of a long literary tradition. Such essays, with their attention to everyday detail, their casual humor, intellectual curiosity, occasional idiosyncratic stance, and mixture of information, criticism, and entertainment, were once known as "familiar" essays. That literary designation disappeared more than a half-century ago; in fact, Fadiman's father, the distinguished American essayist Clifton Fadiman, noted this disappearance back in 1955 when he wrote "A Gentle Dirge for the Familiar Essay." The "familiar" essay took its name from the essayist's use of ordinary topics — such familiar subjects as taking walks or observing facial expressions or table manners — and from an agreeable style or tone that was neither too formal or too informal. Unlike today's confessional or autobiographically oriented personal essays, the familiar essay had a subject other than the self, though the writer usually approached the subject from a decidedly personal perspective. In "Mail," Anne Fadiman looks at a new phenomenon that has become familiar to millions — electronic mail — and ruminates on its relation to her father's old-fashioned habits of letter writing and even the history of the postal service. Along the way, she raises some significant questions about modern technology and the price we sometimes pay for its efficiency and convenience.
    Anne Fadiman's The Spirit Catches You and You Fall Down *(1997) won the National Book Critics Circle Award for general nonfiction. Ex Libris (1998) is a collection of essays on reading and language. A winner of the National Magazine Award for both reporting and essays, she has contributed articles and essays to* Civilization, The New Yorker, Harper's, *and the* New York Times, *among other publications. She lives in western Massachusetts and teaches writing at Yale University. She was the editor of* The Best American Essays 2003. *"Mail" originally appeared in* The

American Scholar, *a magazine she edited for seven years, and was selected
by Kathleen Norris for* The Best American Essays 2001.

Some years ago, my parents lived at the top of a steep hill. My father kept a pair of binoculars on his desk with which, like a pirate
captain hoisting his spyglass to scan the horizon for treasure ships,
he periodically inspected the mailbox to see if the flag had been
raised. When it finally went up, he trudged down the driveway and
opened the extra-large black metal box, purchased by my mother
in the same accommodating spirit with which some wives buy their
husbands extra-large trousers. The day's load — a mountain of letters and about twenty pounds of review books packed in Jiffy bags,
a few of which had been pierced by their angular contents and
were leaking what my father called "mouse dirt" — was always
tightly wedged. But he was a persistent man, and after a brief show
of resistance the mail would surrender, to be carried up the hill in
a tight clinch and dumped onto a gigantic desk. Until that moment, my father's day had not truly begun.

His desk was made of steel, weighed more than a refrigerator,
and bristled with bookshelves and secret drawers and sliding pan-
els and a niche for a cedar-lined humidor. (He believed that cigar-
smoking and mail-reading were natural partners, like oysters and
Muscadet.) I think of it as less a writing surface than a mail-sorting
table. He hated Sundays and holidays because there was nothing
new to spread on it. Vacations were taxing, the equivalent of forced
relocations to places without food. His homecomings were always followed by day-long orgies of mail-opening — feast after
famine—at the end of which all the letters were answered; all the
bills were paid; the outgoing envelopes were affixed with stamps
from a brass dispenser heavy enough to break your toe; the books
and manuscripts were neatly stacked; and the empty Jiffy bags
were stuffed into an extra-large copper wastebasket, cheering confirmation that the process of postal digestion was complete.

"One of my unfailing minor pleasures may seem dull to more
energetic souls: opening the mail," he once wrote.

> Living in an advanced industrial civilization is a kind of near-conquest
> over the unexpected. . . . Such efficiency is of course admirable. It does
> not, however, by its very nature afford scope to that perverse human trait,
> still not quite eliminated, which is pleased by the accidental. Thus to many

tame citizens like me the morning mail functions as the voice of the unpredictable and keeps alive for a few minutes a day the keen sense of the
unplanned and the unplannable. The letter opener is an instrument that
has persisted from some antique land of chance and adventure into our
ordered world of the perfectly calculated.

What chance and adventure might the day's haul contain? My
brother asked him, when he was in his nineties, what kind of mail
he liked best. "In my youth," he replied, "a love letter. In middle
age, a job offer. Today, a check." (That was false cynicism, I think.
His favorite letters were from his friends.) Whatever the accidental
pleasure, it could not please until it arrived. Why were deliveries so
few and so late (he frequently grumbled), when, had he lived in
central London in the late seventeenth century, he could have received his mail between ten and twelve times a day?

We get what we need. In 1680, London had mail service nearly
every hour because there were no telephones. If you wished to invite someone to tea in the afternoon, you could send him a letter
in the morning and receive his reply before he showed up at your
doorstep. Postage was one penny.

If you wished to send a letter to another town, however, delivery
was less reliable and postage was gauged on a scale of staggering
complexity. By the mid-1830s,

> the postage on a single letter delivered within eight miles of the office
> where it was posted was . . . twopence, the lowest rate beyond that limit
> being fourpence. Beyond fifteen miles it became fivepence; after which
> it rose a penny at a time, but by irregular augmentation, to one shilling,
> the charge for three hundred miles. There was as a general rule an addi-
> tional charge of a half penny on a letter crossing the Scotch border;
> while letters to or from Ireland had to bear, in addition, packet rates,
> and rates for crossing the bridges over the Conway and the Menai.

So wrote Rowland Hill, the greatest postal reformer in history, who
in 1837 devised a scheme to reduce and standardize postal rates and
to shift the burden of payment from the addressee to the sender.

Until a few years ago I had no idea that if you sent a letter out of
town — and if you weren't a nobleman, a member of Parliament,
or other VIP who had been granted the privilege of free postal
franking — the postage was paid by the recipient. This dawned on

me when I was reading a biography of Charles Lamb, whose employer, the East India House, allowed clerks to receive letters gratis
until 1817: a substantial perk, sort of like being able to call your
friends on your office's 800 number. (Lamb, who practiced strin-
gent economies, also wrote much of his personal correspondence
on company stationery. His most famous letter to Wordsworth,
for instance — the one in which he refers to Coleridge as "an
Archangel a little damaged" — is inscribed on a page whose heading reads "Please to state the Weights and Amounts of the following Lots.")

Sir Walter Scott liked to tell the story of how he had once had to
pay "five pounds odd" in order to receive a package from a young
New York lady he had never met: an atrocious play called *The
Cherokee Lovers*, accompanied by a request to read it, correct it,
write a prologue, and secure a producer. Two weeks later another
large package arrived for which he was charged a similar amount.
"Conceive my horror," he told his friend Lord Melville, "when out
jumped the same identical tragedy of *The Cherokee Lovers*, with a
second epistle from the authoress, stating that, as the winds had
been boisterous, she feared the vessel entrusted with her former
communication might have foundered, and therefore judged it
prudent to forward a duplicate." Lord Melville doubtless found
this tale hilarious, but Rowland Hill would have been appalled. He
had grown up poor, and, as Christopher Browne notes in *Getting
the Message*, his splendid history of the British postal system, "Hill
had never forgotten his mother's anxiety when a letter with a high
postal duty was delivered, nor the time when she sent him out to
sell a bag of clothes to raise 3*s* for a batch of letters."

Hill was a born Utilitarian who, at the age of twelve, had been so
frustrated by the irregularity of the bell at the school where his father
was principal that he had instituted a precisely timed bell-ringing
schedule. In 1837 he published a report called "Post Office Reform:
Its Importance and Practicability." Why, he argued, should legions of
accountants be employed to figure out the Byzantine postal charges?
Why should Britain's extortionate postal rates persist when France's
revenues had risen, thanks to higher mail volume, after its rates were
lowered? Why should postmen waste precious time waiting for ab-
sent addressees to come home and pay up? A national Penny Post
was the answer, with postage paid by the senders, "using a bit of

paper . . . covered at the back with a glutinous wash, which the bringer might, by the application of a little moisture, attach to the back of the letter."

After much debate, Parliament passed a postal reform act in 1839. On January 10, 1840, Hill wrote in his diary, "Penny Postage extended to the whole kingdom this day! . . . I guess that the number despatched to-night will not be less than 100,000, or more than three times what it was this day twelve-months. If less I shall be disappointed." On January 11, he wrote, "The number of letters despatched exceeded all expectation. It was 112,000, of which all but 13,000 or 14,000 were prepaid." In May, after experimentation to produce a canceling ink that could not be surreptitiously removed, the Post Office introduced the Penny Black, bearing a profile of Queen Victoria: the first postage stamp. The press, pondering the process of cancellation, fretted about the "untoward disfiguration of the royal person," but Victoria became an enthusiastic philatelist, and renounced the royal franking privilege for the pleasure of walking to the local post office from Balmoral Castle to stock up on stamps and gossip with the postmaster. When Rowland Hill — by that time, *Sir* Rowland Hill — retired as Post Office Secretary in 1864, *Punch* asked, "SHOULD ROWLAND HILL have a Statue? Certainly, if OLIVER CROMWELL should. For one is celebrated for cutting off the head of a bad King, and the other for sticking on the head of a good Queen."

The Penny Post, wrote Harriet Martineau, "will do more for the circulation of ideas, for the fostering of domestic affections, for the humanizing of the mass generally, than any other single measure that our national wit can devise." It was incontrovertible proof, in an age that embraced progress on all fronts ("the means of locomotion and correspondence, every mechanical art, every manufacture, every thing that promotes the convenience of life," as Macaulay put it in a typical gush of national pride), that the British were the most civilized people on earth. Ancient Syrian runners, Chinese carrier pigeons, Persian post riders, Egyptian papyrus bearers, Greek *hemerodromes*, Hebrew dromedary riders, Roman equestrian relays, medieval monk-messengers, Catalan *troters*, international couriers of the House of Thurn and Taxis, American mail wagons — what could these all have been leading up to, like an ever-ascending staircase, but the Victorian postal system?

And yet (to raise a subversive question), might it be possible that, whatever the profit in efficiency, there may have been a literary cost associated with the conversion from payment by addressee to payment by sender? If you knew that your recipient would have to bear the cost of your letter, wouldn't courtesy motivate you to write an extra-good one? On the other hand, if you paid for it yourself, wouldn't you be more likely to feel you could get away with "Having a wonderful time, wish you were here"?

I used to think my father's attachment to the mail was strange. I now feel exactly the way he did. I live in an apartment building and, with or without binoculars, I cannot see my mailbox, one of thirteen dinky aluminum cells bolted to the lobby wall. The mail usually comes around four in the afternoon (proving that the postal staircase that reached its highest point with Rowland Hill has been descending ever since), which means that at around three, *just in case*, I'm likely to visit the lobby for the first of several reconnaissance missions. There's no flag, but over the years my fingers have become postally sensitive, and I can tell if the box is full by giving it the slightest of pats. If there's a hint of convexity — it's very subtle, nothing as obvious, let us say, as the bulge of a can that might harbor botulism — I whip out my key with the same excitement with which my father set forth down his driveway.

There the resemblance ends. The thrill of the treasure hunt is followed all too quickly by the glum realization that the box contains only four kinds of mail: (1) junk, (2) bills, (3) work, and (4) letters that I will read with enjoyment, place in a folder labeled "To Answer," leave there for a geologic interval, and feel guilty about. The longer they languish, the more I despair of my ability to live up to the escalating challenge of their response. It is a truism of epistolary psychology that, for example, a Christmas thank-you note written on December 26 can say any old thing, but if you wait until February, you are convinced that nothing less than *Middlemarch* will do.

In October of 1998 I finally gave in and signed up for e-mail. I had resisted for a long time. My husband and I were proud of our retrograde status. Not only did we lack a modem, but we didn't have a car, a microwave, a Cuisinart, an electric can opener, a cellular phone, a CD player, or cable television. It's hard to give up that sort of backward image; I worried that our friends wouldn't have enough to make fun of. I also worried that learning how to use e-mail would be like learning how to program our VCR, an unsuccessful project that had confirmed what excellent judgment we had shown in not purchasing a car, etc.

As millions of people had discovered before me, e-mail was fast. Sixteenth-century correspondents used to write "Haste, haste, haste, for lyfe, for lyfe, haste!" on their most urgent letters; my "server," a word that conjured up a delicious sycophancy, treated *every* message as if someone's life depended on it. Not only did it get there instantly, caromed in a series of analog cyberpackets along the nodes of the Internet and reconverted to digital form via its recipient's modem. (I do not understand a word of what I just wrote, but that is immaterial. Could the average Victorian have diagrammed the mail coach route from Swansea to Tunbridge Wells?) More important, I *answered* e-mail fast — almost always on the day it arrived. No more guilt! I used to think I did not like to write letters. I now realize that what I didn't like was folding the paper, sealing the envelope, looking up the address, licking the stamp, getting in the elevator, crossing the street, and dropping the letter in the postbox.

At first I made plenty of mistakes. I clicked on the wrong icons, my attachments didn't stick, and, not having learned how to file addresses, I sent an X-rated message to my husband (I thought) at gcolt @aol.com instead of georgecolt@aol.com. I hope Gerald or Gertrude found it flattering. But the learning curve was as steep as my father's driveway, and pretty soon I was batting out fifteen or twenty e-mails a day in the time it had once taken me to avoid answering a single letter. My box was nearly always full — no waiting, no binoculars, no convexity checks, no tugging — and when it wasn't, the reason was not that the mail hadn't *arrived*, it was that it hadn't been *sent*. I began to look forward every morning to the festive green arrow with which AT&T WorldNet welcomed me into my father's "antique land of chance and adventure." Would I be invited to purchase Viagra, lose thirty pounds, regrow my thinning hair, obtain electronic spy software, get an EZ loan, retire in three years, or win a Pentium III 500 MHz computer (presumably in order to receive such messages even faster)? Or would I find a satisfying little clutch of friendly notes whose responses could occupy me until I awoke sufficiently to tackle something that required intelligence? As Hemingway wrote to

Fitzgerald, describing the act of letter-writing: "Such a swell way to keep from working and yet feel you've done something."

My computer, without visible distension, managed to store a flood tide of mail that in nonvirtual form would have silted up my office to the ceiling. This was admirable. And when I wished to commune with my friend Charlie, who lives in Taipei, not only could I disregard the thirteen-hour time difference, but I was billed the same amount as if I had dialed his old telephone number on East 22nd Street. The German critic Bernhard Siegert has observed that the breakthrough concept behind Rowland Hill's Penny Post was "to think of all Great Britain as a single city, that is, no longer to give a moment's thought to what had been dear to Western discourse on the nature of the letter from the beginning: the idea of distance." E-mail is a modern Penny Post: the world is a single city with a single postal rate.

Alas, our Penny Post, like Hill's, comes at a price. If the transfer of postal charges from sender to recipient was the first great demotivator in the art of letter-writing, e-mail was the second. "It now seems a good bet," Adam Gopnik has written, "that in two hundred years people will be reading someone's collected e-mail the way we read Edmund Wilson's diaries or Pepys's letters." Maybe — but will what they read be any good? E-mails are brief. (One doesn't blather; an overlong message might induce carpal tunnel syndrome in the recipient from excessive pressure on the Down arrow.) They are also — at least the ones I receive — frequently devoid of capitalization, minimally punctuated, and creatively spelled. E-mail's greatest strength — speed — is also its Achilles' heel. In effect, it's always December 26; you are not expected to write *Middlemarch*, and therefore you don't.

In a letter to his friend William Unwin, written on August 6, 1780, William Cowper noted that "a Letter may be written upon any thing or Nothing." This observation is supported by the index of *The Faber Book of Letters, 1578–1939.* Let us examine some entries from the *d* section:

damnation, 87
dances and entertainments, 33, 48, 59, 97, 111, 275
dentistry, 220
depressive illness, 81, 87

I have never received an e-mail on any of these topics. Instead, I am informed that *Your browser is not Y2K-compliant. Your son left his Pokémon turtle under our sofa. Your column is 23 lines too long.* Important pieces of news, but, as Lytton Strachey (one of the all-time great letter writers) pointed out, "No good letter was ever written to convey information, or to please its recipient: it may achieve both these results incidentally; but its fundamental purpose is to express the personality of its writer." *But wait!* you pipe up. *Someone just e-mailed me a joke!* So she did, but wasn't the personality of the sender slightly muffled by the fact that she forwarded it from an e-mail *she* received, and sent it to seventeen additional addressees?

I also take a dim, or perhaps a buffaloed, view of electronic slang. Perhaps I should view it as a linguistic milestone, as historic as the evolution of Cockney rhyming slang in the 1840s. But will the future generations who reopen our hard drives be stirred by the eloquence of the e-acronyms recommended by a Web site on "netiquette"?

BTDT	been there done that
FC	fingers crossed
IITYWTMWYBMAD	if I tell you what this means will you buy me a drink?
MTE	my thoughts exactly
ROTFL	rolling on the floor laughing
RTFM	read the f —— manual
TAH	take a hint
TTFN	ta-ta for now

Or by the "emoticons," otherwise known as "smileys" — punctuational images, read sideways — that "help readers interpret the e-mail writer's attitude and tone"?

:-)	ha ha
:-(	boo hoo
(-:	I am left-handed
%-)	I have been staring at a green screen for 15 hours straight
:-&	I am tongue-tied

{:-)   I wear a toupee
:-[I am a vampire
:-F   I am a bucktoothed vampire with one tooth missing
=|:-)=   I am Abraham Lincoln

"We are of a different race from the Greeks, to whom beauty was everything," wrote Thomas Carlyle, a Victorian progress-booster. "Our glory and our beauty arise out of our inward strength, which makes us victorious over material resistance." We have achieved a similar victory of efficiency over beauty. I wouldn't give up e-mail if you paid me, but I'd feel a pang of regret if the epistolary novels of the future were to revolve around such messages as

Subject: R U Kidding?
From: Clarissa Harlowe <claha@virtue.com>
To: Robert Lovelace <lovelaceandlovegirlz@vice.com

hi bob, TAH. if u think i'm gonna run off w/ u, :-F, do u really think i'm that kind of girl?? if you're looking 4 a trollop, CLICK HERE NOW: http://www.hotpix.html. TTFN.

I own a letter written by Robert Falcon Scott, the polar explorer, to G. T. Temple, Esq., who helped procure the footgear for Scott's first Antarctic expedition. The date is February 26, 1901. The envelope and octavo stationery have black borders because Queen Victoria had died in January. The paper is yellowed, the handwriting is messy, and the stamp bears the Queen's profile — and the denomination ONE PENNY. I bought the letter many years ago because, unlike a Cuisinart, which would have cost about the same, it was something I believed I could not live without. I could never feel that way about an e-mail.

I also own my father's old wastebasket, which now holds my own empty Jiffy bags. Several times a day I use his stamp dispenser; it is tarnished and dinged, but still capable of unspooling its contents with a singular smoothness. And my file cabinets hold hundreds of his letters, the earliest written in his sixties in small, crabbed handwriting, the last in his nineties, after he lost much of his sight, penned with a Magic Marker in huge capital letters. I hope my children will find them someday, as Hart Crane once found his grandmother's love letters in the attic,

pressed so long
Into a corner of the roof
That they are brown and soft,
And liable to melt as snow.

Reflections and Responses

1. Note the perspective from which Anne Fadiman opens her essay. Can you find other sections of the essay that you think could also have served as a beginning? Why do you think she doesn't begin with the earliest time and end in the present?

2. A portion of the essay is taken up by her brief history of the British postal system. How does she integrate this information into the essay? What associations does she make between that history and our present system of communication? How is her movement between various time periods reflected in the way she crafts her sentences? Find examples of how she constructs single sentences that link various eras.

3. What specific images does Fadiman use to contrast her father's time with her own? How does she evaluate each era? What aspects of her father's time does she appear to prefer? How does she avoid being completely nostalgic about the past? In what ways does Fadiman's essay resemble Scott Russell Sanders's "The Inheritance of Tools"?

VICKI HEARNE

What's Wrong with
Animal Rights

*When people argue for the rights of animals, what exactly do they mean by
"rights"? Does their definition of animal rights take into account the "certain unalienable rights" that Thomas Jefferson wrote into the Declaration of
Independence — the right to "life, liberty and the pursuit of happiness"? In
the following essay, Vicki Hearne skillfully combines personal and professional experience with philosophical reflections on happiness as she builds a
case against the reductive view of animals that typifies the animal-rights
movement. In Hearne's opinion, the problem with animal-rights advocates
is not that they take their position too far; "it's that they've got it all wrong."*

*A professional dog trainer and Yale University professor, Hearne pub-
lished three volumes of poetry,* Nervous Horses *(1980),* In the Absence
of Horses *(1983), and* Parts of Light *(1994); three books of essays,*
Adam's Task: Calling Animals by Name *(1986),* Bandit: Dossier
of a Dangerous Dog *(1991), and* Animal Happiness *(1994); and
a novel,* The White German Shepherd *(1988). "What's Wrong with
Animal Rights" originally appeared in* Harper's Magazine *in 1991 and
was selected by Susan Sontag for* The Best American Essays 1992. *Vicki
Hearne died of lung cancer in August 2001.*

Not all happy animals are alike. A Doberman going over a hurdle
after a small wooden dumbbell is sleek, all arcs of harmonious
power. A basset hound cheerfully performing the same exercise
exhibits harmonies of a more lugubrious nature. There are chim-
panzees who love precision the way musicians or fanatical housekeepers or accomplished hypochondriacs do; others for whom

happiness is a matter of invention and variation — chimp vaudevillians. There is a rhinoceros whose happiness, as near as I can make out, is in needing to be trained every morning, all over again, or else he "forgets" his circus routine, and in this you find a clue to the slow, deep, quiet chuckle of his happiness and to the glory of the beast. Happiness for Secretariat is in his ebullient bound, that joyful length of stride. For the draft horse or the weight-pull dog, happiness is of a different shape, more awesome and less obviously intelligent. When the pulling horse is at its most intense, the animal goes into himself, allocating all of the educated power that organizes his desire to dwell in fierce and delicate intimacy with that power, leans into the harness, and MAKES THAT SUCKER MOVE.

If we are speaking of human beings and use the phrase "animal happiness," we tend to mean something like "creature comforts." The emblems of this are the golden retriever rolling in the grass, the horse with his nose deep in the oats, the kitty by the fire. Creature comforts are important to animals — "Grub first, then ethics" is a motto that would describe many a wise Labrador retriever, and I have a pit bull named Annie whose continual quest for the perfect pillow inspires her to awesome feats. But there is something more to animals, a capacity for satisfactions that come from work in the fullest sense — what is known in philosophy and in this country's Declaration of Independence as "happiness." This is a sense of personal achievement, like the satisfaction felt by a good wood-carver or a dancer or a poet or an accomplished dressage horse. It is a happiness that, like the artist's, must come from something within the animal, something trainers call "talent." Hence, it cannot be imposed on the animal. But it is also something that does not come *ex nihilo.** If it had not been a fairly ordinary thing, in one part of the world, to teach young children to play the pianoforte, it is doubtful that Mozart's music would exist.

Happiness is often misunderstood as a synonym for pleasure or as an antonym for suffering. But Aristotle associated happiness with ethics — codes of behavior that urge us toward the sensation of getting it right, a kind of work that yields the "click" of satisfaction upon solving a problem or surmounting an obstacle. In his *Ethics,* Aristotle wrote, "If happiness is activity in accordance with

---

**ex nihilo:* Latin, "out of nothing." — Ed.

excellence, it is reasonable that it should be in accordance with the highest excellence." Thomas Jefferson identified the capacity for happiness as one of the three fundamental rights on which all others are based: "life, liberty, and the pursuit of happiness."

I bring up this idea of happiness as a form of work because I am an animal trainer, and work is the foundation of the happiness a trainer and an animal discover together. I bring up these words also because they cannot be found in the lexicon of the animal-rights movement. This absence accounts for the uneasiness toward the movement of most people, who sense that rights advocates have a point but take it too far when they liberate snails or charge that goldfish at the county fair are suffering. But the problem with the animal-rights advocates is not that they take it too far; it's that they've got it all wrong.

Animal rights are built upon a misconceived premise that rights were created to prevent us from unnecessary suffering. You can't find an animal-rights book, video, pamphlet, or rock concert in which someone doesn't mention the Great Sentence, written by Jeremy Bentham* in 1789. Arguing in favor of such rights, Bentham wrote: "The question is not, Can they *reason?* nor, can they *talk?* but, can they suffer?"

The logic of the animal-rights movement places suffering at the iconographic center of a skewed value system. The thinking of its proponents — given eerie expression in a virtually sadoporno-graphic sculpture of a tortured monkey that won a prize for its compassionate vision — has collapsed into a perverse conundrum. Today the loudest voices calling for — demanding — the destruc-tion of animals are the humane organizations. This is an inevitable consequence of the apotheosis of the drive to relieve suffering: death is the ultimate release. To compensate for their contradic-tions, the humane movement has demonized, in this century and the last, those who made animal happiness their business: veteri-narians, trainers, and the like. We think of Louis Pasteur as the man whose work saved you and me and your dog and cat from rabies, but antivivisectionists of the time claimed that rabies increased in areas where there were Pasteur Institutes.

---

*Jeremy **Bentham:** British philosopher and social reformer (1748–1832) whose *Introduction to the Principles of Morals and Legislation* appeared in 1789. — Ed.

An anti-rabies public relations campaign mounted in England in the 1880s by the Royal Society for the Prevention of Cruelty to Animals and other organizations led to orders being issued to club any dog found not wearing a muzzle. England still has her cruel and unnecessary law that requires an animal to spend six months in quarantine before being allowed loose in the country. Most of the recent propaganda about pit bulls — the crazy claim that they "take hold with their front teeth while they chew away with their rear teeth" (which would imply, incorrectly, that they have double jaws) — can be traced to literature published by the Humane Society of the United States during the fall of 1987 and earlier. If your neighbors want your dog or horse impounded and destroyed because he is a nuisance — say the dog barks, or the horse attracts flies — it will be the local Humane Society to whom your neighbors turn for action.

In a way, everyone has the opportunity to know that the history of the humane movement is largely a history of miseries, arrests, prosecutions, and death. The Humane Society is the pound, the place with the decompression chamber or the lethal injections. You occasionally find worried letters about this in Ann Landers's column.

Animal-rights publications are illustrated largely with photographs of two kinds of animals — "Helpless Fluff" and "Agonized Fluff," the two conditions in which some people seem to prefer their animals, because any other version of an animal is too complicated for propaganda. In the introduction to his book *Animal Liberation*, Peter Singer says somewhat smugly that he and his wife have no animals and, in fact, don't much care for them. This is offered as evidence of his objectivity and ethical probity. But it strikes me as an odd, perhaps obscene underpinning for an ethical project that encourages university and high school students to cherish their ignorance of, say, great bird dogs as proof of their devotion to animals.

I would like to leave these philosophers behind, for they are inept connoisseurs of suffering who might revere my Airedale for his capacity to scream when subjected to a blowtorch but not for his wit and courage, not for his natural good manners that are a gentle rebuke to ours. I want to celebrate the moment not long ago when, at his first dog show, my Airedale, Drummer, learned that there can be a public place where his work is respected. I want to celebrate his meticulousness, his happiness upon realizing at the dog show that no one would swoop down upon him and swamp him with the goo-goo excesses known as the "teddy-bear complex" but that people actually got out of his way, gave him room to work. I want to say, "There can be a six-and-a-half-month-old puppy who can care about accuracy, who can be fastidious, and whose fastidiousness will be a foundation for courage later." I want to say, "Leave my puppy alone!"

I want to leave the philosophers behind, but I cannot, in part because the philosophical problems that plague academicians of the animal-rights movement are illuminating. They wonder, do animals have rights or do they have interests? Or, if these rightists lead particularly unexamined lives, they dismiss that question as obvious (yes, of course animals have rights, prima facie) and proceed to enumerate them, James Madison style. This leads to the issuance of bills of rights — the right to an environment, the right not to be used in medical experiments — and other forms of trivialization.

The calculus of suffering can be turned against the philosophers of festering flesh, even in the case of food animals, or exotic animals who perform in movies and circuses. It is true that it hurts to be slaughtered by man, but it doesn't hurt nearly as much as some of the cunningly cruel arrangements meted out by "Mother Nature." In Africa, 75 percent of the lions cubbed do not survive to the age of two. For those who make it to two, the average age at death is ten years. Asali, the movie and TV lioness, was still working at age twenty-one. There are fates worse than death, but twenty-one years of a close working relationship with Hubert Wells, Asali's trainer, is not one of them. Dorset sheep and polled Herefords would not exist at all were they not in a symbiotic relationship with human beings.

A human being living in the "wild" — somewhere, say, without the benefits of medicine and advanced social organization — would probably have a life expectancy of from thirty to thirty-five years. A human being living in "captivity" — in, say, a middle-class neighborhood of what the Centers for Disease Control call a Metropolitan Statistical Area—has a life expectancy of seventy or more years. For orangutans in the wild in Borneo and Malaysia, the life expectancy is thirty-five years; in captivity, fifty years. The wild is not a suffering-free zone or all that frolicsome a location.

The questions asked by animal-rights activists are flawed, because they are built on the concept that the origin of rights is in the avoidance of suffering rather than in the pursuit of happiness. The question that needs to be asked — and that will put us in closer proximity to the truth — is not, do they have rights? or, what are those rights? but rather, what is a right?

Rights originate in committed relationships and can be found, both intact and violated, wherever one finds such relationships — in social compacts, within families, between animals, and between people and nonhuman animals. This is as true when the nonhuman animals in question are lions or parakeets as when they are dogs. It is my Airedale whose excellencies have my attention at the moment, so it is with reference to him that I will consider the question, what is a right?

When I imagine situations in which it naturally arises that A defends or honors or respects B's rights, I imagine situations in which the relationship between A and B can be indicated with a possessive pronoun. I might say, "Leave her alone, she's my daughter" or "That's what she wants, and she is my daughter. I think I am bound to honor her wants." Similarly, "Leave her alone, she's my mother." I am more tender of the happiness of my mother, my father, my child, than I am of other people's family members; more tender of my friends' happinesses than your friends' happinesses, unless you and I have a mutual friend.

Possession of a being by another has come into more and more disrepute, so that the common understanding of one person possessing another is slavery. But the important detail about the kind of possessive pronoun that I have in mind is reciprocity: if I have a friend, she has a friend. If I have a daughter, she has a mother. The possessive does not bind one of us while freeing the other; it cannot do that. Moreover, should the mother reject the daughter, the word that applies is "disown." The form of disowning that most often appears in the news is domestic violence. Parents abuse children; husbands batter wives.

Some cases of reciprocal possessives have built-in limitations, such as "my patient/my doctor" or "my student/my teacher" or "my agent/my client." Other possessive relations are extremely limited but still remarkably binding: "my neighbor" and "my country" and "my president."

The responsibilities and the ties signaled by reciprocal possession typically are hard to dissolve. It can be as difficult to give up an enemy as to give up a friend, and often the one becomes the other, as though the logic of the possessive pronoun outlasts the forms it chanced to take at a given moment, as though we were stuck with one another. In these bindings, nearly inextricable, are found the origin of our rights. They imply a possessiveness but also recognize an acknowledgment by each side of the other's existence.

The idea of democracy is dependent on the citizens' having knowledge of the government; that is, realizing that the government exists and knowing how to claim rights against it. I know this much because I get mail from the government and see its "representatives" running about in uniforms. Whether I actually have any rights in relationship to the government is less clear, but the idea that I do is symbolized by the right to vote. I obey the government, and, in theory, it obeys me, by counting my ballot, reading the *Miranda* warning to me, agreeing to be bound by the Constitution. My friend obeys me as I obey her; the government "obeys" me to some extent, and, to a different extent, I obey it.

What kind of thing can my Airedale, Drummer, have knowledge of? He can know that I exist and through that knowledge can claim his happinesses, with varying degrees of success, both with me and against me. Drummer can also know about larger human or dog communities than the one that consists only of him and me. There is my household — the other dogs, the cats, my husband. I have had enough dogs on campuses to know that he can learn that Yale exists as a neighborhood or village. My older dog, Annie, not only knows that Yale exists but can tell Yalies from townies, as I learned while teaching there during labor troubles.

Dogs can have elaborate conceptions of human social structures, and even of something like their rights and responsibilities within them, but these conceptions are never elaborate enough to construct a rights relationship between a dog and the state, or a dog and the Humane Society. Both of these are concepts that depend on writing and memoranda, officers in uniform, plaques and seals of authority. All of these are literary constructs, and all of them are beyond a dog's ken, which is why the mail carrier who doesn't also happen to be a dog's friend is forever an intruder— this is why dogs bark at mailmen.

It is clear enough that natural rights relations can arise between people and animals. Drummer, for example, can insist, "Hey, let's go outside and do something!" if I have been at my computer several days on end. He can both refuse to accept various of my suggestions and tell me when he fears for his life — such as the time when the huge, white flapping flag appeared out of nowhere, as it seemed to him, on the town green one evening when we were working. I can (and do) say to him either, "Oh, you don't have to worry about that" or, "Uh oh, you're right, Drum, that guy looks dangerous." Just as the government and I — two different species of organism — have developed improvised ways of communicating, such as the vote, so Drummer and I have worked out a number of ways to make our expressions known. Largely through obedience, I have taught him a fair amount about how to get responses from me. Obedience is reciprocal; you cannot get responses from a dog to whom you do not respond accurately. I have enfranchised him in a relationship to me by educating him, creating the conditions by which he can achieve a certain happiness specific to a dog, maybe even specific to an Airedale, inasmuch as this same relationship has allowed me to plumb the happiness of being a trainer and writing this article.

Instructions in this happiness are given terms that are alien to a culture in which liver treats, fluffy windup toys, and miniature sweaters are confused with respect and work. Jack Knox, a sheepdog trainer originally from Scotland, will shake his crook at a novice handler who makes a promiscuous move to praise a dog, and will call out in his Scottish accent, "Eh! Eh! Get back, get BACK! Ye'll no be abusin' the dogs like that in my clinic." America is a nation of abused animals, Knox says, because we are always swooping at them with praise, "no gi'ing them their freedom." I am reminded of Rainer Maria Rilke's[*] account in which the Prodigal Son leaves — has to leave — because everyone loves him, even the dogs love him, and he has no path to the delicate and fierce truth of himself. Unconditional praise and love, in Rilke's story, disenfranchise us, distract us from what truly excites our interest.

[*]**Rainer Maria Rilke:** Austrian lyric poet (1875–1926). — Ed.

In the minds of some trainers and handlers, praise is dishonesty. Paradoxically, it is a kind of contempt for animals that masquerades as a reverence for helplessness and suffering. The idea of freedom means that you do not, at least not while Jack Knox is nearby, helpfully guide your dog through the motions of, say, herding over and over — what one trainer calls "explainy-wainy." This is rote learning. It works tolerably well on some handlers, because people have vast unconscious minds and can store complex preprogrammed behaviors. Dogs, on the other hand, have almost no unconscious minds, so they can learn only by thinking. Many children are like this until educated out of it.

If I tell my Airedale to sit and stay on the town green, and someone comes up and burbles, "What a pretty thing you are," he may break his stay to go for a caress. I pull him back and correct him for breaking. Now he holds his stay because I have blocked his way to movement but not because I have punished him. (A correction blocks one path as it opens another for desire to work; punishment blocks desire and opens nothing.) He holds his stay now, and — because the stay opens this possibility of work, new to a heedless young dog — he watches. If the person goes on talking, and isn't going to gush with praise, I may heel Drummer out of his stay and give him an "Okay" to make friends. Sometimes something about the person makes Drummer feel that reserve is in order. He responds to an insincere approach by sitting still, going down into himself, and thinking, "This person has no business pawing me. I'll sit very still, and he will go away." If the person doesn't take the hint from Drummer, I'll give the pup a little backup by saying, "Please don't pet him, he's working," even though he was not under any command.

The pup reads this, and there is a flicker of a working trust now stirring in the dog. Is the pup grateful? When the stranger leaves, does he lick my hand, full of submissive blandishments? This one doesn't. This one says nothing at all, and I say nothing much to him. This is a working trust we are developing, not a mutual congratulation society. My backup is praise enough for him; the use he makes of my support is praise enough for me.

Listening to a dog is often praise enough. Suppose it is just after dark and we are outside. Suddenly there is a shout from the house. The pup and I both look toward the shout and then toward each

other: "What do you think?" I don't so much as cock my head, because Drummer is growing up, and I want to know what he thinks.
He takes a few steps toward the house, and I follow. He listens
again and comprehends that it's just Holly, who at fourteen is
much given to alarming cries and shouts. He shrugs at me and
goes about his business. I say nothing. To praise him for this performance would make about as much sense as praising a human
being for the same thing. Thus:

A. What's that?
B. I don't know. [Listens] Oh, it's just Holly.
A. What a goooooood human being!
B. Huh?

This is one small moment in a series of like moments that will
culminate in an Airedale who on a Friday will have the discrimination and confidence required to take down a man who is attacking
me with a knife and on Saturday clown and play with the children
at the annual Orange Empire Dog Club Christmas party.

People who claim to speak for animal rights are increasingly devoted to the idea that the very keeping of a dog or a horse or a ger-
bil or a lion is in and of itself an offense. The more loudly they
speak, the less likely they are to be in a rights relation to any given
animal, because they are spending so much time in airplanes or
transmitting fax announcements of the latest Sylvester Stallone
anti-fur rally. In a 1988 *Harper's* forum, for example, Ingrid New-
kirk, the national director of People for the Ethical Treatment of
Animals, urged that domestic pets be spayed and neutered and ultimately phased out. She prefers, it appears, wolves — and wolves
someplace else — to Airedales and, by a logic whose interior structure is both emotionally and intellectually forever closed to Drummer, claims thereby to be speaking for "animal rights."
    She is wrong. I am the only one who can own up to my Airedale's
inalienable rights. Whether or not I do it perfectly at any given moment is no more refutation of this point than whether I am perfectly
my husband's mate at any given moment refutes the fact of marriage. Only people who know Drummer, and whom he can know,
are capable of this relationship. PETA and the Humane Society and

the ASPCA and the Congress and NOW — as institutions — do have the power to affect my ability to grant rights to Drummer but are otherwise incapable of creating conditions or laws or rights that would increase his happiness. Only Drummer's owner has the power to obey him — to obey who he is and what he is capable of — deeply enough to grant him his rights and open up the possibility of happiness.

Reflections and Responses

1. How does Hearne define *happiness*? What is its relation to work? Why, in her opinion, are the interrelated concepts of happiness and work not "in the lexicon of the animal-rights movement"?

2. Why does Hearne bring up the life-expectancy statistics of animals living "in the wild"? In what way do these statistics reinforce her argument? How might an animal-rights advocate respond to her use and interpretation of these statistics?

3. The Declaration of Independence reads: "We hold these truths to be self-evident, that all men are created equal, that they are endowed by their Creator with certain unalienable rights, that among these are life, liberty and the pursuit of happiness." Do you think Hearne legitimately or illegitimately extends Jefferson's words to apply to nonhumans? Explain your position.

JAMAICA KINCAID

On Seeing England
for the First Time

*One of the most sinister sides of imperialism is the way it promotes the rul-
ing nation's culture and rejects the colony's. The effect of this on an impres-
sionable young person is vividly described in Jamaica Kincaid's sensitive
and angry autobiographical essay about growing up in Antigua with the
dark shadow of England continually looming over her. England and a reverence for things English invaded every aspect of her daily life and education. Yet it was not until adulthood that she finally journeyed to England
and really saw it for the first time. "The space between the idea of something
and its reality," Kincaid writes, "is always wide and deep and dark." The
real England she finally sees is far different from the other England, whose
maps and history she was made to memorize as a schoolgirl in Antigua.*

Born in Antigua, Kincaid is the author of At the Bottom of the
River *(1983),* Annie John *(1985),* A Small Place *(1988),* Lucy *(1990),*
The Autobiography of My Mother *(1996),* My Brother *(1997), and*
Mr. Potter *(2002). A staff writer for* The New Yorker, *Kincaid has had
stories and essays published in* Rolling Stone, Paris Review, *and other
literary periodicals. She was the editor of* The Best American Essays 1995
*and is a visiting professor of creative writing at Harvard University. "On See-
ing England for the First Time" originally appeared in* Transition *(1991)
and was selected by Susan Sontag for* The Best American Essays 1992.

When I saw England for the first time, I was a child in school sitting
at a desk. The England I was looking at was laid out on a map gently,
beautifully, delicately, a very special jewel; it lay on a bed of sky
blue — the background of the map — its yellow form mysterious,

because though it looked like a leg of mutton, it could not really look like anything so familiar as a leg of mutton because it was England—with shadings of pink and green, unlike any shadings of pink and green I had seen before, squiggly veins of red running in every direction. England was a special jewel all right, and only special people got to wear it. The people who got to wear England were English people. They wore it well and they wore it everywhere: in jungles, in deserts, on plains, on top of the highest mountains, on all the oceans, on all the seas, in places where they were not welcome, in places they should not have been. When my teacher had pinned this map up on the blackboard, she said, "This is England" — and she said it with authority, seriousness, and adoration, and we all sat up. It was as if she had said, "This is Jerusalem, the place you will go to when you die but only if you have been good." We understood then — we were meant to understand then — that England was to be our source of myth and the source from which we got our sense of reality, our sense of what was meaningful, our sense of what was meaningless — and much about our own lives and much about the very idea of us headed that last list.

At the time I was a child sitting at my desk seeing England for the first time, I was already very familiar with the greatness of it. Each morning before I left for school, I ate a breakfast of half a grapefruit, an egg, bread and butter and a slice of cheese, and a cup of cocoa; or half a grapefruit, a bowl of oat porridge, bread and butter and a slice of cheese, and a cup of cocoa. The can of cocoa was often left on the table in front of me. It had written on it the name of the company, the year the company was established, and the words "Made in England." Those words, "Made in England," were written on the box the oats came in too. They would also have been written on the box the shoes I was wearing came in; a bolt of gray linen cloth lying on the shelf of a store from which my mother had bought three yards to make the uniform that I was wearing had written along its edge those three words. The shoes I wore were made in England; so were my socks and cotton undergarments and the satin ribbons I wore tied at the end of two plaits of my hair. My father, who might have sat next to me at breakfast, was a carpenter and cabinet maker. The shoes he wore to work would have been made in England, as were his khaki shirt and trousers, his underpants and undershirt, his socks and brown felt hat. Felt was not the proper material from which a hat that was expected to provide shade from the hot sun should be made, but my father must have seen and admired a picture of an Englishman wearing such a hat in England, and this picture that he saw must have been so compelling that it caused him to wear the wrong hat for a hot climate most of his long life. And this hat — a brown felt hat — became so central to his character that it was the first thing he put on in the morning as he stepped out of bed and the last thing he took off before he stepped back into bed at night. As we sat at breakfast a car might go by. The car, a Hillman or a Zephyr, was made in England. The very idea of the meal itself, breakfast, and its substantial quality and quantity was an idea from England; we somehow knew that in England they began the day with this meal called breakfast and a proper breakfast was a big breakfast. No one I knew liked eating so much food so early in the day; it made us feel sleepy, tired. But this breakfast business was Made in England like almost everything else that surrounded us, the exceptions being the sea, the sky, and the air we breathed.

At the time I saw this map — seeing England for the first time — I did not say to myself, "Ah, so that's what it looks like," because there was no longing in me to put a shape to those three words that ran through every part of my life, no matter how small; for me to have had such a longing would have meant that I lived in a certain atmosphere, an atmosphere in which those three words were felt as a burden. But I did not live in such an atmosphere. My father's brown felt hat would develop a hole in its crown, the lining would separate from the hat itself, and six weeks before he thought that he could not be seen wearing it — he was a very vain man — he would order another hat from England. And my mother taught me to eat my food in the English way: the knife in the right hand, the fork in the left, my elbows held still close to my side, the food carefully balanced on my fork and then brought up to my mouth. When I had finally mastered it, I overheard her saying to a friend, "Did you see how nicely she can eat?" But I knew then that I enjoyed my food more when I ate it with my bare hands, and I continued to do so when she wasn't looking. And when my teacher showed us the map, she asked us to study it carefully, because no test we would ever take would be complete without this statement: "Draw a map of England."

I did not know then that the statement "Draw a map of England" was something far worse than a declaration of war, for in fact a flat-out declaration of war would have put me on alert, and again in fact, there was no need for war — I had long ago been conquered. I did not know then that this statement was part of a process that would result in my erasure, not my physical erasure, but my erasure all the same. I did not know then that this statement was meant to make me feel in awe and small whenever I heard the word "England": awe at its existence, small because I was not from it. I did not know very much of anything then — certainly not what a blessing it was that I was unable to draw a map of England correctly.

After that there were many times of seeing England for the first time. I saw England in history. I knew the names of all the kings of England. I knew the names of their children, their wives, their disappointments, their triumphs, the names of people who betrayed them, I knew the dates on which they were born and the dates they died. I knew their conquests and was made to feel glad if I figured in them; I knew their defeats. I knew the details of the year 1066 (the Battle of Hastings, the end of the reign of the Anglo-Saxon kings) before I knew the details of the year 1832 (the year slavery was abolished). It wasn't as bad as I make it sound now; it was worse. I did like so much hearing again and again how Alfred the Great, traveling in disguise, had been left to watch cakes, and because he wasn't used to this the cakes got burned, and Alfred burned his hands pulling them out of the fire, and the woman who had left him to watch the cakes screamed at him. I loved King Alfred. My grandfather was named after him; his son, my uncle, was named after King Alfred; my brother is named after King Alfred. And so there are three people in my family named after a man they have never met, a man who died over ten centuries ago. The first view I got of England then was not unlike the first view received by the person who named my grandfather.

This view, though — the naming of the kings, their deeds, their disappointments — was the vivid view, the forceful view. There were other views, subtler ones, softer, almost not there — but these were the ones that made the most lasting impression on me, these were the ones that made me really feel like nothing. "When morning touched the sky" was one phrase, for no morning touched the sky where I lived. The mornings where I lived came

on abruptly, with a shock of heat and loud noises. "Evening approaches" was another, but the evenings where I lived did not
approach; in fact, I had no evening — I had night and I had day
and they came and went in a mechanical way: on, off; on, off. And
then there were gentle mountains and low blue skies and moors
over which people took walks for nothing but pleasure, when
where I lived a walk was an act of labor, a burden, something only
death or the automobile could relieve. And there were things that
a small turn of a head could convey — entire worlds, whole lives
would depend on this thing, a certain turn of a head. Everyday life
could be quite tiring, more tiring than anything I was told not to
do. I was told not to gossip, but they did that all the time. And they
ate so much food, violating another of those rules they taught me:
do not indulge in gluttony. And the foods they ate actually: if only
sometime I could eat cold cuts after theater, cold cuts of lamb and
mint sauce, and Yorkshire pudding and scones, and clotted cream,
and sausages that came from upcountry (imagine, "up-country").
And having troubling thoughts at twilight, a good time to have
troubling thoughts, apparently; and servants who stole and left in
the middle of a crisis, who were born with a limp or some other
kind of deformity, not nourished properly in their mother's womb
(that last part I figured out for myself; the point was, oh to have an
untrustworthy servant); and wonderful cobbled streets onto which
solid front doors opened; and people whose eyes were blue and
who had fair skins and who smelled only of lavender, or sometimes
sweet pea or primrose. And those flowers with those names: del-
phiniums, foxgloves, tulips, daffodils, floribunda, peonies; in
bloom, a striking display, being cut and placed in large glass bowls,
crystal, decorating rooms so large twenty families the size of mine
could fit in comfortably but used only for passing through. And
the weather was so remarkable because the rain fell gently always,
only occasionally in deep gusts, and it colored the air various
shades of gray, each an appealing shade for a dress to be worn
when a portrait was being painted; and when it rained at twilight,
wonderful things happened: people bumped into each other unexpectedly and that would lead to all sorts of turns of events — a
plot, the mere weather caused plots. I saw that people rushed:
they rushed to catch trains, they rushed toward each other and
away from each other; they rushed and rushed and rushed. That

word: rushed! I did not know what it was to do that. It was too hot to do that, and so I came to envy people who would rush, even though it had no meaning to me to do such a thing. But there they are again. They loved their children; their children were sent to their own rooms as a punishment, rooms larger than my entire house. They were special, everything about them said so, even their clothes; their clothes rustled, swished, soothed. The world was theirs, not mine; everything told me so.

If now as I speak of all this I give the impression of someone on the outside looking in, nose pressed up against a glass window, that is wrong. My nose was pressed up against a glass window all right, but there was an iron vise at the back of my neck forcing my head to stay in place. To avert my gaze was to fall back into something from which I had been rescued, a hole filled with nothing, and that was the word for everything about me, nothing. The reality of my life was conquests, subjugation, humiliation, enforced amnesia. I was forced to forget. Just for instance, this: I lived in a part of St. John's, Antigua, called Ovals. Ovals was made up of five streets, each of them named after a famous English seaman — to be quite frank, an officially sanctioned criminal: Rodney Street (after George Rodney), Nelson Street (after Horatio Nelson), Drake Street (after Francis Drake), Hood Street, and Hawkins Street (after John Hawkins). But John Hawkins was knighted after a trip he made to Africa, opening up a new trade, the slave trade. He was then entitled to wear as his crest a Negro bound with a cord. Every single person living on Hawkins Street was descended from a slave. John Hawkins's ship, the one in which he transported the people he had bought and kidnapped, was called *The Jesus.* He later became the treasurer of the Royal Navy and rear admiral.

Again, the reality of my life, the life I led at the time I was being shown these views of England for the first time, for the second time, for the one-hundred-millionth time, was this: the sun shone with what sometimes seemed to be a deliberate cruelty; we must have done something to deserve that. My dresses did not rustle in the evening air as I strolled to the theater (I had no evening, I had no theater; my dresses were made of a cheap cotton, the weave of which would give way after not too many washings). I got up in the morning, I did my chores (fetched water from the public pipe for my mother, swept the yard), I washed myself, I went to a woman to have my hair combed freshly every day (because before we were allowed into our classroom our teachers would inspect us, and children who had not bathed that day, or had dirt under their fingernails, or whose hair had not been combed anew that day, might not be allowed to attend class). I ate that breakfast. I walked to school. At school we gathered in an auditorium and sang a hymn, "All Things Bright and Beautiful," and looking down on us as we sang were portraits of the Queen of England and her husband; they wore jewels and medals and they smiled. I was a Brownie. At each meeting we would form a little group around a flagpole, and after raising the Union Jack, we would say, "I promise to do my best, to do my duty to God and the Queen, to help other people every day and obey the scouts' law."

Who were these people and why had I never seen them, I mean really seen them, in the place where they lived? I had never been to England. No one I knew had ever been to England, or I should say, no one I knew had ever been and returned to tell me about it. All the people I knew who had gone to England had stayed there. Sometimes they left behind them their small children, never to see them again. England! I had seen England's representatives. I had seen the governor general at the public grounds at a ceremony celebrating the Queen's birthday. I had seen an old princess and I had seen a young princess. They had both been extremely not beautiful, but who of us would have told them that? I had never seen England, really seen it, I had only met a representative, seen a picture, read books, memorized its history. I had never set foot, my own foot, in it.

The space between the idea of something and its reality is always wide and deep and dark. The longer they are kept apart — idea of thing, reality of thing — the wider the width, the deeper the depth, the thicker and darker the darkness. This space starts out empty, there is nothing in it, but it rapidly becomes filled up with obsession or desire or hatred or love — sometimes all of these things, sometimes some of these things, sometimes only one of these things. The existence of the world as I came to know it was a result of this: idea of thing over here, reality of thing way, way over there. There was Christopher Columbus, an unlikable man, an unpleasant man, a liar (and so, of course, a thief) surrounded by maps and schemes and plans, and there was the reality on the other side of that width, that depth, that darkness. He became obsessed, he became filled with desire, the hatred came later, love was never a part of it. Eventually, his idea met the longed-for reality. That the idea of something and its reality are often two completely different things is something no one ever remembers; and so when they meet and find that they are not compatible, the weaker of the two, idea or reality, dies. That idea Christopher Columbus had was more powerful than the reality he met, and so the reality he met died.

And so finally, when I was a grown-up woman, the mother of two children, the wife of someone, a person who resides in a powerful country that takes up more than its fair share of a continent, the owner of a house with many rooms in it and of two automobiles, with the desire and will (which I very much act upon) to take from the world more than I give back to it, more than I deserve, more than I need, finally then, I saw England, the real England, not a picture, not a painting, not through a story in a book, but England, for the first time. In me, the space between the idea of it and its reality had become filled with hatred, and so when at last I saw it I wanted to take it into my hands and tear it into little pieces and then crumble it up as if it were clay, child's clay. That was impossible, and so I could only indulge in not-favorable opinions.

There were monuments everywhere; they commemorated victories, battles fought between them and the people who lived across the sea from them, all vile people, fought over which of them would have dominion over the people who looked like me. The monuments were useless to them now, people sat on them and ate their lunch. They were like markers on an old useless trail, like a piece of old string tied to a finger to jog the memory, like old decoration in an old house, dirty, useless, in the way. Their skins were so pale, it made them look so fragile, so weak, so ugly. What if I had the power to simply banish them from their land, send boat after boatload of them on a voyage that in fact had no destination, force them to live in a place where the sun's presence was a constant? This would rid them of their pale complexion and make them look more like me, make them look more like the people I love and treasure and hold dear, and more like the people who occupy the near and far reaches of my imagination, my history, my geography, and reduce them and everything they have ever known to figurines as evidence that I was in divine favor, what if all this was in my power? Could I resist it? No one ever has.

And they were rude, they were rude to each other. They didn't like each other very much. They didn't like each other in the way they didn't like me, and it occurred to me that their dislike for me was one of the few things they agreed on.

I was on a train in England with a friend, an English woman. Before we were in England she liked me very much. In England she didn't like me at all. She didn't like the claim I said I had on England, she didn't like the views I had of England. I didn't like England, she didn't like England, but she didn't like me not liking it too. She said, "I want to show you my England, I want to show you the England that I know and love." I had told her many times before that I knew England and I didn't want to love it anyway. She no longer lived in England; it was her own country, but it had not been kind to her, so she left. On the train, the conductor was rude to her; she asked something, and he responded in a rude way. She became ashamed. She was ashamed at the way he treated her; she was ashamed at the way he behaved. "This is the new England," she said. But I liked the conductor being rude; his behavior seemed quite appropriate. Earlier this had happened: we had gone to a store to buy a shirt for my husband; it was meant to be a special present, a special shirt to wear on special occasions. This was a store where the Prince of Wales has his shirts made, but the shirts sold in this store are beautiful all the same. I found a shirt I thought my husband would like and I wanted to buy him a tie to go with it. When I couldn't decide which one to choose, the salesman showed me a new set. He was very pleased with these, he said, because they bore the crest of the Prince of Wales, and the Prince of Wales had never allowed his crest to decorate an article of clothing before. There was something in the way he said it; his tone was slavish, reverential, awed. It made me feel angry; I wanted to hit him. I didn't do that. I said, my husband and I hate princes, my husband would never wear anything that had a prince's any-thing on it. My friend stiffened. The salesman stiffened. They both drew themselves in, away from me. My friend told me that the prince was a symbol of her Englishness, and I could see that I had caused offense. I looked at her. She was an English person, the sort of English person I used to know at home, the sort who was nobody in England but somebody when they came to live among the people like me. There were many people I could have seen England with; that I was seeing it with this particular person, a person who reminded me of the people who showed me England long ago as I sat in church or at my desk, made me feel silent and afraid, for I wondered if, all these years of our friendship, I had had a friend or had been in the thrall of a racial memory.

I went to Bath — we, my friend and I, did this, but though we were together, I was no longer with her. The landscape was almost as familiar as my own hand, but I had never been in this place before, so how could that be again? And the streets of Bath were familiar, too, but I had never walked on them before. It was all those years of reading, starting with Roman Britain. Why did I have to know about Roman Britain? It was of no real use to me, a person living on a hot, drought-ridden island, and it is of no use to me now, and yet my head is filled with this nonsense, Roman Britain. In Bath, I drank tea in a room I had read about in a novel written in the eighteenth century. In this very same room, young women wearing those dresses that rustled and so on danced and flirted and sometimes disgraced themselves with young men, soldiers, sailors, who were on their way to Bristol or someplace like that, so many places like that where so many adventures, the outcome of which was not good for me, began. Bristol, England. A sentence that began "That night the ship sailed from Bristol, England" would end not so good for me. And then I was driving through the countryside in an English motorcar, on narrow winding roads, and they were so familiar, though I had never been on them before; and through little villages the names of which I somehow knew so well though I had never been there before. And the countryside did have all those hedges and hedges, fields hedged in. I was marveling at all the toil of it, the planting of the hedges to begin with and then the care of it, all that clipping, year after year of clipping, and I wondered at the lives of the people who would have to do this, because wherever I see and feel the hands that hold up the world, I see and feel myself and all the people who look like me. And I said, "Those hedges" and my friend said that someone, a woman named Mrs. Rothchild, worried that the hedges weren't

being taken care of properly; the farmers couldn't afford or find
the help to keep up the hedges, and often they replaced them
with wire fencing. I might have said to that, well if Mrs. Rothchild
doesn't like the wire fencing, why doesn't she take care of the
hedges herself, but I didn't. And then in those fields that were now
hemmed in by wire fencing that a privileged woman didn't like
was planted a vile yellow flowering bush that produced an oil, and
my friend said that Mrs. Rothchild didn't like this either; it ruined
the English countryside, it ruined the traditional look of the English countryside.

It was not at that moment that I wished every sentence, everything I knew, that began with England would end with "and then it
all died; we don't know how, it just all died." At that moment, I was
thinking, who are these people who forced me to think of them all
the time, who forced me to think that the world I knew was incomplete, or without substance, or did not measure up because it was
not England; that I was incomplete, or without substance, and did
not measure up because I was not English. Who were these people?
The person sitting next to me couldn't give me a clue; no one person could. In any case, if I had said to her, I find England ugly,
I hate England; the weather is like a jail sentence, the English are a
very ugly people, the food in England is like a jail sentence, the
hair of English people is so straight, so dead looking, the English
have an unbearable smell so different from the smell of people I
know, real people of course, she would have said that I was a person
full of prejudice. Apart from the fact that it is I — that is, the people who look like me — who made her aware of the unpleasantness
of such a thing, the idea of such a thing, prejudice, she would have
been only partly right, sort of right: I may be capable of prejudice,
but my prejudices have no weight to them, my prejudices have no
force behind them, my prejudices remain opinions, my prejudices
remain my personal opinion. And a great feeling of rage and disappointment came over me as I looked at England, my head full of
personal opinions that could not have public, my public, approval.
The people I come from are powerless to do evil on grand scale.

The moment I wished every sentence, everything I knew, that
began with England would end with "and then it all died, we don't
know how, it just all died" was when I saw the white cliffs of Dover.
I had sung hymns and recited poems that were about a longing to

see the white cliffs of Dover again. At the time I sang the hymns and recited the poems, I could really long to see them again because I had never seen them at all, nor had anyone around me at the time. But there we were, groups of people longing for something we had never seen. And so there they were, the white cliffs, but they were not that pearly majestic thing I used to sing about, that thing that created such a feeling in these people that when they died in the place where I lived they had themselves buried facing a direction that would allow them to see the white cliffs of Dover when they were resurrected, as surely they would be. The white cliffs of Dover, when finally I saw them, were cliffs, but they were not white; you would only call them that if the word "white" meant something special to you; they were dirty and they were steep; they were so steep, the correct height from which all my views of England, starting with the map before me in my classroom and ending with the trip I had just taken, should jump and die and disappear forever.

Reflections and Responses

1. Note that Kincaid opens her essay with various images of England. What do these images have in common? How do they reflect colonialism? How do they reflect literature? Why do you think Kincaid begins by placing the images in the context of a classroom?

2. Consider Kincaid's account of her father's hat. In what ways does the "brown felt hat" represent England? How does Kincaid view the hat?

3. When Kincaid finally visits England, what aspects of the country does she dislike the most? What does she mean when she says toward the end of her essay, "I may be capable of prejudice, but my prejudices have no weight to them"? Do you find her opinions prejudiced? In your opinion, has she or has she not "prejudged" England?

DANIELLE OFRI

Living Will

"Living Will" is a fine example of the type of essay that follows a narrative arc as the author describes the process of moving from one state of mind to another, usually from a moral or intellectual dilemma to resolution and insight. Such essays often involve an epiphany. *The Irish novelist James Joyce first used this ancient religious term in a modern literary sense to describe the sudden flash of recognition or the unexpected illumination that can transform our understanding. "Living Will" takes us inside today's medical profession — with its awesome technological capability — and confronts one of medicine's major issues: Why are severely ill and depressed patients who have lost the will to live kept alive at such an enormous cost of time and professional effort?*

Danielle Ofri, MD, PhD, is the author of Singular Intimacies:Becoming a Doctor at Bellevue *(2003) and* Incidental Findings: Lessons from My Patients in the Art of Medicine *(2005). Ofri is editor in chief and cofounder of the* Bellevue Literary Review *and associate chief editor of an award-winning medical textbook,* The Bellevue Guide to Outpatient Medicine. *Her stories have appeared in both literary and medical journals as well in several anthologies. She is an attending physician at Bellevue Hospital and on the faculty of New York University School of Medicine. "Living Will" orginally appeared in* The Missouri Review *and was selected by Susan Orlean for* The Best American Essays 2005.

WILBUR RESTON was already in the intensive care unit of the tiny Florida hospital when I arrived at two-thirty A.M. I had been doing a series of temp jobs after having completed my medical residency at New York City's Bellevue Hospital and now found myself in a small town on the Gulf Coast. The breathing tube in Mr. Reston's throat and his heavy sedation precluded formal introductions. But there was a typewritten summary of his medical history that his wife had left with the nurses; a two-page, single-spaced account that chronicled the rebellion and demise of each organ in this sixty-one-year-old white man. He had survived three heart attacks and seven strokes. One kidney had been removed. He suffered from diabetes, high blood pressure, and congestive heart failure. He had emphysema, glaucoma, severe migraines, and arthritis. His medical history included pancreatitis, diverticulitis, pyelonephritis, sinusitis, cholelithiasis, tinnitus, and ankylosing spondfylitis. The typed paper also mentioned gastroesophageal reflux, vertigo, and depression. I quickly glanced over to the man hooked up to the ventilator to verify that he was indeed alive.

His wife had told the ER physicians that he'd stopped taking his water pills several days ago. Eventually he could no longer breathe. He possessed a living will stating that he did not want any life-sustaining procedures. In the ER, however, he had apparently agreed to be intubated. It had taken an enormous amount of sedation to get the breathing tube in, and then his blood pressure bottomed out. He was now unconscious in the ICU, on multiple pressor medications to support his blood pressure and augment his weak heart. In Bellevue terminology, he was a "train wreck."

Mr. Reston had been admitted to East General Hospital at two A.M. My colleagues in the small private practice where I was working had instructed me *never* to go to the hospital in the middle of the night. "Give your orders over the phone and see the patient in the morning," they advised. But I was still too new at this kind of medicine to be that confident; I had to at least lay eyes on the patient before I could decide on any medical orders.

I couldn't take a history from Mr. Reston, since he was at present unarousable because of all the sedation. My physical exam was brief. Mainly I plowed through the typed medical summary, converting it into a concise admission note. I handed my admitting orders to the nurse, and then there was nothing for me to do. In this small community hospital, the nurses were used to, and entirely comfortable with, working without any doctors around. How unlike Bellevue, where interns and residents roamed the halls twenty-four hours a day, deeply and intricately involved in the minutiae of medical care. Here the nurses took most of the doctors' orders over the phone and did everything themselves: drew blood, inserted IVs, did EKGs, obtained blood and urine cultures, sent patients for x-rays, followed up on test results, and so on. The doctors, with their busy private practices, usually visited once a day, either very early in the morning or late, after their office hours. The emphasis was on remembering to sign verbal orders within twenty-four hours. Not surprisingly, the head nurse was taken aback and almost alarmed when I showed up in the middle of the night for Mr. Reston's admission.

It was now nearly four A.M. as I drove back to the hotel in my rental car. The main roads of the town were deserted. I rolled down the windows and was quickly enveloped in humid, orange-scented fog. Stretches of flat, boring landscape were broken up periodically by strip malls. Neighborhoods of low-slung, white stucco houses were dotted with pickup trucks and palm trees. The smell of blossoms had not been fully eradicated by the burgeoning construction industry.

Southwest Florida was nothing like West Palm Beath, which I had assumed represented all of Florida. This area was rural, with acres of fields farmed by itinerant workers, mostly from Central America. I had just returned from Guatemala, so I was eager to practice my Spanish, but in the private practice where I worked, I rarely had the opportunity, except for the time when I was called upon to explain to a Honduran fruit picker that we couldn't treat his high blood pressure because he didn't have medical insurance. The hospital emergency room had called me when he'd shown up there needing prescriptions, and I'd said sure, send him over right now. When he arrived at the office, however, the practice manager informed me that we could not treat patients without insurance except for medical emergencies. Since I was the only one in the office who spoke passable Spanish, the duty of telling him fell to me. My verb-conjugating ability floundered, and my pronouns disagreed with their antecedents. My vocabulary in Spanish — and in English for that matter — had never included such phrases as "We cannot take care of you. You must go to a different doctor." I suddenly longed for Bellevue, for the chaos of the emergency room there, with its bubbling tumult of languages, ethnicities, colors, and socioeconomic classes, and its assumption that everybody received medical care regardless of ability to pay.

But aside from that one incident, the office was a pleasant place to work. Three doctors had started this practice several years ago, and they were now extremely successful. They had built an impressive clientele of devoted patients, mainly older but many middle-aged. They had equipped their office with a tiny pharmacy and a stress-test machine, and had arranged for weekly visits from an ultrasound technician, who performed all their sonograms. They'd even opened a small gym next door, in which they sponsored exercise classes for the elderly and rehab classes for their patients with emphysema. The doctors were in their forties, looking for ways to cut down on hours and enter semi-retirement. They were more than happy to hand over a third of the office patients and one hundred percent of the inpatient hospital duties. They gladly acceded to my request for paid prep time so that I could read patients' charts in advance of their appointments, all in a comfortable office with an experienced, full-time nurse to assist me. It was the lap of luxury. Within a week they offered me a permanent, full-time position with a salary that was four times what I'd earned as a resident for half the working hours, plus a share in the practice.

The patients were pleasant and apparently particularly happy to have a woman doctor, something new to that practice. And for the first time in *my* life, medicine was not a struggle: I could practice the best medicine I wanted without having to fight for anything. Coming from the trenches of Bellevue, where medicine felt almost like warfare, I found the case of practicing good medicine almost disconcerting. I couldn't deny that the job offer was tempting.

But I could never leave Manhattan — certainly not to live in such a tiny town.

The town was a speck on the map in southwest Florida that no one I knew had ever heard of. The pace was unhurried, and the locals were unceasingly friendly and helpful, traits that were sometimes unsettling to a native New Yorker. Overly polite strangers made me suspicious, though everyone assured me that this was the normal style in the South. There was no place to get sushi, but the two-room library across the street from my office did stock Spanish-lesson tapes, and I was able to study a semester's worth of grammar on my way to work each day. Much to my dismay and disbelief, the library did not subscribe to the *New York Times*. A very weak consolation was the *Wall Street Journal* — only available, however the following day.

The private practice was affiliated with East General, an eighty-eight-bed community hospital. I'd never seen a hospital that small. Eighty-eight beds was one floor at Bellevue, and Bellevue sported twenty-one floors. East General Hospital reminded me of my elementary school — spread out over two wings, each only two stories high. The elevator seemed redundant. Some of the services that I was used to from Bellevue, like twenty-four-hour-a-day access to cardiac catheterization and hemodialysis, were not available, but there were other advantages. With a maximum census of eighty-eight patients, there was never any waiting time for anything I ordered. Stress tests, sonograms, CT scans, pulmonary consults, social-work requests — I had only to jot a request in the chart and it would be completed by the end of the day. The staff was small, but everyone seemed competent and extremely friendly. Within a week even the housekeepers were greeting me by name, and the phone operators recognized my voice when I called.

The following morning Mr. Reston was awake but extremely uncomfortable. He had tried to pull out his breathing tube several times, so the nurses had tied his arms down. I apologized to him for the wrist restraints and explained that I would try to get the tube out as soon as possible. I was self-conscious about my words because Wilbur Reston's body was sentient. He heard and understood everything I said, but the tube and the restraints prevented him from speaking or even gesturing; my awkward reassurances met with no response. I spent the morning in the ICU weaning Mr. Reston off the ventilator and draining fluid from his lungs. When the nurses were rolling him over to change the sheets, he managed to dislodge his own breathing tube and set himself free.

There is an entire scientific literature on the most appropriate time to extubate a patient, based on pulmonary function tests, blood gas values, and chest x-ray findings. But the Bellevue ICU's wisdom was that a patient was ready to be extubated when he or she reached over and yanked the damn tube out. Mr. Reston proved this to be true, since enough fluid had been removed from his lungs that he was able to breathe, if a bit huskily, without the tube. His condition was still tenuous, though, and he was too exhausted from his ordeal to talk much, I waited a while for his wife to arrive, but she never showed up.

Thirty-six hours after his admission I was finally able to actually "meet" Mr. Reston. He was a burly fellow who looked surprisingly robust for a patient with such a thick medical record. I would have expected a shriveled old man, but he had beefy arms and a hefty belly. There was a tattoo of an alligator on his left biceps. The ICU bed sagged slightly under his weight whenever he shifted or turned.

Mr. Reston's face was pulled low on his neck by meaty jowls, and dark bags weighed his eyes down. He had lived his entire life in this small town on the west coast of Florida. He was a veteran of the Korean War, with a specialty in artillery. After the war he'd worked as a police officer and spent some time training guard dogs.

His voice was surprisingly soft and somewhat morose. In slow, deliberate phrases he described a lifetime of progressively declining health. His arthritic pains and severe headaches seemed to have taken a greater toll on him than his many strokes and heart attacks. He was confined to his house, unable even to walk down the driveway to retrieve his mail.

Did he have any hobbies? He heaved a melancholic sigh. "I fancied myself a carpenter. I built miniature furniture for dollhouses. Always used the best wood."

I imagined this bearlike man hunched over delicate divans and bedroom sets.

"Can't do it anymore. My hands." He threw up his gnarled, arthritic paws for inspection.

"I also collect Civil War memorabilia. Once found a belt buckle from the second battle of Bull Run," he said with a puff of pride. "They had it in the museum for a while." But his recollection of his former glory was brief. "My wife thinks it's a stupid hobby," he said.

What about depression? "I've never *not* been depressed," he sighed ruefully. "Ever since college, I suppose." His records showed that he'd been treated at the VA psychiatric clinic with both psychotherapy and antidepressant medications for more than twenty years. His only daughter had died of a brain tumor the year before. His mother and sister had both died in the past five years, So had his dog.

Had he ever attempted suicide? "I'm handy with guns, you know. I have at least five in the house," he said dryly. "Different models. Always keep a loaded one at my bedside."

Did he ever use it? "Well, I stuck the barrel in my mouth. Didn't pull the trigger, though. Too messy. Just stopped taking my pills."

I had an image of Mr. Reston sitting on the side of his bed, shoulders sagging, cradling the gun in his hand. Perhaps he'd raised the gun to his head several times, each time not able to bring it close enough. But then he'd take a quick, dry swallow and, squinting, slide the gun into his mouth. I imagined that he might be startled at how comforting the gun felt in his mouth. But then that very comfort would make him shudder, and he'd rip the gun out, stuff it back into the nightstand drawer, and slam the drawer shut.

Then he'd be left staring at the pill bottles lined up on that nightstand, loaded with promises of good heath. He'd finger them, recalling what ill each was meant to cure. And cure they did. And then what?

I envisioned him opening that drawer again and, with the crook of his clublike arm, sweeping the bottles in, their hard plastic clattering against the gun as they came to rest at the bottom. He'd sink his head into his hands, forgetting to shut the nightstand drawer.

What about his wife, I asked. "She's busy with that volunteer work. She don't have time for me and all my pills," he said sadly. An uneasy silence settled in. I could see moisture accumulating at the edges of his soulful eyes, "We haven't shared a bed in fifteen years," he whispered.

His voice was plaintive but resigned. "Why should I live this life? I can't walk, my wife don't speak to me, I can't do nothing. What's the point?" He fixed his mournful gaze upon me. "*You* tell *me*."

It was both a plea and a demand. His simple statement had caused the space between us to evaporate, and I suddenly felt naked. Without my clinical armor to shield me, I was just one human facing another, squinting before the raw question. What *was* the point? What were the reasons for him to go on living?

I struggled to come up with one. Mr. Reston's body had withered sufficiently to keep him in perpetual pain but not enough to let him die. He had no friends; his wife was estranged. His daughter, mother, and sister had died and abandoned him. He was too weak to walk out of his house. He could no longer do any of the things that brought him pleasure. Why should he want to live? I could see why he had stopped taking his pills.

I didn't have an answer for him, but the law dictated what I had to do: actively suicidal patients must be prevented from harming themselves.

Like all good emergencies, this one occurred late on a Friday afternoon. Unlike Bellevue, there was no residency program in psychiatry to supply immediate consultations. There were several psychiatrists in the community, but they were busy with their private practices during the day and rarely made after-hours calls. But the staff of this tiny hospital was resourceful and helpful. They got me in touch with the local mental health agency, which was able to dispatch a psychiatric nurse practitioner. She agreed with my concerns and helped the nursing staff arrange a round-the-clock "suicide watch" over Mr. Reston. I could have Mr. Reston transferred to a psychiatric hospital once his medical condition stabilized if I felt he was still in danger of hurting himself. The nurse practitioner explained the procedures to invoke the Baker Act, the state legislation that allowed involuntary psychiatric commitment in such circumstances.

Over that weekend Mr. Reston's medical condition slowly improved, but his mood did not, Why should it? I thought. What did he have to look forward to? As much as I tried, I could not bring myself to utter flimsy platitudes about the value of life and how things would be better tomorrow. They weren't going to get better — he knew it and I knew it. Although he was clearly depressed, Mr. Reston was perfectly lucid. Despite his many strokes, his mind seemed to be working just fine. He could do all the tasks in the mental status exam: spell "world" backward, count down from one hundred by sevens, name the president, interpret the proverb "A rolling stone gathers no moss."

Although Mr. Reston seemed to have a reasonably realistic grasp on his situation, I wasn't so sure I had a grasp on mine. Doctors aren't supposed to agree with their patients who say they want to kill themselves, but I found myself overwhelmed by the utterly dismal facts of Mr. Reston's situation. Whom did Mr. Reston have left to live for? Even his dog had died.

I tried to imagine pacing the blank landscape of an empty life. How could I survive if every source of pleasure was denied? How could I live if the flavors, colors, and textures that made life palatable were flattened into a monochrome gray? If I were Mr. Reston, I might have pulled that trigger.

To complicate matters, he was in a rather unique medical situation. Although he had multitudes of medical problems, he was not yet terminally ill. He had a long list of diseases, but none was close to killing him. He was sick enough to be miserable but not sick enough to die. He was still able to eat, care for himself, and communicate with others. There were plenty of services and options for people on the verge of death, but Mr. Reston was not sick enough to qualify. His body, honed from years in the military and police force, was holding on too tenaciously. It left him stranded, strung too far from the shores of either health or death. Mr. Reston had severe physical pain, apparently unresponsive to various treatments, but more important, he was being eaten away by psychic pain.

The medico-legal issues were clear: a suicidal patient is prevented from committing suicide, even against his will, period. But the shades of gray needled me. My patient didn't want his life, and I wasn't sure it was ethical to force him to continue living it.

These issues plagued me for the remainder of the week. Ashamed to reveal my heresies to anyone, I secretly toyed with my doubts, picking at them as one does a loose tooth, perversely finding pleasure in its pain. What if I let him go home to his household of loaded guns? What if I discharged him, knowing full well that he'd stop taking his life-saving medicines? What if I turned my head and let him kill himself, as he so desperately wanted to do? There are those who say that all suicidal thoughts are products of depression, but Mr. Reston had been assiduously treated with medications and psychotherapy for decades. Perhaps he was being entirely rational. Who was I to stand in his way?

Then the toothache would burrow down to the raw nerve: What kind of evil doctor was I to even *consider* not protecting my patient from his violent tendencies? How could I be so negligent?

As I drove back and forth to work each day, this dilemma nagged at me. Lulled by the bland landscape, my mind would wander from the Spanish vocabulary coming from the car's tape deck to Mr. Reston languishing in his bare hospital room. Could there ever be any happiness for him? What if I found him a new hobby, one that he could manage with his disabilities? Stamp collecting — that wouldn't require much mobility. But probably his fingers couldn't manipulate the fragile paper stamps. Maybe he could take up painting. Large, easy brushes with hefty tubs of paint—he could manage that. Perhaps there was an artist waiting inside his weary body.

Traffic was stopped as a cumbersome tractor-trailer backed out of a construction site, attempting to turn around. A grove of orange trees had just been plowed, probably for a new strip mall. The trailer was open on top, and I could see the stacks of shimmering steel girders. The driver backed up a few feet, and then the trailer swung in the opposite direction, blocking his turn. The workers on the road waved their hands, shouting contradictory instructions: "Pull back a bit." "Swing to the right." "Turn your wheels on a sharp left." The driver edged forward and back, craning his neck out the window, then up toward his rearview mirror, as he tried to extricate himself from the tight spot. The steel girders flashed in the sunlight each time he changed angles. The smell of fresh, damp earth blended with the intoxicating sweetness of the orange blossoms, something I'd never smelled in New York City.

The metallic clanking and the competing shouts, along with the glare of the sunlight and the overpowering fragrance, made me feel heady and somewhat faint. I leaned my head into the steering wheel, and suddenly I saw the hole in Mr. Reston's armor: he had let himself be intubated. This man, who possessed a living will explicitly refusing all life-sustaining procedures, had *voluntarily* allowed a breathing tube to thrust air into his drowning lungs. He had reached for a life preserver.

I picked my head back up, feeling the murkiness begin to clear. Despite all of Wilbur Reston's misgivings and doubts, a desire to live had somehow percolated through.

As I leaned back in my seat, I wondered how that had come to pass. Was it simply the life-grabbing instinct that springs forward in such moments of near doom? Or was it truly evidence of Mr. Reston's ambivalence, of a desire to be saved and cared for?

Clearly, I had no way to know — I doubted if he himself would even know — but it seemed to me that Mr. Reston had given himself permission for a second chance. Now that he had done so, I had the opportunity, perhaps even the obligation, to allow that chance to flourish. If this second chance wasn't nourished, there probably wouldn't be a third. As if to confirm my realization, the tractor-trailer veered to the left and finally pulled itself out of its trap. The traffic snarl cleared, and I jammed on the accelerator, flying down the road with the breath of orange blossoms sweeping against my face.

When his medical condition stabilized, Mr. Reston was involuntarily committed to a VA psychiatric facility. He didn't protest when I informed him. He just nodded his head, his baggy jowls bobbing. During his entire stay, I'd never once met his wife; her occasional visits never seemed to coincide with mine.

The VA doctors assumed care of Mr. Reston, and I had no more contact. The private practice was busy, and I saw many patients every day. My mind was filled with Shana Elron's brittle diabetes and Henry Shaw's uncontrolled hypertension. There was the couple who lived in Pennsylvania during the summer but spent winters down south, and I was helping them coordinate his prostate cancer treatment between the two locations. I had recommitted myself to Spanish and spent my evenings conjugating verbs. I planned to leave for Mexico as soon as this stint in Florida was over, and I wanted to have the conditional tense under my belt. I had to decide if I wanted to start my trip in Guadalajara and end it in Chiapas, or vice versa. Or maybe just fly straight to Oaxaca and enroll in the Spanish school there. And then there was that shell-beach peninsula set against a tangle of mangroves twenty minutes from my hotel which beckoned me every night after work. I soon forgot about Mr. Reston.

Several weeks later, as my assignment in Florida was drawing to a close, some paperwork concerning Mr. Reston's original hospital admission turned up in my office needing a signature. Wilbur Reston's morose face flickered in my mind, and I thought about his miniature doll furniture. I wished I were still his doctor.

Besides giving himself a second chance, Mr. Reston had granted me the opportunity to tease out some of the more subtle aspects of medicine. He forced me to see beyond his imposing résumé of disease to his simple, hurting human self. The patient is not simply the sum of his illnesses, Wilbur Reston taught me. It is far more — blessedly far more — intricate than that.

After a labyrinth of phone calls through the VA bureaucracy, I finally tracked down his psychiatrist. Mr. Reston had just been discharged a few days ago. The psychiatrist described the long weeks and the laborious effort it had required to get Mr. Reston to take responsibility for simple things like brushing his teeth. By the end, though, he was showing up at the group meetings, even if he rarely spoke. Once in a while he even went to arts and crafts. Mr. Reston did not beome an effusive, energetic person, but according to the psychiatrist he no longer actively expressed the wish to die. That was considered a major success. And once he was continue involuntarily hospitalized. He could go home to his wife and no longer suicidal, there was no justification for keeping him with his regular outpatient therapy.

The psychiatrist commiserated with me over the many painful but immutable realities of Mr. Reston's life. A social worker was trying to help Mr. Reston get a new dog — that was about the only thing they could remedy.

I flew to Mexico the following week. In the end I'd decided to fly directly to Oaxaca for a month of Spanish lessons. Afterward I'd trek to Chiapas to see the Mayan ruins. I plunged into my classes, determined not to speak a word of English for six weeks, if that was possible. I rented a room from a family that spoke no English; I purchased Spanish editions of *Jonathan Livingston Seagull* and *The Little Prince* as my reading material; I tried to minimize my social contacts with the other foreigners in my classes and instead hang out at local cafés.

But I still thought about Wilbur Reston and wondered how he was doing. Those thoughts could only be in English. I imagined that he was sitting alone in his house, his wife at yet another volunteer function, his bones still aching, his weak heart preventing him from even getting the mail. But maybe there was now a puppy yapping at his feet, freely dispensing and demanding love. When the headaches and joint pains became overwhelming, maybe Mr. Reston would again consider ending his life. But then he might stop and think: Who would feed the puppy?

Reflections and Responses

1. Consider Danielle Ofri's title for her essay. What two meanings does it possess simultaneously? How are these two meanings in

opposition to each other? How are both of these meanings relevant to the essay as a whole?

2. What dilemma prompts Ofri's "epiphany" — the realization that her patient actually has the will to live? How and where does this sudden realization occur? In what ways is the specific context in which the epiphany occurs appropriate? How does it help to trigger the sudden insight?

3. Note the number of times that Ofri imagines her patient's life and activities. Why do you think she does this? Reexamine the final paragraph, for example. How would you evaluate this conclusion? How would a reader know whether it's at all accurate? Do you find the conclusion satisfying from a narrative point of view? Explain why or why not? How else might the essay have ended?

[handwritten notes]

will to live
Is his living will greater than his desire to die?

why should he live this life? or is his life worth living?

what circumstances or not conditions will to live is strong?

ASHRAF RUSHDY

Exquisite Corpse

*When Emmett Till — a fourteen-year-old from Chicago visiting relatives in
Mississippi — was viciously murdered and then tossed into the Tallahatchie
River in 1955, his mother insisted on an open-coffin funeral that allowed
photographs of her son's horribly mutilated corpse to be published across the
nation. It was a momentous political gesture; it shocked the country and
the photographs had an enormous impact on the course of the civil rights
movement. But why didn't the public see photographs of James Byrd, who
in 1998 was brutally dragged from a pickup truck in Texas until his body
was dismembered? Would such photos, however sickening, have had a positive effect by making us vividly see what racial hatred is capable of? In
"Exquisite Corpse," African American scholar Ashraf Rushdy compares
these two racial incidents, separated by nearly a half-century, and examines the moral authority of photography. "So why do we need to see the
corpse?" he asks. His essay provides a compelling answer.*

*Ashraf Rushdy is professor of African American Studies and English
Literature at Wesleyan University. He is the author of one book on John
Milton,* The Empty Garden *(1992), and two books on contemporary
African American cultural and literary history,* Neo-Slave Narratives
(1999) and Remembering Generations *(2001). Written while he was a
Fellow at the National Humanities Center, "Exquisite Corpse" first appeared
in* Transition *and was selected by Kathleen Norris for* The Best American
Essays *2001.*

In an earlier time, a lynch mob would display the body of its victim
with impunity, often gathering around it for a group photograph.
These images, and the bodies they represented, were the icons of
white supremacy. Circulated in newspapers, the pictures displayed

Min want in the proper edition

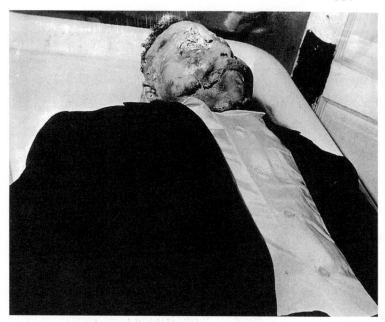

Some fifty thousand mourners filed past the open casket of lynching victim Emmett Till between September 3 and September 6, 1955. Used with permission of Chicago Defender

the power of the white mob and the powerlessness of the black community. After the highly publicized lynching of Claude Neal in 1934, photographers took hundreds of shots of his mutilated body and sold them for fifty cents each. The photograph of Neal's hanging body eventually became a postcard. One group of white people, gathered around a burned black body, was communicating to another group in another county: they had done their part, asserted their place in the world. The image was certain to incite other communities to follow their example: this was the golden age of lynching.

The body of the victim assumed a magical quality for the lynch mob: the corpse was an object to be tortured, mutilated, collected, displayed. To snuff out life was rarely enough: more ritual was required. In 1937, when a Georgia mob was unable to lynch Willie Reid because the police had already killed him, they broke into the funeral home where he lay, carried his body to a baseball diamond, and burned it. Even a mob that had already hanged, maimed, and burned a man might still feel compelled to exhume his body in order to inflict further indignities; so it was with the corpse of George Armwood, in 1933.

As the historian Jacquelyn Dowd Hall has noted, the spectacle of lynching dramatized a social hierarchy where whites and blacks, women and men, knew their place. Blacks were terrorized, white women were vulnerable, and white men were on top, invulnerable and free. Still, whites projected immense sexual power onto blacks; the terror of lynching reflected their own anxieties.

Indeed lynching also seems to be the expression of a peculiar necrophilia, manifest in the desire to possess the bodies of victims, in the passion with which dead bodies were handled and displayed — as if they were talismans of life itself. The East Texas lynch mob that killed David Gregory in 1933 pulled out his heart and cut off his penis before tossing his body onto a pyre: those were the most potent emblems of vitality. Such actions bespeak nothing so much as a perverse fondness for the dead body.

While lynch mobs subjected the corpses of their victims to the most spectacular abuse, victims' families were more concerned with matters of the spirit. Most often they buried their loved ones in silence: for these families, the corpse was less important than the soul.

The same can be said of those families who refused to bury lynch victims. In 1889, after a mob broke into a Barnwell, South Carolina, jail and lynched eight African American men, the local black community displayed its solidarity at the funeral. More than five hundred people lined the street, and several women implored the Lord to "burn Barnwell to the ground." The community refused to bury six of the men, claiming that the whites who killed them should bear that responsibility. In Virginia, Joseph McCoy's aunt refused to bury the body of her nephew, who was lynched in 1897. "As the people killed him, they will have to bury him," she explained. The body, whether buried or left to the elements, had become a symbol of the injustice and barbarism of the white community, the failure of the nation's founding principles: let the dead bury their dead.

When Emmett Till was lynched in 1955, Mamie Till Bradley refused to hide her son's corpse. His mutilated and decomposed body was found in the Tallahatchie River three days after he died. Despite the sheriff's opposition, she insisted that her son be returned to Chicago. Bradley opened the casket as soon as it arrived at Illinois Central Terminal and promptly announced that she wanted an open-casket funeral so everyone could "see what they did to my boy." On the first day the casket was open for viewing, ten thousand people saw it; on the day of the funeral, at least two thousand mourners stood outside the packed church where the services were held. The body of Emmett Till — "his head . . . swollen and bashed in, his mouth twisted and broken" — became a new kind of icon. Emmett Till showed the world exactly what white supremacy looked like.

According to one report, Till's funeral created an "emotional explosion": "thousands of cursing, shrieking, fainting Negroes" responded to the "corpse . . . displayed 'as is.'" The Southern media denounced Bradley's decision as "macabre exhibitionism" and cheap political "exploitation." But African Americans who attended the funeral or saw pictures of Till's body were transformed. One reader congratulated the *Amsterdam News* for "putting the picture of the murdered Till boy on the front page"; a writer for the *Pittsburgh Courier* predicted that Mrs. Bradley's decision might "easily become an opening gun in a war on Dixie which can reverberate around the world." A photo-essay in *Jet* proved electrifying: Representative Charles Diggs remarked that the "picture in *Jet* magazine showing Emmett Till's mutilation . . . stimulated . . . anger on the part of blacks all over the country." A black sociologist later wrote that "the *Jet* magazine photograph of Emmett Till's grotesque body left an indelible impression on young Southern blacks"; they went on to become "the vanguard of the Southern student movement."

The influence of the *Jet* photographs has been well documented. As a girl, civil rights activist Joyce Ladner kept clippings in a scrapbook. She responded to the picture of Till's bloated body in the magazine "with horror that transformed itself into a promise to alter the political and racial terrain where such a crime could happen." Cleveland Sellers, an activist and field director in the Student Nonviolent Coordinating Committee, remembers how pictures of the corpse in black newspapers and magazines—showing "terrible gashes and tears in the flesh . . . [giving] the appearance of a ragged, rotting sponge" — created a stir about civil rights when he was a youth in South Carolina. A thirteen-year-old boy named Cassius Clay stood on a street corner in Louisville, transfixed by pictures of Emmett Till in black newspapers and magazines: in one picture, smiling and happy; in the other, a gruesome mockery of a face. Muhammad Ali says he admired Mrs. Bradley, who had "done a bold thing" in forcing the world to look at her son. Fifteen years later, Ali met Brother Judge Aaron, a man who had survived a Klan lynching attempt in the 1960s. (They had carved the letters *KKK* into his chest and castrated him to send a "message" to "smart-alecky . . . niggers like Martin Luther King and Reverend Shuttleworth.") Ali responded by dedicating all his future fights to "the unprotected people, to the victims."

By the time of Emmett Till's murder, lynching had begun to decline, and pictures of lynching victims were becoming scarce. What had once been viewed with pride now seemed like barbarity: the victim's body became less an icon of white supremacy than a denunciation of it. As popular opinion turned against lynching, the sight of lynched bodies became an embarrassment for white communities squirming under the glare of national and international scrutiny. In fact, these corpses became potent weapons in the political struggle to enact a law against lynching — a struggle that continues today.

The 1959 murder of Mack Charles Parker was representative of this new climate. The lynch mob wore masks to hide the identity of its members; they gave up on their original plan to castrate their victim and hang the body from a bridge: instead, they weighted the body and dumped it into the river. When Parker's body was recovered ten days later, town officials worked furiously to keep it from being entered as evidence before the Senate during deliberations on antilynching legislation. Police officers and state troopers guarded the body in a funeral home, and after *Chicago Defender* reporter Tony Rhoden managed to sneak in and take a picture of the badly mutilated body, there was a frantic search for him and his camera. Two hours after the coroner's inquest, before Parker's mother had even heard that his body had been recovered, he was buried in a hasty ceremony.

It is not clear what happened to Rhoden's photograph of Parker's body. If it was not published, it might have been because of the censorship that has restrained mainstream photojournalism in times of extremity. *Life* magazine had to wait eight months while government censors debated whether it could publish a picture of a dead American soldier on Buna Beach, New Guinea, in 1943. While pictures of dead bodies were widely published during the Vietnam War, a *Detroit Free Press* photographer had to beg military censors to approve a photograph of an American soldier crying over a body bag during the Persian Gulf War. And even in the absence of official censorship, Americans' delicate sensibilities have prevented the widespread dissemination of gruesome pictures. A *New York Times* reader wrote an angry letter to complain about a photograph of a Kosovo massacre victim in October 1998. His brief comment — "This is not something I wish to see alongside my breakfast" — aptly characterizes a reading public that does not expect graphic violence in the responsible media.

In June 1998 an African American named James Byrd was murdered in Jasper, Texas, by a white ex-con named John William King and two accomplices. It was determined that Byrd's body had been dragged from a pickup truck and that the body had been dismembered along the route: the head, neck, and right arm were severed from the torso. During King's trial in February 1999, the prosecution presented photographs that documented Byrd's suffering: his knees, heels, buttocks, and elbows were ground to the bone; eight of his left ribs and nine of his right were broken; his ankles were cut to the bone by the chains that attached him to the truck. A pathologist testified that Byrd's "penis and testicles [were] shredded from his body," and we learned, with horror, that "Mr. Byrd was alive up to the point where he hit the culvert and his head separated from his body." For months, the story of James Byrd's brutal slaying transfixed the nation.

No picture of James Byrd's corpse has ever been published. Indeed, when the *New York Times* interviewed several editors for a story on newspaper photography, none had seen the prosecution's photographs. In a strange twist of fate, however, King's own body served as evidence in the state's case against him: it seems he had a passion for racist tattoos. Prosecutors showed thirty-three slides and photographs of the images inscribed on King's body: a cross with a black man hanging from it, a swastika, the insignia of Hitler's SS, a woodpecker peeking out from a Ku Klux Klan hood, the Virgin Mary holding a horned baby Jesus, images of Church of

Satan founder Anton La Vey, goat heads, Valentine hearts turned upside down, playing cards showing eights and aces (the dead man's poker hand), a dragon emblazoned with the words *Beto I* (the Texas prison where King was incarcerated from 1995 to 1997), the slogan *Aryan Pride*, and several allusions to "peckerwoods" — rednecks — in prison. (It had been reported earlier that King had a tattoo of Tinkerbell on his penis; the DA declined to mention this.) It was King's body, not Byrd's, that became an advertisement for white supremacy, and judging by the John William King tribute pages that have sprung up on the Internet, the advertisement has been successful.

It is not likely that anyone other than the lawyers, the jury, and the courtroom spectators will ever see the photographs that the court accepted as evidence. In the only well-known image of Byrd, he is wearing a Colorado Rockies baseball cap, looking directly into the camera. The most graphic picture appeared on the cover of the *Boston Globe* on June 12, 1998: it showed the dried blood that stained the Jasper street where Byrd's torso had been dragged.

The Byrd family was singularly gracious in promoting reconciliation and defusing racial hatred in the aftermath of the murder, and it may have been out of respect for their feelings that photographs of James Byrd's body were not published. Indeed, for about six weeks after the murder, the major story in Jasper was the tension between the Byrd family's desire for privacy and activists' eagerness for publicity. Even as reporters set up a media circus around the funeral, they wrote compassionately of the pain that politicians and political advocacy groups created for the Byrds. When the Klan gathered for a rally to distance themselves from John William King and his cohorts, and the Dallas-based New Black Panthers gathered to respond to the Klan, the Byrd family tried to remain above the fray. As the *Houston Chronicle* reported, "Byrd's family was uncomfortable with the idea of turning him into a national symbol, and would have preferred to have had a quieter service without the political rallying cries."

Despite these pleas, this case demanded national attention. In newspaper stories that pit a grieving family wishing for peace and quiet against a flock of politically motivated vultures intent on creating a self-serving spectacle, the true complexity of the Jasper saga is lost. It is despicable, of course, to use Byrd's funeral to promote racism, as the Klan did; and it is wrongheaded to use the event to promote armed self-defense, as the New Black Panthers did. But there are other considerations — considerations that are at least as compelling as a family's grief. Those who attempted to situate the murder in its historical context, while respecting the family's wishes for a degree of privacy, should be praised.

At James Byrd's funeral, Jesse Jackson said that "Brother Byrd's innocent blood alone could very well be the blood that changes the course of our country, because no one has captured the nation's attention like this tragedy." Jackson asked the town of Jasper to erect a monument in Byrd's memory, "as a tangible protest against hate crimes." I applaud Jackson's sense of urgency, but his proposal is in the wrong tenor. Indeed, I would suggest that Jackson went wrong precisely when he departed from his insight: spilled blood is a valuable representation of the search for justice. In his resolve to create a monument, he shifted his focus from blood to image, from body to stone. *policy & more abstract; less real*

The connections between the Till and Byrd lynchings are striking. Part of the evidence against King was an *Esquire* article on the Till lynching that he had kept in his apartment: this suggested that his actions were premeditated. Mamie Till Bradley spoke about the Jasper murder on a New York radio talk show; two weeks later, she held the hand of James Byrd's father at a Harlem memorial service. There were some coincidences, too: after the trial of Till's lynchers, newspapers reported that Till's father had been hanged in 1944, after he was convicted of rape and murder while stationed in Italy with the army; after the trial in the Jasper case, it was revealed that John William King's uncle had been acquitted of kill ing a gay man in 1939. More than half a century of hate crimes has ensnared these families — the Tills, the Byrds, the Kings — in America's quiet history of guilt and grief.

But there are disparities. In 1955, the American public learned about Emmett Till's life and they saw his death: the contrast between a vibrant youth and a violent end helped ignite the outcry that followed. In 1998, even as contemporary readers learned about James Byrd's life, they were denied the pictures that might have inspired a greater and more productive outrage. On February

24, 1999, the same day the *New York Times* reported the jury's verdict in the Jasper trial, it ran two other stories about hate crimes: in
Virginia, a jury convicted a white teenager of burning a cross on
the lawn of an interracial couple; and in Louisiana, a white man
was sentenced to twenty years in prison for trying to set fire to two
cars and their African American occupants. Hatred is far more
pervasive than we would like to admit, and representations of it are
critical to the education of the majority of white Americans who
believe that racism was a phenomenon that ended sometime in the
sixties.

ital

Of course, publishing pictures of James Byrd's corpse might fan
the flames of white supremacy. There were reports of copycat
crimes within a week of Byrd's murder: in Louisiana, where three
white men taunted a black man with racial epithets while trying to
drag him alongside their car; and in Illinois, where three white boys
assaulted a black teenager in almost exactly the same way. Three
months later, New York City police officers and firefighters parodied
Byrd's murder by imitating it in a Labor Day parade float. And while
the trial was under way, a Washington, D.C., radio announcer —
the "Greaseman" — responded to a clip from a song by soul singer
Lauryn Hill by commenting, "No wonder people drag them behind
trucks." (He was fired the next day.) In a climate where people still
respond to lynching with jokes and mimicry, pictures of James
Byrd's body might have fed this evil appetite.

So why do we need to see the corpse? It is possible that pictures
of graphic violence still have the power to make an impression.

cancel/ital

At least one member of the jury found the pictures of Byrd's body
almost unbearable; she had to force herself to turn each page. Indeed, one Jasper resident suggested that the lynchers should be
sentenced to life in a cell "with pictures of James Byrd's body parts
pasted all over the walls" — expressing the hope that even the murderers would find such images sickening. This kind of shock therapy might work for the public at large. It would have been difficult
for policemen and firemen in New York, or a DJ in Washington, to
joke about the murder of James Byrd if their jokes summoned images of the horrific crimes they were taking so lightly.

These photographs could also turn the tide of history once
again. African American men have long been portrayed as comic
buffoons or dangerous criminals, and a large segment of this

nation remains incapable of imagining black suffering. A study concerning the effects of race on the death penalty found that there is "neither strong nor consistent" evidence of discrimination against black defendants in death penalty trials. But the study also concluded that the race of the victim matters greatly in juries' decisions to sentence a murderer to death. Convicted murderers who kill a white victim are more than four times as likely to be condemned to death as those who kill a black victim. Only 8 whites have been executed for murdering black Americans since the death penalty was reinstated in 1977, but 123 blacks have been put to death for murdering whites. Predominantly white juries seem unable to sympathize with black crime victims. It is possible that this crime, fixed in memory, could transform the nation's moral imagination.

To have wounded the Byrd family any more would have been intolerable; and pictures of their relative's body would have wounded them. To have created conditions that satisfied the blood lust of white supremacists would have been criminal; and photographs of the remains of James Byrd would have given them glee. To lower the already low level of public discourse would be shameful; and publishing more photographs of violence is not likely to elevate it. But our primary concern must be to prevent another family from feeling as the Byrd family now feels; we cannot determine how best to combat hatred by focusing on the response of the most incorrigible purveyors of hatred. The past teaches us that images of terror — used responsibly — can foster a climate in which terror is no longer tolerated. I suggest that we aspire to the courageous example of Mamie Till Bradley, not the cautious compromises of newspaper editors who fear to offend their readerships. A citizenry alert to the horror of hate crimes would be compensation enough.

Reflections and Responses

---

1. Why is Emmett Till's murder important to the argument Rushdy constructs? Do you think the two incidents are similar enough to make his case, or do you think important distinctions can be made?

2. Why do you think Rushdy avoids simply contrasting only the Till and Byrd murders? Why does he introduce many other examples of lynchings and murders? What historical point is he making?

3. Note that Rushdy's argument does not merely dismiss those who opposed publishing the Byrd photographs. What are their arguments? Why might Byrd's family not want to publicize the photos? Why would newspapers oppose? What other reasons does Rushdy offer in favor of those who oppose making the photos available? Do you agree with Rushdy, or do you think Byrd's photos would have served no useful purpose?

ELAINE SCARRY

Citizenship in Emergency

The terrorist attacks on September 11, 2001, are depicted in two 2006 films — the TV movie Flight 93 *and the feature* United 93 *— both of which relate in realistic fashion the events that occurred aboard the hijacked plane that was brought down by the action of passengers near Shanksville, Pennsylvania. For some reason, this particular event — though just one of many on that disastrous day — has captured the public's imagination. Although written a few years before the two movies, the essay "Citizenship in Emergency" offers an interesting explanation of why this incident has received so much attention. In contrasting two of that day's hijacked flights, American Airlines Flight 77 that struck the Pentagon and United Flight 93, Elaine Scarry examines "two different conceptions of national defense: one model is authoritarian, centralized, top-down; the other, operating in a civil frame, is distributed and egalitarian." That one model was far more effective than the other, Scarry believes, should convince us of the superiority of a* civilian-based homeland defense.

  Elaine Scarry is the Walter M. Cabot professor of Aesthetics and the General Theory of Value at Harvard University. She is the author of The Body in Pain *(1985),* Literature and the Body *(1988),* On Beauty and Being Just *(1999),* Dreaming by the Book *(1999), and* Who Defended the Country? *(2003). She has also written many articles on war and the social contract. "Citizenship in Emergency, written only a year after the attack of 9/11," originally appeared in* The Boston Review *and was selected by Anne Fadiman for* The Best American Essays 2003.

FOR THE PAST YEAR, we have spoken unceasingly about the events of September 11, 2001. But one aspect of that day has not yet been the topic of open discussion: the difficulty we had as a country

ʒ๑๑ʒ

defending ourselves; as it happened, the only successful defense was carried out not by our professional defense apparatus but by the passengers on Flight 93, which crashed in Pennsylvania. The purpose of this essay is to examine that difficulty, and the one success, and ask if they suggest that something in our defense arrangements needs to be changed. Whatever the ultimate answer to that question, we at least need to ask it, since defending the country is an obligation we all share.

The difficulty of defense on September 11 turned in large part on the pace of events. We need to look carefully at the timelines and timetables on that day. But as we do, it is crucial to recall that the word "speed" did not surface for the first time on September 11. It has been at the center of discussions of national defense for the last fifty years. When we look to any of our literatures on the subject, we find in the foreground statements about the speed of our weapons, of our weapons' delivery systems, and of the deliberations that will lead to their use.

Throughout this period, the heart of our defense has been a vast missile system, all parts of which are described as going into effect in "a matter of minutes": a presidential decision must be made in "a matter of minutes"; the presidential order must be transmitted in "a matter of minutes"; the speed of the missile launch must be carried out in "a matter of minutes"; and the missile must reach its target in "a matter of minutes."

The matter-of-minutes claim is sometimes formally folded into the names of our weapons (as in the Minuteman missile) and other times appears in related banner words such as "supersonic" and "hair-trigger." Thousands of miles separating countries and continents can be contracted by "supersonic" missiles and planes that carry us there in "a matter of minutes"; and thousands of miles separating countries and continents can be contracted by focusing on the distance that has to be crossed not by the weapon itself but by the hand gesture that initiates the launch — the distance of a hair.

"Speed" has occupied the foreground not only of our *descriptive* statements about our national defense but also our *normative* statements. Our military arrangements for defending the country have often been criticized for moving increasingly outside the citizenry's control. The constitutional requirement for a congressional declaration of war has not been used for any war since World War II: the Korean War, the Vietnam War, and the war in former Yugoslavia were all carried out at the direction of the president and without a congressional declaration, as were the invasions of Panama, Grenada, and Haiti; the recent "Authorization for the Use of Military Force Against Iraq" once again fails to fulfill the requirement for a congressional declaration. Speed has repeatedly been invoked to counter ethical, legal, or constitutional objections to the way our weapons policies and arrangements have slipped further and further beyond democratic structures of self-governance.

This bypassing of the Constitution in the case of conventional wars and invasions has been licensed by the existence of nuclear weapons and by the country's formal doctrine of "presidential first use," which permits the president, acting alone, to initiate nuclear war. Since the president has genocidal injuring power at his personal disposal, obtaining Congress's permission for much lesser acts of injury (as in conventional wars) has often struck presidents as a needless bother: President Bush Sr. boasted, "I didn't have to get permission from some old goat in the United States Congress to kick Saddam Hussein out of Kuwait." The most frequent argument used to excuse the setting aside of the Constitution is that the pace of modern life simply does not allow time for obtaining the authorization of Congress, let alone the full citizenry. Our ancestors who designed the Constitution — so the argument goes — could not have envisioned the supersonic speed at which the country's defense would need to take place. So the congressional requirement is an anachronism. With planes and weapons traveling faster than the speed of sound, what sense does it make to have a lot of sentences we have no time to hear?

Among the many revelations that occurred on September 11 was a revelation about our capacity to act quickly. Speed — the realpolitik that has excused the setting aside of the law for fifty years — turns out not to have been very *real* at all. The description that follows looks at the timetables of American Airlines Flight 77 — the plane that hit the Pentagon — and United Airlines Flight 93 — the plane that crashed in Pennsylvania when passengers successfully disabled the hijackers' mission. Each of the two planes was a small piece of U.S. ground. Their juxtaposition indicates that a form of defense that is external to the ground that needs to be defended

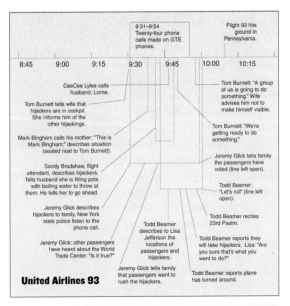

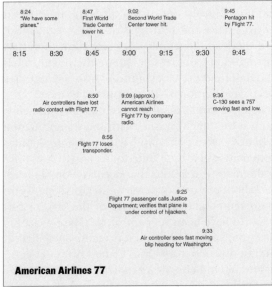

Charts detailing timeline of events for two 9/11 hijacked jetliners,
United Airlines 93 and American Airlines 77. © *Boston Review*

does not work as well as a form of defense that is internal to the ground that needs to be protected. This outcome precisely matches the arguments that were made at the time of the writing of the Constitution about why the military had to be "held within a civil frame": about why military actions, whether offensive or defensive, must be measured against the norms of civilian life, must be brought into contact with the people with whom one farms or performs shared labor, or the people with whom one raises children, or the people with whom one goes to church or a weekly play or movie. Preserving such a civil frame was needed to prevent the infantilization of the country's population by its own leaders, and because it was judged to be the only plausible way actually to defend the home ground.

When the plane that hit the Pentagon and the plane that crashed in Pennsylvania are looked at side by side, they reveal two different conceptions of national defense: one model is authoritarian, centralized, top-down; the other, operating in a civil frame, is distributed and egalitarian. Should anything be inferred from the fact that the first form of defense failed and the second succeeded? This outcome obligates us to review our military structures and to consider the possibility that we need a democratic, not a top-down, *proportion* form of defense. At the very least, the events of September 11 cast doubt on a key argument that, for the past fifty years, has been used to legitimize an increasingly centralized, authoritarian model of defense — namely, the argument based on speed.

American Airlines Flight 77 was originally scheduled to fly from Washington to Los Angeles. The plane approached the Pentagon at a speed of 500 miles per hour. It entered the outermost of the building's five rings, ring E, then cut through ring D and continued on through ring C, and eventually stopped just short of ring B. Two million square feet were damaged or destroyed. Before September 11, the Pentagon was five corridors deep, five stories high, and in its overall shape five-sided. Three of the Pentagon's five sides were affected (one had to be leveled and rebuilt; the other two were badly damaged by smoke and water).

One hundred and eighty-nine people died — 64 on the plane, 125 working in the Pentagon. Many others were badly burned. Twenty-three thousand people work in the Pentagon. Two factors prevented many more people from being killed or badly burned. First, the building is stacked horizontally, not vertically like the World Trade Center towers — it is built like layers of sedimentary rock that have been turned on their side and lie flush with the ground. Second, one of the sections hit was being renovated and was therefore relatively empty of people when the plane entered.

While we continue to lament the deaths and injuries, and continue to find solace in the fact that the number of deaths and injuries was not higher, one key fact needs to be held on to and stated in a clear sentence: on September 11, the Pentagon could not defend the Pentagon, let alone the rest of the country.

The U.S. military had precious little time to respond on September 11 (and this fact has been accurately acknowledged by almost everyone, both inside and outside the country, who has spoken about the day). But by the standards of speed that have been used to justify setting aside constitutional guarantees for the last fifty years, the U.S. military on September 11 had a great deal of time to protect the Pentagon. It had more than minutes. The pilots of the F-15s and F-16s that flew on that day made no mistakes, displayed no inadequacies, and showed no lack of courage — but what they tried to do now appears to have been a structural impossibility.

One hour and twenty-one minutes go by between the moment FAA controllers learn that multiple planes have been taken and the moment the Pentagon is struck. Controllers hear the hijackers on the first seized plane (American Flight 11) say "we have some planes" at 8:24 A.M., a sentence indicating that the plane from which the voice comes is not the sole plane presently imperiled. The information that "some planes" have been taken is available one hour and twenty-one minutes before the Pentagon is hit by the third seized plane at 9:45 A.M.

Fifty-eight minutes go by between the attack on the first World Trade Center tower (at 8:47 A.M.) and the crash into the Pentagon (9:45 A.M.). This means that for almost one hour before the Pentagon is hit, the military knows that the hijackers have multiple planes and that those hijackers have no intention to land those planes safely.

The crash of American Flight 77 into the Pentagon comes fifty-five minutes after that plane has itself disappeared from radio contact (at 8:50 A.M.). So for *fifty-five minutes*, the military knows three things:

1. the hijackers have multiple planes;
2. the hijackers, far from having any intention of landing the planes safely, intend to injure as many people on the ground as possible; and
3. Flight 77 has a *chance* of being one of those planes, since it has just disappeared from radio.

When, six minutes later, the plane loses its transponder (so that its radar image as well as its radio contact is now lost), the chance that it is one of the seized planes rises.

By the most liberal reading, then, the country had *one hour and twenty-one minutes* to begin to respond. By the most conservative reading, the country had *fifty-five minutes* to begin to respond. The phrase "begin to respond" does not mean that an F-15 or F-16 could now attack the plane that would hit the Pentagon. At the one-hour-and-twenty-one-minute clock time, the plane that will eventually hit the Pentagon is only four minutes into its flight and has not yet been hijacked. It means instead that a warning threshold has just been crossed and a level of readiness might therefore begin: at one hour and twenty-one minutes, fighter pilots could be placed on standby on the ground with engines running; at fifty-five minutes, fighter planes could be following the third plane, as well as any other planes that are wildly off course and out of radio contact.

One hour and twenty-one minutes and *fifty-five minutes* are each a short time — a short, short time. But by the timetables that we have for decades accepted as descriptive of our military weapons, by the timetables we have accepted as explanations for why we must abridge our structures of self-governance — by the intoxicating timetables of "rapid response," the proud specifications of eight minutes, twelve minutes, four minutes, one minute — by these timetables, the September 11 time periods of one hour and twenty-one minutes or of fifty-five minutes are very long periods indeed.

The transition from the moment Flight 77's radio is off (at 8:50 A.M.) to the moment it disappears from secondary radar (8:56 A.M.) is crucial, for it begins to confirm the inference that this is one of the hijacked planes. A sequence of confirmations now follows. While the FAA controllers have been unable to reach the plane, now the airline company also discovers its inability to reach Flight 77 on a separate radio (shortly after 9 A.M.). At 9:25 a passenger, Barbara Olson, places a phone call to her husband, Theodore Olson, in the U.S. Justice Department, stating that the plane is under the control of hijackers. Because the passenger is well known to the Justice Department listener, no time need be lost assessing the honesty and accuracy of the report. This means that twenty minutes prior to the moment the Pentagon is hit, the Justice Department has direct, reliable voice confirmation of the plane's seizure.

So for *twenty minutes* prior to the hitting of the Pentagon, the military is in a position to know three things (the third of which differs decisively from what it knew at the fifty-five-minute marker):

1. the hijackers have multiple planes;
2. the hijackers intend to injure as many people as possible;
3. Flight 77 is *certainly* one of the hijacked planes: it has disappeared from radio, disappeared from secondary radar, disappeared from the company radio, and has been described to the Justice Department as "hijacked" by a passenger whose word cannot be doubted.

The steadily mounting *layers of verification* listed in number 3 continue. At 9:33 A.M., an FAA air traffic controller (according to the *New York Times*) sees on radar a "fast moving blip" or "fast moving primary target" making its way toward Washington airspace: this level of verification comes *twelve minutes* prior to the plane's crash into the Pentagon. At 9:36 A.M. an airborne C-130 sees the plane and identifies it as a "757 moving low and fast." This further confirmation comes *nine minutes* prior to the collision. No one can suppose that in nine minutes planes could be scrambled and reach the hijacked plane (even if we have, for decades, listened dutifully to descriptions of much more complicated military acts occurring in nine minutes). But certainly the layers of alert, of scrambling, of takeoff, of tracking, could have begun one hour and twenty minutes earlier, or fifty-five minutes earlier, not nine minutes earlier. Nine minutes is presumably the time frame in which only the last act of military defense need be carried out by the fighter planes — if there is any reasonable last act to be taken, a question to which I will return.

During much of its flight, American Flight 77 was over countryside (rather than over densely populated urban areas). Here is a list of the six successive layers of verification, which will help us picture where the plane was at each stage:

- loss of radio (55 minutes remain)
- loss of transponder (49 minutes remain)
- loss of contact with the airline company (approximately 36 minutes remain)
- a passenger calls the Justice Department (20 minutes remain)
- a radar image is seen moving toward Washington whose source is not using its secondary radar (12 minutes remain)
- a C-130 sights a Boeing 757 flying fast and low (9 minutes remain)

Assuming an air speed of 500 miles an hour, we can infer that at the time we learn that both the radio and the transponder are off (*the second layer of confirmation*), the plane would be 410 miles from Washington with many miles of sparsely populated land beneath it. By *the fourth confirmation* (Barbara Olson's phone call), it would be 166 miles from Washington. By *the sixth confirmation*, that given by the C-130, the plane destined for the Pentagon would still be 75 miles from Washington and the possibility of minimizing injury to those on the ground would be rapidly vanishing with each passing mile.

Again, the point here is not to say, "Why couldn't these airmen shoot down the plane?" Time made that extremely difficult. But much smaller units of time have been invoked to explain our battle readiness over the last fifty years and to license the centralization of injuring power rather than a decentralized and distributed authorization across the full citizenry, which is, according to the U.S. Constitution, our legal right and our legal responsibility to protect. There is a second, profound reason the act could not be (ought not to have been) carried out — the problem of consent, to which I will return when we come to United Flight 93.

Let us see what actions the military undertook during this time (actions described in the *New York Times* and *Aviation Week and Space Technology*). Fourteen National Guard planes are responsible for defending the country. Five of those planes — two F-15s from Otis Air Force Base on Cape Cod and three F-16s from Langley in Virginia — were called into action on September 11. These five planes were not the only military planes in the air that day. Once the Pentagon was hit, the FAA ordered all aircraft down — a beautifully choreographed landing of 4,546 planes over a period of three hours. When the FAA announced the order, 206 military planes were in U.S. airspace (most engaged in routine exercises, actions unconnected to the immediate defense of the country); 90 remained in the air after the grounding (their duties have not been entered into the public record). But it is only the five National Guard planes that were called into action against the seized passenger airliners that will be described here.

The two National Guard F-15s that took off from Otis attempted to address the events taking place in New York City. They were called into action one minute before the first World Trade Center tower was hit; by the time the second tower was hit, they were seventy-one miles — eight minutes — away from Manhattan. Should they then have continued down to the Washington area? (By this time, the plane destined for the Pentagon had its radio and transponder off and was reachable by neither air controllers nor the airline company.) The answer is no. The two F-15s needed to stay near New York City, where it was reasonable to worry that a third hijacked plane could approach. From September 11, 2001, until March 21, 2002, New York airspace was protected twenty-four hours a day by F-15s, F-16s, and AWACS planes.

The three F-16s at Langley received their first order from Huntress Defense Section at 9:24 A.M. This is a late start: twenty-two minutes after the second World Trade Center tower has been hit, thirty-four minutes after the plane destined for the Pentagon has lost its radio, twenty-eight minutes after it has disappeared from secondary radar, and fifteen minutes after the airline company has failed to reach the plane on its own radio. By 9:30 A.M. the Langley F-16s are in the air, traveling at 600 miles per hour toward New York City. Soon they are instructed to change their course and are told that Reagan National Airport is the target. They are flying at 25,000 feet. The hijacked plane is flying at 7,000 feet. The F-16s reach Washington, DC, at some unspecified time after the 9:45 A.M. collision of Flight 77 into the Pentagon. As they pass over the city, they are asked to look down and confirm that the Pentagon is on fire — confirmation that by this point civilians on the ground have already provided.

There are profoundly clear reasons why the military could not easily intercept the plane and bring it down in a rural area. But each of those reasons has counterparts in our long-standing military arrangements, which should now be subjected to rigorous questioning. First, Flight 77's path was hard to track, since its transponder had been turned off. Yes, that's true — and so, too, any missiles fired on the United States or its allies will surely be traveling without a transponder; their paths will not be lucid; their tracking will not be easy. Second, the fact that Flight 77's radio was not working couldn't be taken as a decisive sign that it was a hijacked plane, since at least eleven planes then in the skies had nonworking radios (nine of the eleven were unconnected to the hijackings). Yes, that's true — and with missile defense there are likely to be not eleven but hundreds of decoys and false targets that will have to be nimbly sorted through. As difficult as it was to identify the third seized plane, it must be acknowledged that the flight had elements that made it far easier to identify than the enemy missiles our nation has spoken blithely about for decades: the direct voice confirmation provided by the passenger phone call to the Justice Department, most notably, will not have any counterpart in a missile attack, nor can we reasonably expect six layers of verification of any one enemy plane or missile.

A third crucial explanation for the failure to protect the Pentagon is that an F-16 cannot shoot down a passenger plane by arrogating the right to decide whether the lives on board can be sacrificed to avert the *possibility* of even more lives being lost on the ground. Yes, that is true — and yet for decades we have spoken about actions that directly imperil the full American citizenry (including presidential first use of nuclear weapons against a population that the president acting alone has decided is "the enemy") without ever obtaining the American citizenry's consent to those actions.

Each of these three explanations for why the attack on the Pentagon could not be easily averted raises key questions about our long-standing descriptions of the country's defense, and yet so far does not appear to have in any way altered those descriptions. September 11 has caused the United States and its allies to adjust their timetables only in those cases where the scenario imagined closely approximates the events that occurred in the terrorist attack itself. In England, the *Observer* reports, "MI5 has warned Ministers that a determined terrorist attempt to fly a jet into the Sellafield nuclear plant in Cumbria could not be prevented because it is only *two minutes'* flying time from transatlantic flight paths."

While two minutes' time makes it impossible to defend Cumbria against terrorists, two minutes is apparently plenty of time for the United States and its NATO allies to carry out missile defense. Here is a post–September 11 description of England's Joint Rapid Reaction Force, described in the *Scotsman:* "A new satellite communications system has been installed to allow planners in Northwood to transmit target co-ordinates to the royal Navy's nuclear submarines equipped to fire Tomahawk cruise missiles. HMS *Trafalgar* and HMS *Triumph* in the Indian Ocean both have this system. *Within minutes* of the Prime Minister giving permission to fire from Downing Street, General Reith could pass on the orders to the submarine nominated to launch the precision attack." What would be the response by Western democracies if a terrorist used chemical, biological, or even nuclear weapons? In an article in *News of the World* describing advice given to Tony Blair by his defense ministers, we learn that "one of his most trusted advisers believes that a highly effective way of preventing such an attack is to threaten states that succor the terrorists with a nuclear wipe-out, within minutes of such an attack, without waiting for intelligence reports, United Nations resolutions or approval from NATO." Does the Bush administration have plans in place for such an attack? Might it be our duty to inquire?

The plane that took the Pentagon by surprise could not be stopped despite a *one-hour-and-twenty-one-minute* warning that multiple planes had been hijacked, despite a *fifty-eight-minute* warning that the hijackers intended to maximize the number of casualties, despite a *fifty-five-minute* warning that Flight 77 might *possibly* be a hijacked flight, and despite a *twenty-minute* warning that Flight 77 was *certainly* a hijacked flight. Yet so confident are we of our ability to get information, of our power to decipher complex lines of responsibility, of the existence of evil and of the transparency of that evil, that we are still today talking about two or three minutes to send cruise missiles and even nuclear genocide to foreign populations. This despite eleven months — 475,000 minutes — in which we have been unable to determine who sent anthrax to the U.S. Senate and various television communication centers.

United Airlines Flight 93 was a small piece of American territory — roughly 600 cubic meters overall. It was lost to the country for approximately forty minutes when terrorists seized control. It was restored to the country when civilian passengers who became citizen soldiers regained control of the ground — in the process losing their own lives.

The passengers on Flight 93 were able to defend this ground for two reasons. First, they were able to identify the threat accurately because it was in their immediate sensory horizon (unlike the F-16s that hoped to intercept the plane that hit the Pentagon, the passengers on Flight 93 did not need to decipher their plane's flight path from the outside, nor make inferences and guesses about lost radio contact). The passengers were also able to get information from unimpeachable sources external to the plane: crucially, they did not rely on information from a single central authority but obtained it from an array of sources, each independent of the others. Second, it was their own lives they were jeopardizing, lives over which they exercised authority and consent. On the twin bases of sentient knowledge and authorization, their collaborative work met the democratic standard of "informed consent."

When the U.S. Constitution was completed it had two provisions for ensuring that decisions about warmaking were distributed rather than concentrated. The first was the provision for a congressional declaration of war — an open debate in both the House and the Senate involving what would today be 535 men and women. The second was a major clause of the Bill of Rights — the Second Amendment right to bear arms — that rejected a standing executive army (an army at the personal disposal of president or king) in favor of a militia, a citizens' army distributed across all ages, geography, and social classes. Democracy, it was argued, was impossible without a distributed militia: self-governance was perceived to be logically impossible without self-defense (exactly what do you "self-govern" if you have ceded the governing of your own body and life to someone else?).

United Flight 93 was like a small legislative assembly or town meeting. The assembly structure is audible in the public record of conversations (a detailed record that was made available by the *Pittsburgh Post-Gazette* and *U.S. News & World Report*). The residents on that ground conferred with one another, as well as with people not on the plane. Records from the onboard telephones show that twenty-four phone calls were made between 9:31 A.M. and 9:54 A.M.; additional calls were made from cell phones. In approximately *twenty-three minutes,* the passengers were able collectively to move through the following sequence of steps:

1. *Identify the location throughout the plane of all hijackers and how many people each is holding.* We know that passengers registered this information in detail because they voiced the information to people beyond the plane: Todd Beamer relayed the information to Lisa Jefferson (a Verizon customer-service operator); Jeremy Glick relayed it to his wife; Sandy Bradshaw to her husband; Mark Bingham to his mother; Marion Britton to a close friend; Elizabeth Wainio to her stepmother; and CeeCee Lyles to her husband.

In terms of democratic self-defense, these conversations are crucial (both at step 1 and at each of the seven steps listed below) to preserving the civil frame that the founders identified as so essential to military defense. The conversations enabled extraordinary events to be tested against the norms of everyday life. They were both intimate and an act of record-making — how else to explain Mark Bingham's self-identification to his mother: "This is Mark Bingham"? He both gave his mother the statement that the plane had been seized by hijackers ("You believe me, don't you?") and in effect notarized the statement by giving a verbal signature.

2. *Hear from sources outside the plane the story of the World Trade Center.* This information was key: it informed the passengers that they would almost certainly not be making a safe landing; it also informed them that many people on the ground would also suffer death or injury from their plane.

3. *Verify from multiple sources outside the plane the World Trade Center story.* Jeremy Glick, for example, told his wife that the account of the World Trade Center attacks was circulating among the passengers. He explicitly asked her to confirm or deny its truth: "Is it true?"

4. *Consult with each other and with friends outside the plane about the appropriate action.* Jeremy Glick told his family the passengers were developing a plan "to rush" the hijackers, and he asked their advice. Todd Beamer told Lisa Jefferson the passengers will "take" the terrorists. (She cautioned: "Are you sure that's what you want to do?") Tom Burnett told his wife "[a group of us] is going to do something." (She urged him to lay low and not make himself visible.) Sandy Bradshaw told her husband she was at that moment

filling coffee pots with boiling water, which she planned to throw at the hijackers; she asked if he had a better plan. (He told her she had the best plan, and to go ahead.)

5. *Take a vote.* Jeremy Glick described the voting process to his wife as it was under way.

6. *Prepare themselves for taking a dire action that may result in death.* CeeCee Lyles, unable to reach her husband, left a recorded message of herself praying, then later reached him and prayed with him; Tom Burnett asked his wife to pray while he and others on the plane acted; Todd Beamer and Lisa Jefferson together recited the Twenty-third Psalm.

7. *Take leave of people they love.* Each of the passengers who was in conversation with a family member stated aloud his or her love for the listener; Todd Beamer asked Lisa Jefferson to convey his love to his family. The family members reciprocated: "I've got my arms around you," Elizabeth Wainio's stepmother told her.

8. *Act.*

Many passengers described the plan to enter the cockpit by force. Not every passenger assumed death was certain. Jeremy Glick left his phone off the hook, telling his wife, "Hold the phone. I'll be back." Todd Beamer also left the phone line open — either because he expected to come back or as an act of public record-keeping. The two open lines permitted members of the Glick household and Lisa Jefferson to overhear the cries and shouts that followed, indicating that action was being taken. CeeCee Lyles, still on the phone with her husband, cried, "They're doing it! They're doing it!" Confirmation is also provided by Sandy Bradshaw's sudden final words to her husband: "Everyone's running to first class. I've got to go. Bye."

The passengers on United Flight 93 could act with speed because they resided on the ground that needed to be defended. Equally important, they could make the choice — formalized in their public act of an open vote — between certain doom and uncertain (but possibly more widespread) doom. They could have hoped that the hijackers would change their planned course; they could have known that death by either avenue was certain, but one avenue would take them to their deaths in several minutes (rushing the hijackers and crashing the plane) and the other avenue would perhaps give them another half hour or hour of life (waiting for

power;
choice

the plane to reach its final target). They could have chosen the second; many people have chosen a delayed death when given the same choice. It is, in any event, the right of the people who themselves are going to die to make the decision, not the right of a pilot in an F-16 or the person giving orders to the pilot in the F-16 — as both civilian and military leaders have repeatedly acknowledged since September 11.

It may be worth noting that the hijackers themselves correctly foresaw that the threat to their mission would come from the passengers ("citizen soldiers") and not from a military source external to the plane. The terrorists left behind multiple copies of a manual, five pages in Arabic. The manual is a detailed set of instructions for the hours before and after boarding the plane — what its translators and interpreters have described (in the *New York Review of Books*) as "an exacting guide for achieving the unity of body and spirit necessary for success." The ritualized set of steps includes: taking a mutual pledge to die; carrying out a ritual act of washing, invocation, and prayer; and dressing according to prescribed recommendations on the tightness or looseness of clothing.

The manual does not tell the terrorists what to do if an F-15 or F-16 approaches the plane they have seized. It instead gives elaborate instructions on what to do if passengers offer resistance. We should not ordinarily let ourselves be schooled by terrorists. But terrorists who seek to carry out a mission successfully have to know what the greatest threat to their mission is — and the handbook indicates that the great obstacles were perceived to be, first, the passengers, and second, the reluctance the hijackers might feel about killing any resisting passengers. They are instructed at length and in elaborate detail to kill any resister and to regard the killing as "a sacred drama," a death carried out to honor their parents. (That the hijackers would unblinkingly crash into a skyscraper, taking thousands of lives, yet balk at the idea of killing people with their own hands, and therefore require detailed counseling to get them through it, is perhaps no more surprising than the fact that we listen every day to casualty rates brought about by the military yet would not keenly kill in hand-to-hand combat.)

I have intended here to open a conversation about our general capacity for self-defense. I have compared the fates of the plane that hit the Pentagon and the plane that crashed in Pennsylvania. The military was unable to thwart the action of Flight 77 despite fifty-five minutes in which clear evidence existed that the plane might be held by terrorists, and despite twenty minutes in which clear evidence existed that the plane was certainly held by terrorists. In the same amount of time — twenty-three minutes — the passengers of Flight 93 were able to gather information, deliberate, vote, and act.

September 11 involved a partial failure of defense. If ever a country has been warned that its defense arrangements are defective, the United States has been warned. Standing quietly by while our leaders build more weapons of mass destruction and bypass more rules and more laws (and more citizens) simply continues the unconstitutional and — as we have recently learned — ineffective direction we have passively tolerated for fifty years. We share a responsibility to deliberate about these questions, as surely as the passengers on Flight 93 shared a responsibility to deliberate about how to act.

The failures of our current defense arrangements put an obligation on all of us to review our procedures for protecting the country. "All of us" means "all of us who reside in the country," not "all of us who work at the Pentagon" or "all of us who convene when there is a meeting of the Joint Chiefs of Staff." What the Joint Chiefs think, or what analysts at the Pentagon think, is of great interest (as are the judgments of men and women who by other avenues of expertise have thoughtful and knowledgeable assessments of security issues); it would be a benefit to the nation if such people would begin to share those views with the public. But such views can in no way preempt or abridge our own obligation to review matters, since the protection of the country falls to everyone whose country it is.

More particularly, September 11 called into question a key argument that has been used to legitimate the gradual shift from an egalitarian, all-citizen military to one that is external to — independent of — civilian control: the argument about speed. The egalitarian model turned out to have the advantage of swiftness, as well as obvious ethical advantages. This outcome has implications for three spheres of defense.

1. *Defense against aerial terrorism.* To date, the egalitarian model of defense is the only one that has worked against aerial terrorism.

It worked on September 11 when passengers brought down the plane in Pennsylvania. It worked again on December 22, 2001, when the passengers and crew on an American Airlines flight from Paris to Miami prevented a terrorist (called "the shoe bomber") from blowing up the plane with plastic explosives and killing the 197 people on board. Two F-15s escorted the plane to Boston and, once the plane landed, FBI officials hurried aboard, but the danger itself was averted not by the fighter jets or the FBI but by men and women inside the plane, who restrained the six-foot-four-inch man using his own hair, leather belts, earphone wires, and sedatives injected by two physicians.

When a passenger plane is seized by a terrorist, defense from the outside (by a fighter jet, for example) appears to be structurally implausible from the perspective of time, and structurally impossible from the perspective of consent. The problem of time — time to ascertain that a plane has been seized, time to identify accurately which plane it is, time to arrive in the airspace near the seized plane — was dramatically evident in the case of the plane that hit the Pentagon, even though much more time and many more layers of verification were available that day than are likely to be available in any future instance. The time difficulty was evident again on January 5, 2002, when a fifteen-year-old boy took off without authorization from St. Petersburg–Clearwater International Airport, crossed the airspace of MacDill Air Force Base (headquarters for the U.S. war in Afghanistan), and crashed into the twenty-eighth floor of a forty-two-story skyscraper in Tampa. Two F-15s "screamed" toward him from the south (as the *Tampa Tribune* reported), but reached him only after he had completed his twenty-five-minute flight. The time problem was visible once more on June 19, 2002, when a pilot and passenger in a Cessna 182 accidentally crossed into forbidden airspace near the Washington Monument, flew there for twelve miles (coming within four miles of the White House), and then crossed out again before armed F-16s from Andrews Air Force Base could reach the plane.

Even if the nearly insurmountable problems of time and perfect knowledge can one day be solved, how can the problem of consent be solved? There is no case in war when a soldier is authorized to kill two hundred fellow soldiers; how can an airman be authorized to kill two hundred fellow citizens? How can anyone other than the passengers themselves take their lives in order to save some number of the rest of us on the ground? During the seven months that F-15s and F-16s, armed with air-to-air missiles, flew round-the-clock over New York and Washington, what instructions did they have in the event that a passenger plane was seized? What instructions do they now have for their more intermittent flights? Are such instructions something only high-ranking officials should be privy to, or might this be something that should be candidly discussed in public?

It seems reasonable to conclude that on September 11 the Pentagon could have been defended in one way and one way only, by the passengers on the American Airlines flight. This would have required three steps: that multiple passengers on the plane be informed about the World Trade Center attacks; that the passengers decide to act, or not to act; and that, in the event they choose to act, they be numerous enough to carry out their plan successfully. As far as we know, none of these steps took place — in part because, as far as we know, there were not enough passengers on board who knew about the World Trade Center. It is possible that one or more of these steps did take place, even though they were not recorded.

In stating that the egalitarian model is our best and only defense against aerial terrorism, I do not mean that passengers in any one case *must* choose to act, or that, having so chosen, they will be successful. I mean only that this is the one form of defense available to us as a country, which passengers are at liberty to exercise or refrain from exercising. Measures taken by the nation that are internal to the plane (locks on cockpit doors, the presence of air marshals, the cessation of round-the-clock fighter jets over New York and Washington) are compatible with this form of defense.

2. *National defense in the immediate present.* The contrast between the plane that hit the Pentagon and the plane that crashed in Pennsylvania invites consideration of the need to return to an egalitarian and democratic military, not only in the specific case of aerial terrorism but in all measures we take for the nation's defense in the present year. Some may argue that we cannot generalize from one day. Can we generalize from zero days? One day is what we have. What makes this non-risky is that rather than requiring us to come up with some new system of government, all it requires is returning to, and honoring, the framework of our own laws.

Since September 11 we have witnessed many actions taken in the name of homeland defense that are independent of, or external to, civilian control. Foreign residents have been seized and placed in circumstances that violate our most basic laws; the war against Afghanistan was under way before we had even been given much explanation of its connection to the terrorists, who were from Saudi Arabia or Lebanon or Egypt or the United Arab Emirates, not from Afghanistan; that war now seems to be over, even though we don't know whether we eliminated the small circle around Osama bin Laden, for whose sake we believed we were there; we are now tripping rapidly ahead to the next war, listening passively to weekly announcements about an approaching war with Iraq that has no visible connection to the events of September 11; the president's formulation of this future war sometimes seems to include (or at least not to exclude) the use of nuclear weapons and the animation of our nuclear first-use policy. The decoupling of all defense from the population itself lurches between large outcomes (presidential declaration of war) and the texture of everyday life. According to the former chairman of the Federal Communications Commission, the federal agency called the National Communications System has "proposed that government officials be able to take over the wireless networks used by cellular telephones in the event of an emergency," thereby preempting the very form of defense that did work (the citizenry) and giving their tools to the form of defense that did not work (the government).

We are defending the country by ceding our own powers of self-defense to a set of managers external to ourselves. But can these powers be ceded without relinquishing the very destination toward which we are traveling together, as surely as if our ship had been seized? The destination for which we purchased tickets was a country where no one was arrested without his or her name being made public, a country that did not carry out wars without the authorization of Congress (and the widespread debate among the population that such a congressional declaration necessitates), a country that does not threaten to use weapons of mass destruction. Why are we sitting quietly in our seats?

In the short run, returning to an egalitarian model of defense means: no war with Iraq unless it has been authorized by Congress and the citizenry; no abridgment of civil liberties; no elimination of the tools that enable citizens to protect themselves and one another (such as cell phones) — and, above all, no contemplated use of nuclear weapons.

3. *National defense in the long run.* Europeans often refer to nuclear weapons as "monarchic weapons" precisely because they are wholly external to any powers of consent or dissent exercised by the population. In the long run, the return to an egalitarian model of national defense will require the return to a military that uses only conventional weapons. This will involve a tremendous cost: it will almost certainly, for example, mean the return of a draft. But a draft means that a president cannot carry out a war without going through the citizenry, and going through the citizenry means that the arguments for going to war get tested tens of thousands of times before the killing starts.

Our nuclear weapons are the largest arsenal of genocidal weapons anywhere on earth. These weapons, even when not in use, deliver a death blow to our democracy. But even if we are willing to give up democracy to keep ourselves safe, on what basis have we come to believe that they keep us safe? Their speed? A Cessna plane (of the kind that proved impossible to intercept in Florida and Washington) travels at approximately 136 feet per second; a Boeing 757 (of the kind that proved impossible to intercept as it approached the Pentagon) travels at 684 feet per second; a missile travels at 6,400 feet per second. On what have we based our confidence about intercepting incoming missiles, since the problem of deciphering information and decoupling it from decoys will (along with speed) be much greater in the case of the missile than in the cases of the planes?

Nuclear weapons are an extreme form of aerial terrorism. It is with good reason that we have worked to prevent the proliferation throughout the world of nuclear weapons (and also biological and chemical weapons of mass destruction). But in the long run, other countries will agree to abstain from acquiring them, or to give them up in cases where they already have them, only when and if the United States agrees to give them up. The process of persuading Iraq, China, North Korea, India, Pakistan, as well as our immediate allies to give them up will commence on the day we agree to restore within our own country a democratic form of self-defense.

Reflection and Responses

1. Why does Elaine Scarry place such an emphasis on "speed" in her opening paragraphs? What "argument based on speed" does she think 9/11 cast into doubt? How is that argument related to the main contention of her essay? How does "speed" help establish the validity of her argument?

2. At the center of Scarry's essay is the contrast between Flight 77 and Flight 93. What does this contrast demonstrate for her? Do you consider the contrast valid? Why didn't the passengers of Flight 77 behave similarly to those of Flight 93? If we praise the passengers of Flight 93 for their actions, need we blame the passenger of Flight 77 for not helping to deter their flight? Explain why or why not?

3. Scarry believes that the American citizenry needs to return to an "egalitarian model of national defense." Explain what you think she means by this? Do you think she wants the United States to have no standing army and instead return to having state militias? According to Scarry, how can citizens defend the country, and why is Flight 93 a model of homeland defense?

PETER SINGER

The Singer Solution
to World Poverty

*Philosophy can sometimes be quite practical: the following essay, which argues
for our moral responsibility to behave altruistically, even contains two toll-free
telephone numbers the reader can use to make a two-hundred-dollar contribu-
tion. Peter Singer, the famous and controversial ethical philosopher, sincerely
hopes that his argument will convince you to contribute. He reinforces his
argument with several intriguing hypothetical situations that put readers in
the driver's seat of a moral dilemma. How will you respond? Would you agree
not to buy another hooded Gap sweatshirt or that new Eminem CD that you
don't really need and instead give the money to UNICEF?*

*Peter Singer was born in Melbourne, Australia, and studied philosophy there
and at the University of Oxford. One of the leading thinkers of the animal-rights
movement, Singer has written influential books on ethical issues, including*
Animal Liberation *(1975),* Practical Ethics *(1979), and* Rethinking
Life and Death *(1995). Among his recent publications are* Writings on an
Ethical Life *and* A Darwinian Left: Politics, Evolution, and Coopera-
tion, *both of which appeared in 2000;* One World: Ethics and Globaliza-
tion *(2002);* The President of Good and Evil *(2004); and* The Way We
Eat *(with Jim Mason, 2006). He is currently DeCamp professor of Bioethics in
the Center for Human Values, Princeton University. "The Singer Solution to
World Poverty" originally appeared in* The New York Times Magazine *and
was selected by Alan Lightman for* The Best American Essays, 2000.

In the Brazilian film *Central Station*, Dora is a retired schoolteacher
who makes ends meet by sitting at the station writing letters for illit-
erate people. Suddenly she has an opportunity to pocket a thousand

dollars. All she has to do is persuade a homeless nine-year-old boy to follow her to an address she has been given. (She is told he will be adopted by wealthy foreigners.) She delivers the boy, gets the money, spends some of it on a television set, and settles down to enjoy her new acquisition. Her neighbor spoils the fun, however, by telling her that the boy was too old to be adopted — he will be killed and his organs sold for transplantation. Perhaps Dora knew this all along, but after her neighbor's plain speaking, she spends a troubled night. In the morning Dora resolves to take the boy back.

Suppose Dora had told her neighbor that it is a tough world, other people have nice new TVs too, and if selling the kid is the only way she can get one, well, he was only a street kid. She would then have become, in the eyes of the audience, a monster. She redeems herself only by being prepared to bear considerable risks to save the boy.

At the end of the movie, in cinemas in the affluent nations of the world, people who would have been quick to condemn Dora if she had not rescued the boy go home to places far more comfortable than her apartment. In fact, the average family in the United States spends almost one third of its income on things that are no more necessary to them than Dora's new TV was to her. Going out to nice restaurants, buying new clothes because the old ones are no longer stylish, vacationing at beach resorts — so much of our income is spent on things not essential to the preservation of our lives and health. Donated to one of a number of charitable agencies, that money could mean the difference between life and death for children in need.

All of which raises a question: in the end, what is the ethical distinction between a Brazilian who sells a homeless child to organ peddlers and an American who already has a TV and upgrades to a better one, knowing that the money could be donated to an organization that would use it to save the lives of kids in need?

Of course, there are several differences between the two situations that could support different moral judgments about them. For one thing, to be able to consign a child to death when he is standing right in front of you takes a chilling kind of heartlessness; it is much easier to ignore an appeal for money to help children you will never meet. Yet for a utilitarian philosopher like myself — that is, one who judges whether acts are right or wrong by their consequences — if the upshot of the American's failure to donate the money is that one more kid dies on the streets of a Brazilian city, then it is in some sense just as bad as selling the kid to the organ peddlers. But one doesn't need to embrace my utilitarian ethic to see that at the very least, there is a troubling incongruity in being so quick to condemn Dora for taking the child to the organ peddlers while at the same time not regarding the American consumer's behavior as raising a serious moral issue.

In his 1996 book, *Living High and Letting Die,* the New York University philosopher Peter Unger presented an ingenious series of imaginary examples designed to probe our intuitions about whether it is wrong to live well without giving substantial amounts of money to help people who are hungry, malnourished, or dying from easily treatable illnesses like diarrhea. Here's my paraphrase of one of these examples:

Bob is close to retirement. He has invested most of his savings in a very rare and valuable old car, a Bugatti, which he has not been able to insure. The Bugatti is his pride and joy. In addition to the pleasure he gets from driving and caring for his car, Bob knows that its rising market value means that he will always be able to sell it and live comfortably after retirement. One day when Bob is out for a drive, he parks the Bugatti near the end of a railway siding and goes for a walk up the track. As he does so, he sees that a runaway train, with no one aboard, is running down the railway track. Looking farther down the track, he sees the small figure of a child very likely to be killed by the runaway train. He can't stop the train and the child is too far away to warn of the danger, but he can throw a switch that will divert the train down the siding where his Bugatti is parked. Then nobody will be killed—but the train will destroy his Bugatti. Thinking of his joy in owning the car and the financial security it represents, Bob decides not to throw the switch. The child is killed. For many years to come, Bob enjoys owning his Bugatti and the financial security it represents.

Bob's conduct, most of us will immediately respond, was gravely wrong. Unger agrees. But then he reminds us that we too have opportunities to save the lives of children. We can give to organizations like UNICEF or Oxfam America. How much would we have to give one of these organizations to have a high probability of saving the life of a child threatened by easily preventable diseases? (I do not believe that children are more worth saving than adults, but since no one can argue that children have brought their poverty on themselves, focusing on them simplifies the issues.) Unger called up some experts and used the information they provided to offer some plausible estimates that include the cost of raising money, administrative expenses, and the cost of delivering aid where it is most needed. By his calculation, $200 in donations would help a sickly two-year-old transform into a healthy six-year-old — offering safe passage through childhood's most dangerous years. To show how practical philosophical argument can be, Unger even tells his readers that they can easily donate funds by using their credit card and calling one of these toll-free numbers: (800) 367-5437 for UNICEF; (800) 693-2687 for Oxfam America.

Now you too have the information you need to save a child's life. How should you judge yourself if you don't do it? Think again about Bob and his Bugatti. Unlike Dora, Bob did not have to look into the eyes of the child he was sacrificing for his own material comfort. The child was a complete stranger to him and too far away to relate to in an intimate, personal way. Unlike Dora too, he did not mislead the child or initiate the chain of events imperiling him. In all these respects, Bob's situation resembles that of people able but unwilling to donate to overseas aid and differs from Dora's situation.

If you still think that it was very wrong of Bob not to throw the switch that would have diverted the train and saved the child's life, then it is hard to see how you could deny that it is also very wrong not to send money to one of the organizations listed above. Unless, that is, there is some morally important difference between the two situations that I have overlooked.

Is it the practical uncertainties about whether aid will really reach the people who need it? Nobody who knows the world of overseas aid can doubt that such uncertainties exist. But Unger's figure of $200 to save a child's life was reached after he had made conservative assumptions about the proportion of the money donated that will actually reach its target.

One genuine difference between Bob and those who can afford to donate to overseas aid organizations but don't is that only Bob can save the child on the tracks, whereas there are hundreds of millions of people who can give $200 to overseas aid organizations. The problem is that most of them aren't doing it. Does this mean that it is all right for you not to do it?

Suppose that there were more owners of priceless vintage cars — Carol, Dave, Emma, Fred, and so on, down to Ziggy — all in exactly the same situation as Bob, with their own siding and their own switch, all sacrificing the child in order to preserve their own cherished car. Would that make it all right for Bob to do the same? To answer this question affirmatively is to endorse follow-the-crowd ethics — the kind of ethics that led many Germans to look away when the Nazi atrocities were being committed. We do not excuse them because others were behaving no better.

We seem to lack a sound basis for drawing a clear moral line between Bob's situation and that of any reader of this article with $200 to spare who does not donate it to an overseas aid agency. These readers seem to be acting at least as badly as Bob was acting when he chose to let the runaway train hurtle toward the unsuspecting child. In the light of this conclusion, I trust that many readers will reach for the phone and donate that $200. Perhaps you should do it before reading further.

Now that you have distinguished yourself morally from people who put their vintage cars ahead of a child's life, how about treating yourself and your partner to dinner at your favorite restaurant? But wait. The money you will spend at the restaurant could also help save the lives of children overseas! True, you weren't planning to blow $200 tonight, but if you were to give up dining out just for one month, you would easily save that amount. And what is one month's dining out compared to a child's life? There's the rub. Since there are a lot of desperately needy children in the world, there will always be another child whose life you could save for another $200. Are you therefore obliged to keep giving until you have nothing left? At what point can you stop?

Hypothetical examples can easily become farcical. Consider Bob. How far past losing the Bugatti should he go? Imagine that Bob had got his foot stuck in the track of the siding, and if he diverted the train, then before it rammed the car it would also amputate his big toe. Should he still throw the switch? What if it would amputate his foot? His entire leg?

As absurd as the Bugatti scenario gets when pushed to extremes, the point it raises is a serious one: only when the sacrifices become very significant indeed would most people be prepared to say that

Bob does nothing wrong when he decides not to throw the switch. Of course, most people could be wrong; we can't decide moral issues by taking opinion polls. But consider for yourself the level of sacrifice that you would demand of Bob, and then think about how much money you would have to give away in order to make a sacrifice that is roughly equal to that. It's almost certainly much, much more than $200. For most middle-class Americans, it could easily be more like $200,000.

Isn't it counterproductive to ask people to do so much? Don't we run the risk that many will shrug their shoulders and say that morality, so conceived, is fine for saints but not for them? I accept that we are unlikely to see, in the near or even medium-term future, a world in which it is normal for wealthy Americans to give the bulk of their wealth to strangers. When it comes to praising or blaming people for what they do, we tend to use a standard that is relative to some conception of normal behavior. Comfortably off Americans who give, say, 10 percent of their income to overseas aid organizations are so far ahead of most of their equally comfortable fellow citizens that I wouldn't go out of my way to chastise them for not doing more. Nevertheless, they should be doing much more, and they are in no position to criticize Bob for failing to make the much greater sacrifice of his Bugatti.

At this point various objections may crop up. Someone may say, "If every citizen living in the affluent nations contributed his or her share, I wouldn't have to make such a drastic sacrifice, because long before such levels were reached the resources would have been there to save the lives of all those children dying from lack of food or medical care. So why should I give more than my fair share?" Another, related objection is that the government ought to increase its overseas aid allocations, since that would spread the burden more equitably across all taxpayers.

Yet the question of how much we ought to give is a matter to be decided in the real world—and that, sadly, is a world in which we know that most people do not, and in the immediate future will not, give substantial amounts to overseas aid agencies. We know too that at least in the next year, the United States government is not going to meet even the very modest United Nations — recommended target of 0.7 percent of gross national product; at the moment it lags far below that, at 0.09 percent, not even half of Japan's 0.22 percent or a tenth of Denmark's 0.97 percent. Thus, we know that the money we can give beyond that theoretical "fair share" is still going to save lives that would otherwise be lost. While the idea that no one need do more than his or her fair share is a powerful one, should it prevail if we know that others are not doing their fair share and that children will die preventable deaths unless we do more than our fair share? That would be taking fairness too far.

Thus, this ground for limiting how much we ought to give also fails. In the world as it is now, I can see no escape from the conclusion that each one of us with wealth surplus to his or her essential needs should be giving most of it to help people suffering from poverty so dire as to be life-threatening. That's right: I'm saying that you shouldn't buy that new car, take that cruise, redecorate the house, or get that pricy new suit. After all, a thousand-dollar suit could save five children's lives.

So how does my philosophy break down in dollars and cents? An American household with an income of $50,000 spends around $30,000 annually on necessities, according to the Conference Board, a nonprofit economic research organization. Therefore, for a household bringing in $50,000 a year, donations to help the world's poor should be as close as possible to $20,000. The $30,000 required for necessities holds for higher incomes as well. So a household making $100,000 could cut a yearly check for $70,000. Again, the formula is simple: whatever money you're spending on luxuries, not necessities, should be given away.

Now, evolutionary psychologists tell us that human nature just isn't sufficiently altruistic to make it plausible that many people will sacrifice so much for strangers. On the facts of human nature, they might be right, but they would be wrong to draw a moral conclusion from those facts. If it is the case that we ought to do things that, predictably, most of us won't do, then let's face that fact head-on. Then, if we value the life of a child more than going to fancy restaurants, the next time we dine out we will know that we could have done something better with our money. If that makes living a morally decent life extremely arduous, well, then that is the way things are. If we don't do it, then we should at least know that we are failing to live a morally decent life — not because it is good to wallow in guilt but because knowing where we should be going is the first step toward heading in that direction.

When Bob first grasped the dilemma that faced him as he stood by that railway switch, he must have thought how extraordinarily unlucky he was to be placed in a situation in which he must choose between the life of an innocent child and the sacrifice of most of his savings. But he was not unlucky at all. We are all in that situation.

Reflections and Responses

1. Do you find Singer's hypothetical examples convincing? If you place yourself in the situations he describes, do you reach the same conclusions he does? Can you refute his hypothetical situations?

2. At one point, Singer identifies himself as a "utilitarian philosopher," that is, "one who judges whether acts are right or wrong by their consequences." Do you find any limitations with this manner of evaluating right and wrong? Can you rewrite Singer's hypothetical examples in such a way that the "right" decision would perhaps lead to a bad consequence? Suppose, for example, that Bob pulled the switch and saved the boy's life, but another child hiding in the runaway train was killed in the collision with Bob's fancy automobile. Would that child's death be a direct consequence of Bob's apparently generous act? Would criminal charges be filed against Bob? Consider other variations.

3. Note that throughout the essay Singer argues for just one cause — child poverty. Why do you think he chose this and not a different sort of cause? What if he had selected AIDS research or Amnesty International as likely ways to help human suffering? Would these be just as effective? Why or why not? And if you did give your money to relieve child poverty, would you be making a conscious decision NOT to assist the causes of AIDS or cancer research or the Red Cross or any other legitimate charitable organization?

PAULA SPECK

Six Seconds

Do we live "in the final triumph of the market economy," in which everything, even the "fear of death," has a price tag? That's a question that a young attorney is forced to ask herself after she researches what may seem a macabre legal question: How much should a jury award individuals for their "last-minute mental fear and anguish"? In "Six Seconds," Paula Speck recalls how she handled this assignment in 1988, after Pan Am Airlines appealed a jury award for a 1982 New Orleans crash that killed 154 passengers. How much, she finds herself obliged to calculate, are six seconds of suffering truly worth?

Paula Speck has published essays in The Gettysburg Review, The Literary Review, *and* The Massachusetts Review, *among other literary journals. Her essays have been cited as notable works in both* The Best American Essays *and* The Best American Travel Writing *series. A lawyer, Speck is a frequent instructor at the Writer's Center in Bethesda, Maryland.*

A few days after September 11, 2001, newspapers carried an interview with the wife of a passenger who died on the flight that lifted out of Boston for Los Angeles and, fifty-one minutes later, slammed into the World Trade Center. Her husband's business, she said, had led him to take this flight regularly, once or twice a month. His routine was to rise early, drive to the airport, check in, take his seat, and promptly fall asleep until nearing his destination. That day, his destination was a fireball ninety stories above lower Manhattan. The grieving wife told reporters: "I hope that's what he did on September 11. I hope he just went to sleep and never realized what happened."

What it life worth? See fn [handwritten note]

Reading this story, I found myself remembering the day nearly two decades earlier when I had to put a price on the last six seconds of the lives of two airplane passengers.

On July 9, 1982, a Pan Am jet carrying 154 passengers and crew clipped a tree just after takeoff from New Orleans International Airport and smashed into the runway. Everyone on board died. Four to six seconds passed between the moment the plane struck the tree and the instant the pilot's desperate efforts to bring the nose up ended on the hard tarmac. In 1986, a jury decided that the children of two of the passengers should receive $20,000 for the mental anguish each of their parents felt during those last four to six seconds. In 1988, the airline appealed this award.

The appeal landed in my inbox. The judge I worked for wanted me to go over the figure the jury had arrived at. He needed a reason to dissent or concur in a draft opinion that was circulating.

In a professional sense, this was a routine assignment. To start with, I had the jury's verdict. And the strong reluctance — going back to medieval English law — to revisit the hard questions the jury had decided. No judge was supposed to fiddle with the jury's numbers unless, as one opinion I read put it, they fell outside "the universe of possible awards" that a "reasonable jury" could assign. So my task settled into a straightforward research job: all I had to do was find every case in the last twenty years or so in which a jury had priced last-minute mental fear and anguish, compare that amount with the one assigned here, and report to my judge whether this jury's number fell within that range.

I set to work. Conveniently, a legal indexing system had a computer-searchable category for what I was looking for: "Death," subcategory number 77, "Preimpact Pain and Suffering."

A lawyer doesn't read cases the way he or she reads a novel or a newspaper article. If reading a novel is a stroll along a winding path through a meadow, reading a case is the circling of a hawk hundreds of feet above that meadow, interrupted by a downward swoop to snatch at the barely perceptible scurry of a field mouse. Focused on one question — what is the range of damages that may be awarded for an air crash victim's preimpact pain and suffering? — I skimmed over discussions of weather conditions, control-tower negligence, pilot drug use, mechanical failures, future earnings. Not my concern whether the judge should have allowed the jury to read a wind-shear expert's report, whether a nephew could win damages for the loss of an aunt under Illinois law, how much money a medical student would have made over the course of a lopped-off career — or how much to subtract for the cost of finishing medical school and buying stethoscopes and eye charts. But despite my narrow lens, despite the deliberate impersonality of the opinion writers' language, details from one opinion, and then another, broke through:

The woman's body found with every inch of its skin charred by the fire that swept the cabin, but with internal organs and bones intact; this showed she did not die when the plane hit the runway, but survived for several seconds afterward. The two minutes a pilot spent desperately trying to right a bucking plane after a wing clipped a baggage truck, while the passengers rattled like dice in a cup. The businessman sucked out of a hole punched in the plane's skin by a bomb, dropping for three conscious seconds to the ground. The elderly couple who sat in the back of the vintage plane they had rented for a wedding-anniversary flight over the Caribbean, listening while their pilot (who, it seemed, had misread the gas gauge) desperately radioed for an airport within gliding distance. The helpless ground witnesses who heard screams coming from inside a burning fuselage.

And, because judges will hunt out analogies when they can't find enough cases directly "on point": the oil worker who put his foot on empty air near the top of an offshore oil platform and took a long two seconds to descend to the platform's deck. The woman struck by a train who bled to death for seventeen minutes on the tracks while a panicked stationmaster tried to get an ambulance. The crewmen seen through fog clinging for long minutes to the upturned hulk of their wrecked ship.

I read only the passage in each case that described the victims' last moments. When I learned how the judge and jury dealt with damages in that case, I moved on to the next. One anecdote of terror and delayed death trod on the heels of another. Suddenly it was too much. I had to break off research and find an errand that would take me out of the office.

Returning to my notes, I realized that in order to make comparisons among cases, I'd have to convert the damages I found into per-second figures. Luckily, the figures slotted into a rough chart:

$138.89 per second (twelve minutes for $100,000)
$208 per second (two minutes for $25,000)
$333.34 per second (thirty seconds for $10,000)
$833 per second (six seconds for $5,000)
$1,250 per second (six seconds for $7,500)
$2,500 per second (six seconds for $15,000)
$5,000 per second (two seconds for $10,000)
$7,955 per second (eleven seconds for $87,500)
$10,625 per second (eight seconds for $85,000)
$15,000 per second ("death was almost instantaneous")

All right, I thought, let's assume that the two passengers in the case I was working on had each lived six seconds, the longest time possible. If so, the jury had priced their fear at $3,334 per second. Since this was within the range that other juries had awarded — and there was no other objection to that part of the verdict — my job was done. I summarized the research and explained my conclusion to the judge. He sent in his concurrence. I moved on to another assignment.

Everyone working on this case — the lawyers, the judges, myself — assumed that the unlucky couple who died on the runway in New Orleans had been wronged when they were forced to stare at their own deaths for six seconds, more wronged than if they had died without warning. But it could have been otherwise.

In the Middle Ages, books on the *ars moriendi* — the art of dying — instructed the faithful on how to achieve a "good death" and exhorted them to imagine their own deaths in detail as a spur to resist sin and practice for the always-too-soon. Holbein, Dürer, and dozens of lesser-known artists painted "Dances of Death," showing Death prancing bawdily through palaces and marketplaces. Hamlet was almost as angry with his uncle for killing his father during an afternoon nap — "grossly, full of bread; with all his crimes broad blown, as flush as May" — as for the murder itself. That's why Hamlet let pass the opportunity to kill Claudius at prayer; such a death would be too good for him.

The Victorians carefully photographed dead children nested like wax dolls in satin-lined coffins and displayed the pictures in their parlors. Thousands rushed newsstands to buy the last installment of *The Old Curiosity Shop* and join worldwide weeping over the drawn-out final minutes of Dickens's Little Nell. A man's last seconds gave him a chance to apologize to God, to reconcile with loved ones, to balance a life's books.

Even the law grants special status to last moments. Evidently codes recognize an exception to the hearsay rule for a "dying declaration." It's a strangely medieval provision. If Hamlet tells Horatio, "It was Claudius who poisoned the King," and then gallops off to Heidelberg, Horatio cannot testify about Hamlet's statement in court. That would be hearsay. But Horatio can repeat Hamlet's same speech in court if it's a dying declaration, panted out as Hamlet expires in Horatio's arms from the thrust of that poisoned sword tip in the fifth act. The official commentary to the rule in the federal code notes coyly that "the original religious justification for the exception" — no man wants to meet his Creator with a lie on his lips — "may have lost its conviction for some persons over the years." But, the commentary continues, "it can scarcely be doubted that powerful psychological pressures are present."

What exactly are those "powerful psychological pressures"? Do we still believe that people who are about to die are less likely to lie than the rest of us? Do we want to hope that they stand on the threshold of a realm of eternal truth above the sphere of lies and deceit where the rest of us live?

And why, then, is it an injury — compensated in countable cash — for an airline passenger to be forced to watch (and, yes, feel) the last seconds of his life hurtle into the past? Whereas a medieval man might have been grateful for the chance to pray, and a Victorian might have choked out a last word for his family, we sue.

An easy answer, and not necessarily a false one, is that we live in the final triumph of the market economy and that everything, including fear of death, has a price in such an economy. We are materialist to our core, buying and selling our last breaths and heartbeats.

Or perhaps we're just humble. Medieval man thought he could ingratiate himself with the power that rules the universe if he said the right words and thought the right thoughts for a few minutes at the end of his life. Nineteenth-century man thought he could fix lifelong hatreds and misunderstandings with heartfelt words and hands clasped across death-sweated sheets.

We have lower hopes, more reasonable goals. A life's mistakes can't be set right in a few moments, we tell ourselves. But money is undoubtedly useful to a family that has lost a father, a daughter, a brother, a wife.With money, they can pay for therapists, college tuition, fresh flowers in the dining room. Salvation or reconciliation are not in our power to give. We can, however, give $3,334 a second. And so we do.

I have given up trying to decide whether the society I live and earn my living in is wise or shallow in its approach to death. I have only tentative conclusions, subject to revision and applicable only to myself. One is that I'd like to look my death in the face when and however it comes. If I get my wish, I hope my family won't ask to be paid for it. Although I'd prefer to postpone the meeting.

Reflections and Responses

1. Paula Speck calls the assignment of putting a "price on the last six seconds of the lives of two airline passengers" a "routine assignment." Why would it be "routine"? How does she manage to make the experience less routine? Point to elements of her essay that make her topic seem not routine but instead unusual.

2. Why do Speck's thoughts shift from the twentieth century to the Middle Ages and then to the Victorian era? What central point does she want to establish? How, in a sentence, would you summarize the main point of her essay?

3. Speck at the essay's end says that she has only arrived at "tentative conclusions." Why do you think this is the case? Do you think that she might have come to a more definite conclusion? What conclusion — given her reflections on the case — might that be? Explain what conclusions you personally draw from her essay?

Is it an injury to be compensated w/ cash? Is cash an adequate or even appropriate compensation? Explain why it is or is not. (what's life worth?)

ELLEN ULLMAN

Dining with Robots

Even essays that posit ideas — ideas such as the future of artificial intelligence — can feature a personal voice and vision and can demonstrate a remarkable pattern of imagery. In other worlds, the essay can be a form of literature, no matter how scientific or philosophic its subject. In "Dining with Robots," Ellen Ullman moves seamlessly from ordinary activities in her own life — grocery shopping and preparing for a large dinner party — to speculations about computer programming and the likelihood of robots that would be indistinguishable from human beings. It is a model essay — at once covering science, society, and the self.

Ellen Ullman is the author of Close to the Machine *(1997), a memoir about her twenty years of experience as a software engineer; and* The Bug *(2003), a novel. Her essays about the emotional and social effects of computing have appeared in* Harper's *Magazine,* Salon, Wired, *and the* New York Times. *She was a contributing editor of* The American Scholar, *where "Dining with Robots" first appeared. It was chosen by Susan Orlean for* The Best American Essays 2005.

On the first day of the first programming course I ever took, the instructor compared computer programming to creating a recipe. I remember he used the example of baking a cake. First you list the ingredients you'll need — flour, eggs, sugar, butter, yeast — and these, he said, are like the machine resources the program will need in order to run. Then you describe, in sequence, in clear declarative language, the steps you have to perform to turn those ingredients into a cake. Step one: preheat the oven. Two: sift together dry ingredients. Three: beat the eggs. Along the way were decisions he likened to the if/then/else branches of a program: if using a countertop electric mixer, then beat three minutes; else if using a hand electric mixer, then beat four; else beat five. And there was a reference he described as a sort of subroutine: go to page 117 for details about varieties of yeast (with "return here" implied). He even drew a flow chart that took the recipe all the way through to the end: let cool, slice, serve.

I remember nothing, however, about the particulars of the cake itself. Was it angel food? Chocolate? Layered? Frosted? At the time, 1979 or 1980, I had been working as a programmer for more than a year, self-taught, and had yet to cook anything more complicated than poached eggs. So I knew a great deal more about coding than about cakes. It didn't occur to me to question the usefulness of comparing something humans absolutely must do to something machines never do: that is, eat.

In fact, I didn't think seriously about the analogy for another twenty-five years, not until a blustery fall day in San Francisco, when I was confronted with a certain filet of beef. By then I had learned to cook. (It was that or a life of programmer food: pizza, takeout, whatever's stocked in the vending machines.) And the person responsible for the beef encounter was a man named Joe, of Potter Family Farms, who was selling "home-raised and butchered" meat out of a stall in the newly renovated Ferry Building food hall.

The hall, with its soaring, arched windows, is a veritable church of food. The sellers are small, local producers; everything is organic, natural, free-range; the "baby lettuces" are so young one should perhaps call them "fetal" — it's that sort of place. Before shopping, it helps to have a glass of wine, as I had, to prepare yourself for the gasping shock of the prices. Sitting at a counter overlooking the bay, watching ships and ferries ply the choppy waters, I'd sipped down a nice Pinot Grigio, which had left me with lowered sales resistance by the time I wandered over to the Potter Farms meat stall. There Joe greeted me and held out for inspection a large filet — "a beauty," he said. He was not at all moved by my remonstrations that I eat meat but rarely cook it. He stood there as a man who had — personally — fed, slaughtered, and butchered this cow, and all for me, it seemed. I took home the beef.

I don't know what to do with red meat. There is something appalling about meat's sheer corporeality — meat meals are called *fleishidich* in Yiddish, a word that doesn't let you forget that what you are eating is *flesh*. So for help I turned to *The Art of French Cooking*, volume 1, the cookbook Julia Child* wrote with Louisette Bertholle and Simone Beck. I had bought this book when I first decided I would learn to cook. But I hadn't been ready for it then. I was scared off by the drawings of steer sides lanced for sirloins, porterhouses, and T-bones. And then there was all that talk of blanching, deglazing, and making a roux. But I had stayed with it, spurred on by my childhood memories of coming across Julia on her TV cooking show, when I'd be zooming around the dial early on weekend mornings and be stopped short at the sight of this big woman taking whacks at red lumps of meat. It was the physicality of her cooking that caught me, something animal and finger-painting- gleeful in her engagement with food.

And now, as rain hatched the windows, I came upon a recipe that Julia and her coauthors introduced as follows:

SAUTÉ DE BOEUF À LA PARISIENNE
[Beef Sauté with Cream and Mushroom Sauce]

This sauté of beef is good to know about if you have to entertain important guests in a hurry. It consists of small pieces of filet sautéed quickly to a nice brown outside and a rosy center, and served in a sauce. In the variations at the end of the recipe, all the sauce ingredients may be prepared in advance. If the whole dish is cooked ahead of time, be very careful indeed in its reheating that the beef does not overcook. The cream and mushroom sauce here is a French version of beef Stroganoff, but less tricky as it uses fresh rather than sour cream, so you will not run into the problem of curdled sauce.

Serve the beef in a casserole, or on a platter surrounded with steamed rice, *risotto*, or potato balls sautéed in butter. Buttered green peas or beans could accompany it, and a good red Bordeaux wine.

And it was right then, just after reading the words "a good red Bordeaux wine," that the programming class came back to me: the instructor at the board with his flow chart, his orderly procedural

*Julia Child (1912–2004) is perhaps America's best-known cook. Her enormously successful cookbook, *Mastering the Art of French Cooking*, was published in 1961, and her popular television show, *The French Chef*, first aired in 1963.— Ed.

steps, the if/then decision branches, the subroutines, all leading to the final "let cool, slice, serve." And I knew in that moment that my long-ago instructor, like my young self, had been laughably clueless about the whole subject of cooking food.

If you have to entertain important guests.

A nice brown outside.

Rosy center.

Stroganoff.

Curdled.

Risotto.

Potato balls in butter.

A good red Bordeaux.

I tried to imagine the program one might write for this recipe. And immediately each of these phrases exploded in my mind. How to tell a computer what "important guests" are? And how would you explain what it means to "have to" serve them dinner (never mind the yawning depths of "entertain")? A "nice brown," a "rosy center": you'd have to have a mouth and eyes to know what these mean, no matter how well you might translate them into temperatures. And what to do about "Stroganoff," which is not just a sauce but a noble family, a name that opens a chain of association that catapults the human mind across seven centuries of Russian history? I forced myself to abandon that line of thought and stay in the smaller realm of sauces made with cream, but this inadvertently opened up the entire subject of the chemistry of lactic proteins, and why milk curdles. Then I wondered how to explain "risotto": the special short-grained rice, the select regions on earth where it grows, opening up endlessly into questions of agriculture, its arrival among humans, the way it changed the earth. Next came the story of potatoes, that Inca food, the brutalities through which it arrives on a particular plate before a particular woman in Europe, before our eponymous Parisienne: how it is converted into a little round ball, and then, of course, buttered. (Then, Lord help me, this brought up the whole subject of the French and butter, and how can they possibly get away with eating so much of it?)

But all of this was nothing compared to the cataclysm created by "a good red Bordeaux."

The program of this recipe expanded infinitely. Subroutine opened from subroutine, association led to exploding association.

It seemed absurd even to think of describing all this to a machine. The filet, a beauty, was waiting for me.

Right around the time my programming teacher was comparing coding to cake-making, computer scientists were finding themselves stymied in their quest to create intelligent machines. Almost from the moment computers came into existence, researchers believed that the machines could be made to think. And for the next thirty or so years, their work proceeded with great hope and enthusiasm. In 1967, the influential MIT computer scientist Marvin Minsky declared, "Within a generation the problem of creating 'artificial intelligence' will be substantially solved." But by 1982, he was less sanguine about the prospects, saying, "The AI problem is one of the hardest science has ever undertaken."

Computer scientists had been trying to teach the computer what human beings know about themselves and the world. They wanted to create inside the machine a sort of mirror of our existence, but in a form a computer could manipulate: abstract, symbolic, organized according to one theory or another of how human knowledge is structured in the brain. Variously called "micro worlds," "problem spaces," "knowledge representations," "classes," and "frames," these abstract universes contained systematized arrangements of facts, along with rules for operating upon those — theoretically all that a machine would need to become intelligent. Although it wasn't characterized as such at the time, this quest for a symbolic representation of reality was oddly Platonic in motive, a computer scientist's idea of the pure, unchanging forms that lie behind the jumble of the physical world.

But researchers eventually found themselves in a position like mine when trying to imagine the computer program for my *boeuf à la Parisienne:* the network of associations between one thing and the next simply exploded. The world, the actual world we inhabit, showed itself to be too marvelously varied, too ragged, too linked and interconnected, to be sorted into any set of frames or classes or problem spaces. What we hold in our minds is not abstract, it turned out, not an ideal reflection of existence, but something inseparable from our embodied experience of moving about in a complicated world.

Hubert L. Dreyfus, a philosopher and early critic of artificial intelligence research, explained the problem with the example of a simple object like a chair. He pointed out the futility of trying to create a symbolic representation of a chair to a computer, which had neither a body to sit in it nor a social context in which to use it. "Chairs would not be equipment for sitting if our knees bent backwards like those of flamingoes, or if we had no tables, as in traditional Japan or the Australian bush," he wrote in his 1979 book *What Computers Can't Do.* Letting flow the myriad associations that radiate from the word "chair," Dreyfus went on:

> Anyone in our culture understands such things as how to sit on kitchen chairs, swivel chairs, folding chairs; and in arm chairs, rocking chairs, deck chairs, barber's chairs, sedan chairs, dentist's chairs, basket chairs, reclining chairs . . . since there seems to be an indefinitely large variety of chairs and of successful (graceful, comfortable, secure, poised, etc.) ways to sit in them. Moreover, understanding chairs also includes social skills such as being able to sit appropriately (sedately, demurely, naturally, casually, sloppily, provocatively, etc.) at dinners, interviews, desk jobs, lectures, auditions, concerts . . .

At dinners where one has to entertain important guests . . . at the last minute . . . serving them beef in a French version of Stroganoff . . . with buttered potatoes . . . and a good red Bordeaux.

*   *   *

Several weeks after making Julia's *boeuf,* I was assembling twelve chairs (dining chairs, folding chairs, desk chair) around the dining table, and I was thinking not of Dreyfus but of my mother. In her younger days, my mother had given lavish dinner parties, and it was she who had insisted, indeed commanded, that I have all the necessary equipment for the sort of sit-down dinner I was giving that night. I surveyed the fancy wedding-gift stainless she had persuaded me to register for ("or else you'll get a lot of junk," she said), the Riedel wine glasses, also gifts, and finally the set of china she had given me after my father's death, when she sold their small summer house — "the country dishes" is how I think of them, each one hand-painted in a simple design, blue cornflowers on white.

It wasn't until I started setting the table, beginning with the forks, that I thought of Dreyfus. Salad forks, fish forks, crab forks, entrée forks, dessert forks — at that moment it occurred to me that the paradigm for an intelligent machine had changed, but what remained was the knotty problem of teaching a computer what it needed to know to achieve sentience. In the years since Dreyfus wrote his book, computer scientists had given up on the idea of intelligence as a purely abstract proposition — a knowledge base and a set of rules to operate upon it — and were now building what are called social robots, machines with faces and facial expressions, who are designed to learn about the world the way human beings do: by interacting with other human beings. Instead of being born with a universe already inscribed inside them, these social machines will start life with only basic knowledge and skills. Armed with cute faces and adorable expressions, like babies, they must inspire humans to teach them about the world. And in the spirit of Dreyfus, I asked myself: If such a robot were coming to dinner, how could I, as a good human hostess and teacher, explain everything I would be placing before it tonight?

Besides the multiple forks, there will be an armory of knives: salad knife, fish knife, bread knife, dessert knife. We'll have soup spoons and little caviar spoons made of bone, teaspoons, tiny demitasse spoons, and finally the shovel-shaped ice cream spoons you can get only in Germany — why is it that only Germans recognize the need for this special ice cream implement? My robot guest could learn in an instant the name and shape and purpose of every piece of silverware, I thought; it would instantly understand the need for bone with caviar because metal reacts chemically with roe. But its mouth isn't functional; the mouth part is there only to make us humans feel more at ease; my robot guest doesn't eat. So how will it understand the complicated interplay of implement, food, and mouth — how each tool is designed to hold, present, complement the intended fish or vegetable, liquid or grain? And the way each forkful or spoonful finds its perfectly dimensioned way into the moist readiness of the mouth, where the experience evanesces (one hopes) into the delight of taste?

And then there will be the wineglasses: the flutes for champagne, the shorter ones for white wine, the pregnant Burgundy glasses, the large ones for Cabernet blends. How could I tell a machine about the reasons for these different glasses, the way they cup the wine, shape the smell, and deliver it to the human nose? And how to explain wine at all? You could spend the rest of your life tasting wine and still not exhaust its variations, each bottle a little ecosystem of grapes and soils and weather, yeast and bacteria, barrels of wood from trees with their own soil and weather, the variables cross-multiplying until each glassful approaches a singularity, a moment in time on earth. Can a creature that does not drink or taste understand this pleasure? A good red Bordeaux!

I went to the hutch to get out the china. I had to move aside some of the pieces I never use: the pedestaled cigarette holders, the little ashtrays, the relish tray for the carrots, celery, and olives it was once de rigueur to put on the table. Then I came to the coffeepot, whose original purpose was not to brew coffee — that would have been done in a percolator — but to serve it. I remembered my mother presiding over the many dinners she had given, the moment when the table was scraped clean of crumbs and set for dessert, the coffee cups and saucers stacked beside her as she poured out each cup and passed it down the line. Women used to serve coffee at table, I thought. But my own guests would walk over and retrieve theirs from the automatic drip pot. My mother is now ninety-one; between her time as a hostess and mine, an enormous change had occurred in the lives of women. And, just then, it seemed to me that all that upheaval was contained in the silly fact of how one served coffee to dinner guests. I knew I would never want to go back to mother's time, but all the same I suddenly missed the world of her dinner parties, the guests waving their cigarettes as they chatted, my mother so dressed up, queenly by the coffeepot, her service a kind of benign rule over the table. I put the pot in the corner of the hutch and thought: It's no good trying to explain all this to my robot guest. The chain of associations from just this one piece of china has led me to regret and nostalgia, feelings I can't explain even to myself.

The real problem with having a robot to dinner is pleasure. What would please my digital guest? Human beings need food to survive, but what drives us to choose one food over another is what I think of as the deliciousness factor. Evolution, that good mother, has seen fit to guide us to the apple instead of the poison berry by our attraction to the happy sweetness of the apple, its fresh crispness, and, in just the right balance, enough tartness to make it complicated in the mouth. There are good and rational reasons why natural selection has made us into creatures with fine taste discernment — we can learn what's good for us and what's not. But this very sensible survival imperative, like the need to have sex to reproduce, works itself out through the not very sensible, wilder part of our nature: desire for pleasure.

Can a robot desire? Can it have pleasure? When trying to decide if we should confer sentience upon another creature, we usually cite the question first posed by the philosopher Jeremy Bentham: Can it suffer? We are willing to ascribe a kind of consciousness to a being whose suffering we can intuit. But now I wanted to look at the opposite end of what drives us, not at pain but at rapture: Can it feel pleasure? Will we be able to look into the face of a robot and understand that some deep, inherent need has driven it to seek a particular delight?

According to Cynthia Breazeal, who teaches at MIT and is perhaps the best known of the new social-robot researchers, future digital creatures will have drives that are analogous to human desires but that will have nothing to do with the biological imperatives of food and sex. Robots will want the sort of things that machines need: to stay in good running order, to maintain physical homeostasis, to get the attention of human beings, upon whom they must rely, at least until they learn to take care of themselves. They will be intelligent and happy the way dolphins are: in their own form, in their own way.

Breazeal is very smart and articulate, and her defense of the eventual beingness of robotic creatures is a deep challenge to the human idea of sentience. She insists that robots will eventually become so lifelike that we will one day have to face the question of their inherent rights and dignity. "We have personhood because it's granted to us by society," she told me. "It's a status granted to one another. It's not innately tied to being a carbon-based life form."

So challenged, I spent a long time thinking about the interior life of a robot. I tried to imagine it: the delicious swallowing of electric current, the connoisseurship of voltages, exquisite sensibilities sensing tiny spikes on the line, the pleasure of a clean, steady flow. Perhaps the current might taste of wires and transistors, capacitors and rheostats, some components better than others, the way soil and water make up the *terroir* of wine, the difference between a good Bordeaux and a middling one. I think robots will delight in discerning patterns, finding mathematical regularities, seeing a world that is not mysterious but beautifully self-organized. What pleasure they will take in being fast and efficient — to run without cease! — humming along by their picosecond clocks, their algorithms compact, elegant, error-free. They will want the interfaces between one part of themselves and another to be defined, standardized, and modular, so that an old part can be unplugged, upgraded, and plugged back in their bodies forever renewed. Fast, efficient, untiring, correct, standardized, organized: the virtues we humans strive for but forever fail to achieve, the reasons we invented our helpmate, the machine.

The dinner party, which of course proceeded without a single robot guest, turned out to be a fine, raucous affair, everyone talking and laughing, eating and drinking to just the right degree of excess. And when each guest rose to pour his or her own cup of coffee, I knew it was one of those nights that had to be topped off with a good brandy. By the time the last friend had left, it was nearly two A.M., the tablecloth was covered with stains, dirty dishes were everywhere, the empty crab shells were beginning to stink, and the kitchen was a mess. Perfect.

Two days later I was wheeling a cart through the aisles at Safeway — food shopping can't always be about fetal lettuces — and I was thinking how neat and regular the food looked. All the packaged, prepared dinners lined up in boxes on the shelves. The meat in plastic-wrapped trays, in standard cuts, arranged in orderly rows. Even the vegetables looked cloned, identical bunches of spinach and broccoli, perfectly green, without an apparent speck of dirt. Despite the influence of Julia Child and California-cuisine guru Alice Waters, despite the movement toward organic, local produce, here it all still was: manufactured, efficient, standardized food.

But of course it was still here, I thought. Not everyone can afford the precious offerings of the food hall. And even if you could, who really has the time to stroll through the market and cook a meal based on what looks fresh that day? I have friends who would love to spend rainy afternoons turning a nice filet into *boeuf à la Parisienne*. But even they find their schedules too pressed these days; it's easier just to pick something up, grab a sauce out of a jar. Working long hours, our work life invading home life through e-mail and mobile phones, we all need our food-gathering trips to be brief and organized, our time in the kitchen efficiently spent, our meals downed in a hurry.

As I picked out six limes, not a bruise or blemish on them, it occurred to me that I was not really worried about robots becoming sentient, human, indistinguishable from us. That long-standing fear — robots who fool us into taking them for humans — suddenly seemed a comic-book peril, born of another age, as obsolete as a twenty-five-year-old computer.

What scared me now were the perfect limes, the five varieties of apples that seemed to have disappeared from the shelves, the dinner I'd make and eat that night in thirty minutes, the increasing rarity of those feasts that turn the dining room into a wreck of sated desire. The lines at the checkout stands were long; neat packages rode along on the conveyor belts; the air was filled with the beep of scanners as the food, labeled and bar-coded, identified itself to the machines. Life is pressuring us to live by the robots' pleasures, I thought. Our appetites have given way to theirs. Robots aren't becoming us, I feared; we are becoming them.

In memory of Julia Child

Reflections and Responses

1. Note that Ellen Ullman opens her essay with an analogy that was used by an instructor in her first computer programming course. What is the intended meaning of the analogy as the instructor sees it? What meaning does it have for Ullman? How does this opening analogy prepare us for the rest of the essay?

2. Ullman's essay contains a number of deliberately repeated details. For example, observe the several times she refers to a "good red Bordeaux wine." Why do you think she does this? What effect does it have? What does the Bordeaux wine signify as the essay proceeds?

3. Ullman's essay concludes with a surprising realization and twist. How does she prepare the reader for this? How would you describe the essay's ultimate message? How is that message embedded in the essay's title?

JOY WILLIAMS

The Killing Game

In today's world, survival is a theme that includes all of nature, not merely human life. When the following angry attack on hunting originally appeared in a popular men's magazine, the editors were deluged with equally angry letters from hundreds of subscribers. As you read the essay, you'll see at once why it enraged hunters and hunting advocates. Williams did not choose to write a calm, composed, and gently persuasive critique of hunting but went all out in a savage and often sarcastic attack on American hunters, a group she considers "overequipped . . . insatiable, malevolent, and vain."

Williams is the author of several novels and two collections of stories, Taking Care *(1982) and* Escapes *(1989), as well as a 1987 history and guide to the Florida Keys. Her nonfiction includes articles on sharks, James Dean, the environment, and the electric chair. In 1993, she received the Strauss Living Award from the American Academy of Arts and Letters, and in 1999, the prestigious Rea Award for the Short Story. Her recent books include a novel,* The Quick and the Dead *(2000); and an essay collection,* Ill Nature: Rants and Reflections on Humanity and Other Animals *(2001). "The Killing Game" originally appeared in* Esquire *(1990) and was selected by Joyce Carol Oates for* The Best American Essays 1991.

Death and suffering are a big part of hunting. A big part. Not that you'd ever know it by hearing hunters talk. They tend to downplay the killing part. To kill is to put to death, extinguish, nullify, cancel, destroy. But from the hunter's point of view, it's just a tiny part of the experience. *The kill is the least important part of the hunt,* they often say, or, *Killing involves only a split second of the innumerable hours we spend surrounded by and observing nature . . .* For the animal, of course, the killing part is of considerable more importance. José Ortega y Gasset, in *Meditations on Hunting*, wrote, *Death is a sign of reality in hunting. One does not hunt in order to kill; on the contrary, one kills in order to have hunted.* This is the sort of intellectual blather that the "thinking" hunter holds dear. The conservation editor of *Field & Stream*, George Reiger, recently paraphrased this sentiment by saying, *We kill to hunt, and not the other way around,* thereby making it truly fatuous. A hunter in West Virginia, one Mr. Bill Neal, blazed through this philosophical fog by explaining why he blows the toes off tree raccoons so that they will fall down and be torn apart by his dogs. *That's the best part of it. It's not any fun just shooting them.*

Instead of monitoring animals — many animals in managed areas are tagged, tattooed, and wear radio transmitters — wildlife managers should start hanging telemetry gear around hunters' necks to study their attitudes and listen to their conversations. It would be grisly listening, but it would tune out for good the *suffering as sacrament* and *spiritual experience* blather that some hunting apologists employ. *The unease with which the good hunter inflicts death is an unease not merely with his conscience but with affirming his animality in the midst of his struggles toward humanity and clarity,* Holmes Rolston III drones on in his book *Environmental Ethics.*

There is a formula to this in literature — someone the protagonist loves has just died, so he goes out and kills an animal. This makes him feel better. But it's kind of a sad feeling-better. He gets to relate to Death and Nature in this way. Somewhat. But not really. Death is still a mystery. Well, it's hard to explain. It's sort of a semireligious thing . . . Killing and affirming, affirming and killing, it's just the cross the "good" hunter must bear. The bad hunter just has to deal with postkill letdown.

Many are the hunter's specious arguments. Less semireligious but a long-standing favorite with them is the vegetarian approach: you eat meat, don't you? If you say no, they feel they've got you — you're just a vegetarian attempting to impose your weird views on others. If you say yes, they accuse you of being hypocritical, of allowing your genial A&P butcher to stand between you and reality. The fact is, the chief attraction of hunting is the pursuit and murder of animals—the meat-eating aspect of it is trivial. If the hunter chooses to be *ethical* about it, he might cook his kill, but the meat of most animals is discarded. Dead bear can even be dangerous! A bear's heavy hide must be skinned at once to prevent meat spoilage. With effort, a hunter can make okay chili, *something to keep in mind,* a sports rag says, *if you take two skinny spring bears.*

As for subsistence hunting, please . . . Granted that there might be one "good" hunter out there who conducts the kill as spiritual exercise and two others who are atavistic enough to want to supplement their Chicken McNuggets with venison, most hunters hunt for the hell of it.

For hunters, hunting is fun. Recreation is play. Hunting is recreation. Hunters kill for play, for entertainment. They kill for the thrill of it, to make an animal "theirs." (The Gandhian doctrine of nonpossession has never been a big hit with hunters.) The animal becomes the property of the hunter by its death. Alive, the beast belongs only to itself. This is unacceptable to the hunter. *He's yours . . . He's mine . . . I decided to . . . I decided not to . . . I debated shooting it, then I decided to let it live . . .* Hunters like beautiful creatures. A "beautiful" deer, elk, bear, cougar, bighorn sheep. A "beautiful" goose or mallard. Of course, they don't stay "beautiful" for long, particularly the birds. Many birds become rags in the air, shredded, blown to bits. *Keep shooting till they drop!* Hunters get a thrill out of seeing a plummeting bird, out of seeing it crumple and fall. *The big pheasant folded in classic fashion.* They get a kick out of "collecting" new species. *Why not add a unique harlequin duck to your collection?* Swan hunting is satisfying. *I let loose a three-inch Magnum. The large bird only flinched with my first shot and began to gain altitude. I frantically ejected the round, chambered another, and dropped the swan with my second shot. After retrieving the bird I was amazed by its size. The swan's six-foot wingspan, huge body, and long neck made it an impressive trophy.* Hunters like big animals, trophy animals. A "trophy" usually means that the hunter doesn't deign to eat it. Maybe he skins it or mounts it. Maybe he takes a picture. *We took pictures, we took pictures.* Maybe he just looks at it for a while. The disposition of the "experience" is up to the hunter. He's entitled to do whatever he wishes with the damn thing. It's dead.

Hunters like categories they can tailor to their needs. There are the "good" animals — deer, elk, bear, moose — which are allowed to exist for the hunter's pleasure. Then there are the "bad" animals, the vermin, varmints, and "nuisance" animals, the rabbits and raccoons and coyotes and beavers and badgers, which are disencouraged to exist. The hunter can have fun killing them, but the pleasure is diminished because the animals aren't "magnificent."

Then there are the predators. These can be killed any time, because, hunters argue, they're predators, for godssakes.

Many people in South Dakota want to exterminate the red fox because it preys upon some of the ducks and pheasant they want to hunt and kill each year. They found that after they killed the wolves and coyotes, they had more foxes than they wanted. The ring-necked pheasant is South Dakota's state bird. No matter that it was imported from Asia specifically to be "harvested" for sport, it's South Dakota's state bird and they're proud of it. A group called Pheasants Unlimited gave some tips on how to hunt foxes. *Place a small amount of larvicide* [a grain fumigant] *on a rag and chuck it down the hole . . . The first pup generally comes out in fifteen minutes . . . Use a .22 to dispatch him . . . Remove each pup shot from the hole. Following gassing, set traps for the old fox who will return later in the evening . . .* Poisoning, shooting, trapping — they make up a sort of sportsman's triathlon.

In the hunting magazines, hunters freely admit the pleasure of killing to one another. *Undeniable pleasure radiated from her smile. The excitement of shooting the bear had Barb talking a mile a minute.* But in public, most hunters are becoming a little wary about raving on as to how much fun it is to kill things. Hunters have a tendency to call large animals by cute names — "bruins" and "muleys," "berry-fed blackies" and "handsome cusses" and "big guys," thereby implying a balanced jolly game of mutual satisfaction between the hunter and the hunted — *Bam, bam, bam, I get to shoot you and you get to be dead.* More often, though, when dealing with the nonhunting public, a drier, businesslike tone is employed. Animals become a "resource" that must be "utilized." Hunting becomes "a legitimate use of the resource." Animals become a product like wool or lumber or a crop like fruit or corn that must be "collected" or "taken" or "harvested." Hunters love to use the word *legitimate*. (Oddly, Tolstoy referred to hunting as "evil legitimized.") *A legitimate use, a legitimate form of recreation, a legitimate escape, a legitimate pursuit.* It's a word they trust will slam the door on discourse. Hunters are increasingly relying upon their spokesmen and supporters, state and federal game managers and wildlife officials, to employ the drone of a solemn bureaucratic language and toss around a lot of questionable statistics to assure the nonhunting public (93 percent!) that there's nothing to worry about. The pogrom is under control. The mass murder and manipulation of wild animals is just another business. Hunters are a tiny minority, and it's crucial to them that the millions of people who don't hunt not be awakened from their long sleep and become antihunting. Nonhunters are okay. Dweeby, probably, but okay. A hunter *can respect the rights* of a nonhunter. It's the "antis" he despises, those *misguided, emotional, not-in-possession-of-the-facts, uninformed zealots who don't understand nature . . . Those dime-store ecologists cloaked in ignorance and spurred by emotion . . . Those doggy-woggy types, who under the guise of being environmentalists and conservationists are working to deprive him of his precious right to kill.* (Sometimes it's just a *right;* sometimes it's a *God-given* right.) Antis can be scorned, but nonhunters must be pacified, and this is where the number crunching of wildlife biologists and the scripts of *professional resource managers* come in. Leave it to the professionals. They know what numbers are the good numbers. Utah determined that there were six hundred sandhill cranes in the state, so permits were issued to shoot one hundred of them. Don't want to have too many sandhill cranes. California wildlife officials reported "sufficient numbers" of mountain lions to "justify" renewed hunting, even though it doesn't take a rocket scientist to know the animal is extremely rare. (It's always a dark day for hunters when an animal is adjudged *rare.* How can its numbers be "controlled" through hunting if it scarcely exists?) A recent citizens' referendum prohibits the hunting of the mountain lion in perpetuity — not that the lions aren't killed anyway, in California and all over the West, hundreds of them annually by the government as part of the scandalous Animal Damage Control Program. Oh, to be the lucky hunter who gets to be an official government hunter and can legitimately kill animals his buddies aren't supposed to! Montana officials, led by K. L. Cool, that state's wildlife director, have definite ideas on the number of buffalo they feel can be tolerated. Zero is the number. Yellowstone National Park is the only place in America where bison exist, having been annihilated everywhere else. In the winter of 1988, nearly six hundred buffalo wandered out of the north boundary of the park and into Montana, where they were immediately shot at point-blank range by lottery-winning hunters. It was easy. And it was obvious from a video taken on one of the blow-away-the-bison days that the hunters had a heck of a good time. The buffalo, Cool says, threaten ranchers' livelihoods by doing damage to property — by which he means, I guess, that they eat the grass. Montana wants zero buffalos; it also wants zero wolves.

Large predators — including grizzlies, cougars, and wolves — are often the most "beautiful," the smartest and wildest animals of all. The gray wolf is both a supreme predator and an endangered species, and since the Supreme Court recently affirmed that ranchers have no constitutional right to kill endangered predators — apparently some God-given rights are not constitutional ones — this makes the wolf a more or less lucky dog. But not for long. A small population of gray wolves has recently established itself in northwestern Montana, primarily in Glacier National Park, and there is a plan, long a dream of conservationists, to "reintroduce" the wolf to Yellowstone. But to please ranchers and hunters, part of the plan would involve immediately removing the wolf from the endangered-species list. Beyond the park's boundaries, he could be hunted as a "game animal" or exterminated as a "pest." (Hunters kill to hunt, remember, except when they're hunting to kill.) The area of Yellowstone where the wolf would be restored is the same mountain and high-plateau country that is abandoned in winter by most animals, including the aforementioned luckless bison. Part of the plan, too, is compensation to ranchers if any of their far-ranging livestock is killed by a wolf. It's a real industry out there, apparently, killing and controlling and getting compensated for losing something under the Big Sky.

Wolves gotta eat — a fact that disturbs hunters. Jack Atcheson, an outfitter in Butte, said, *Some wolves are fine if there is control. But there never will be control. The wolf-control plan provided by the Fish and Wildlife Service speaks only of protecting domestic livestock. There is no plan to protect wildlife . . . There are no surplus deer or elk in Montana . . . Their numbers are carefully managed. With uncontrolled wolf populations, a lot of people will have to give up hunting just to feed wolves. Will you give up your elk permit for a wolf?*

It won't be long before hunters start demanding compensation for animals they aren't able to shoot.

Hunters believe that wild animals exist only to satisfy their wish to kill them. And it's so easy to kill them! The weaponry available is staggering, and the equipment and gear limitless. *The demand for big boomers has never been greater than right now, Outdoor Life crows, and the makers of rifles and cartridges are responding to the craze with a variety of light artillery that is virtually unprecedented in the history of sporting arms* . . . Hunters use grossly overpowered shotguns and rifles and compound bows. They rely on four-wheel-drive vehicles and three-wheel ATVs and airplanes . . . *He was interesting, the only moving, living creature on that limitless white expanse. I slipped a cartridge into the barrel of my rifle and threw the safety off* . . . They use snowmobiles to run down elk, and dogs to run down and tree cougars. It's easy to shoot an animal out of a tree. It's virtually impossible to miss a moose, a conspicuous and placid animal of steady habits . . . *I took a deep breath and pulled the trigger. The bull dropped. I looked at my watch: 8:22. The big guy was early. Mike started whooping and hollering and I joined him. I never realized how big a moose was until this one was on the ground. We took pictures* . . . Hunters shoot animals when they're resting . . . *Mike selected a deer, settled down to a steady rest, and fired. The buck was his when he squeezed the trigger. John decided to take the other buck, which had jumped up to its feet. The deer hadn't seen us and was confused by the shot echoing about in the valley. John took careful aim, fired, and took the buck. The hunt was over* . . . And they shoot them when they're eating . . . *The bruin ambled up the stream, checking gravel bars and backwaters for fish. Finally he plopped down on the bank to eat. Quickly, I tiptoed into range* . . . They use decoys and calls . . . *The six-point gave me a cold-eyed glare from ninety steps away. I hit him with a 130-grain Sierra boat-tail handload. The bull went down hard. Our hunt was over* . . . They use sex lures . . . *The big buck raised its nose to the air, curled back its lips, and tested the scent of the doe's urine. I held my breath, fought back the shivers, and jerked off a shot. The 180-grain spire-point bullet caught the buck high on the back behind the shoulder and put it down. It didn't get up* . . . They use walkie-talkies, binoculars, scopes . . . *With my 308 Browning BLR, I steadied the 9X cross hairs on the front of the bear's massive shoulders and squeezed. The bear cartwheeled backward for fifty yards* . . . *The second Federal Premium 165-grain bullet found its mark. Another shot anchored the bear for good* . . . They bait deer with corn. They spread popcorn on golf courses for Canada geese and they douse meat baits with fry grease and honey for bears . . . *Make the baiting site redolent of inner-city doughnut shops.* They use blinds and tree stands and mobile stands.

They go out in groups, in gangs, and employ "pushes" and "drives." So many methods are effective. So few rules apply. It's fun! . . . *We kept on repelling the swarms of birds as they came in looking for shelter from that big ocean wind, emptying our shell belts* . . . A species can, in the vernacular, be *pressured by hunting* (which means that killing them has decimated them), but that just increases the fun, the *challenge.* There is practically no criticism of conduct within the ranks . . . *It's mostly a matter of opinion and how hunters have been brought up to hunt* . . . Although a recent editorial in *Ducks Unlimited* magazine did venture to primly suggest that one should *not fall victim to greed-induced stress through piggish competition with others.*

But hunters are piggy. They just can't seem to help it. They're overequipped . . . insatiable, malevolent, and vain. They maim and mutilate and despoil. And for the most part, they're inept. Grossly inept.

Camouflaged toilet paper is a must for the modern hunter, along with his Bronco and his beer. Too many hunters taking a dump in the woods with their roll of Charmin beside them were mistaken for white-tailed deer and shot. Hunters get excited. They'll shoot anything — the pallid ass of another sportsman or even themselves. A Long Island man died last year when his shotgun went off as he clubbed a wounded deer with the butt. Hunters get mad. They get restless and want to fire! They want to use those assault rifles and see foamy blood on the ferns. Wounded animals can travel for miles in fear and pain before they collapse. Countless gut-shot deer — *if you hear a sudden, squashy thump, the animal has probably been hit in the abdomen* — are "lost" each year. "Poorly placed shots" are frequent, and injured animals are seldom tracked, because most hunters never learned how to track. The majority of hunters will shoot at anything with four legs during deer season and anything with wings during duck season. Hunters try to nail running animals and distant birds. They become so overeager, so *aroused,* that they misidentify and misjudge, spraying their "game" with shots but failing to bring it down.

The fact is, hunters' lack of skill is a big, big problem. And nowhere is the problem worse than in the new glamour recreation, bow hunting. These guys are elitists. They doll themselves up in camouflage, paint their faces black, and climb up into tree stands from which they attempt the penetration of deer, elk, and

turkeys with modern, multiblade, broadhead arrows shot from sophisticated, easy-to-draw compound bows. This "primitive" way of
hunting appeals to many, and even the nonhunter may feel that
it's a "fairer" method, requiring more strength and skill, but bow
hunting is the cruelest, most wanton form of wildlife disposal of
all. Studies conducted by state fish and wildlife departments repeatedly show that bow hunters wound and fail to retrieve as many
animals as they kill. An animal that flees, wounded by an arrow,
will most assuredly die of the wound, but it will be days before he
does. Even with a "good" hit, the time elapsed between the strike
and death is exceedingly long. *The rule of thumb has long been that we
should wait thirty to forty-five minutes on heart and lung hits, an hour or
more on a suspected liver hit, eight to twelve hours on paunch hits, and
that we should follow immediately on hindquarter and other muscle-only
hits, to keep the wound open and bleeding,* is the advice in the magazine *Fins and Feathers.* What the hunter does as he hangs around
waiting for his animal to finish with its terrified running and dying
hasn't been studied — maybe he puts on more makeup, maybe he
has a highball.

Wildlife agencies promote and encourage bow hunting by per-
mitting earlier and longer seasons, even though they are well
aware that, in their words, *crippling is a by-product of the sport,* making archers pretty sloppy for elitists. The broadhead arrow is a very
inefficient killing tool. Bow hunters are trying to deal with this
problem with the suggestion that they use poison pods. These poisoned arrows are illegal in all states except Mississippi *(Ah'm gonna
get ma deer even if ah just nick the little bastard),* but they're widely
used anyway. You wouldn't want that deer to suffer, would you?

The mystique of the efficacy and decency of the bow hunter is as
much an illusion as the perception that a waterfowler is a refined
and thoughtful fellow, a *romantic aesthete,* as Vance Bourjaily put it,
equipped with his faithful Labs and a love for solitude and wild
places. More sentimental drivel has been written about bird shooting than any other type of hunting. It's a soul-wrenching pursuit,
apparently, the execution of birds in flight. Ducks Unlimited — an
organization that has managed to put a spin on the word *conservation* for years — works hard to project the idea that duck hunters
are blue bloods and that duck stamps with their pretty pictures are

responsible for saving all the saved puddles in North America. *Sportsman's conservation* is a contradiction in terms (We protect things now so that we can kill them later) and is broadly interpreted (Don't kill them all, just kill most of them). A hunter is a conservationist in the same way a farmer or a rancher is: he's not. Like the rancher who kills everything that's not stock on his (and the public's) land, and the farmer who scorns wildlife because "they don't pay their freight," the hunter uses nature by destroying its parts, mastering it by simplifying it through death.

George ("We kill to hunt and not the other way around") Reiger, the conservationist-hunter's spokesman (he's the best they've got, apparently), said that the "dedicated" waterfowler will shoot other game "of course," but *we do so much in the same spirit of the lyrics, that when we're not near the girl we love, we love the girl we're near.* (Duck hunters practice tough love.) The fact is, far from being a "romantic aesthete," the waterfowler is the most avaricious of all hunters . . . *That's when Scott suggested the friendly wager on who would take the most birds . . .* and the most resistant to minimum ecological decency. Millions of birds that managed to elude shotgun blasts were dying each year from ingesting the lead shot that rained down in the wetlands. Year after year, birds perished from feeding on spent lead, but hunters were "reluctant" to switch to steel. They worried that it would impair their shooting, and ammunition manufacturers said a changeover would be "expensive." State and federal officials had to weigh the poisoning against these considerations. It took forever, this weighing, but now steel-shot loads are required almost everywhere, having been judged "more than adequate" to bring down the birds. This is not to say, of course, that most duck hunters use steel shot almost everywhere. They're traditionalists and don't care for all the new, pesky rules. Oh, for the golden age of waterfowling, when a man could measure a good day's shooting by the pickup load. But those days are gone. Fall is a melancholy time, all right.

Spectacular abuses occur wherever geese congregate, Shooting Sportsman notes quietly, something that the more cultivated Ducks Unlimited would hesitate to admit. Waterfowl populations are plummeting and waterfowl hunters are out of control. "Supervised" hunts are hardly distinguished from unsupervised ones. A biologist with the Department of the Interior who observed a hunt at Sand Lake in South Dakota said, *Hunters repeatedly shot over the line at incoming flights where there was no possible chance of retrieving. Time and time again I was shocked at the behavior of hunters. I heard them laugh at the plight of dazed cripples that stumbled about. I saw them striking the heads of retrieved cripples against fence posts.* In the South, wood ducks return to their roosts after sunset when shooting hours are closed. Hunters find this an excellent time to shoot them. Dennis Anderson, an outdoors writer, said, *Roost shooters just fire at the birds as fast as they can, trying to drop as many as they can. Then they grab what birds they can find. The birds they can't find in the dark, they leave behind.*

Carnage and waste are the rules in bird hunting, even during legal seasons and open hours. Thousands of wounded ducks and geese are not retrieved, left to rot in the marshes and fields . . . *When I asked Wanda where hers had fallen, she wasn't sure.* Cripples, and there are many cripples made in this pastime, are still able to run and hide, eluding the hunter even if he's willing to spend time searching for them, which he usually isn't . . . *It's one thing to run down a cripple in a picked bean field or a pasture, and quite another to watch a wing-tipped bird drop into a huge block of switch grass.* Oh nasty, nasty switch grass. A downed bird becomes invisible on the ground and is practically unfindable without a good dog, and few "waterfowlers" have them these days. They're hard to train — usually a professional has to do it — and most hunters can't be bothered. Birds are easy to tumble . . . *Canada geese — blues and snows — can all take a good amount of shot. Brant are easily called and decoyed and come down easily. Ruffed grouse are hard to hit but easy to kill. Sharptails are harder to kill but easier to hit . . .* It's just a nuisance to recover them. But it's fun, fun, fun swatting them down . . . *There's distinct pleasure in watching a flock work to a good friend's gun.*

Teal, the smallest of common ducks, are really easy to kill. Hunters in the South used to practice on teal in September, prior to the "serious" waterfowl season. But the birds were so diminutive and the limit so low (four a day) that many hunters felt it hardly worth going out and getting bit by mosquitoes to kill them. Enough did, however, brave the bugs and manage to "harvest" 165,000 of the little migrating birds in Louisiana in 1987 alone. *Shooting is usually best on opening day. By the second day you can sometimes detect a decline in local teal numbers. Areas may deteriorate to virtually no action by the third day . . .* The area *deteriorates.* When a flock is wiped out, the skies are empty. *No action.*

Teal declined more sharply than any duck species except mallard last year; this baffles hunters. Hunters and their procurers—wildlife agencies—will *never* admit that hunting is responsible for the decimation of a species. John Turner, head of the federal Fish and Wildlife Service, delivers the familiar and litanic line. Hunting is not the problem. *Pollution* is the problem. *Pesticides, urbanization, deforestation, hazardous waste,* and *wetlands destruction* are the problem. And drought! There's been a big drought! Antis should devote their energies to solving these problems if they care about wildlife, and leave the hunters alone. While the Fish and Wildlife Service is busily conducting experiments in cause and effect, like releasing mallard ducklings on a wetland sprayed with the insecticide ethyl parathion (they died—it was known they would, but you can never have enough studies that show guns aren't a duck's only problem), hunters are killing some 200 million birds and animals each year. But these deaths are incidental to the problem, according to Turner. A factor, perhaps, but a *minor* one. Ducks Unlimited says the problem isn't hunting, it's *low recruitment* on the part of the birds. To the hunter, *birth* in the animal kingdom is *recruitment.* They wouldn't want to use an emotional, sentimental word like *birth.* The black duck, a very "popular" duck in the Northeast, so "popular," in fact, that game agencies felt that hunters couldn't be asked to refrain from shooting it, is scarce and getting scarcer. Nevertheless, it's still being hunted. *A number of studies are currently under way in an attempt to discover why black ducks are disappearing, Sports Afield* reports. Black ducks are disappearing because they've been shot out, their elimination being a dreadful example of game management, and managers who are loath to "displease" hunters. The skies — *flyways* — of America have been divided into four administrative regions, and the states, advised by a federal government coordinator, have to agree on policies.

There's always a lot of squabbling that goes on in flyway meetings — lots of complaints about short-stopping, for example. Short-stopping is the deliberate holding of birds in a state, often by feeding them in wildlife refuges, so that their southern migration is slowed or stopped. Hunters in the North get to kill more than hunters in the South. This isn't fair. Hunters demand equity in opportunities to kill.

Wildlife managers hate closing the season on anything. Closing the season on a species would indicate a certain amount of mismanagement and misjudgment at the very least — a certain reliance on overly optimistic winter counts, a certain overappeasement of hunters who would be "upset" if they couldn't kill their favorite thing. And worse, closing a season would be considered victory for the antis. Bird-hunting "rules" are very complicated, but they all encourage killing. There are shortened seasons and split seasons and special seasons for "underutilized" birds. (Teal were very recently considered "underutilized.") The limit on coots is fifteen a day — shooting them, it's easy! They don't fly high — giving the hunter something to do while he waits in the blind. Some species are "protected," but bear in mind that hunters begin blasting away one half hour before sunrise and that most hunters can't identify a bird in the air even in broad daylight. Some of them can't identify birds in hand either, and even if they can (*#%*! I got me a canvasback, that duck's frigging protected...*), they are likely to bury unpopular or "trash" ducks so that they can continue to hunt the ones they "love."

Game "professionals," in thrall to hunters' "needs," will not stop managing bird populations until they've doled out the final duck (*I didn't get my limit but I bagged the last one, by golly...*). The Fish and Wildlife Service services legal hunters as busily as any madam, but it is powerless in tempering the lusts of the illegal ones. Illegal kill is a monumental problem in the not-so-wonderful world of waterfowl. Excesses have always pervaded the "sport," and bird shooters have historically been the slobs and profligates of hunting. *Doing away with hunting would do away with a vital cultural and historical aspect of American life,* John Turner claims. So, do away with it. Do away with those who have already done away with so much. Do away with them before the birds they have pursued so relentlessly and for so long drop into extinction, sink, in the poet Wallace Stevens's words, "downward to darkness on extended wings."

"Quality" hunting is as rare as the Florida panther. What you've got is a bunch of guys driving over the plains, up the mountains, and through the woods with their stupid tag that cost them a couple of bucks and immense coolers full of beer and body parts. There's a price tag on the right to destroy living creatures for play, but it's not much. *A big-game hunting license is the greatest deal going since the Homestead Act,* Ted Kerasote writes in *Sports Afield. In many* *states residents can hunt big game for more than a month for about $20.* It's cheaper than taking the little woman out to lunch. It's cheap all right, and it's because killing animals is considered *recreation* and is underwritten by state and federal funds. In Florida, state moneys are routinely spent on "youth hunts," in which kids are guided to shoot deer from stands in wildlife-management areas. The organizers of these events say that these staged hunts *help youth to understand man's role in the ecosystem.* (Drop a doe and take your place in the ecological community, son . . .)

Hunters claim (they don't actually believe it but they've learned to say it) that they're doing nonhunters a favor, for if they didn't use wild animals, wild animals would be useless. They believe that they're just *helping Mother Nature control populations (you wouldn't want those deer to die of starvation, would you?*). They claim that their tiny fees provide *all* Americans with wild lands and animals. (People who don't hunt get to enjoy animals all year round while hunters get to enjoy them only during hunting season . . .) Ducks Unlimited feels that it, in particular, is a selfless provider and environmental champion. Although members spend most of their money lobbying for hunters and raising ducks in pens to release later over shooting fields, they do save some wetlands, mostly by persuading farmers not to fill them in. *See that little pothole there the ducks like? Well, I'm gonna plant more soybeans there if you don't pay me not to . . .* Hunters claim many nonsensical things, but the most nonsensical of all is that they *pay their own way.* They do not pay their own way. They *do* pay into a perverse wildlife-management system that manipulates "stocks" and "herds" and "flocks" for hunters' killing pleasure, but these fees in no way cover the cost of highly questionable ecological practices. For some spare change . . .*the greatest deal going*. . .hunters can hunt on public land — national parks, state forests — preserves for hunters! — which the nonhunting and antihunting public pay for. (Access to private lands is becoming increasingly difficult for them, as experience has taught people that hunters are obnoxious.) Hunters kill on millions of acres of land all over America that are maintained with general taxpayer revenue, but the most shocking, really twisted subsidization takes place on national wildlife refuges. Nowhere is the arrogance and the insidiousness of this small, aggressive minority more clearly demonstrated. Nowhere is the murder of animals, the manipulation of language, and the distortion of public intent more flagrant. The public perceives national wild life refuges as safe havens, as sanctuaries for animals. And why wouldn't they? The word *refuge* of course *means* shelter from danger and distress. But the dweeby nonhunting public — they tend to be so literal. The word has been reinterpreted by management over time and now hunters are invited into more than half of the country's more than 440 wildlife "sanctuaries" each year to bang them up and kill more than half a million animals. This is called *wildlife-oriented recreation*. Hunters think of this as being no less than their due, claiming that refuge lands were purchased with duck stamps (. . .*our duck stamps paid for it . . .our duck stamps paid for it . . .*). Hunters equate those stupid stamps with the mystic, multiplying power of the Lord's loaves and fishes, but of 90 million acres in the Wildlife Refuge System, only 3 million were bought with hunting-stamp revenue. Most wildlife "restoration" programs in the states are translated into clearing land to increase deer habitats (so that too many deer will require hunting . . .you wouldn't want them to die of starvation, would you?) and trapping animals for restocking and study (so hunters can shoot more of them). Fish and game agencies hustle hunting — instead of conserving wildlife, they're killing it. It's time for them to get in the business of protecting and preserving wildlife and creating balanced ecological systems instead of pimping for hunters who want their deer/duck/pheasant/turkey — animals stocked to be shot.

Hunters' self-serving arguments and lies are becoming more preposterous as nonhunters awake from their long, albeit troubled, sleep. Sport hunting is immoral; it should be made illegal. Hunters are persecutors of nature who should be prosecuted. They wield a disruptive power out of all proportion to their numbers, and pandering to their interests — the special interests of a group that just wants to kill things — is mad. It's preposterous that every year less than 7 percent of the population turns the skies into shooting galleries and the woods and fields into abattoirs. It's time to stop actively supporting and passively allowing hunting, and time to stigmatize it. It's time to stop being conned and cowed by hunters, time to stop pampering and coddling them, time to get them off the government's duck-and-deer dole, time to stop thinking of wild animals as "resources" and "game," and start thinking of them as sentient beings that deserve our wonder and respect, time to stop allowing hunting to be creditable by calling it "sport" and "recreation." Hunters make wildlife *dead, dead, dead*. It's time to wake up to this indisputable fact. As for the hunters, it's long past check-out time.

Reflections and Responses

1. In her sixth paragraph, Williams introduces the following quotes: *"He's yours . . . He's mine . . . I decided to . . . I decided not to . . . I debated shooting it, then I decided to let it live . . ."* Who is supposedly saying these things? What point is Williams making about hunters?

2. Williams criticizes not only the morality of hunting but also the "manipulation of language" by "hunting apologists." To what extent does she focus her argument on language? What aspects of the pro-hunting language does she most dislike? What euphemisms does she satirize? Do you think she criticizes this language fairly? Explain.

3. Go through the essay systematically and list the pro-hunting arguments Williams introduces. How many can you identify? How do you think she handles them? For example, do you agree with her refutation of the position that people who eat meat are hypocritical in their criticism of hunters?

CREDITS